DATE DUE

FEB 2 9 1996	
MAR 1 4 1996	
Mar 28/96	
FEB - 3 1998	
Mar 6	
MAR 2 3 2001	

BRODART   Cat. No. 23-221

The Soviet system has undergone a dramatic transformation: from communist monopoly to multiparty politics, from Marxism to competing values, from centralisation to fragmentation, and from state ownership to a mixed economy. This book, by three of the West's leading scholars of Soviet and post-Soviet affairs, traces the politics of transition in the late 1980s and early 1990s from its origins to its uncertain post-communist future. The authors analyse the full impact of transition on official and popular values, central and local political institutions, the post-Soviet republics, the CPSU and the parties which replaced it, and political participation. A final chapter considers the problematic nature of this form of 'democracy from above'. Detailed but clearly and accessibly written, *The politics of transition* provides an ideal guide to the changes that have been taking place in the politics of the newly independent nations that together constitute a sixth of the world's land surface.

The politics of transition

The politics of transition: shaping a post-Soviet future

Stephen White
University of Glasgow

Graeme Gill
University of Sydney

Darrell Slider
University of South Florida

CAMBRIDGE
UNIVERSITY PRESS

Published by the Press Syndicate of the University of Cambridge
The Pitt Building, Trumpington Street, Cambridge CB2 1RP
40 West 20th Street, New York, NY 10011-4211, USA
10 Stamford Road, Oakleigh, Victoria 3166, Australia

First published 1993

Printed in Great Britain at the University Press, Cambridge

A catalogue record for this book is available from the British Library

Library of Congress cataloguing in publication data applied for
White, Stephen, 1945–
From Soviet to post-Soviet politics / Stephen White, Graeme Gill, Darrell Slider.
    p.   cm.
Includes index.
ISBN 0 521 44094 7. – ISBN 0 521 44634 1 (pbk.)
1. Soviet Union – Politics and government – 1985–1991.
2. Former Soviet republics – Politics and government.
I. Gill, Graeme J.   II. Slider, Darrell.   III. Title
DK288.W45   1993
947.085'4–dc20   92–42520–CIP

ISBN 0 521 44094 7   hardback
ISBN 0 521 44634 1   paperback

CE

Contents

		page	viii
Preface			
1	Beyond Marxism		1
2	Reforming the electoral system		20
3	Structures of government		39
4	The Presidency and central government		60
5	From union to independence		79
6	Patterns of republic and local politics		98
7	The withering away of the party		117
8	The emergence of competitive politics		140
9	The politics of economic interests		164
10	Public opinion and the political process		178
11	Letters and political communication		193
12	The Soviet transition and 'democracy from above'		212
Index			274

Preface

The establishment of communist rule in the USSR has reasonably been regarded as the main turning-point of twentieth-century world history. The collapse of that system of government, first in Eastern Europe and then in the USSR itself, marks a turning-point that will hardly be less significant. For more than seven decades a single party had exercised a political monopoly across a sixth of the world's land surface. It dominated the electoral system and the soviets in whose name the revolution had originally taken place. It decided all key appointments, directed the work of government, controlled the mass media, and could draw if it wished upon the assistance of a security apparatus as well as the police and army. All of this was the party's 'leading role', confirmed in the Constitution that was adopted under Leonid Brezhnev's guidance in 1977. The Communist Party, as a party, exercised a broader influence through its relationship with more than 100 communist or workers' parties in other countries; and the USSR, as a state, was the centre of a political and military system that dominated the destinies of about a third of the world's population.

All of this came to an end in the late 1980s, as first of all its East European allies and then the USSR itself abandoned the various characteristics of communist rule. Communist rule in Eastern Europe had been largely an outside imposition and its demise was less remarkable in those countries than the collapse of party authority in the USSR itself, more than seventy years after a revolution that the party had itself precipitated. The stages of that transition were played out before a world-wide media audience: the ideology became less restrictive, the economy less state controlled, the political system less dominated by the Communist Party. In 1989 and 1990, the first competitive elections under Soviet rule saw the widespread rejection of official candidates and the establishment, in at least six of the formerly united Soviet republics, of overtly nationalist administrations. The Communist Party lost members and influence, and in March 1990 its constitutionally guaranteed leading role. After an attempted coup had collapsed in August 1991, the party was itself suppressed. In December 1991 the USSR was replaced by an ill-defined Commonwealth, and post-communist patterns of politics began to develop in what were now fifteen independent states.

We have attempted, in this book, to outline and analyse this momentous transition from Soviet to post-Soviet politics. We begin with changes in ideology and values, and then consider in turn the electoral and representative system, the central government and presidency, the transition from a federation to independent states and the patterns of politics that have developed in these new states. Further chapters consider the decline of the authority of the CPSU, and the rise of alternative organisations – first of all 'informals', and then fully fledged parties – to challenge its formerly dominant position. The newer forms of organised politics that have emerged in post-communist Russia are the focus of a further chapter, with particular emphasis upon business and labour, and we also consider the conclusions that are suggested by opinion polls and by letters to the newspapers and to public institutions during the Soviet and now post-Soviet years. We conclude with some more broadly conceived reflections on the nature of a transition of the Soviet kind in the context of a wider literature on democratic development.

This book has been some time in the making and, although the chapters were written by individual authors (Stephen White in the case of chapters 1, 2, 3 and 11, Graeme Gill in the case of chapters 4, 7, 8 and 12, and Darrell Slider in the case of chapters 5, 6, 9 and 10), it is a genuinely collective endeavour. It was planned in the late 1980s when the three authors arranged to share a platform at the 1990 Harrogate World Congress for Soviet and East European Studies. First drafts of three of the chapters in the book were presented at Harrogate, and three further chapters at a convention of the American Association for the Advancement of Slavic Studies in Miami in 1991. We have circulated our drafts for comment, and met and corresponded on other occasions so as to ensure that the outcome was a coherent book-length study of the Soviet transition. It remains to thank Michael Holdsworth of Cambridge University Press for his interest and encouragement, and the discussants and others who have contributed directly to our work over these years: particularly David Wedgwood Benn, Ronald Hill and Viktor Sheinis. Our own institutions also deserve thanks for having helped to make possible a scholarly collaboration over several years across three continents.

Finally, a note on conventions. In respect of transliteration we have followed the system employed by the Library of Congress, modified in cases where different usages have become familiar to a Western reader (for instance, Alexander rather than Aleksandr, and Yeltsin rather than El'tsin). Glasnost and perestroika have been regarded as English words and are not italicised. And the post-Soviet successor states have been given their current official designations: for instance, Belarus rather than Belorussia, Kyrgyzstan rather than Kirgizia. These and other changes reflect the political transformation with which our volume is itself concerned.

STEPHEN WHITE
GRAEME GILL
DARRELL SLIDER

1   Beyond Marxism

The Soviet system that Gorbachev inherited was 'ideocratic' in character.[1] It was a system, in other words, in which a single ideology – Marxism-Leninism – was fundamental to political life and not open to legitimate challenge. It was, in fact, some time before the varied teachings of Marx, Engels and Lenin were synthesised into Soviet Marxism-Leninism, and some time more before that doctrine in its turn became the only framework of discussion that could be employed in all spheres of public life. As late as 1930 the philosopher Losev could refer to dialectical materialism as a 'lamentable absurdity',[2] and it was not until the years of fully-fledged Stalinism that literature and art, education and public life more generally were brought under close party control. Editors of all newspapers and journals, from these years onwards, were appointed on party instructions; an elaborate system of censorship monitored whatever they produced; and the doctrine of 'socialist realism' (in fact, uncritical support of regime policies) became mandatory in all fields of cultural life. For the theorists of totalitarianism an official ideology of this kind was one of the essential features of a communist system (as it was of Nazi Germany); for others, the regime was simply an 'ideology' or 'utopia in power'.[3]

The place of this official ideology was established, in the Brezhnev years, in the Constitution that was adopted under his guidance in October 1977. The 'highest goal of the Soviet state', its preamble explained, was the 'building of a classless communist society', and it was at this time that the Communist Party was given a correspondingly dominant position in Article 6. There has been a long and inconclusive debate about the extent to which this official ideology was simply a rationalisation of leadership choices, and about the extent to which it actually guided public policy.[4] It was certainly clear, in the post-Stalin era, that this was an ideology that could not openly be contested: it informed the educational system, determined the parameters of public debate, and set limits to all fields of cultural endeavour. It was clear, moreover, that although an official ideology of this kind might not provide a set of unambiguous directives for policymakers, it certainly ruled out a number of options that might otherwise have attracted support. In the

1970s and 1980s these options probably included the dissolution of the collective farms, private ownership of large-scale industry and the establishment of a multiparty system (although it was sometimes pointed out that a limited choice of parties, as in Eastern Europe and in Russia itself after the revolution, was not ruled out indefinitely[5]).

The changes that took place during the Gorbachev years, accordingly, required some reconsideration of official theory. Equally, the reconsideration of official theory that took place during these years encouraged a search for policy alternatives that often might lie outside the boundaries of Marxism, and legitimated a range of options that had been maturing among scholars and practitioners during the years of Brezhnevite stagnation. Many of these were 'children of the 20th Congress', proponents of a more democratic and pluralist socialism of the kind that Khrushchev had encouraged in the late 1950s. Georgii Arbatov, for instance, director of the USA and Canada Institute of the Academy of Sciences, had prepared a lengthy report on the implications of the scientific-technical revolution in the early 1970s. Brezhnev, in the event, locked it away and the proposal to hold a special Central Committee discussion was quietly forgotten, but the report itself eventually reached Gorbachev.[6] A later and better-known example was the 'Novosibirsk report', produced in 1983 by a group of economists under the direction of Tatiana Zaslavskaia, and then leaked to the West; it located the source of Soviet difficulties in bureaucratic, over-centralised forms of management and called directly for perestroika.[7] Zaslavskaia, who met Gorbachev at this time, found him a receptive and understanding audience.[8] Debates of this kind became legitimate once Gorbachev had assumed the party leadership; they facilitated the search for a 'humane, democratic socialism' in the late 1980s, and then – in the early 1990s – a search for societal alternatives that extended well beyond Marxism (indeed, many of these writings identified Marxism itself as the problem).

The end of orthodoxy

Gorbachev's early speeches, in fact, had given relatively little attention to the longer-term objectives he had in mind for Soviet society. His acceptance speech, in March 1985, promised that the strategy worked out at the 26th Party Congress of 1981 would remain unchanged: a policy of the 'acceleration of the country's socioeconomic development [and] the perfection of all aspects of the life of the society'.[9] His first full address to the Central Committee in April 1985 again emphasised the importance of the 26th Congress and called for a 'steady advance' rather than a clear break with earlier policies. There had been 'major successes' in all spheres of public life, Gorbachev insisted; the new state had reached the 'summits of economic and social progress', while the working man had for the 'first time in history' become the maker of his own destiny. The party's general line, as he explained it, involved the 'perfection of developed socialist society', a characterisation that was thoroughly Brezhnevian in tone. Gorbachev did call for 'further changes and transformations' and for the establishment of a 'qualitatively new state of society, in the broadest sense of the word'; he was also concerned to activate the 'human factor'. It was changes in the economy, however, that would be decisive in any development of this kind, and the speech was largely preoccupied with familiar matters such as technological innovation, labour productivity, waste and financial self-sufficiency.[10]

The most authoritative statement of the party's longer-term purposes was its programme, first adopted in 1903 and then in further editions in 1919 and 1961.[11] The 1961 Programme, hailed by Khrushchev as a 'Communist Manifesto of the modern era', was best known for its promise that the achievement of a fully communist society had become an 'immediate practical task for the Soviet people', and that it would 'in the main' be completed by 1980.[12] These optimistic assumptions were quickly abandoned by Khrushchev's successors, and under Brezhnev it began to be claimed that the USSR had achieved no more than the construction of a 'developed socialist society', whose further evolution into full communism might take half a century or more.[13] The Party Programme of 1961 was clearly difficult to reconcile with these very different perspectives, and the 26th Congress in 1981 agreed with Brezhnev that it was time for a new edition to be prepared. The essentials of the existing programme, Brezhnev explained, were still valid, but twenty years had elapsed since its adoption and there were many developments it had failed to record, among them the fact that Soviet society was proceeding to communism through the stage of 'developed socialism'.[14] Both Andropov and Chernenko, who succeeded Brezhnev as chairmen of the committee that was responsible for preparing a new programme, pointed out that the USSR was 'only at the beginning' of developed socialism and that the transition to the fully communist society of the future would be 'protracted'.[15]

Gorbachev succeeded Chernenko not only as general secretary but also, it emerged, as chairman of the commission preparing the new programme. A draft was published in the central press for public discussion in October 1985; there were many, even within the leadership, who thought the changes so considerable that the new version should be called a fourth Party Programme, not just a revision.[16] Perhaps the most striking single change in the new programme was the abandonment of the optimistic perspectives of its Khrushchevian predecessor. The 1961 Programme, for instance, had defined itself as a 'programme for the building of communist society'; the revised version of 1986 was no more than a programme for the 'perfection of socialism' and claimed only that it offered 'advantages' as compared with capitalism (the 1961 Programme had promised that socialism alone could 'abolish the exploitation of man by man'). The dates and stages by which communism was to be reached disappeared entirely (indeed there was originally some pressure for the Programme to be entirely 'deideologised' with any references to communism confined to the introduction or conclusion).[17] The 1986 Programme, on the contrary, noted that the party did 'not attempt to foresee in detail the features of full communism' and warned that any attempt to advance too rapidly was 'doomed to failure and might cause both political and economic damage'. The collectivist emphases of the 1961 Programme – more and more services such as transport and housing to be provided free of charge, more public catering and shared upbringing of children – found no place in the new text, nor did the promise of a minimum one-month paid holiday for all citizens. The 1986 Programme, similarly, contained no reference to the historic goal of the withering away of the state; its main emphasis was upon practical and short-term objectives, and it struck a disciplinarian rather than utopian note in its references to careerism, nepotism and profiteering.[18]

Both the new version of the programme and a revised set of party rules, which were also approved at the 27th Congress, included a reference to 'developed socialism' (during the period since the 1960s, as the Party Programme put it, the USSR had 'entered the stage of developed socialism'[19]). There had been more than six million letters in connection with the draft programme, Gorbachev told the Congress; some of these had suggested the removal of all references to developed socialism, and others had suggested that the subject to considered at greater length. Yegor Ligachev, at this time a Central Committee Secretary, had gone still further, arguing for the 'all-round perfection of developed socialism', and this formulation was retained until the very last minute.[20] In the end the Programme retained one of the two references in the draft to developed socialism;[21] but the concept did not subsequently figure in the General Secretary's speeches or in party documents, and it was replaced later the same year by the term 'developing socialism' (*razvivaiushchiisia sotsializm*),[22] implying a still earlier stage in the transition towards the communist society of the future. Another term, 'integral socialism' (*tsel'nyi sotsializm*), made a brief appearance in the draft version of the Programme. Soviet society, it was explained, had achieved a 'qualitatively new state of development, in Lenin's words, "integral socialism"';[23] but the reference disappeared entirely in the final version of the Programme and was not subsequently revived.

As Gorbachev told the 19th Party Conference in 1988, they were looking for a socialism that 'renounced everything that deformed socialism in the

1930s and that led to its stagnation in the 1970s', a socialism that would inherit the 'best elements' of the thinking of its founding fathers together with the constructive achievements of other countries and social systems.[24] Gorbachev expanded upon this 'new image of socialism' in an address to party functionaries in July 1989. It would, he explained, be a 'society of free people, a society of and for the working people, built on the principles of humanism, socialist democracy and social justice'. It would be based on a variety of forms of public ownership, which would enable people to be masters of their own lives and give full play to their energy and abilities. Economic development would be based upon self-regulation, with the centre playing a purely coordinating role. It would be a society in which the people would have 'absolute power and the full range of rights', and it would be based on both the 'finest traditions of Soviet democracy and the experience of mankind's democratic evolution'. And in turn, it would be an 'important stage in the advance to communism'. This, however, was no more than a 'general outline', and he called for the scholarly community to develop it in the kind of detail that was required.[25]

Gorbachev himself contributed to this task in an extended statement, 'The socialist idea and revolutionary perestroika', which appeared in *Pravda* in November 1989, drawing upon a series of speeches the Soviet leader had made in the late autumn. If at first he had thought it would be sufficient simply to eliminate various shortcomings in Soviet life, Gorbachev explained, he was now in no doubt that nothing less than a radical reconstruction of the whole of society was necessary. There was no detailed plan to guide this work, nor could there be; but it would certainly avoid the command-administrative methods of the Soviet past and the capitalist methods of the West. A process of this kind – perestroika – would occupy a 'lengthy stage in the historical development of socialism'; its ultimate objective was the establishment of a 'genuinely democratic and self-governing social organism' in place of the bureaucratic system that had come into existence during the Stalin years. Gorbachev had no doubt that the socialist choice in October 1917 had been the right one; and the alternative would almost certainly have been a military dictatorship rather than liberal democracy. Socialism, in any case, had to be conceived as a 'global process'. The experience of other countries and movements, particularly European social democracy, provided much from which they could learn; and the future lay in a cooperative rather than confrontational relationship between the USSR and the wider world from which both sides could benefit.[26]

Official perspectives of this kind were summed up in the 'Programmatic Declaration' adopted by the 28th Party Congress in July 1990. Entitled 'Towards a humane, democratic socialism', the Declaration insisted, as

Gorbachev had done, that the origins of Soviet difficulties were to be found, not in any deficiency of the socialist idea itself, but in the deformations to which it had been subjected in the past. Party dictatorship had led to tyranny and lawlessness; nature had been plundered without restraint; and dogmatism had reigned supreme in the arts. The Declaration included a set of 'urgent anti-crisis measures' to deal with some of these immediate difficulties; for the longer term it envisaged the strengthening of civil liberties, a 'stage-by-stage transition to a market system', international cooperation and democratisation of the party itself.[27] Gorbachev, in his own contribution to the discussion, spoke of a 'civil society of free men and women' with a multiparty system, freedom of thought and information, and 'real government by the people'.[28] He resisted the idea that objectives of this kind could be set down in a textbook, a kind of Stalinist *Short Course*;[29] elsewhere he had rejected the idea of a programme as a kind of 'railway timetable', with routes and dates set out in advance, and resisted all attempts to 'force real life into Procrustean schemes'.[30] Continuing the work of the 20th Congress of 1956, the purpose of the socialism of which Gorbachev conceived was rather different: to 'profoundly democratise and humanise society' and to provide freedom in place of the 'stifling and repressive atmosphere of Stalinism and stagnation'.[31]

The Congress agreed to begin work on a new, fourth Party Programme, replacing the document approved in 1986. There was, in the end, no fourth Programme, because the party had been suspended before its 29th Congress could be convened. In July 1991, however, the Central Committee approved the draft of a new Programme entitled 'Socialism, Democracy, Progress' and made it available for public discussion. Several writers, in the discussion, had urged the CPSU to undertake a 'Bad Godesberg', after the German Social Democratic Programme of 1959 in which the last vestiges of that party's Marxist heritage had been abandoned.[32] The published draft did still commit the party to communism as an 'historic perspective'; but this, as the Leningrad party leader Boris Gidaspov commented, was in the spirit of an 'epitaph on a tombstone' (the version considered by the plenum had in fact originally left out all references of this kind[33]). The draft Programme was much briefer than its immediate predecessors; it was also very different in character. It committed the party to a set of basic principles including 'democracy and freedom in all their varied forms', the rule of law, human rights, social justice and international integration, and to a series of more immediate policy objectives. The longer-term aim was the construction of a society based on a mixed economy, political pluralism and 'genuine people's power', which in turn could only be formed in association with a 'new world civilisation'.[34] The new Programme was intended to provide a 'plan of concrete action for today and tomorrow'; it was also, in Gorbachev's words, an admission that the Soviet model of socialism had suffered a 'strategic defeat' and that the communist ideal was unrealisable in the foreseeable future.[35]

If there was a single concept that was central to this progression, it was political pluralism. For earlier Soviet leaders and writers pluralism had been little more than the ideology of the bourgeoisie.[36] Even Andropov, prepared in other contexts to reconsider some of the central elements of Marxism, saw '"pluralism"' as an 'artificial attempt to create an organised opposition to socialism'.[37] Gorbachev, at least from the summer of 1987, began to suggest a very different conceptualisation. The term first appeared in a discussion with media workers in which he had urged them to ensure that 'socialist pluralism, so to speak', was 'present in every publication'.[38] Speaking to a group of French public figures two months later, he described them as a 'pluralistic complex' and went on, in discussion, to agree that Soviet society was increasingly pluralistic, provided only that it was qualified as 'socialist'.[39] In February 1988 Gorbachev spoke approvingly to the Central Committee of the 'socialist pluralism of opinions' they had begun to experience, and there were even positive references, later in the year, to a 'pluralism of opinions' and a 'pluralism of interests'.[40] There were further supporting references to pluralism, 'socialist' or otherwise, at the 19th Party Conference in the summer of 1988,[41] and at a meeting in Poland Gorbachev even attempted to explain what he meant by the term – it was, at any rate, the opposite of 'uniformity' or 'spiritual conformity'.[42]

In early 1989 Gorbachev was still opposed to 'political pluralism', together with a multiparty system and private property.[43] In the summer of 1989, however, there were positive references, at the First Congress of People's Deputies, to the 'pluralism of opinion' for which it made provision, and then in early 1990, at the same time as the leading role of the party was being abandoned, there were the first positive references to 'political pluralism' itself. Party theorists were meanwhile explaining that 'pluralism' was increasingly being used to refer to aspects of perestroika, above all the 'deep and comprehensive democratisation of society', and pointing up the contrast between 'political pluralism' and the 'political monopolism' of the recent past.[44] The draft Programme of 1991 completed the process by referring to 'political and ideological pluralism' as one of the features of the humane and socialist society that the party would seek to establish in the future, one that would incorporate the notion of a 'civil society' and the opportunity for groups to defend their various interests within a framework of law and guaranteed rights and freedoms for the individual.[45]

Debating socialist and post-socialist futures

This broad vision of a Soviet, post-Soviet or indeed global future was carried forward in the late 1980s and early 1990s by a group of reform-minded academics and commentators, among them Fedor Burlatsky, Boris Kurashvili, Anatolii Butenko and Georgii Shakhnazarov. Burlatsky, a people's deputy as well as scholar and journalist, attacked the authoritarian, statist socialism that went back beyond Stalin to Peter the Great, and argued instead in favour of a decentralised, self-managing system which drew upon the experience of the New Economic Policy of the 1920s, and which explicitly 'subordinated the state to civil society'. In a society of this kind, as Burlatsky outlined it, there would be a planned but commodity-based economy, a separation of powers between party, state and social organisations, a greater role for public opinion, and the gradual development of a more participatory culture based on what Engels had called the 'associated producers'.[46] For the jurist Boris Kurashvili the future socialist society would still be based upon the elected soviets, but they would be combined with some of the features of a parliamentary and representative system so that government was 'by the people' as well as 'for the people', and so that the 'support democracy' of the past became a 'democracy of participation'.[47] Kurashvili elsewhere expressed support for a form of 'democratic socialism' which would include respect for minority rights, a separation of powers, genuine federalism and a 'socialist multiparty system'.[48] Writing in 1990, Kurashvili continued to support a multiparty system as a means of balancing the presidency and reviving the CPSU, but he was also concerned to maintain the dominance of public ownership and to maximise social equality – an objective that, in his view, was most readily achieved within a socialist framework.[49]

Another contributor to the discussion was Anatolii Butenko, a department head at the Institute of Economics of the World Socialist System at the USSR Academy of Sciences. In his writings of the early 1980s, which were strongly influenced by the Polish crisis, Butenko argued that Soviet-type societies did not eliminate 'contradictions', in particular those between the sectional interests of managers and the working people they directed.[50] Writing subsequently and at greater length, Butenko set out a vision of the Soviet future that was based upon the concept of 'socialist popular self-management' and which involved the abolition of the *nomenklatura* appointments system and a wide-ranging electoral reform.[51] Interviewed in *Pravda* in 1989, Butenko placed the greatest emphasis upon the emancipation of labour as the goal of socialism. This meant more than the elimination of exploitation, which had already been achieved in the Stalinist period: it meant the elimination of the oppression of man by man, which could be achieved only by the working class itself and not by a bureaucracy on its behalf. Butenko called in particular for the establishment of a socialist civil society, based upon a wide dispersal of ownership (so long as workers depended upon their employers, even under public ownership, they could never become the agents of their own destiny). This meant individual and private as well as state and municipal ownership; and in the political sphere it meant 'genuine popular rule – rule of the people by the people themselves'.[52]

Butenko was one of a group of leading scholars that met regularly in the late 1980s under party auspices with a view to formulating a 'contemporary concept of socialism'.[53] The results of their labours appeared in the party press in 1989; they summed up the perspectives of the most strongly reformist section of the social science community. Lenin's 'new model of socialism', they argued, had been put into effect during the 1920s, but then replaced by a Stalinist system which had 'created an alienation of the individual from ownership, from power and from the results of his work'. Liberating society from this legacy was no easy matter, because not only officials but wide strata of the population thought this Stalinist model was in fact the very essence of socialism. The statement distinguished, as Butenko had done, between exploitation (which had been eliminated by public ownership) and oppression, which had continued. More controversially, and following Hayek and other critics of socialist collectivism,[54] the group went on to argue that complete state ownership led to 'totalitarian forms of government', and that a wide variety of forms of property, including private ownership, was necessary if the personal liberties of citizens were to be securely protected. Economic life, more generally, was to be regulated through a 'socialist market', but with an improved system of social benefits to protect the disadvantaged from its worst effects. It would, finally, be a society based upon the rule of law, and upon universal human values such as honesty, decency and a sense of duty.[55]

A statement of equal influence was 'Towards a new image of socialism', published in the party theoretical journal *Kommunist* in 1989 by its editorial staff and a seminar group from the Academy of Sciences. The statement also placed its emphasis upon forms of ownership, warning that excessive concentration of resources in the hands of the state could lead to the alienation of ordinary people from political as well as economic life; and it called for a shift from 'state paternalism' and towards a regulated market, the 'free movement of labour' and socialist entrepreneurship. So long as employment was dominated by a 'Leviathan state', it warned, there could be no basis for a self-governing civil society, and no basis either for political democratisation.[56] The connection between democracy and private property was a crucial one, and it was one that appeared to have persuaded the General

Secretary himself. Speaking in Odessa in August 1990, Gorbachev called for the development of small businesses and the 'spirit of enterprise', and described free enterprise as the 'motor' of economic growth. It was the first speech in which the Soviet leader referred approvingly to 'privatisation'; more remarkably, he went on to argue that the market and private property were important not only in themselves but also because they alone could guarantee democracy and human rights.[57]

Scholarly thinking on these and other issues became still more outspoken in the early 1990s. Indeed little of what had been unchallengeable orthodoxy since the 1920s remained untouched. The rector of the party's Institute of Social Sciences, Yuri Krasin, insisted that Marxism had represented a 'gigantic leap forward' in the understanding of social development, but deplored the assumption that its prescriptions were valid for all time. There was still some value in its emphasis upon social justice and equality, but not necessarily in the view that force was the midwife of history, or that socialism had no need of market mechanisms.[58] Sergei Alekseev, chairman of the Constitutional Supervision Committee, pointed out that the proletariat of which Marx and Engels had written no longer existed, and that reforms were a more satisfactory form of progress than 'bloody revolutions'. Alekseev was particularly concerned to retain the heritage of social democracy; Lenin, after all, had been a Social Democrat for twenty years but a Communist for only four, and if they failed to incorporate values of this kind they would be left with little more than Stalinism.[59] Georgii Shakhnazarov, head of the Soviet political science association and a Gorbachev adviser, went still further in a series of articles on the 'new model of socialism' in *Kommunist*. For Shakhnazarov, socialism would continue as long as mankind pursued a better world; but he rejected the idea of 'stages' of human history and the primary of economic factors, and saw communism itself as a 'hypothesis' or even a 'dream'.[60]

While Shakhnazarov and others were attempting to define a democratic socialism, many others, from the late 1980s, were moving beyond socialism altogether and (in some cases) identifying socialism as the problem rather than a part of any possible solution. One of these controversies concerned the nature of the USSR itself. Was it, in fact, to be considered a socialist society at all? Some of these articles took as their point of departure Gorbachev's slogan of 'More socialism! More democracy!'. Socialism, it was noted, had officially been established in the USSR in the late 1930s. But if this was the case, how could more of it be needed in the late 1980s? And if what had been established was not socialism, how was it to be classified?[61] There were all kinds of suggestions in this respect, including 'a new form of serfdom', 'departmental feudalism', an 'extrahistorical socioeconomic formation', even a 'new and hitherto unknown mode of production'.[62] A related issue was the necessity of the October revolution and, intimately connected with it, the validity of Leninism. Had the October revolution, as some were prepared to argue, prevented a normal pattern of peaceful and democratic development after Tsardom had been overthrown? How much blame should be attached to Lenin for the repressive, overcentralised system that had succeeded him? And how much was Marxism itself to blame for the economic inefficiency and political authoritarianism that had characterised at least a substantial part of Soviet history?[63]

A celebrated series of articles by the philosopher Alexander Tsipko, in this connection, traced the roots of Stalinism back to pre-revolutionary society, and more particularly to Marxism itself. It was from Marx, for instance, that Stalin had taken the principle of collectivising small-scale peasant agriculture; and his hostility to the market was not very different from that of other Marxists, nor indeed from the thinking of Marx, Engels and Lenin themselves. The deformation of socialism, for Tsipko, had doctrinal as well as other origins; it was pointless, for instance, to pretend that there could be firm guarantees of democracy if all were employed by the state, or of liberty if it was believed that the revolution was its 'own justification and its own law'.[64] Another scholar, the sociologist Igor Kliamkin, argued similarly that Stalinism was not the aberration of a single man but the logical result of Lenin's single-party system, which had prized unity more than democracy and had remained largely intact ever since.[65] For the economist Vasilii Seliunin the origins of their difficulties lay still deeper, in the utopian nature of Marxism itself, which led almost inevitably to the forcible direction of labour in the absence of other means of motivation. Seliunin, criticising Lenin, went on to argue that there was a close relationship between the freedom to sell one's labour and human freedoms in general, and between total state ownership and the 'temptation to expropriate the individual personality'.[66]

Were these kinds of distinctions, in any case, of much value? In the view of several other writers, the assumption that capitalism and socialism were polar opposites was itself exaggerated and out of date. Advanced capitalism, as the economist Oleg Bogomolov pointed out, had evolved towards the 'practical realisation of many socialist principles'. Property was increasingly regulated in the public interest, and planning mechanisms were being strengthened at the national level and within individual firms. The development of democracy, at the same time, allowed ordinary people to express their preferences more freely than ever before; human rights were better protected, and living standards and social security were steadily improving.[67] Writing elsewhere, Bogmolov suggested that countries like Sweden and Austria might have found the 'only realistic way to put many socialist ideas into practice in the current world context'.[68] For others still the differences between socialism and capitalism, in an interdependent world, were 'relative'. Socialism, in this view, was better understood as 'post-capitalism' than its opposite; nor was there necessarily any incompatibility between socialism and capitalist private property.[69] Shakhnazarov, similarly, felt it was unhelpful to divide societies into two dichotomous categories, 'socialist' or 'capitalist', when in reality all known societies were 'mixed'.[70] Gorbachev, speaking after his enforced retirement, took the same view.[71]

For still others, forms of property and government were in the end much less important than a change in values and in human relations. This view found eloquent expression in the speeches and writings of Alexander Iakovlev, a Politburo member from 1987 to 1990 and before that director of the important Institute of the World Economy and International Relations of the Academy of Sciences. Speaking in Perm' in December 1988, Iakovlev insisted there was no alternative to the 'economic bloodflow' of the 'socialist market'. The 'absolute monopoly of the state', under the planning system, left the consumer 'absolutely defenceless', and was a form of social organisation that went back to Peter the Great rather than Karl Marx. Lenin, by contrast, had insisted (at least after 1921) that socialism was a society with 'commodity production, a market, competition, money [and] democracy'.[72] Speaking to Moscow automobile workers in June 1989, Iakovlev argued that Marx's 'utopia' of non-commodity production had simply not justified itself. No other way had yet been found to relate supply and demand; but more than this – the market was also the 'foundation of democracy', since it provided an economic basis for the exercise of choice by ordinary citizens. It was just as important to transfer ownership from the state to the producers themselves; only in this way would it be possible to overcome the alienation of ordinary people from their society and from the political system through which it was managed.[73]

The larger purposes of perestroika, as these remarks suggested, were ethical. For Iakovlev, it must revive moral norms, honesty and decency, encouraging a shift from 'passive expectancy to the creation of a new life based on a new morality; from the worship of a Holy Writ serving an authoritarian regime to man's spiritual elevation'.[74] Writing in May 1991, Iakovlev thought the Soviet experience had made it tragically clear how an indifference to moral considerations could undermine a social order that had been constructed with very different intentions. Nothing, in particular, had discredited the Soviet experience more than the use of force and the assumption that all differences must be antagonistic. The whole Bolshevik tradition had been one of combat, since they had manned the barricades in the 1905 revolution: first with Tsarism, then with the provisional government, and finally with their own people.[75] Iakovlev, speaking elsewhere, attacked the 'enemy syndrome' that had led to seventy years of struggle with real or imaginary opponents, and he deplored the tendency in the French as well as the Russian revolution towards the forcible resolution of political differences.[76] The 'most dangerous crisis in our society', he argued in late 1991, was the 'loss, the erosion of all morality'; and speaking after the collapse of communist rule, he continued to insist upon the importance of dialogue, consensus and respect for the interests and opinions of others.[77]

Iakovlev's writings pointed towards a Christian, ethical dimension to Russian and post-Soviet choices in the early 1990s; and this was one of the value systems that became more widely available towards the end of communist rule, as religious festivals began to be celebrated and as spiritual writings began to be circulated through the regular book trade as well as through the churches themselves (more than half of the Soviet population, in 1991, described themselves as religious believers[78]). Alexander Solzhenitsyn's writings were close to many of these values; his *Gulag Archipelago*, reprinted in several of the literary journals, was reportedly the most-read book of 1991,[79] and a controversial manifesto enjoyed considerable attention when it appeared in the Komsomol newspaper in 1990. The manifesto, 'How to reconstruct Russia', called for the formation of a purely Slavic state, the return of women to their families, the protection of young people from 'streams of filth', and a political system suited to the 'specific needs of our own country'.[80] There was some overlap between these writings and literature of a more chauvinistic character, which argued that the Russian people were threatened by Jews and Freemasons and attacked Yeltsin as a 'puppet of the Zionists';[81] there was some overlap too with orthodox communism, which saw the country threatened by foreign (and not simply Jewish) imperialism.

Bookstalls and underpasses also made available a range of literature of a very different kind. Article 228 of the Criminal Code ostensibly forbade pornography, but it did not prevent the appearance of poorly reproduced pamphlets with such titles as *Brezhnev's Mistresses, Swedish Threesome* and *Twelve Sex Rules for the Revolutionary Proletariat*. Works of this kind were occasionally prosecuted, but such 'classics' as the Marquis de Sade or *Lady Chatterley's Lover* – published by the State Publishing House of Political Literature – were distributed without restriction.[82] A further contribution was made by 'video houses', of which there were two thousand in Moscow alone in the early 1990s.[83] Spiritualist writings were also very popular, including Madame Blavatsky and Nostradamus, together with self-help guides on subjects like emigration, self-defence and folk medicine. Dale Carnegie's *How to Make Friends and Influence People* was serialised in the Communist Party's organisational fortnightly, without much obvious effect; extracts from Hitler's *Mein Kampf* appeared in 1990, and Goebbels' diaries in 1992.[84] An ideology of a very different kind was business, which was strongly represented on the bookstalls in the early 1990s: from the writings of Peter Drucker, Paul Samuelson and Lee Iacocca to more practically oriented guides like *How to Become a Millionaire in the CIS, How to Establish a Private Enterprise, The Fundamentals of Marketing* and S. N. Bonk's *English for International Collaboration*.

A particular contribution to this ferment of ideas was made by the writings of an earlier generation of Russians, now republished for a modern audience. The influential prerevolutionary collection, *Vekhi* (Landmarks), was reprinted in various forms, together with its 1918 successor *Iz glubiny* (From the Depths). The main philosophy journal carried the religious writer S. L. Frank, exiled in 1922, and the Kadet politician and philosopher S. N. Bulgakov, in emigration after 1923. The religious writer and historian Nikolai Berdiaev, another to be exiled in 1922, was reprinted in the same journal, together with writers in the socialist tradition like Mikhail Bakunin and Leon Trotsky. The main sociology journal, in a series of publications of prerevolutionary or unapproved classics, included the scientist and philosopher A. A. Bodganov, the religious writer P. A. Florensky and the sociologist Pitirim Sorokin, exiled after 1922, as well as Bukharin and Trotsky. There was also room, in the early 1990s, for contemporary European debates. In 1990 the monthly journal *Voprosy filosofii* carried an extract from Francis Fukuyama's 'End of history' with a critical rejoinder; and space was found for other contemporary writings such as Ralph Dahrendorf's *Reflections on the Revolution in Eastern Europe*. This recovery of prerevolutionary traditions, and of an earlier association with developments in the outside world, had an influence on public and cultural life that was at least as great as the examination of Stalinism and other 'blank spots' of the Soviet period.

Political choices and public responses

What, finally, did the public at large make of these competing philosophies? The general response in the late 1980s and early 1990s was certainly a gloomy one, if the survey evidence was any guide. When, for instance, would Russia emerge from its socioeconomic crisis? In two or three years, according to 26 per cent of Muscovites in early 1992, but in the view of another 31 per cent it would take five to ten years, and others thought it would take 'up to twenty years' or 'decades' (6 and 7 per cent respectively), or that it would 'never' happen (7 per cent).[85] What did Soviet rule provide for its citizens, the National Public Opinion Centre asked in 1991? A quarter of those who were polled said 'peace', but for 65 per cent – the largest number – it meant 'shortages, queues and poverty', and for 28 per cent it meant 'powerlessness, constant insults and humiliation'.[86] Asked 'what is perestroika?', 29 per cent found it hard to say; but of those that did have an answer, the largest group (18 per cent) thought it was an 'attempt by the ruling group to hold on to their power by a certain degree of democratisation', and 14 per cent found it an 'out of date and exhausted slogan'.[87] Asked in 1991 what the main results of perestroika had been, 43 per cent mentioned their 'loss of certainty in the future', and 37 per cent the 'crisis of inter-ethnic relations'; for 29 per cent the main result was 'chaos and disorganisation in government' and for 28 per cent it was the 'deepening of economic crisis'. As many as 38 per cent, in early 1992, thought it was positively irresponsible to bring children into a society whose future was so alarming.[88]

It did not necessarily follow, however, that there was overwhelming support for capitalism or the institutions of liberal democracy. For 22 per cent (the largest number), in a national poll in late 1990, the October revolution had 'opened a new era' in Russian history, and for another 22 per cent it had 'stimulated the country's social and economic development'. Asked what they would do if the October revolution took place a second time, 43 per cent told pollsters they would largely or entirely have supported the Bolsheviks, and only 6 per cent would have opposed them (a further 10 per cent would have emigrated, and 13 per cent would have tried to avoid becoming involved). When it came to a choice among the major parties active during the revolutionary year, by far the largest proportion (39 per cent) would have supported the Bolsheviks; a further 8 per cent would have supported the Mensheviks, and only 3 per cent would have supported the Constitutional Democrats (support for the monarchists was lower still, at 1 per cent). The largest group (39 per cent) thought the October revolution 'reflected the wishes of the peoples of the Russian empire', and a majority were prepared to accept that it had been necessary to use force to take power, though fewer thought the Constituent Assembly should have been dissolved or the royal family executed, and many more regretted the losses that had been suffered by Russian culture and business during the revolutionary years.[89]

So far as forms of rule in general were concerned, the largest group (38 per cent), in a national poll in 1991, thought socialism had been shown to be deficient in principle. But when asked what kind of a society should be constructed in the Russian Federation, 29 per cent said a socialist one, 56 per cent thought it should be a Swedish-style combination of the best features of capitalism and socialism, and only 3 per cent opted for unreconstructed capitalism.[90] Surveys conducted for the Western press in early 1991 (see table 1.1) found similarly that there was substantial support for 'a more democratic type of socialism'.[91] In late 1991, according to a national

Table 1.1. *'What kind of society would you like to see in your country?'* *(percentages)*

	European Russia	Ukraine	Lithuania
'A socialist society along the lines we have had in the past'	10	10	3
'A more democratic type of socialism'	36	27	9
'A modified form of capitalism such as found in Sweden'	23	26	38
'A free market form of capitalism such as found in the US or Germany'	17	23	29
No opinion	14	14	21

Source: Adapted from the Times-Mirror survey, Washington DC, 1991, mimeo.

poll, a democratic socialist society of the Swedish kind was again the most popular option (23 per cent), together with a 'unique path to the future' (23 per cent); and a socialist system of the kind that had existed before perestroika (14 per cent) was more popular than American capitalism (11 per cent).[92] Socialism, in fact, retained considerable support into the post-communist era, according to surveys conducted in the summer of 1992. More than two-thirds of those who were asked were 'largely' (32 per cent) or 'entirely' (35 per cent) in agreement that socialism as a system had 'undoubted advantages', with only 18 per cent in disagreement; and about half (49 per cent) thought Stalin a 'great leader'.[93]

Nor, according to the polls, was there much tendency to blame Lenin, founder of the Soviet system, for the multiplicity of ills to which that system had given rise. In a national poll in late 1990, Lenin was the figure of the revolutionary era who aroused the greatest sympathy (64 per cent), followed – surprisingly – by Dzerzhinsky (41 per cent), Bukharin (27 per cent) and Trotsky (15 per cent). The Tsar (5 per cent) and Kerensky (4 per cent) were some distance behind.[94] More than half of those polled, moreover, thought they had come to evaluate Lenin more positively as a result of perestroika, notwithstanding the publication of a letter of Lenin's of 1922 in which he had called for the shooting of as many reactionary priests as possible and new evidence that he might have instigated the murder of the Tsar and his family in 1918.[95] In a poll in late 1990 in which respondents were asked which figure would make the greatest difference to the Soviet Union by the year 2000, Jesus Christ came first with 58 per cent and Andrei Sakharov second with 48 per cent, but Lenin was a creditable third with 36 per cent.[96]

In another national poll in late 1991, Peter the Great was chosen by 13 per cent as the 'greatest figure of all times and nations'; Jesus Christ came second with 11 per cent; but Lenin and Albert Einstein were a joint third with 8 per cent support, and ahead of Sakharov, Alexander Nevsky, the pre-revolutionary prime minister Stolypin and Napoleon Bonaparte.[97]

More generally, the evidence that was available in the early 1990s suggested only a limited and qualified commitment to the values of liberal democracy. It was certainly clear, if the polls were any guide, that the attempted coup of August 1991 was seen as an illegal one: 62 per cent throughout the USSR took this view, according to a survey conducted at the time, and 73 per cent in Moscow.[98] It was also clear that, in the public view, Gorbachev should not have been displaced by the State Emergency Committee: 55 per cent, according to another contemporary poll, thought his dismissal improper, as compared with 22 per cent that were willing to support it. A large majority were opposed to the establishment of the Emergency Committee, and as many as 92 per cent were hostile towards its members individually. And for a substantial proportion (60 per cent, among the urban population as a whole) the success of the coup would have led to political repression on a significant scale.[99] Nor were these impressions misplaced. Thousands of forms, it subsequently emerged, had been prepared for mass arrests; and just before the coup itself there was a sudden order for 250,000 pairs of handcuffs.[100] In the abstract, there was certainly no doubt of the strength of popular support for glasnost and for democratisation;[101] and even in the difficult circumstances of August 1991, just after the coup had been defeated, only 33 per cent were in favour of banning meetings and demonstrations on a temporary basis, as compared with 44 per cent that were opposed.[102]

This notwithstanding, there was substantial support for the coup and its apparent objectives. According to Gorbachev himself, speaking shortly afterwards to journalists, support for the coup ran as high as 40 per cent.[103] Polls in 1992 found that a quarter saw the coup leaders as criminals, but many more (46 per cent) saw them as the 'victims of times and circumstances', and 60–70 per cent of the letters that reached the Russian prosecutor's office were openly in their support.[104] Nor, at the same time, had newly-established and more democratic institutions of government succeeded in developing a high level of support for their activities. Only 13 per cent, in the spring of 1992, thought deputies had justified the hopes that had been invested in them, with 56 per cent taking the opposite view;[105] and only 12 per cent were satisfied with the work of the Russian parliament, with as many as 70 per cent dissatisfied.[106] The question most Muscovites wanted to ask their deputy, in the spring of 1992, was 'Do they, the deputies, know how people are living at the moment, and when will such a life end?'.[107] Half of those who were asked, in the summer of 1992, thought government should be entrusted to experienced nonparty specialists, not to the democrats (14 per cent) or communists (5 per cent);[108] and fully 70 per cent were prepared to agree that 'Russia's salvation would be a person able to lead the people and bring order to the country'[109] – a view that was reminiscent of much older orientations to government, in which parties and representative institutions had generally had little place.

The survey evidence of the early 1990s also suggested a relatively low level of attachment to minority rights and a number of the other conventions that sustain a democratic order. In the summer of 1991, for instance, 30 per cent favoured the death penalty for homosexuals. Another 30 per cent supported compulsory medical treatment, and only 10 per cent regarded it as a private matter (in Central Asia support for the death penalty ran as high as 85 per cent).[110] A similar proportion, in a 1990 survey, were in favour of the 'liquidation' of prostitutes (28.4 per cent); 28 per cent favoured the liquidation of drug addicts, 23 per cent the liquidation of the handicapped, 21 per cent the liquidation of all 'rockers', and 17 per cent the liquidation of all AIDS victims.[111] There was substantial support for the death penalty, with 34 per cent supporting its use on the basis of the existing law and 28 per cent favouring an extension of its application;[112] and there was substantial support for the Communist Party to be put on trial, with some calls – as in Eastern Europe – for its former members or at least officials to be denied the right to seek or hold public office.[113] No more than 10 per cent, according to surveys conducted in 1992, had an adequate understanding of the nature of democracy, and many more were prepared to support public order (49 per cent) than individual liberties (28 per cent).[114]

There was equally strong support, according to Western surveys carried out in 1992, for many other values of long standing (see table 1.2). There was little backing, in these inquiries, for the official doctrine of Marxism-Leninism, and little more for 'socialism', but 'capitalism' was scarcely more popular. The most strongly supported principles, by a very wide margin, were Christianity, a 'united and indivisible Russia', and 'freedom' – understood, presumably, as the long-standing Russian aspiration for liberty from external constraint. Support for values of this kind, moreover, was consistent across the generations, although among those aged under 30 there was less support for Marxism-Leninism and rather more for capitalism; and it was consistent across the genders, across the regions, and across national, educational, occupational and income groups. Even present or former Communist Party members, while less positive towards Christianity than nonmembers or former members, were still overwhelmingly favourable, and they were more supportive of the idea of a 'unitary and indivisible Russia' than they were of socialism or Marxism-Leninism.[115]

Table 1.2. *'We often hear the following words. What feelings do they evoke?'* *(percentages)*

	Positive	Negative	Difficult to answer
Christianity	73	3	24
Marxism-Leninism	15	37	46
Socialism	24	33	42
Capitalism	25	28	46
Glasnost	63	16	21
'Unitary and indivisible Russia'	75	5	20
Perestroika	21	45	33
Freedom	78	4	17

Source: Adapted from Irina Boeva and Viacheslav Shironin, *Russians between State and Market* (Glasgow: Centre for the Study of Public Policy, 1992), pp. 30–1.

Russians, moreover, were very different as a group from the other 'new democracies' of Eastern Europe. Russians, according to surveys conducted in 1992, were much more likely than members of the other new democracies to have a low opinion of their current economic situation, and much less likely to expect an improvement. More of them supported the economic system that had obtained before perestroika than the system they expected to have in five years' time, whereas among East Europeans the reverse was true. Russians, similarly, were more positively disposed towards the unreformed political system of the pre-perestroika years than towards their current political system, or the one that they expected to have in five years' time; East Europeans, again, took the opposite view.[116] This certainly reflected the fact that in Eastern Europe, generally speaking, living standards had fallen less rapidly than they had in post-communist Russia, and parties and political leaders had generally been more successful in outlining and then implementing a strategy of transformation. But it also reflected a much longer-standing difference in orientations towards government, and a much greater predisposition in Russia towards state control, central leadership and public ownership. The process of political transition with which we are concerned in this book had a number of common features, beyond as well as within the post-communist world; but communist rule in Russia had been longer and more indigenous than in Eastern Europe, and the system that succeeded it was marked by specifically Russian as well as more general characteristics.

2 Reforming the electoral system

Elections were not traditionally an important form of linkage between regime and public in the USSR, or indeed in its Tsarist predecessor.[1] Representative institutions of any kind were slow to develop in pre-revolutionary Russia: the first elected assembly, the State Duma, came into existence as late as 1906, and although it had begun to develop some independent authority by the First World War it operated upon an extremely limited franchise and appears to have engaged little public interest or support by the time of its dissolution. Political parties became legal at the same time, but they operated under severe restrictions and there was little public awareness of the distinctive positions they had assumed – or even of their existence.[2] The short period of Provisional Government from February to October 1917 saw the emergence of legal political contestation, with up to fifty parties competing in relatively free elections both to local authorities and to the Constituent Assembly.[3] The Bolshevik revolution of November 1917, however, although ostensibly intended to transfer 'All power to the Soviets', soon led to the formation of a single-party dictatorship within which political power became increasingly centralised and elections an increasingly empty formality.

The adoption of a new constitution in December 1936 appeared at first to hold out the prospect of significant change. Elections to the newly-established Supreme Soviet became direct and secret; and Stalin, in an interview with an American journalist, went so far as to predict that there would be a 'very lively electoral struggle' among the candidates.[4] Needless to say, nothing of the kind took place, and it was in fact during the Stalin years that the notorious pattern of 99 per cent support for a single list of candidates became established. Stalin himself recorded a favourable vote of more than 100 per cent on one occasion, when voters in neighbouring constituencies insisted on casting their ballot in the Moscow constituency in which the 'leader of leaders' was standing.[5] The Khrushchev years saw a brief and limited discussion of the possibility of a choice of candidate, if not of party;[6] but no formal changes were made, and the Soviet electoral system throughout the Brezhnev period remained the *locus classicus* of what

W. J. M. Mackenzie described as 'acclamatory elections', providing its citizens with little more than an opportunity to approve the choices that had been made beforehand by the party authorities (the Politburo, it later emerged, actually approved the reports of the Central Electoral Commission before the elections themselves had taken place[7]).

The accession of Gorbachev in 1985, by contrast, led to a series of reforms that probably represented the most radical reconstruction of the Soviet political system since the revolution itself. There was, at the outset, little to suggest this would be one of the chief emphases of the programme of perestroika that the new General Secretary put forward. At the 27th Party Congress, in early 1986, a more rapid rate of economic growth was the 'key to all our problems',[8] and the Central Committee meetings which took place later that year devoted more attention to economics than to politics. Gorbachev himself accepted, in a speech to the Polish Sejm in July 1988, that he had initially failed to appreciate the crucial significance of political reform, both for its own sake and for the contribution it could make to economic and other objectives.[9] A brief passage in his speech to the 27th Party Congress did however refer to the need to make 'necessary corrections' in the electoral system; the Congress itself, in its resolution on the report, agreed it was 'correct and timely' to raise the issue; and the revised version of the Party Programme, adopted at the Congress, referred to the 'perfection of the electoral system' and to the development of its 'democratic principles'.[10] Electoral and political reform more generally in turn became an explicit objective at the January 1987 Central Committee plenum as part of a much larger programme of 'democratisation' in all areas of Soviet life.

The critique of past practice

It was widely accepted, in the debate on political reform to which these remarks gave rise, that the existing electoral system had outlived its usefulness.[11] One of the most serious shortcomings in that system was the absence of a choice of candidate, let alone of party. Since at least the early 1920s no more candidates had been nominated than seats available; in the 1984 elections to the USSR Supreme Soviet there was not even this degree of choice as one of the candidates died shortly before the poll, leaving 1,499 contenders to fight it out for the 1,500 seats available.[12] The candidates, moreover, conformed to social and occupational quotas that had been set in advance by the central authorities. As the chairman of a local soviet from Minsk explained, the district instructed him to nominate 'so many mechanisers, so many milkmaids, so many with a higher education and so many with a secondary education'.[13] In another case a local party official had been told to ensure that 4.6 per cent of the candidates in his area were managers, that 1.1 per cent were employed in culture and the arts, and that 45.9 per cent had not previously held representative office.[14] Voters, understandably, had little interest in a set of candidates that had been selected for them in advance by local officials, and often knew no more about them than their biographical data.[15] Deputies, for their part, felt more accountable towards the officials that had nominated them than towards the public that had nominally secured their election.[16]

Voters could, in theory, delete the name of the single candidate standing for election, and at the local level popular nominations were sometimes defeated in this way. Such a practice, however, was strongly discouraged by the need to make use of the screened-off booth in the polling station for this purpose. As V. Timofeev, a war and labour veteran, told *Izvestiia* in early 1987:

You get your ballot – everyone is looking at you. You pull a pencil out of your pocket – everyone can guess your intentions. Young Pioneers or poll attendants are standing by the polling booth. If you go into the booth, it's clear that you voted against the candidate. Those who don't want to vote against go straight to the ballot box. It's the same at plant trade union elections and party election conferences. You can't even go off into a corner by yourself before a curious eye is peering over your shoulder.[17]

The level of turnout was in any case improbably high, even allowing for absentee ballots and other circumstances. In 1984, in the last national elections upon this basis, 99.99 per cent of voters were reported to have taken part, with just a single abstention in Turkmenia out of an electorate of 1.5 million.[18] Part of the explanation, certainly, was 'absentee certificates', which allowed potential non-voters to remove themselves from the register; but there was also abundant evidence of personation and other abuses, with family members voting on behalf of others 'particularly common'.[19] The results were so predictable that (in the Stalin period) they were once announced in advance, and (rather later) newspapers could be prepared with pictures of the successful candidates before the elections themselves had taken place.[20]

There were still further criticisms. Far too many deputies, for instance, secured their position by virtue of the office they held. In the 1984 Supreme Soviet, it was calculated, as many as 39 per cent of the deputies were ministers, party secretaries or others who held their seats more or less *ex officio*. These were balanced by a substantial proportion of ordinary workers and peasants, leaving very few deputies to represent the white-collar professions. Would it be so bad, asked commentators, if there were no milkmaids in the new Supreme Soviet and only a few regional party secretaries, but rather more of the popular and articulate economists, journalists and writers who were doing so much to advance perestroika?[21] Perhaps most worrying of all for the authorities, electoral arrangements of this formalistic kind appeared to be losing their ability to mobilise, still less convince the mass public, with an increase in non-voting, especially among the better educated and urbanised,[22] and falling levels of attendance at nomination meetings in spite of video shows, buffets and other incentives.[23] Gorbachev drew attention to the 'alienation' of working people from the state that supposedly represented their interests in his speech to the 19th Party Conference,[24] and both he and other leaders appear to be well aware of the political danger to the regime if such indifference were allowed to continue indefinitely.

Gorbachev and electoral reform

As well as the now familiar critique of the 'negative tendencies' and 'stagnation' that had characterised the 1970s and early 1980s, Gorbachev's speech to the January 1987 Central Committee plenum placed much greater emphasis than had previously been the case upon the elimination of these and other faults through the 'democratisation' of Soviet society. This involved the workplace and cooperatives together with the CPSU itself, including the principle of secret and competitive ballots for lower (and perhaps eventually for higher) level positions in the party apparatus. Above all, however, it involved reform of the electoral system. 'The Politburo', Gorbachev explained, 'considers the perfection of the Soviet electoral system to be one of the main means of democratising our society'. The essence of the proposals that were reaching the leadership from working people, Gorbachev told the plenum, was that there should be greater popular involvement at all stages of the electoral and pre-electoral process. More particularly, electors should be able to consider several candidacies, in larger constituencies returning several members; this would allow electors to express their own view of the candidates, and in turn give party and state officials a better understanding of the wishes and intentions of the mass public. The fate of the country, as Gorbachev put it in his concluding address, was now 'in the hands of the people'.[25]

Exactly how different these local elections would be became apparent at the end of March 1987 when it was announced that an 'experiment' would take place under which a choice of candidates would be nominated in a number of enlarged constituencies each of which would return several members. In the event, just over 1 per cent of the constituencies were formed on this new multimember basis, and these returned no more than 4 per cent of all the deputies elected on 21 June 1987. Press reports made it clear that this was nonetheless a somewhat different exercise from those that had preceded it: there were greater difficulties than usual in securing nomination, and in the election itself there were some notable casualties, including party and state officials, factory directors and collective farm chairmen. For many senior officials the whole experience was evidently an unwelcome and even distressing one; in Karaganda 'the embarrassed chairman of the district electoral commission did not know how to report the unheard-of news in a delicate way'.[26] At the popular level, however, the response was much more favourable: there was a 'real feeling that the people were choosing', according at least to press reports, and surveys found that while only 55 per cent of those asked took a positive view of the new arrangements before they had been put into effect, fully 77 per cent supported them afterwards.[27]

Gorbachev, in his report to the 19th Party Conference a year later, concluded that competitiveness had made the elections 'more lively, the voters more interested and the deputies more conscious of their responsibilities', and called for the new principles to be applied more widely. It should be possible, for instance, for an unlimited number of candidates to be nominated, and for their respective merits to be freely discussed. The choice from among those nominated should then be made by a 'lively and free expression of the will of the electorate', leading to the election of 'principled, vigorous and experienced deputies' who could effectively represent their constituencies and work energetically on government bodies.[28] There was no further discussion of the electoral system at the Conference itself, apart from a call by Boris Yeltsin for direct and secret elections to all party and state bodies,[29] but the resolution on political reform with which the Conference concluded did commit the party to a 'substantive renewal of the electoral system' in line with Gorbachev's report and in line with the Theses that had been published by the Central Committee in advance of the Conference itself.[30] A Supreme Soviet by-election in January 1988 had already taken place on the basis of these new principles; so too did republican by-elections in October 1988.[31]

The new electoral law, which was published in draft on 23 October and formally adopted on 1 December 1988 after a public discussion, made it clear that electoral choice was now to become a normal rather than exceptional practice at all levels of government. Under Article 38, an unlimited number of candidates could be nominated for each of the seats available (the draft had specified that 'as a rule' there should be a choice of candidate; the final version made no specific provision either way). The right to nominate was extended to voters' meetings of 500 or more, in addition to the Communist Party and other public organisations (Art. 37); and at the elections themselves voters had to pass through a booth or room before casting their ballot (Art. 52). Deputies, for their part, had normally to live or work in the area they represented (Art. 37); there had been some notable absentees in the past including General Bagramian, who had lived in Moscow since the end of World War II while continuing to represent a constituency in Armenia. Candidates, under the new law, had to present 'programmes' to the electorate (Art. 45), and had the right to nominate up to ten campaign staff to assist them (Art. 46).[32] The new legislation was to apply to all future elections at local or national level; together with a working parliament and other reforms, it laid the basis for a combination of party dominance and voter sovereignty that had no obvious precedent in Soviet history or Leninist theory.

The practice of competitive elections

The first real test of political reform was the elections which took place in March 1989 to the USSR Congress of People's Deputies.[33] Under the new law the campaign was to proceed in two stages. In the first, nominations were to be made and then approved by a selection conference in the constituency or social organisation for which the candidate was seeking election. In the second, the candidates that had been 'registered' in this way were to compete for the support of their respective electorates: in the ordinary constituencies up to polling day, which was fixed for 26 March 1989, or in the social organisations up to an election meeting at some point during the previous fortnight. This was a new, elaborate and largely unfamiliar set of procedures; it was also one to which many citizens had strong objections. The representation that had been given to social organisations, in particular, appeared to violate the principle of 'one person, one vote', and the holding of selection conferences to approve a final list of candidates was also unpopular (who needed such 'elections before elections?', it was asked?).[34] It was pointed out in reply that some exercise of this kind was necessary to reduce the number of nominations to manageable proportions; and in any case this stage in the proceedings was bypassed in Estonia, most of Lithuania and some districts of Moscow in order to leave such choices to the electorate.[35]

The selection of candidates in the social organisations took a variety of forms. At one extreme was the Council of Collective Farms, which approved 58 candidates for its 58 seats by open vote in half an hour.[36] The Communist Party itself caused some controversy by nominating no more than 100 candidates for the 100 seats it had been allocated: a 'no-lose lottery', as a disgruntled member described it.[37] The list included most of the Politburo and Secretariat, together with a wide range of figures from science, education, culture and the arts (the Bolshoi soloist Yevgenii Nesterenko was perhaps the most unlikely inclusion).[38] A somewhat more open process took place in the trade unions, which took seven hours and several rounds of voting to produce a list of 114 candidates for the 100 seats that were available.[39] The Writers' Union also had some difficulty reducing its 92 nominations to a final list of 12 candidates. The meeting lasted three days and several ballots were necessary; the leading conservative, Yuri Bondarev, failed in the end to gain a place on the ballot paper, but so too did liberals such as Yevgenii Yevtushenko and Andrei Voznesensky.[40] There was still greater controversy in the Academy of Sciences, where 23 candidates were chosen at a meeting of the Academy's Presidium to contest the 20 seats available. The list did not include Andrei Sakharov, the space scientist Roald Sagdeev and several other well-known reformers, and a vigorous (and eventually successful) campaign took place to secure their nomination at a later stage.[41]

The selection of candidates in the constituencies took a still wider variety of forms. A selection conference at Melitopol in the Ukraine, for instance, was packed out by officials to such an extent that it reminded one participant of a conference of party activists. Of the 33 who asked to speak only 5 were chosen, all of whom supported the Zaporozh'e first secretary, Grigorii Kharchenko; indeed only one of them even raised the possibility that there might be another candidate. The party secretary was duly registered by an overwhelming majority.[42] There were many cases of pressure by party secretaries on other candidates to withdraw: so successful were these efforts in Kazakhstan that all 17 of the republic's first secretaries were unopposed – a 'strange monopoly' as *Pravda* described it.[43] Alternative candidates found it hard to obtain accommodation for their meetings, or to print their publications; at one of their meetings in Leningrad angry speeches were drowned by 'loud dance music'.[44] One hopeful self-nominee was fired from his work just a month before the election; as work collectives could nominate only their own members he could not, as a result, legally become a candidate.[45] Attempts to nominate *Ogonek*'s controversial editor Vitalii Korotich in Moscow's Dzerzhinsky district led to particularly disorderly scenes. A first attempt to hold a meeting was barracked by *Pamiat'* members and in any case fell below the legal quorum; a second meeting, also attended by *Pamiat'*, was packed out and accompanied by 'din, shouts and chaos' according to Yevtushenko, one of the editor's sponsors.[46] Korotich, in the end, had to seek a nomination elsewhere.

In other constituencies, however, a rather more open atmosphere prevailed. In Leningrad's Vasilevsky Island constituency, for instance, the seat had been represented for fifty years by a worker from the local shipyard. In 1989 the University's Law Faculty decided to put forward six of its own nominations, one of them law professor Anatolii Sobchak. Sobchak, whose programme had emphasised legality and human rights, was in turn the single name put forward by the University to the local selection conference. Sobchak had a sceptical view himself of the 'cumbersome and not over-democratic' system of elections that had been devised, and he was urged not to waste his time on a futile challenge. A local party official bet a bottle of cognac on his defeat. Colleagues insisted there could be no chance of real elections under Soviet conditions. And how could a single professor, even if he was elected, hope to defeat the System? Sobchak, however, took his cue from Martin Luther King's speech 'I have a dream', and persuaded the selection conference to include him and three others on the ballot paper. He spoke at more than a hundred public meetings, turning the local under-ground station into a 'political club'. And he took part in television debates between the candidates, the first of their kind that had ever taken place.[47]

Sobchak 'saw life as he had not seen it in fifty years' during the two-month electoral struggle. He was accused himself of demanding the favours of girl students if they were to be admitted to the Faculty. His wife was told to her face that Sobchak had heartlessly refused to visit his spouse, who was 'dying in hospital'. It was even suggested that he wanted to 'castrate the working class' (a colleague had suggested that alcoholics and drug addicts should be persuaded to undergo sterilisation on a voluntary basis). At public meetings Sobchak was asked if he supported proposals of this kind, what he thought about the leading role of the Communist Party, if he was a Jew, and why there were no heroes of capitalist labour while there were plenty of heroes of socialist labour. In these, the 'most democratic, "most alter-native" elections' that had ever taken place in the city, Sobchak fell just short of victory in the first round and then took three-quarters of the vote in a run-off with a single opponent. Elsewhere in Leningrad the city party secretary, Anatolii Gerasimov, was apparently assured of an uncontested nomination until there was a call from an agitated member of the selection conference for another nomination, as this might be their 'last chance'. At the end of the meeting it was announced that the speaker had died; in the elections themselves the alternative nomination, a young worker called Yuri Boldyrev, was overwhelmingly successful.[48]

The most celebrated single contest, that between Boris Yeltsin and Yevgenii Brakov, director of the Zil factory in Moscow, demonstrated both the changes that had taken place and the extent to which even this reformed electoral system could still be manipulated from above. Although he had been nominated by party branches Yeltsin was not one of the 100 candidates recommended for adoption by the CPSU leadership. According to Yeltsin himself there was strong pressure from party officials not to allow him to be put forward as a candidate anywhere else.[49] Nominated eventually for the Moscow national-territorial seat No. 1 after a 13-hour selection conference, Yeltsin found it difficult to develop an electoral campaign: he appeared only once on central television and production of his election material was hindered by party officials.[50] The Central Committee, unprecedentedly in modern times, established a subcommittee at its meeting on 16 March to determine if his outspoken views were compatible with party membership, and published the record of the October 1987 plenum at which his views had been declared 'politically mistaken'.[51] Despite (or perhaps because of) these difficulties, an increasingly charismatic Yeltsin drew enormous crowds for a series of public meetings at which he attacked party privileges, demanded improvements in food and housing, and called for the establishment of an all-union Popular Front as a means of countering the lack of debate within the CPSU and 'apathy' within the wider society.[52]

The public organisations began to choose their deputies on 11 March, and the CPSU made its choice (all 100 candidates were duly elected) on 15 March. The first results in the constituencies were in at about midnight on 26 March; Soviet spacemen had already appeared, ballots in hand, on the evening television news. By the afternoon of the following day about half the results had been declared and special telegrams despatched to the Central Electoral Commission, where staff deputed from the State Statistical Committee entered them into computers.[53] The first and in some ways most significant result was the turnout. The election law and official commentaries had made it clear that the abuses of former years would not be tolerated: fathers voting for families, friends for their neighbours, and officials for anyone who stood in the way of a swift and all but universal turnout. Voting took place over a slightly shorter period than had been customary in earlier years, and the date coincided with the introduction of summer time, which meant an earlier start. In some areas, notably Armenia, an active boycotting campaign had been conducted, and the results of the December 1988 earthquake were still in evidence: voting in Leninakan, for instance, had to take place in prefabricated huts or even tents.[54] In these circumstances an overall turnout of 89.8 per cent could be regarded as a considerable success, modest though it was compared with the artificially inflated totals of previous years.[55]

The results, constituency by constituency, were still more remarkable: a Moscow election official was so overwhelmed when he began to read them that he suffered a heart attack.[56] Some 2,884 candidates had been selected to contest the 1,500 constituencies; in 384 of them, despite the intentions of the new law, there was just a single nomination, but elsewhere there was a choice and in one Moscow constituency as many as 12 candidates were competing for the support of voters. In the event, in 76 of the constituencies where three or more candidates had been nominated none secured more than half the votes and a run-off (*povtornoe golosovanie*) between the two most successful candidates had to be announced, to be held within the following two weeks. Under the election law the result would be determined by a relative majority, not an absolute one, and there was therefore unlikely to be much difficulty in finding a winner. Unexpectedly, however, even 'sensationally' for *Izvestiia*, in 195 constituencies where only one or two candidates were standing none of them secured more than half the vote and no result could be declared. This meant that in these constituencies the whole exercise would have to be repeated (*povtornye vybory*), beginning with the nomination of new and normally different candidates, within a two-month period. In a further three constituencies there would have to be a repeat ballot because fewer than half of the registered electors had voted.[57]

Still more unexpected was the number of defeats suffered by leading party and state officials. A whole series of local leaders, admittedly, were successfully returned, among them the party first secretaries and prime ministers of Belarus, Estonia, Georgia, Kazakhstan, Moldova, the Ukraine, Turkmenia, Uzbekistan and the Russian Republic. And there were some striking victories for individual party leaders: the Astrakhan first secretary, for instance, won more than 90 per cent of the vote, the Tambov first secretary won over 92 per cent, and the first secretary in earthquake-stricken Spitak obtained more than 93 per cent of the vote in his constituency.[58] But the defeats that were suffered by local party and state leaders were even more remarkable. The prime minister of Latvia was defeated, and the prime minister and president of Lithuania; so too were 38 regional and district party secretaries throughout the country.[59] The mayors of Moscow and Kiev were defeated, and the party first secretaries of Kiev, Minsk, Kishinev, Alma Ata and Frunze. The runaway success of Yeltsin in Moscow – with a majority so large it entered the Guinness Book of Records – was a particular snub to the party authorities, given the attempts that had been made to frustrate his campaign.[60] The most spectacular defeats of all, however, were in Leningrad, where the list of casualties included the regional first secretary (a candidate member of the Politburo) and the second secretary, the chairman of the city soviet and his deputy, the chairman of the regional soviet and the city party secretary. Nothing of this kind had happened before in Soviet history.

Further reform and the republican elections

The experience of partly competitive elections to the Congress of People's Deputies led to a further consideration of the system under which they had been conducted. There was strong support, in the discussion, for dispensing with some of the features of the new system that had given rise to the greatest number of objections, particularly selection conferences and the representation of social organisations. Selection conferences (or 'constituency pre-election meetings') were still defended by Barabashev and Vasil'ev, two of the jurists most closely involved in devising the new arrangements. There had been relatively few attempts to exclude controversial candidates; more positively, the conferences had given voters a chance to compare the candidates at first hand and to reduce the number of names on the ballot paper to manageable proportions. The representation of social organisations had been equally unpopular, and some candidates had promised, if elected, to campaign for the removal of this provision from the legislation. Barabashev and Vasil'ev, once again, thought the innovation had been justified by its results: the elections had encouraged a greater degree of activism in the organisations concerned, and they had acted as a 'compensation' mechanism, helping (for instance) to improve the representation of women and young people.[61]

Arguments of this kind, however, hardly disposed of the central issue, which was that members of social organisations enjoyed additional representation in a way that was quite inconsistent with the principle of 'one person, one vote'. And it was arguments of this kind that appeared to carry the greatest weight with the Soviet public. Letters in the press certainly supported the view that candidates should be nominated exclusively by other citizens, with no rights of this kind for social organisations.[62] A poll conducted by the All-Union Centre for the Study of Public Opinion, similarly, found strong support in most parts of the country for the view that the CPSU and other social organisations should be required to nominate candidates in the ordinary way. Far fewer (17 per cent in the Russian Republic) thought the organisations concerned should have a guaranteed number of seats in the national legislature, and a substantial minority (13 per cent in Russia and 22 per cent in the Ukraine) thought such organisations should take no part at all in the electoral process. There was strong support for the principle that candidates should be required to live or work within the constituency for which they sought a nomination. Overwhelming majorities, again, thought a choice of candidate should be compulsory, and very substantial minorities thought selection conferences were unnecessary (although in Russia and Armenia, as compared to the Baltic and Ukraine, they had more supporters than opponents).[63] These and other views were clearly taken into account when the electoral law and constitution were revised again a year later.

Speaking to the Supreme Soviet in October 1989, its then Vice-Chairman Anatolii Luk'ianov explained that this reconsideration involved both changes in general procedures and a greater tolerance of local variation in practices and institutions. Ukraine and the Russian Republic, for instance, both intended to convene Congresses of People's Deputies from which a working Supreme Soviet would be elected; the other republics intended to elect a Supreme Soviet by direct and popular ballot. The formation of presidia would also vary from republic to republic (some would be entirely elected, some entirely *ex officio*, and others still a combination); and there were differences on the representation of social organisations, with some republics proposing to retain and others to abandon it. Different views had similarly been expressed about the idea of selection conferences, and this would be left to the republics to decide. The right to nominate candidates would, however, be extended to universities and colleges, and equal conditions should be established for the candidates – 'far from all' had competed under such circumstances in the March elections. On the question of electoral choice, finally, the existing constitutional provisions would be left unchanged, allowing but not requiring the nomination of more candidates than seats available. This, thought Luk'ianov, was 'more democratic'.[64]

These and other changes were passed into law at the Second Congress of People's Deputies in December 1989.[65] Congresses of Deputies, it was made clear, would not be obligatory at the republican level; there had been some objection to arrangements of this kind from the Baltic republics at the time of their adoption, and in the event only the Russian Republic introduced the complicated two-tier parliament that continued to operate at the national level. It was decided to remove all references to the representation of social organisations from the Constitution; the Congress of People's Deputies, Luk'ianov explained, would continue to be composed in the same way as before, but republics would be free to make their own arrangements. In the event, two of them – Kazakhstan (where a quarter of the seats were allocated on this basis) and Belarus (where handicapped and veterans' organisations were given 50 of the 360 seats) – decided to retain such representation in their republican parliament;[66] the Ukrainian law retained the principle in draft but discarded it in the final version.[67] The reference to selection conferences, similarly, was dropped, allowing republics to make their own arrangements; only four Central Asian republics, in the end, retained them. Despite further suggestions for a change, finally, the number of candidates that were to be nominated remained as before: there could be any number, leaving the decision (at least in principle) to the electorate.[68]

The republican and local elections that took place upon the basis of this amended law were held over a period of months and often on different dates – a further deviation from established practices, which left republican parliaments in some cases to vote themselves an extended period of office.[69] Among the first to vote were the Baltic republics, in February and March 1990; nationalist candidates were overwhelmingly successful, particularly in Lithuania, and the three republics began to move towards independence under non-communist administrations.[70] The Slavic republics voted in early March 1990. In the Russian Federation, over 6,700 candidates competed for the 1,068 seats, with up to 28 candidates in a single constituency. The turnout was 77 per cent, substantially lower than the corresponding

Table 2.1. *Republican elections, 1990*

Republic	Date	Seats	Candidates	Index of competition candidates/seats)	Turnout (%)
Turkmenia	7 Jan.	175	526	3.0	93.6
Uzbekistan	18 Jan.	500	1,094	2.2	93.5
Lithuania	24 Feb.	141	471	3.3	75.0
Kyrgyzstan	25 Feb.	350	878	2.5	92.0
Tajikistan	25 Feb.	230	1,035	4.5	91.2
Moldova	25 Feb.	380	1,892	5.0	83.4
Belarus	4 Mar.	310	1,473	4.8	86.5
Russia	4 Mar.	1,068	6,705	6.3	77.0
Ukraine	4 Mar.	450	3,901	6.9	84.7
Latvia	18 Mar.	201	395	2.0	81.2
Estonia	18 Mar.	105	392	3.7	78.2
Kazakhstan	25 Mar.	270	1,031	3.8	83.9
Armenia	20 May	259	1,390	5.4	60.4
Azerbaijan	30 Sept.	350	n.a.	n.a.	81.0
Georgia	28 Oct.	250	n.a.	n.a.	69.9

Source: Based upon central and republican press reports.

figure a year earlier, and only 121 seats could be filled after the first round of voting; among them, once again, was Boris Yeltsin, chosen by over 80 per cent of those voting in his home town of Sverdlovsk.[71] In the Ukraine, over 3,000 candidates competed for the 450 seats available; turnout was relatively high, at 85 per cent, with nationalist and 'green' candidates enjoyed some success, particularly in the western regions.[72] In Belarus, which also conducted its elections in March, over 1,400 candidates were standing for the 310 seats available; turnout again was relatively high, at 87 per cent.[73]

Elections in the other republics took place at various times: in Armenia, for instance, in May 1990, and in Georgia the date was first postponed and then set for October 1990.[74] The Armenian elections were obviously complicated by the situation in Nagorno-Karabakh, most of whose residents decided to take part in elections to the Armenian Supreme Soviet although they were formally resident in Azerbaijan. The formation of twelve Armenian constituencies within the area was a clear violation of the Soviet constitution, under which a republic could only exercise authority within its own territory; and the elections took place despite a formal ban imposed by the Soviet government and by the Azerbaijani authorities. Ballot papers from Yerevan were seized at Stepanakert airport, which was later closed, and election agents and candidates were placed under house arrest. On election day, 20 May, troops patrolled potential polling stations, but the election took place in apartment blocks and most of the population, except Azerbaijanis and servicemen's families, were able to take part; the reported turnout was 95 per cent.[75] In Armenia itself the 'political indifference' of voters was more apparent; the turnout, already the lowest in 1989, was lower still – 'just over 60 per cent'.[76] In Georgia, a nationalist coalition took 54 per cent of the vote in late October, ahead of local Communists with 30 per cent, and shortly afterwards the veteran dissident Zviad Gamsakhurdia was elected republican president on a programme of transition to complete independence.[77]

As before, there was least competition in Central Asia. In Uzbekistan, for instance, about a third of seats in the February 1990 elections had only one candidate, and a 'good half' of all the candidates were managers or executives. The candidates, moreover, were distributed rather unevenly: in 39 seats there were more than five candidates and in 11 seats there were more than three, but many of the remaining seats had 'alternativeless' candidates who were disproportionately regional and district party secretaries. No fewer than 94.6 per cent of the successful candidates were party members or candidates.[78] The elections in Turkmenia, on the other hand, produced at least one minor sensation when a collective farm milkmaid defeated the head of the ideology department of the republican Central Committee; voters, apparently, were attracted by her 'principled position'.[79] Elections to the Kyrgyz parliament took place in February 1990; so too did elections to the Tajik parliament, where over a third of the successful candidates were party or state officials, and only five were women. The turnout was over 90 per cent.[80] In Azerbaijan, which voted in September 1990, over a thousand candidates were in contention for the 360 seats in the republican parliament; Communist Party candidates secured an overwhelming share of seats, in part because of the harassment of their opponents, but oppositional candidates won at least 26 places in the new parliament and a legitimate place in the political process.[81]

The republican elections that took place in 1990 showed a number of common features. In the first place, turnout levels were down on those that had been recorded a year earlier; later rounds of voting, as before, had still lower levels of turnout than in the first round, and turnout levels were lower in the towns than in the countryside. Turnout levels, as in March 1989, were highest in the Central Asian republics and lowest in Armenia. Secondly, there was a significantly higher level of party or organised group activity, with the beginnings of coordinated platforms across or within republics. This was particularly true of the Baltic republics, which voted by party lists, and major cities, where radical groupings such as 'Democratic Russia' enjoyed their greatest support. Thirdly, there was a greater degree of electoral choice than in the elections to the Congress of People's Deputies the previous year, although levels of choice remained much lower in Central Asia and to local rather than republican levels of government. As a result, larger numbers of seats remained unfilled after the first round of balloting than ever before; the whole exercise became a lengthier one, and (incidentally) a more expensive one.[82] And finally, the candidates remained overwhelmingly CPSU members, but a greater share of seats than ever before went to managers, executives, academics and clerics, and the representation of workers, collective farmers, women and young people declined even further (in the Russian Federation, for instance, the proportion of workers and collective farmers fell from 21.2 to 5.9 per cent[83]).

Electoral reform: some unresolved issues

Elections are to a large extent a matter of procedure: they require a set of conventions to be established which will allow candidates to stand without undue impediment, voters to express their views as between one candidate and another, and the preferences of voters to be reflected at least approximately in the formation of a subsequent government.[84] The adoption of a new election law in 1988, and its amendment in 1989, did not necessarily establish such a set of conventions and indeed sometimes presented its own difficulties of interpretation. What, for instance, was a 'labour collective' with the right to nominate: could it include the apparatus of a local state or Communist Party committee?[85] What kind of citizens' associations had the right to nominate – was it only those that had been 'approved' under an act of 1932, the only existing piece of legislation on nongovernmental bodies in the Russian republic?[86] What about independent trade unions, which did not have to 'register' in this way but still appeared to enjoy the right to nominate that had been granted to such organisations in general?[87] What, *Izvestiia* was asked, about the requirement that candidates 'as a rule' live or work in the constituency they sought to represent: was this a formal requirement or not?[88] And who should determine if proposals for a multiparty system or private property contradicted the Constitution and thus electoral regulations?[89]

Still more serious were the questions that arose in relation to the size of constituencies. Nominally, under the electoral law, territorial and national-territorial constituencies were to have an 'equal number of electors' (Arts. 16 and 17). This was clearly not the case in Latvia, as one of its elected deputies, Viktor Alksnis, told the first Congress of People's Deputies. The number of voters in fact varied between 28,800 and 127,300 as compared with a 'norm' of 62,000. The smaller constituencies were generally in the countryside, giving rural areas more seats than urban ones although 71 per cent of the republic's population lived in the towns. Not only this: ten of the eleven Popular Front leaders had stood in rural constituencies rather than in the towns, which were disproportionately Russian-speaking. Where was the equality of electors of which the law had spoken?[90] There were similar disproportions in Estonia, where the number of electors in a single constituency varied between 3,500 and 6,000 in rural areas, but between 12,000 and 14,000 in the towns, where Russian speakers were again disproportionately concentrated.[91] Nor was the problem confined to the Baltic. In Moscow, for instance, the Veshniakov constituency had 139,236 voters but the Leningrad constituency no fewer than 379,906, as compared with a norm of 257,300.[92]

A more formal analysis prepared by Soviet geographers found that the distribution of seats by republic was improper in the first place: at least 14 constituencies should have been transferred elsewhere, using the 1979 census, or 28 constituencies, if the preliminary results of the 1989 census had been employed. Much more serious distortions were found in the allocation of seats within territorial units, based on a wish not to cut across regional boundaries. And there were regions with a smaller number of electors but a greater number of seats than others – Irkutsk, for instance, had 1,890,000 voters and 7 seats, while Novosibirsk had 1,846,300 voters but 8 seats. The Pskov region, to quote another example, had 635,700 voters and 3 seats, while the Yakut republic had 668,900 voters but only 2 seats.[93] Variations of this kind appeared to arise in part because constituency boundaries had followed existing administrative divisions. But in Estonia, where this was not the case, the number of electors per constituency varied from 3,900 to as much as 15,600.[94] It was hoped that there would at least be some improvement following the adoption by all the republics (except Lithuania) of regulations requiring the publications of lists of constituencies with the number of electors that they included: public opinion, it was thought, would help to keep the number of gross distortions to a minimum.[95] It is nonetheless difficult to believe that the system will evolve much further without an element of judicial process and probably a set of boundary commissioners.

There was a still greater level of concern about the requirement that candidates compete under equal conditions. During the elections to the Congress of People's Deputies some candidates had the assistance of their workplaces, allowing them to print a wide variety of colourful material, while others had much more limited resources at their disposal. As Luk'-ianov later acknowledged, the result had often reflected the candidates' access to resources, not their personal or other qualities.[96] A member of the Central Electoral Commission suggested, during the campaign, that less favoured candidates should be allowed to collect donations in order to assist them in their efforts.[97] Another member of the Commission produced a more considered response a few days later, making clear that any donations of this kind would be improper as they would give some candidates an unfair advantage.[98] The Commission also established that campaign staff, up to the maximum number permitted, would be recompensed out of public funds.[99] The electoral law was amended at the end of 1989 in an effort to ensure more equal 'start positions': candidates, it made clear, took part in the elections on an equal basis, and their electoral expenses were to be paid out of a single fund created by the state as well as by the voluntary donations of enterprises, organisations and citizens.[100] These important principles, reflected or even strengthened in the corresponding republican election laws, were none the less insufficient to prevent what could sometimes be gross violations of the principle of equal competition.

Some candidates, for instance, found their efforts hindered by administrative influences of various kinds. One of them, in the Dnepropetrovsk region, found it very difficult to obtain accommodation in which to hold his meeting, and then found it occupied at the time that had been arranged. Nor could he find a printer that was prepared to print a leaflet with his picture and programme. The other candidate, who was openly supported by two district party secretaries, had no difficulties of this kind and indeed found himself nominated by eight collectives where he was more or less unknown.[101] In the Bashkir republic the local party secretary was able to circulate a poster of his own a month earlier than his competitors, and then arranged for a biography and interview to appear in the local paper, which had evidently 'made its choice'. The republican paper *Sovetskaia Bashkiriia* itself devoted the whole of its front page to the party leader, printing a large portrait as well as an extended interview.[102] Party officials were even prepared to intervene in the electoral campaigns of the clergy. The party secretary of a plant in Elektrostal', it was reported, went to local churches two days before the ballot and demanded that a prayer service be held for one of the Orthodox priests who was competing, but not for the priest who was his competitor. In two other villages, leaflets in favour of this candidate were distributed together with church candles and holy objects.[103]

Many of the candidates who occupied important positions also attempted to boost their support by 'material incentives'. The director of a bread factory, also in the Bashkir republic, arranged for the constituency in which he was a candidate to be provided with four years' supply of buckwheat.[104] In Frunze, local residents were surprised to receive an invitation – the first of its kind they had ever seen – to the local stomatological clinic from 'T. Sel'piev, candidate for constituency no. 32'. An elderly bachelor was even more surprised to receive a printed invitation to a gynaecological clinic.[105] In Minsk, the director of a medical institution appeared at a voters' meeting with a team of well-equipped doctors and announced: 'If you vote for me I'll look after your health. What can my opponents offer you?'.[106] In Khabarovsk, the director of the 'Sputnik' confectionery works distributed coupons for boxes of chocolates at the polling station at which he was a candidate (in the event he failed to gain election).[107] Here, as elsewhere, publicity efforts by candidates themselves were formally prohibited lest any of them enjoy an unfair advantage; the result, in the view of several commentators, was that the candidates were all but unknown to the electorate that was supposed to choose between them – not 'equal opportunities' but 'equal restrictions'.[108]

In apparent violation of this constitutional provision, the electoral law in Lithuania did permit candidates to open a bank account and to accept up to a thousand rubles in donations from individuals, labour collectives, public organisations and movements. The legality of all such operations was to be monitored by the local electoral commission, and any unspent balance was to be transferred after the elections to the republican electoral commission.[109] A decree of the Estonian Supreme Soviet of September 1989 made similar provision for workplaces and public bodies to allocate up to a thousand rubles for the purpose of electoral campaigning within a given town or district. At the same time other republics simply prohibited any financial or material support of candidates by enterprises or individuals, even if it was made available through a single state fund.[110] Regulations on campaign funding were widely agreed to be unsatisfactory, as well as different from one republic to another. Given the virtual impossibility of preventing direct or indirect support being given to candidates, two jurists, Piskotin and Smirnov, suggested it might be better to allow such contributions but to make every effort (as in other countries) to prevent them exercising an undue influence on the electoral outcome;[111] and candidates, it was argued elsewhere, should be required to declare their sources of financial support.[112]

There was of course no shortage of open violations of the electoral law, some of which were sufficiently grave to lead to the invalidation of the results. There were cases of falsification of the records of nomination meetings: two documents of this kind were presented in the Moscow national-territorial seat in which Boris Yeltsin was a candidate.[113] A voter in Alma Ata was allowed to vote for the whole of his family at the very outset of elections to the Congress of People's Deputies;[114] another was given a set of ballot papers only to find that the name of one of the candidates had already been deleted.[115] In a constituency in the Chechen-Ingush republic, 1,163 ballot papers were returned although only 699 had been distributed; the same occurred in other constituencies in the same republic, and in at least one case members of the electoral commission were found to be directly related to the candidates.[116] In another case, in the Moscow region, voters' choices marked in pencil had been erased and 'new' votes had been cast in ink.[117] An electoral commission in the Bashkir republic had to be dissolved when 130 falsified ballots were detected; the chairman of the commission, who was drunk when the investigating committee arrived, turned out to be related to one of the candidates, whose electoral support had originally fallen short of what was needed by exactly the same number of votes.[118] In the Russian presidential elections the following year, the vote in one Novosibirsk constituency took place – apparently an innocent mistake – a day early.[119]

Looking forward to the post-Soviet elections of the future, Russian commentators have drawn several lessons from the partly competitive elections that took place during the last years of communist rule. One suggestion was that future elections should place on a proportional basis so that minorities could be properly represented, and so that successive rounds of voting could be avoided.[120] There were calls for limits on electoral expenditure, with any surplus transferred to other candidates, and for more effective measures to protect electoral commissions from the pressures that are still placed upon them by the 'higher levels of the *nomenklatura*'.[121] Future elections, it was generally accepted, would have to take account of the existence of alternative parties, but it would hardly be appropriate to base the whole exercise upon party lists given that so many voters had no clear affiliation of this kind. The Georgian electoral law of 1990, it was suggested, might offer a way forward: half the seats available were allocated to single member constituences, with plurality voting; the other half was allocated to party lists, with voting by proportional representation.[122] Many questions have nonetheless remained open. Should there, for instance, be a second chamber; and if so, how should it be composed? Should parties be required to obtain a minimum percentage of the vote in order to obtain parliamentary representation; and if so, at what level should the threshhold be set? And if proportional representation was employed, which of its various forms should be adopted?[123] All that was clear, in the early 1990s, was that the answer to such questions was more likely to be found in the practice of other countries than in the lamentable experience of the Soviet system of representation.

3   Structures of government

Electoral reform clearly made little sense without a corresponding change in structures of government themselves. The Soviet parliament, in particular, had for more than thirty years since its foundation been much less than the 'highest body of state authority' for which the Constitution ostensibly provided.[1] The USSR Supreme Soviet was required to meet twice a year but did so for only two or three days on each occasion, making it one of the world's least frequently convened assemblies.[2] Its deputies were all part-timers, reflecting the official view that political representation should form part of ordinary life and not a separate, 'parasitic' profession. There was an elaborate procedure for resolving differences between the Supreme Soviet's two chambers, but its votes had almost always been unanimous: the only recorded exception was in 1955 when an elderly lady delegate, overcome by shock, failed to register her approval of the resignation of Prime Minister Malenkov.[3] Deputies were told when to speak, and – broadly speaking – what to say;[4] and parliamentary journalists could file their copy before the session they were reporting had taken place.[5] There was some attempt, in the late 1960s, to strengthen the Supreme Soviet through the development of its committee system;[6] but for the most part the assembly Gorbachev inherited was – like its predecessors – an 'ornamental' rather than operational part of the political system, its purpose to invest party decisions with the 'garb of constitutional legality'.[7]

There were, in fact, some limits to the value of institutions of this kind of party leaders. Ministers were immune from challenge, not just to their policies, but also to their personal competence. Legislation that received so little attention was frequently poorly drafted or misconceived; this could lead to expensive mistakes, and often to a multitude of sublegislative acts in which the intentions of the original law were clarified. And the Soviet public were generally sceptical of the effectiveness of political action through channels of this kind, making their point (when they chose to do so) in a less conventional or even violent manner. As early as the 1950s, under Khrushchev, there was some attempt to strengthen the authority of local soviets,[8] and in the early 1970s there was a further attempt to strengthen the authority of deputies at all levels.[9] The Supreme Soviet, at the apex of the representative system, was relatively little affected by these developments. Oppositionists and liberals, however, continued to press for changes that would allow it to become an 'effective working body with longer sessions at more frequent intervals';[10] and under Yuri Andropov, in the early 1980s, some attempt was made to reduce the number of party and state officials in the Supreme Soviet and to expand its committee system still further.[11] Even Brezhnev, as he explained in the late 1970s, was concerned to ensure that 'every, I repeat every, Soviet citizen should feel involved in state affairs, that his opinion, his voice will be heard and taken into account in the making of both large and small decisions'.[12]

Reform of representative institutions gathered pace with Gorbachev's accession, and particularly after the January 1987 meeting of the CPSU Central Committee. Addressing that meeting, Gorbachev made clear that economic reform was conceivable only in association with a far-reaching 'democratisation' of the political system, designed to reverse the 'social corrosion' that had developed over the Brezhnev years. The leadership of the time, he argued, had failed to see the changes that were required. 'Crisis phenomena' had been allowed to accumulate, and social problems like crime and drug abuse had worsened. Party leaders had become increasingly intolerant of criticism or even of discussion; some had abused their trust and permitted – even encouraged – openly criminal activities. Whole republics, regions and ministries had been affected. All of this, in Gorbachev's view, argued the need for a 'profound democratisation' of Soviet society, designed to ensure that ordinary people once again felt able to associate themselves with its objectives. Only through the broadening of the democratic forms inherent in socialism, Gorbachev suggested, could they achieve the break-throughs that were needed in economic and social life; there would still be leadership 'from above', but it should be balanced by effective democratic control 'from below'. The further democratisation of Soviet society accordingly became the party's 'most urgent task'.[13]

Gorbachev elaborated upon the reasons for these changes in subsequent speeches. The purpose of the reforms, he told a meeting in Latvia, was to 'fling open the doors to the broad democratisation of all spheres of Soviet society'.[14] Only democratisation, he told the trade unions in February 1987, could provide a guarantee against the repetition of past errors, and consequently a guarantee that the restructuring process was irreversible.[15] The June 1987 Central Committee plenum agreed with his proposal that a party conference – the first for nearly fifty years – should be called in the summer of 1988 to take this programme of democratic reform further.[16] In his address on the seventieth anniversary of the revolution the following November Gorbachev returned to the theme. There were two key problems in the development of perestroika, he told his audience: the democratisation of social life, and radical economic reform. Democratisation in particular was 'at the core of perestroika', vital to its success and indeed to the future of socialism in general. It would advance through the soviets, which must 'live up to their role as sovereign and decision-making bodies'.[17] Democratisation was 'the main thing', he explained in February 1988, the 'decisive means of achieving the aims of perestroika'. Only through democratisation could the 'human factor' be given full play; only through democratisation and glasnost could apathy be ended and ordinary people encouraged to take a part in managing their own society.[18]

By May 1988, speaking to the media, Gorbachev was ready to argue that democratisation was the 'key to everything'. Unless they created a permanent democratic mechanism of this kind, 'involving the people in all of society's affairs', the reform process would grind to a halt.[19] By June 1988, in his speech to the 19th Party Conference, Gorbachev called for 'radical reform' of the political system, not just 'democratisation', and went on to argue that it was 'crucial' to the solution of all the other problems that faced Soviet society. The political system established by the October revolution, he told the Conference, had undergone 'serious deformations'. This had made possible the omnipotence of Stalin and his entourage, and a 'wave of repressive measures and lawlessness'. The 20th Party Congress in 1956 had begun to eliminate these distortions, but had not succeeded in doing so because the importance of democratic change had been underestimated. A 'bloated administrative apparatus' had taken over the management of economic as well as political life; about a third of the population had been elected to local government bodies of various kinds, but most of them had been deprived of real influence. Society had been 'straitjacketed' by political control, and ordinary working people had become 'alienated' from public ownership and management. It was this 'ossified system of government, with its command-and-pressure mechanism', that was now the main obstacle to perestroika.[20]

The debate was taken further in the general and specialist press, and at conferences and meetings. As three prominent jurists, Barabashev, Sheremet and Vasil'ev, pointed out in the legal journal *Sovetskoe gosudarstvo i pravo*, surveys had found low levels of satisfaction with the work of the Soviets, and even deputies themselves appeared to be unsure of their own usefulness. There had been encouraging signs recently, such as the criticism and amendment of legislation that had taken place in the Supreme Soviet, 'probably for the first time in its history', in the summer of 1987. But deputies were allowed access to legislation only in its final stages, when it was difficult to make any changes, and the brevity of Supreme Soviet sessions meant that even the annual plan and budget could hardly be seriously discussed. So far as the number of legal directives was concerned, the Presidium and Council of Ministers were far more important sources than the Supreme Soviet itself; and its own laws were poorly drafted, at least in part because deputies had little influence upon their preparation. The Supreme Soviet could hardly hope to act as guardian of the constitution without a committee on legality within its structure; and there was no constitutional court. Nor had the Supreme Soviet ever exercised its right to hear a report by the Soviet government, the USSR Council of Ministers; the last such report, according to a writer in *Pravda*, was as long ago as 1935.[21]

There was very general agreement among contributors to the discussion, which extended throughout the late 1980s, that the elected soviets should become (as Barabashev, Sheremet and Vasil'ev put it) 'genuine centres of the elaboration and adoption of all major state decisions in the field of legislation and administration'. This meant, for instance, that deputies should be chosen for their professional competence rather than their social origins, and that they should be able to devote much more of their time to representative duties. Few of them, if any, should hold government office. The party, equally, should work exclusively through its representatives in the Soviets and make no attempt to discipline them unless a decision was taken which was entirely at variance with CPSU policy.[22] A more radical view, put forward by the jurist Boris Kurashvili in *Kommunist* in May 1988, was that nothing less than 'Soviet parliamentarianism' was likely to be sufficient. This would involve a separation of powers with a constitutional court that could strike down government decisions, and a parliament that excluded ministers from its membership (how, he asked, could they 'report to themselves and monitor themselves?'). Kurashvili also favoured a system of smaller, virtually full-time Soviets staffed by salaried politicians, working largely through standing committees, and sustained by a research staff and wide-ranging powers of investigation. All of this, in Kurashvili's view, was necessary if there was to be a move from the 'support democracy' of earlier years to a 'democracy of participation'.[23]

A number of these proposals found a place in Gorbachev's speech at the 19th Party Conference a month later. The resumption of full authority by the soviets was indeed the General Secretary's central proposal. The soviets, he made clear, must have more adequate, independent and stable sources of revenue, and greater control over local enterprises; and they should work, so far as possible, 'in full view of the electorate'. Some of the deputies should be freed from their ordinary work and allowed to become full-time representatives; and they should be allowed to choose their executive committees by secret ballot from a plurality of candidates. There should be limitations upon the period of time for which an executive office could be held – two terms, or three in exceptional circumstances (the absence of such restrictions in the past had been a 'prime cause of abuses of power both centrally and locally'). The most unexpected of Gorbachev's proposals concerned the USSR Supreme Soviet, which was to become a smaller working body of 400–450 deputies elected from a much larger Congress of People's Deputies, which would meet annually. The whole state structure would be headed by a Chairman of the USSR Supreme Soviet, who would nominate the Chairman of the Council of Ministers and guide the work of a reconstituted Presidium.[24]

These proposals were broadly endorsed by the Conference and in turn found reflection in the constitutional amendments that were adopted on 1 December 1988 after an extended public discussion.[25] There was 'broad support' for the changes, according to official sources,[26] but also a number of specific criticisms. Who really needed the Congress of People's Deputies, for a start? A strange, almost medieval 'assembly of estates', its only purpose seemed to be to '"filter" the will of the electorate'.[27] Would it not be better to elect the new Supreme Soviet directly, thus keeping the distance between deputies and their constituents to a minimum?[28] The relationship between the two bodies was in any case unclear, argued a Moscow professor. Was the new Supreme Soviet equal in constitutional authority to the Congress of People's Deputies, or simply its organ? Which was 'supreme' – and if it was the Congress of People's Deputies, should the Supreme Soviet not be renamed?[29] And how was the working Supreme Soviet to be chosen from the 2,250 deputies that had been elected to the Congress of People's Deputies?[30] There was also some resistance to the idea of full-time deputies. Workplaces, faced with the loss of their services, would nominate their least effective members,[31] and the deputies, involved in parliamentary duties in the capital, would lose touch with those who had elected them. What about deputies that had small children?[32] And how were constituents supposed to find their deputy in these new circumstances: by travelling up to Moscow?[33]

The draft legislation, these criticisms notwithstanding, was duly adopted by the Supreme Soviet on 1 December 1988; Gorbachev, with some poetic licence, called this the 'last act in its rich political biography'.[34] The changes that were agreed made clear, among other things, that all soviets were to be elected for a five-year term (Art. 90), and that no deputy could serve on more than two soviets at the same time (Art. 96). Much more controversially, the Supreme Soviet accepted Gorbachev's proposal (made originally at the Party Conference) that the new supreme state body, the USSR Congress of People's Deputies, should be elected not only by the population at large and by national-territorial areas but also by public organisations like the Communist Party and the trade unions (Art. 109). The Congress, it was agreed, would elect a Supreme Soviet which would meet for a spring and autumn session every year, each of three or four months' duration (Art. 112).

A fifth of its members would stand down every year (Art. 111), as would a fifth of the membership of its standing committees (Art. 122). Wide-ranging powers were given to a new Chairman of the USSR Supreme Soviet, who would exercise 'general guidance' over the work of state bodies and issue his own directives (Art. 121). Similar changes were instituted in the union and autonomous republics (Arts. 137–42, 143–4); local soviets, in addition, were to have their own presidia and chairmen, who were to account once a year to the soviet that had elected them and to the population at large (Arts. 145–50).

The Congress of People's Deputies and Supreme Soviet

The representative institutions that emerged from these reforms were very different from the 'supreme state organs' that had preceded them. There were, in fact, more party members in the Congress of People's Deputies than in the outgoing Supreme Soviet: 88 per cent of the new deputies were CPSU members or candidates, well above the previous level, and higher even than the proportion of party members and candidates among those that had contested the election.[35] Officials, despite the reform's intentions, were also better represented: 65 per cent of the new deputies were paid administrators of some kind, as compared with 48 per cent in the outgoing Supreme Soviet, and this despite the fact that ministers were no longer eligible for election (the main increase was in lower administrative positions). Equally, however, the scientific and cultural intelligentsia was much more fully represented in the new Congress than in the old Supreme Soviet. Apart from Sakharov, Sagdeev and others, the deputies included the eminent literary scholar Dmitrii Likhachev, the political commentators Fedor Burlatsky and Roy Medvedev, sociologist Tatiana Zaslavskaia, economists Gavriil Popov, Nikolai Shmelev and Oleg Bogomolov, and writers such as Valentin Rasputin, Chingiz Aitmatov and Yevgenii Yevtushenko. There were seven religious leaders, the first ever elected to a Soviet legislative body; rural leaseholders and commercial cooperators were also represented for the first time; and there was a substantial detachment of pensioners. This was no longer an assembly of officials and token representatives of the working class and peasantry.

In line with the new doctrine that deputies should be chosen for their political qualities rather than their social characteristics, the Congress was also less representative in a sociological sense of the population that had elected it. The proportion of women deputies, most notably, was down by about half, from 32.8 to 15.7 per cent,[36] and would have been lower still but for the 75 seats specifically reserved for the Soviet Women's Committee. The CPSU, with 100 seats at its disposal, chose only 12 women; the Komsomol, more than half of whose members were women, chose 11 out of

Table 3.1. *Social composition of the USSR Supreme Soviet (1984),*
Congress of People's Deputies (1989) and the USSR Supreme Soviet (1989)

	Supreme Soviet, 1984 (%)	Congress 1989 (%)	Supreme Soviet, 1989 (%)	No.
Top political leadership	1.5	0.7	0.2	1
Top and middle-level managerial personnel*	40.0	39.8	32.8	178
Lower echelon managerial personnel†	6.6	25.3	35.3	191
Workers, collective farmers, non-professional office employees	45.9	22.1	18.3	99
Highly professional intellectuals	6.0	10.2	12.5	68
Priests	0.0	0.3	0.0	0
Pensioners	0.0	1.6	0.9	5
Total	100.0	100.0	100.0	542

* Republican, regional and territorial-level party leaders, responsible employees of the CPSU Central Committee, leaders of the Supreme Soviets of the USSR and the union republics, government ministers, top military leaders, directors of research and educational institutions, etc.
† Chiefs of workshops, departments, work teams, laboratories, collective and state farms, etc.
Source: Moskovskie novosti, 1989, no. 24, p. 8.

75. Even the teaching profession, more than two-thirds female, chose only one woman among its four representatives. What hope could this provide that women would play an equal part with men in shaping public policy in the coming years?[37] The proportion of workers and collective farmers, equally, was down by about half: workers from 34.3 per cent in the outgoing Supreme Soviet to 17.9 per cent in the new Congress, and collective farmers from 10.6 to 4.9 per cent.[38] To look at the composition of the new Supreme Soviet, a trade union deputy remarked, you would think the country was made up of 'nothing but intellectuals, scientists, Academicians and professors'.[39] The Kyrgyz party leader, Absamat Masaliev, went so far as to suggest a constitutional amendment that would ensure more adequate representation of the working class, peasantry and 'our respected veterans' in the future.[40] 'Now the workers will understand they have been fooled', a party secretary in Odessa is reported to have remarked;[41] and if this was too simple a verdict, the 1989 elections did none the less mark the end of the USSR as a state where policies were at least nominally determined by ordinary working people rather than by white-collar professionals claiming to speak on their behalf.

The Congress of People's Deputies, which held its first session on 25 May 1989, made a number of further innovations in Soviet political and constitutional practice. It began with a call for a minute's silence in memory of the peaceful demonstrators that had died in Tbilisi the previous month, and demanded that the guilty men be publicly identified.[42] Gorbachev, as expected, was elected to the newly-established post of Chairman of the Supreme Soviet, but two candidates were nominated to stand against him and he secured election, in the end, by a less than unanimous vote (2,123 in favour, but 87 against).[43] Deputies went on to suggest that he resign the General Secretaryship and leave the Politburo on assuming these new responsibilities of state.[44] His recent speeches, it was complained had 'lacked the clarity and boldness that used to characterise them'.[45] What was his position on the sovereignty of the republics, Baltic deputies wanted to know?[46] Had he a dacha in the Crimea, other deputies enquired?[47] And was he able, unlike Napoleon, to avoid the 'adulation and influence of his wife'?[48] Anatolii Luk'ianov, who was elected First Vice-Chairman of the Supreme Soviet four days later, faced a still more extended inquisition from deputies, including questions about his responsibility, while in the Central Committee apparatus, for the fact that the country had been 'engulfed in crime'.[49]

Gorbachev addressed the Congress on 30 May 1989, and prime minister Ryzhkov on 7 June. Most of the remainder of the session, which lasted until 9 June 1989, was given over to speeches, initially on procedural issues, but latterly on all aspects of party and state policy, and often of a sharply critical character. For Pavel Bunich, for instance, the USSR led the world in the number of resolutions it adopted about the economy, but also in the length of its queues. He called for the Ministry of Finance to be given a 'last chance'.[50] The head of the Soviet women's committee, Zoia Pukhova, asked why more women than men were working on night shifts, and called for 'more profundity' in the speeches of Gorbachev and other leaders on these matters.[51] Boris Yeltsin, in an explosive contribution, complained that power was still monopolised by the party and state apparatus and warned that the head of state had accumulated so much authority that a 'new dictatorship' was possible.[52] The economist Emel'ianov, supporting him, argued that an 'elite stratum' was 'wallowing in luxury' while tens of millions were living below the poverty line. No ruling class, he warned, had ever surrendered its position voluntarily.[53] Yevtushenko referred to the problem as the 'cult of personality of the state' and called for a constitutional amendment which would give non-party members equal treatment in appointments instead of 'thumbing through the same old greasy *nomenklatura* pack'.[54]

Another target was the KGB. Yuri Vlasov, an Olympic weightlifter, in an astonishing speech, listed the sites in which its victims had been buried and accused it of crimes 'unknown in the history of humanity'. He went on to describe the contemporary KGB as an 'underground empire', all-powerful and largely uncontrolled, and called for its headquarters to be moved from central Moscow and its activities to be directly subordinated to the Congress and Supreme Soviet.[55] Andrei Sakharov, himself criticised for his remarks about the conduct of the war in Afghanistan, read out an alternative programme which included the removal of the CPSU and its leading role from the Constitution.[56] Chingiz Aitmatov, one of the party's deputies to the Congress, compared Soviet living standards unfavourably with those of Sweden, Finland, Austria, Holland, and 'Canada over the ocean', not to speak of Switzerland.[57] The writer Yuri Kariakin called for Solzhenitsyn to be given back his Soviet citizenship, and went on to propose that Lenin be reburied in Leningrad and that the names of all the victims of Stalinist repression be engraved on the Lubianka.[58] Moscow University economist Gavriil Popov called for half the economy to be handed over to private ownership; another deputy, television commentator Yuri Chernichenko, asked why responsibility for agriculture had been given to someone (Ligachev) who knew nothing about it and had already 'made a mess of things in ideology'. With five times as many tractors and ten times as many combine harvesters, Chernichenko remarked, they were still producing half as much bread as the United States.[59]

Other issues that were repeatedly aired included the national question and the ecological situation. A. A. Grakhovsky, a Belarusian deputy, wanted a state programme to deal with the aftermath of the Chernobyl explosion.[60] A. V. Iablokov, speaking more generally, pointed out that 20 per cent of the population lived in ecological disaster zones, and that a further 35–40 per cent lived in areas that were seriously polluted. Every third man in these areas contracted cancer, and every year the number of cases increased. The same was true of the food supply: more than 30 per cent of the food consumed in what was then Leningrad was unhealthy, and more than 42 per cent of children's dairy products (although not quite a secret, the report in which these disturbing facts had appeared had been published in a print-run of just 18 copies).[61] The writer Sergei Zalygin, who dealt with the same issues, identified the Aral Sea as a 'global catastrophe'; another deputy, O. O. Suleimenov from Kazakhstan, mentioned the harmful consequences of the nuclear tests that had taken place in Semipalatinsk.[62] The Congress, responding to these appeals, decided to increase pensions at once rather than wait for the adoption of a new law; it also set up a committee to investigate the sensitive question of privileges. Two other questions were entrusted to commissions: one, headed by Alexander Iakovlev, was to examine the 1939 Nazi-Soviet pact, and the other was to review the circumstances which had led to the brutal suppression of a peaceful demonstration in Tbilisi on 9 April.[63]

One of the Congress's first acts was to set up the new-style Supreme Soviet, a much smaller body which was expected to remain in session for most of the year. The elections were based in part on a regional quota system; Boris Yeltsin, nominated for the Russian Republic, failed at first to secure election but then obtained a place when another deputy stood down in his favour.[64] Despite historian Yuri Afanas'ev's criticism that it was a 'Stalinist-Brezhnevite' body with an 'aggressively obedient majority',[65] the new Supreme Soviet when it met for the first time on 3 June soon showed that it would be a very different institution from its unlamented predecessor. One sign of this was the elaborate committee system that was set up, including committees of the Supreme Soviet as a whole and commissions attached to each of its two chambers. One of the Supreme Soviet's new committees dealt with defence and state security, including the KGB; another with glasnost and citizens' rights. Taken together, about two-thirds of the work of the new parliament was expected to take place under their auspices.[66] Another sign was the difficulty with which the new Council of Ministers was formed. Ryzhkov himself was elected relatively easily to the premiership, with nine against and thirty-one abstentions,[67] but all the other nominations were intensively questioned and ten of Ryzhkov's original candidates were rejected.[68] This 'parliamentary marathon' took about three weeks; Ryzhkov later described it as the most unusual process of government formation in the history of Soviet rule.[69]

There were four more sessions of the Congress of People's Deputies, and parallel sessions of the new-style Supreme Soviet. None of them had the impact of the first Congress, but all of them marked important stages in the progress of reform. The second Congress of People's Deputies, in December 1989, gave its main attention to a programme of economic recovery proposed by Nikolai Ryzhkov on behalf of the Soviet government.[70] The programme, in the end, was overwhelmingly approved, but not before the government had been accused of 'administrative narcosis' with the introduction of a market 'systematically put off'.[71] A Lithuanian deputy insisted that the socialist economy had failed, 'not only in our country and not only in Eastern Europe but in all countries of a socialist orientation'.[72] For a Georgian deputy, Ryzhkov was offering no more than 'socialist starvation'.[73] There were further calls for the government to 'go green': they were all living five or six years less than they should, it was pointed out, and only 14 per cent of school leavers were healthy.[74] Yeltsin, in another vigorous speech, complained of the 'indecisiveness, compromises and tightrope-walking between the interests of the apparatus and those of the society' which had led to an 'all-round crisis';[75] and there was further pressure, particularly from the radical Inter-Regional Group, for the abolition of reform of Article 6, which enshrined the party's 'leading role'.[76]

Table 3.2. *Committees and Standing Commissions of the USSR Supreme Soviet, 1989–91*

Committees of the Supreme Soviet of the USSR

Public Health Committee
Committee on Ecology and the Rational Use of Natural Resources
International Affairs Committee
Committee on Glasnost and Citizens' Rights and Appeals
Committee on Women and the Protection of the Family, Maternity and Childhood
Committee on Veterans and Disabled Persons
Committee on Science, Public Education, Upbringing, and Culture
Committee on Economic Reform
Committee on Agriculture and Food
Committee on Construction and Architecture
Committee on the Activity of the Soviets of People's Deputies and the Development of
    Administration, Management and Self-Government
Committee on Legislation, Legality, Law and Order
Committee on Defence and State Security

Standing Commissions of the Chambers of the USSR Supreme Soviet

Council of the Union	Council of Nationalities
Commission on Labour, Prices and Social Policy	Commission on Consumer Goods, Trade, Utilities and Other Services
Commission on Planning, Budget and Finance	
Commission on Transport, Communications and Information	Commission on the Development of Culture, Language, National and International Traditions, and the Protection of Historical Heritage
Commission on the Development of Industry, Power Engineering, and Technology	Commission on the Social and Economic Development of Union and Autonomous Republics, Autonomous Regions and Areas
	Commission on the Nationalities Policy and Inter-Ethnic Relations

Source: Vedomosti S"ezda narodnykh deputatov i Verkhovnogo Soveta SSSR, 1989, no. 1, arts. 33, 36 and 40.

The third Congress, in March 1990, was described as an 'extraordinary' one; it was certainly exceptional, in that it authorised a presidential system for the first time in Soviet or Russian political practice. The presidency was opposed by Yuri Afanas'ev, on behalf of the Inter-Regional Group of deputies; it would, he warned, be a 'very grave political mistake' to institute such a position before there had been a more general constitutional reform.[77] Another speaker warned of the danger of a 'return to dictatorship'.[78] Others supported the new system as a means of ending a dangerous 'vacuum of power', and there were suggestions that it be extended to the republics as well.[79] Anatolii Luk'ianov, proposing the change, argued that it would help to end the impasse that had developed between parliament and government, and added that there would be guarantees against the abuse of presidential power, including an age limit and the ability of the Congress of People's Deputies to revoke his mandate.[80] In the end the vote was overwhelmingly favourable: 1,817 in favour of the presidency, with 133 against and sixty-one abstentions;[81] and Gorbachev was duly elected to the new position, after others had withdrawn their nominations, with 71 per cent of the vote.[82] The Congress at the same time approved the modification of Article 6 of the constitution, ending the Communist Party's guaranteed monopoly, and of Article 7, making clear that all parties and movements would have to work within the Soviet constitution and laws.[83]

The fourth Congress, in December 1990, saw further constitutional changes. 'Life itself', Gorbachev suggested, had brought them to a presidential system; the Congress saw that system consolidated, with the establishment of a Cabinet of Ministers directly subordinate to the President. Gorbachev had talked, in March, of the need for a new union treaty; at the fourth Congress he suggested that a referendum be held to approve it, and at the same time to undermine the 'destructive actions of separatist and nationalist forces'. Several measures of economic reform were approved, including a sales tax and a 'stabilisation fund', cuts in military spending, and the sale of state assets.[84] A new union treaty, in the event, was approved in principle,[85] but Yeltsin (now chairman of the Russian Supreme Soviet) insisted that the 'revolution from above' had ended and refused to accept any reimposition of the *diktat* of the centre.[86] Nikolai Ryzhkov, in his last speech as prime minister, conceded that perestroika in its original form had failed.[87] Eduard Shevardnadze unexpectedly resigned as foreign minister, warning in a dramatic speech that 'dictatorship [was] advancing';[88] a Ukrainian deputy warned similarly that a '*coup d'état*' was taking place – a 'quiet, "creeping", right-wing, reactionary *coup d'état*'.[89] The KGB chairman Vladimir Kriuchkov, who also addressed the meeting, sounded a different note with his warnings about the work of Western intelligence services and economic 'sabotage'.[90]

The fifth and final Congress, which met in September 1991 just after the coup had collapsed, was also an 'extraordinary' one. Indeed its business was unprecedented: it consisted largely in establishing a new form of government for what was expected to be a short transitional period. The Congress of People's Deputies disappeared entirely. In its place, and fulfilling its functions, was a modified Supreme Soviet, with two chambers both made up of republican nominees. A new State Council was established, consisting of the USSR President and the heads of state of each of the republics, to give overall direction to the affairs of the states that were still members of the union.[91] This new and inter-republican Supreme Soviet met for a single session later in the year; the parliamentary experiment that had begun so hopefully finally ended on 26 December when one of the two chambers, which was in fact inquorate, voted to liquidate the USSR altogether and with it this transitional system of representation.[92] *Izvestiia*'s journalists, watching it depart, felt neither joy nor sorrow, just a feeling that it was an 'historical inevitability'; it had been divided from the outset between radicals and conservatives, and failed, in the end, to rally to its own defence during the short-lived coup. And yet it had been here, in the first Soviet parliament, that the transition to democracy had been initiated.[93]

The Soviet parliament: some indicators of performance

One measure of the increased authority of the new Soviet parliament was the number of days on which it convened. The 1977 Constitution had specified that the Supreme Soviet should be convened 'twice a year' (Art. 112). The number of days on which the Supreme Soviet held its meetings did in fact increase after the exceptional war and postwar period up to the fourth convocation of the mid 1950s, when to some writers at least it seemed that it was gradually evolving into an influential and genuinely parliamentary institution. There were still some years, however, in which the Supreme Soviet met only once, despite the requirements of the constitution;[94] and after the Khrushchev years it met less and less frequently, with occasional variations such as when an exceptional four-day session (with nearly 100 speeches) was held to consider the new Constitution in October 1977. The Supreme Soviet met less frequently than ever before during the Brezhnev years, convening only once – despite the Constitution – in 1967, 1971, 1976 and 1982. Throughout the 1970s and early 1980s (see table 3.3) the Supreme Soviet was normally in session for no more than four or five days of the year, significantly below its long-term average.

In 1988, the year of the 19th Party Conference, the outgoing Supreme Soviet met in four separate sessions, considering a law on cooperatives, constitutional reform and the plan and budget as well as a series of personnel changes. The decisive transition, however, was in 1989, when the Congress of People's Deputies together with the new Supreme Soviet began to meet over extended periods. The Congress was supposed to meet in regular session 'once a year' (Art. 110); in fact it met twice in 1989, twice again in 1990, and for a final session in 1991. The Supreme Soviet that it constituted

Table 3.3. *The USSR Supreme Soviet and Congress of People's Deputies: some indicators of performance, 1938–90*

Convocations	Days of meeting p.a.	Speeches p.a.	Laws p.a.	Interpellations p.a.
1st (1938–46)	7.1	72.6	10.8	0
2nd (1946–50)	6.0	76.0	14.8	0
3rd (1950–54)	5.5	62.0	9.8	0
4th (1954–58)	9.8	142.5	32.0	3
5th (1958–62)	6.3	132.3	34.5	2
6th (1962–66)	5.5	116.8	28.0	3
7th (1966–70)	5.5	85.3	25.8	0
8th (1970–74)	4.5	77.3	21.0	0
9th (1974–79)	5.4	92.4	21.0	0
10th (1979–84)	5.0	73.0	11.8	0
11th (1984–89)	5.2	114.4	9.2	5
1st–4th (1989–90)	19.0	1,024.0	35.5	1

Source: Calculated from *Zasedaniya Verkhovnogo Soveta SSSR*, 1938–88, and *Pervyi – Chervertyi s"ezd narodnykh deputatov SSSR*, 1989–90.

as a 'working organ' met more frequently still, though less than the six to eight months the Constitution now specified; and by the early 1990s, the Congress and Supreme Soviet were meeting, taken together, at least as frequently as parliaments in the major liberal democracies.[95] The work of parliamentary committees was also an intensive one: in their first two years the committees and commissions attached to the new Supreme Soviet held 1,250 formal sessions, very much more than the twenty or so meetings that had been held every year by standing commissions attached to its predecessor.[96] The committees, as before, invited experts and specialists to take part in their work, and between thirty and 100 deputies who were not at the time members of the Supreme Soviet itself were also present at every meeting.[97]

Deputies, for their part, became more assertive and outspoken public representatives. There were about seventy or eighty speeches a year in the old Supreme Soviet, rather more during the Khrushchev years (see table 3.3). A substantial and, in the 1970s, increasing proportion of speeches were made by ministers or committee chairmen, rather than by deputies themselves; and most legislation was adopted after a perfunctory discussion, sometimes after no discussion at all. The new statute on people's control, for instance, was adopted in 1979 after a minister had spoken in its favour, and the law on the legal position of foreigners in 1981 was approved after a single committee chairman had responded.[98] And no use at all was made, after

1965, of the interpellation or *zapros*. The 1977 Constitution provided that deputies had the right 'to address inquiries to the Council of Ministers of the USSR, and to Ministers and the heads of other bodies formed by the Supreme Soviet of the USSR'. A verbal or written reply had to be tendered 'within three days at the given session of the Supreme Soviet of the USSR' (Art. 117). From 1965 until the late 1980s, however, there were no inquiries of this kind in either chamber, although the practice continued at the local level. Earlier interpellations had usually provided no more than a platform for foreign policy pronouncements by the Soviet government. It was difficult, nonetheless, to argue that the Supreme Soviet had actually gained in authority by their apparent abandonment.

The position since the late 1980s has been very different. The interpellation returned in 1987. The same year, during a debate on the taxation of newly-established enterprises, there were the first open disagreements.[99] In 1988 the new cooperative law had to be referred back to committee for further discussion, and then later in the year two Presidium edicts were opposed and (in December) there were votes against the constitutional amendments – so unexpected the chairman failed to see them and then initially recorded them as abstentions.[100] In 1988 the number of speeches was back to the levels of the Khrushchev years; and from 1989 onwards there were several hundred speeches every year to the Congress of People's Deputies, as well as several hundred briefer contributions to debate (*preniia* rather than *vystupleniia*) and contributions to the smaller working Supreme Soviet. Predictably, perhaps, the Slavic republics contributed more than their share to these discussions, and the Central Asian republics rather less.[101] Deputies, from the late 1980s, were organised into loose groupings or fractions: the largest, in December 1990, was the Communist group (with 730 deputies), followed by the hard-line 'Soiuz' group (562), the 'agrarians' (431), the 'workers' (400), those from the autonomous republics (239), the radical Inter-Regional Group (229), and an ecological grouping (220). Some deputies, however, belonged to more than one group, and voting patterns showed little evidence of group cohesion.[102]

The legislative output of the old Supreme Soviet showed a similar pattern, rising sharply in the Khrushchev years, and then falling sharply in the 1970s and 1980s. During the first three convocations (1938–54) the Supreme Soviet met irregularly and was concerned almost exclusively with the annual budget, which was usually presented for consideration after the beginning of the year to which it referred. The Supreme Soviet's legislative output was also fairly meagre during these years, with an average output of no more than four statute laws (*zakony*) a year. With the fourth convocation (1954–8), however, the first to be elected after the death of Stalin, the picture changes considerably. Meetings became more frequent and more deputies were involved in the formal proceedings; the range of discussion widened, with the annual plan being considered as well as the budget and other matters; and the annual output of legislation doubled or even trebled as compared with earlier convocations. It was during this period, especially from 1957 onwards, that many of the basic post-Stalin legal codes were adopted, and it has for this reason sometimes been known as the 'second period' of Soviet legislative activity, the first being the period of the early 1920s immediately before and after the death of Lenin.[103]

A third period may be distinguished, covering the seventh, eighth, ninth and tenth convocations (1966–84). During this period the Supreme Soviet met somewhat less often and heard fewer speeches, and its legislative output also fell, although not to the levels of the wartime or immediate postwar years. The diminishing volume of legislation, however, was in part a consequence of the delegation of more matters to subordinate levels of authority; and there was a modest increase in the proportion of laws that were considered by the Supreme Soviet itself, rather than adopted on its behalf by the Presidium.[104] It was during the late 1960s, moreover, that the committee system was expanded. When the Supreme Soviet was initially established in 1938 there were only four standing commissions attached to each of its two chambers, with just 8 per cent of the deputies serving on their membership. An economic commission attached to the Council of Nationalities was established in 1957, and some of the other commissions set up sub-commissions to assist them in their work. Apart from this there were no substantial changes until 1966, when the whole system was reconstructed. By the late 1970s, with further additions, there were sixteen commissions attached to each of the two chambers with 76 per cent of all deputies represented upon them; the commissions met up to three times a year, in addition to meetings of the Supreme Soviet itself.[105]

The volume of legislation expanded enormously after 1989: so much so, indeed, that it was no longer necessary to ratify decrees of the Presidium taken between formal parliamentary sessions. In its first two years the new parliament adopted over 100 laws; Luk'ianov, who chaired its sessions, identified the constitutional amendments, a series of laws on land, leasing, property and entrepreneurship, and a further series of laws covering the press, freedom of conscience, emigration and citizenship as the most important. Nor was it necessarily true that these laws had little influence. There were already more than 32,000 leaseholders and 60,000 independent farms, Luk'ianov pointed out, less than a year after the Law on Land had permitted their establishment. And more than 8,000 periodicals had registered under the Law on the Mass Media, of which more than half had made their first appearance in the same year. There had been progress, at the same time, in parliamentary monitoring of government, even in formerly 'forbidden zones' like foreign policy, security and atomic energy. In its first two years the Minister of Defence had addressed the Supreme Soviet five times, and the Chairman of the KGB and the Minister of Internal Affairs had each addressed it four times. Over fifty international treaties had been ratified, with some of the committee hearings – for instance on the INF treaty and the German settlement – carried on national television. These, Luk'ianov accepted, were still no more than the 'first steps' towards a fully effective parliament.[106]

The politics of parliamentary practice

Reflecting on its history shortly after the USSR itself had disappeared, the editor of the parliamentary journal *Narodnyi deputat* had to remind its readers that it was the old Supreme Soviet that had given political reform its first impulse. As founded in 1936, the Supreme Soviet had been a 'cover for party-state dictatorship'. But it had been the unreformed Supreme Soviet that had carried out the country's first democratic revolution. The initiators of democratisation, certainly, had been a group of politicians headed by Mikhail Gorbachev. They had based themselves, however, on the Soviet parliament. In December 1988 it had adopted a new electoral law, leading to the relatively open and competitive elections of March 1989. Those elections had given rise to the Congress of People's Deputies, which had 'turned political life in the country upside down'. The Congress, and the Supreme Soviet it elected, had become the country's first genuinely parliamentary institutions; their existence had been an 'important stage in the history of our democracy', and a 'school of politics not only for the deputies themselves but for the country as a whole'.[107] For Anatolii Luk'ianov, speaking more officially, the Congress and Supreme Soviet had encouraged a whole new generation of politicians to make themselves known; for Nikolai Ryzhkov, similarly, a new group of parliamentary 'professionals' had grown up through the work of the Congress itself.[108]

The new parliamentary institutions certainly acquired a large popular following in their early stages. The First Congress of People's Deputies, according to a series of telephone polls conducted as it was meeting, was followed closely throughout the country: from 61 per cent (in the Kazakh capital Alma Ata) up to 92 per cent (in the Georgian capital Tbilisi) claimed to be watching or listening to its proceeedings 'constantly' or 'more or less constantly'. Between 79 and 88 per cent of those polled, in various republican capitals, thought the Congress was operating 'completely' or 'more or less democratically'.[109] Over 141,000 members of the public, prompted no doubt by the continuous television coverage of its proceedings, were sufficiently moved to send telegrams or other communications to the Congress as it was meeting.[110] Readers of *Izvestiia* voted its parliamentary reports the best publication of the year;[111] indeed, so close was the attention to the proceedings of the new Soviet parliament that there was a fall of 20 per cent in output when it was meeting and television coverage had to be rescheduled for the evenings.[112] Asked for their views in May, only 31 per cent had thought the First Congress would be a success. By June, after it had met, fully 70 per cent thought it had justified their expectations,[113] and 93 per cent, in a separate survey, were familiar to a greater or lesser extent with its activities.[114]

Public support for the new parliament, however, steadily declined as its deputies argued endlessly about procedure while the living standards of ordinary people deteriorated. The Second Congress of People's Deputies, meeting at the end of 1989, had the support of no more than 49 per cent of those who were polled.[115] By the end of 1990 only 18 per cent of those who were asked still took a positive view of the new Supreme Soviet, and 37 per cent were negative; the new Soviet government was even more unpopular, with 15 per cent support but a disapproval rating of 65 per cent. Only 26 per cent were willing to vote for the same deputies again, and 42 per cent were sure to vote against them, with a further 17 per cent unlikely to vote at all.[116] By 1992 no more than 8 per cent of Muscovites felt the deputies they had elected two years earlier had justified their hopes, and 43 per cent refused to trust any politician whatsoever.[117] Support for the Russian Congress of People's Deputies had meanwhile fallen to 12 per cent,[118] and only 4 per cent thought there would be 'significant improvements' in public life as a result of its deliberations.[119] Surveys of the mass public found 'political apathy and scepticism', together with a 'general distrust of all power structures'.[120] The question most Muscovites wanted to put to their deputy was a very simple one: 'Do you know how people are living at the moment, and how much longer will it go on?'.[121]

Deputies themselves were dissatisfied with their new role. For Viktor Sheinis, the Congress and Supreme Soviet had confirmed the worst predictions of their critics and become less and less productive, the voters more and more disillusioned.[122] Another deputy, Gennadii Lisichkin, found himself powerless both as a deputy and as a Central Committee member.[123] Between 53 and 55 per cent of deputies, at various dates, were satisfied with the work of the first Congress; by the time of the Second Congress, in December 1989, just 41 per cent were satisfied, and the attitudes of deputies varied widely: 'from optimism and calm to pessimism and despair'. Of all the factors that affected their work, the 'culture of political discussion' was criticised the most frequently (73 per cent); 59 per cent were dissatisfied with the level of agreement between the different parliamentary factions, and 42 per cent were unhappy with the 'psychological atmosphere at the

Congress'.[124] By the end of 1989, only 37 per cent of the deputies wished to stand for election to the next Supreme Soviet; indeed, when the time came for membership of the Supreme Soviet to be rotated, some difficulty was caused when the number of deputies that wished to retire greatly exceeded the number that were due to be replaced.[125] In the end about 40 per cent, not the intended 20 per cent, stood down.[126]

There were other causes of dissatisfaction. One of them was the inability of more than a small minority of deputies to address the chamber in the time that was available. At the second Congress of People's Deputies, for instance, only 461 deputies were able to speak of the 2,083 that had indicated a wish to do so; this left no opportunity for all the republics to be represented in the discussion of issues like the new union treaty, and there were complaints of 'favouritism' in the selection of speakers.[127] Absenteeism was one sign of disillusion: the number of deputies absent for key votes varied between sixty and 160, and sessions were frequently inquorate.[128] Some deputies, attempting to get round the problem, were found pressing the voting buttons of their absent neighbours in what was described as a 'mutual assistance system'.[129] Another source of dissatisfaction was the way in which the parliament continued to be bypassed when important matters of state were being decided. Why, for instance, had the Soviet parliament been excluded from the 'nine plus one' agreement between Gorbachev and republican leaders in April 1991, and from the process of discussion to which it had led?[130] Why, asked a reader in *Izvestiia*, was the future of the USSR being decided at a dacha near Moscow and not at the supposedly sovereign Congress of People's Deputies?[131] And why did the President so rarely bother to visit parliament?[132]

There were deeper, more structural reasons for the failure of the new parliament to make the impact its members had hoped it would have. One of these was the curious relationship between the Supreme Soviet and the Congress of People's Deputies that elected it. The relationship between the two bodies had been queried at the very outset, when some had argued that the Congress was the 'parliament' and the Supreme Soviet only its 'working organ', while others had seen the Supreme Soviet itself as a 'working, constantly functioning parliament' and the Congress as no more than the body that elected it.[133] Experience gradually made clear that the two-tier parliament was an unworkable as well as an ambiguous institution; Congress meetings acquired the character of a 'public meeting'[134] or a 'hockey field' for the conduct of political campaigns.[135] The relationship had certainly to be rethought, in the view of two leading jurists; both Congress and Supreme Soviet had assumed similar functions, and who needed such a system of 'dual power'?[136] For another jurist, Boris Kurashvili, the Congress resembled nothing so much as the Zemskii Sobor, the 16th century 'Assembly of the Land'; far better to have a proper and directly elected parliament.[137] For the radical deputy Sergei Stankievich, similarly, the Congress had shown the need for a working, professional and directly elected parliament.[138] Drafts of a new union treaty, even before the USSR itself had disappeared, made it clear that any future association of republics would have a single and directly elected parliament, as in other states; and this was the form chosen by all the post-Soviet republics.[139]

Most fundamental of all, the parliament could hardly hope to function effectively in the absence of a properly developed party system capable of linking citizen, deputy and government. Candidates at the elections put forward their own priorities, and could hardly offer a coherent programme of government for the country as a whole. Nor could they, as isolated legislators, put forward a list of deputies who might form a unified administration or an alternative to it. In most liberal democracies, it was political parties that performed these functions: sponsoring candidates at elections, formulating a medium-term programme of government, and then securing a stable majority of deputies to ensure its fulfilment. The Soviet and then the Russian experience of political reform had generated a legislature that could articulate complaints, and that could sometimes agree to vote additional expenditure on matters of interest to their constituents. Discussion of the pensions law in 1990, for instance, found deputy after deputy calling for 'special consideration' for the interest he represented; the result was to raise pensions to a record 17.5 per cent of national income, the highest level in the world.[140] In 1992, similarly, the Russian parliament voted an additional 70 billion rubles for food subsidies and housing, despite warnings that this would increase the budgetary deficit alarmingly.[141] Why should deputies worry when reconciling the priorities of government was someone else's responsibility?

The establishment of a Soviet, and then a Russian presidency was designed to overcome the deadlock between government and parliament that had developed in the late communist period. But it could hardly do so without the support of a 'presidential party', or at least a legal system that was capable of enforcing its resolutions. The old and now discredited Soviet system had incorporated a parliament that was far from sovereign, but at least its decisions – through the single ruling party that sponsored them – had enjoyed some legal authority. The post-communist system that replaced it incorporated a parliament that was no longer subject to party control, but it was also a parliament that had few means of committing government and society to its decisions. Yeltsin himself referred to the impasse between parliament and the presidency as a 'constitutional crisis',[142] and there were continuing tensions in the early 1990s on ministerial appointments, public spending, control of the press and other matters.

The Russian tradition had been one of strong and centralised government; in the divided society of the early 1990s, however, it seemed more important to develop a broadly based consensus incorporating an effective parliament and a citizenry that was prepared to identify with its activities.

4   The Presidency and central government

The history of the Soviet system has usually been written in terms of its leaders. Lenin, Stalin, Khrushchev, Brezhnev and Gorbachev are the names with which distinct periods of Soviet development are associated. This practice captures one of the essential elements of the Soviet system, the prominent place played by the leading political figure. However for more than seventy years of the system's existence, there was a fundamental ambiguity with regard to the top job, reflected most importantly in the low level of institutionalisation of leading positions in the political structure.

The traditional presidency

The source of this ambiguity lay in the leading and guiding role which the party played in the Soviet period. In practical terms this meant that the most powerful figure in the political structure was neither the head of state nor the prime minister, but the party General (from September 1953 until April 1966 first) Secretary. From May 1940 until his death in March 1953 Stalin was Chairman of the Council of People's Commissars (from March 1956 Council of Ministers) as well as General Secretary, a practice emulated by Khrushchev between September 1958 and October 1964, but in neither case was their state position the principal source of their power. Under both, the position of head of state, or Chairman of the Presidium of the Supreme Soviet, was occupied by such second-rank leaders as Kalinin, Shvernik, Voroshilov, Brezhnev (at the time) and Mikoian. In these conditions, the head of state, or presidency, was a formal position with little independent power. This remained true even when this post was occupied by the leading political figure in the land from 1977–85. From 1977 until his death in 1982, Brezhnev combined occupancy of the posts of General Secretary and Chairman of the Presidium of the Supreme Soviet. This practice was followed by his two immediate successors, Andropov and Chernenko. However it is not clear that the assumption of the state posts added any substantial power to that which these leaders possessed by virtue of their party posts. Thus while the combination of these positions may have eased some of the protocol

60

problems involved in the party leader engaging in international diplomacy on behalf of his country, it did not reflect any shift in relative power between state and party organs. Nor did it clear up the ambiguity stemming from the party's predominant role.

When Gorbachev was elected to the leading party position, the precedent therefore existed for his occupation of the state presidency as well. It surprised many when, in July 1985, instead of taking up this post, Gorbachev nominated veteran foreign minister Andrei Gromyko. In explanation, he declared that the occupation of both posts had been fully appropriate in earlier times, but that now a range of issues and challenges confronted the party, most particularly in the lead-up to the approaching 27th Congress and in the economy. These demanded a further strengthening of the role of the party in society and an increase in the intensity of the work of the CC and Politburo. Under such conditions, the General Secretary should concentrate his efforts in the organisation of the work of the central party organs and in coordinating the efforts of all organisations in the pursuit of the desired course.[1] Gorbachev's thinking, at least publicly, was thus to concentrate the vision of the General Secretary on party matters and the role of the party in the society. Perhaps paradoxically, this was consistent with the position he was later to adopt about the separation of party and state functions. More immediately, this had the political bonus for Gorbachev of removing Gromyko from the Foreign Ministry and enabling his replacement by the more reformist Eduard Shevardnadze. Gorbachev's rejection of the state presidency may thus in part have been tactical in nature.

In the new state Constitution adopted in 1977, the formal powers ascribed to the Presidium of the Supreme Soviet were wide-ranging. As well as the power to promulgate decrees and adopt decisions, the Presidium was vested with the power of judicial review of the constitutionality of all laws of the Union and of the republics (including republican constitutions), amendment of laws, appointment and removal of governmental officers, formation of the Defence Council, ratification of international treaties, proclamation of martial law, and formation and abolition of state ministries and committees.[2] But while the collective body was vested with such extensive powers, the post of Chairman remained undefined in the Constitution. In formal terms, the Chairman seemed to be conceived as having little more than the function of a normal committee chairman; he was part of the collective body with no special individual role to play. Indeed, as the office was used under Brezhnev and his successors, it is doubtful whether the Chairman even performed this role. The deputy chairman seems to have done much of the administrative work while the Chairman played the more public, and honorific, role on the national and international stage. This kind of profile continued to apply to the Chairmanship of the Presidium of the Supreme Soviet until late 1988.[3]

Chairman of the Supreme Soviet: a new presidency

At the 19th Conference of the party in June-July 1988, decisions were taken which were to have an important bearing upon the way in which the presidency developed. Championed by Gorbachev and enshrined in a resolution of the conference,[4] the party was called upon to withdraw from direct involvement in affairs of the state and to concentrate upon exercising its leading role through the influence of party members in state organs. Although this clear principle of eliminating the overlap in functions was obscured somewhat by the assertion that party leaders should also be recommended as chairmen of the soviets,[5] if implemented fully this implied a shifting of at least administrative power from the party to the state apparatus, and therefore from the party General Secretary to a leading position located in the state structure. To facilitate this (as we have seen) a new state structure was envisaged, consisting of the USSR Congress of People's Deputies as the supreme body of authority, a smaller standing Supreme Soviet which was to have legislative, administrative and supervisory functions and a Chairman of the Supreme Soviet, who was to be elected by secret ballot. The official resolution of the conference gave no details about what the position of Chairman of the Supreme Soviet was to entail. Gorbachev was more expansive in his report. He declared that the establishment of such a post would enhance the role played by the representative bodies, strengthen the rule of law basis of government, and improve the representation of the USSR in international affairs. The chairman was to be accountable to the Congress of People's Deputies and to exercise broad state powers. In particular the Chairman was to give overall guidance to the drafting of legislation and major socio-economic programmes, decide key foreign policy, defence and national security issues, chair the Defence Council, and submit proposals nominating the Chairman of the Council of Ministers. He was also to guide the work of the Presidium of the Supreme Soviet.[6]

Measures to introduce these changes were adopted at a special session of the Supreme Soviet convened in November 1988. In the interim, the proposals were accorded little attention in Gorbachev's key address to the Central Committee plenum at the end of July or in the major decision emanating from that meeting.[7] Nevertheless, the proposals were doubtless the subject of much discussion behind the scenes. Their political import may be reflected in the fact that at the beginning of October Gromyko formally resigned from the Chairmanship of the Presidium of the Supreme

Soviet, and Gorbachev was elected unanimously to the post.[8] As the incumbent, Gorbachev's claim to the new presidential position when it was created was strengthened.

The formal amendments to the Constitution introducing the changes foreshadowed at the 19th Conference were adopted at the Supreme Soviet meeting in November 1988. In his address to that body, Gorbachev devoted little attention to the new post of Chairman of the Supreme Soviet.[9] His comments did, however, reflect a recognition of the reservations some people had expressed about the excessive concentration of power in that office. While confirming collectivism in decision-making, Gorbachev declared that the Chairman could 'have sufficient powers to organise the work of the Supreme Soviet and its Presidium, while ruling out excessive concentration of power in one person'. Although this danger was highlighted by some participants in the national debate on the constitutional changes, it was not a major concern in the published debate in the Supreme Soviet.

Under the new provisions of the Constitution, the Chairman of the Supreme Soviet was declared to be the highest ranking official in the Soviet state and to represent the USSR both inside the country and in the international sphere. The Chairman was to be elected by the Congress of People's Deputies from among the People's Deputies by secret ballot for a term of five years. No individual was to hold that office for more than two consecutive terms. Although the Chairman was declared to be accountable to both the Congress of People's Deputies and the Supreme Soviet, only the Congress of People's Deputies could recall a Chairman, and this through a secret ballot (Art. 120). Provision was also made for vice-chairmen to carry out some of the functions of the Chairman when directed to do so and to stand in for the Chairman when that person was absent or unable to perform his duties (Art. 121). The Chairman was also allocated a number of specific responsibilities:

1 To exercise general guidance over the preparation of questions to be examined in the Congress or Supreme Soviet and to sign laws adopted by leading state organs.
2 To submit reports on the state of the country and important policy issues to the Congress and the Supreme Soviet.
3 To propose to the Congress a nominee for election as First Vice-Chairman of the Supreme Soviet and members of the Constitutional Inspection Committee.
4 To suggest to the Supreme Soviet candidates for appointment as Chairman of the Council of Ministers, of the Public Inspection Committee and Supreme Court, the Procurator-General and Chief State Arbitrator.
5 To head the Defence Council.
6 To conduct negotiations and sign international treaties.

In addition, the Chairman was given the power to issue directives (Art. 121), although these could be revoked by the Supreme Soviet (Art. 113), to chair meetings of the Congress of People's Deputies (Art. 110) and joint sittings of the two chambers of the Supreme Soviet (Art. 111), to convene the Supreme Soviet (Art. 112) and to initiate legislation (Art. 114).

The powers accorded the Chairman seem extensive, particularly compared with the 1977 Constitution, but these need to be offset against the system of checks and balances instituted at this time. While the establishment of checks and balances signifies the attempt to move toward a presidential type of system, the result was not a presidency along the lines of the French or American models because there was no provision for the separation of powers: the Chairman continued to come from within the legislature. This meant that the Chairman had no power to dissolve either legislative organ, although the Congress of People's Deputies had the power to remove the Chairman. The directives the Chairman was empowered to issue could be over-ridden by the Supreme Soviet and his proposals for filling leading posts were subject to legislative ratification. On a range of issues he had to coordinate his actions with the Presidium of the Supreme Soviet, a body which retained extensive powers in foreign and domestic affairs and which was formed independently of his will.[10] These were real constraints upon the power of the Chairman, with no equivalent measures available to him to restrain the legislative organs. The Chairman's power to sign laws and acts adopted by the leading state organs may, by implication, have meant a power not to sign and thereby to frustrate the will of these assemblies, although the failure of the Constitution to specify a means of resolving the resulting deadlock suggests that this may not have been the intention of the drafters. Alternatively, it may reflect sloppy drafting. In any case, the real power of the Chairman in the legislative arena lay in his capacity to set the agenda and, through his role as chairman of and presenter of reports to the meetings, to direct the course of those meetings and shape the parameters of debate. But the capacity of a Chairman to utilise these potential sources of power depended upon two things, neither of which was wholly within his control: the shaping of the broad political agenda for the society as a whole, and the moral authority which the Chairman was able to summon.

Gorbachev was elected Chairman of the Supreme Soviet at the second session of the Congress of People's Deputies on 25 May 1989.[11] He was the only candidate whose name was on the ballot, although two others (A. M. Obolensky and Boris Yeltsin) were nominated but their names were withdrawn before the ballot. During the debate on Gorbachev's candidacy, two major issues were raised. The first concerned whether the ballot should be characterised by more than one candidate. Most who addressed this issue supported the principle of competitive elections, but agreed that in the current circumstances there was no realistic alternative to Gorbachev. The second issue concerned the combination of the positions of Chairman of the Supreme Soviet and General Secretary of the Central Committee of the CPSU. Some argued that the positions should be separated in order to protect the Chairman from being subject to the influence of the party apparatus exercised through the operation of party discipline, and that the combination of these posts had led to the formation of cults.[12] Another declared that the responsibilities attached to both positions would be too great for one individual to perform and that they should therefore be divided.[13] One delegate even referred to Gorbachev's speech of April 1985 in which he argued for the separation of these posts.[14] But others argued that the positions should remain combined. In the view of one delegate, Gorbachev played a role in controlling the party apparatus and that role would be best served by maintaining both posts.[15] According to others, the situation in the country was so serious that the combination of both posts was essential for the future welfare of all.[16] One delegate supported the principle of separating the posts, but declared that in the current climate they should be combined in the person of Gorbachev in order to ensure the conduct of democratic elections at all levels.[17] Gorbachev's own expressed view was that the combination of posts was necessary in the current climate because the process of perestroika was in its early stages and that the support of the party was essential to its ultimate success.[18] In the end, no move was made to separate these posts.

The concern underlying these two issues, and in particular that of the combination of both posts, was that it would concentrate excessive power in the hands of the Chairman. Gorbachev was alert to this worry and addressed it directly in his concluding speech to the Congress. Acknowledging the sensitivity of the question of the concentration of excessive power in the hands of one leader, he declared:

As a communist, I categorically reject the hints, albeit veiled, that I am trying to concentrate all power in my hands. This is alien to my views, to my world outlook and even my character. It was not for this that a sharp turn to a new policy was made at the April plenum, it is not for this that the party and people have begun the difficult work of democratisation, glasnost, purification and renewal of our society, of public life. As General Secretary and Chairman of the Supreme Soviet, I have no other policy than perestroika, democratisation and glasnost. . .[19]

Gorbachev's attempt to defuse this issue was, in an institutional sense, fatally flawed. He proposed no institutional measures to prevent the excessive concentration of power in his hands; the only guarantee lay in his personal commitment. This could have meaning for the delegates and the people at large only while the Chairman retained the moral authority to command acceptance of his word. In this sense, the barriers against the centralisation of power were weak and subject to human frailty. This was to be realised during 1989.

During 1989 the course of events in the USSR was significantly radicalised and thereby wrenched out of the hands of the central leadership. Important in this was the escalation of national tension, with three developments of particular significance. The events in Georgia in April in which the army attacked and killed a number of civilians was greeted with dismay right across the Soviet Union by those hoping for significant, and peaceful, change from perestroika. Despite denials of foreknowledge of this action on the part of Gorbachev, many suspected that the military would not have acted without direction from Moscow. This tarnished Gorbachev's image. So too did the handling of the Nagorno-Karabakh dispute which burst forth in 1988–9. The central government temporised, placing the area under special jurisdiction and thereby avoiding making a decision about the ultimate location of the area. Unrest and fighting went largely unstopped for some time, and then in January 1990 the Soviet army forced its way into Baku with significant destruction and loss of life. The image of Gorbachev, the leader of the central government, which this course of events projected was not flattering: from someone who was dithering in the face of a difficult (indeed, intractable) problem, he was transformed into someone who had resorted to excessive military force in an arbitrary fashion. The third development was the move towards independence in the Baltic states. With unforeseen rapidity, events in these three republics moved towards a rejection of rule from Moscow and the reassertion of national independence, with many local communists supporting this process. Gorbachev's response was to bluster, to deny the legitimacy of these moves and to threaten reprisals. In other republics also, nationalist movements began to stir and gather strength.

The effect of these was reinforced by the emergence of independent activity elsewhere in the Union. The most striking example of this was the miners' strike in summer 1989, but also important was the emergence of the range of informal groups which came to throng the Soviet public stage (see chapter 8). This was accompanied by the erosion of the position and prestige of the formerly dominant CPSU. Reflected in the party's poor performance in the election to the Congress of People's Deputies in many areas early in 1989, the popular disillusionment and turning away from the party that became particularly evident in 1990 was making its presence felt during 1989. The declaration of independence from the CPSU made by the Lithuanian party in December merely reflected a more general problem: the party was disintegrating as the dominant force in Soviet society.

This combination of events had an important effect on Gorbachev's standing in the legislature. Gorbachev sought to play the role of an active, interventionist and directive chairman. In the absence of clearly understood standing orders or traditions of parliamentary procedure to structure proceedings within the chamber, Gorbachev sought to use his position as chairman to guide the course of debate in the directions he preferred. This relied upon his own personal authority; the office he held carried little in the way of mystique to bolster the authority of its incumbent. In the early period Gorbachev was able to play this role successfully. However, when the events noted above began to accumulate in the collective consciousness of the deputies, their effect was to erode Gorbachev's personal standing. Many deputies were unconvinced by Gorbachev's protestations of innocence about the violence in Georgia and disturbed by his inability to assert Moscow's power and bring the Nagorno-Karabakh issue to a resolution. His performance in the face of the challenge from the Baltic republics did little to add lustre to his authority: to conservatives he appeared vacillating and weak, while to reformers he lacked the courage to accept the legitimate aspirations of the Baltic peoples. His authority was directly challenged by walk-outs on the part of Armenian and Azeri deputies and by the refusals to participate on the part of some of the Baltic deputies. The handling of the miners' strike and the ambivalence already evident in some sectors of official policy projected an image of Gorbachev as weak and lacking in firm policy direction. His continued position as party General Secretary tied him in many people's minds to an organisation whose days had passed, and his refusal to break that tie raised real questions about his judgement, if not his basic intentions.

The accumulation of these sorts of images, added to the emergence of a string of other prominent national politicians (including Yeltsin and Sakharov) with whom he had to share the limelight, combined to erode the personal authority that was so central to the exercise of his role. The deterioration in the public situation throughout 1989 reinforced this development: continuing economic malaise, the rise of ethnic conflict, the increasingly divisive nature of political debate compared with what it had been before and the palpable demoralisation within the ranks of the party, all against a background of a government which was unable to come up with the sorts of innovative policies which could break out of this malaise, continued to erode Gorbachev's position. This occurred both in the legislative arena and among the populace at large. It also encouraged pressures favouring a strengthening of central power.

A presidential system

At the extraordinary Third Congress of People's Deputies in March 1990, amendments to the Constitution were debated and eventually adopted. One of the chief issues here was the introduction of a new post, President of the

USSR. The major issues of concern were the same as those involved in the earlier discussion of Gorbachev's candidacy for the Chairmanship of the Supreme Soviet, the excessive concentration of power in one person and the desirability or otherwise of the President being an officer of a political party. The report on the proposed changes was delivered by Anatolii Luk'ianov.[20] He advocated the introduction of a state president as a means of creating a more clearly defined system of power relations in a context within which the party would no longer play the directive administrative role it had played in the past. However, he declared, this would not lead to the establishment of a 'regime of authoritarian personal power'. The draft constitutional changes contained, in his view, 'an entire system of guarantees' against such a development. He listed five of these:

a) Direct election of the President in a universal, secret ballot in which the President must obtain more than half the votes cast both overall and in a majority of republics.[21]

b) An individual would be unable to hold the Presidency for more than two terms and would be subject to an age limit.

c) The President was to be under the control of the Congress of People's Deputies, which had the right to recall him should he violate the Constitution or laws.

d) The President must act within the Constitution and the law.

e) The Congress of People's Deputies had the right to annul presidential decrees while the Constitutional Review Committee must supervise their legality.

Many deputies appear to have been unconvinced by Luk'ianov's assurances. Some emphasised the need to have a real balancing of the arms of the state, the legislative, executive and judicial, in order to make the new system function effectively and in an acceptable fashion.[22] Others were concerned that the institution of the presidency and the powers that would be accorded to it would infringe upon the sovereignty of the union republics,[23] while one deputy declared that although Gorbachev was trusted, who would come after him was uncertain and in the crisis conditions, the sentiment in favour of a 'little father' would increase.[24]

There was a strong feeling among the deputies that the President should not simultaneously be the leader of the party, for the same sorts of reasons that had been advanced earlier. However the combination of the presidency with party leadership was defended on a number of grounds. Party Secretary Vadim Medvedev argued that in no other countries which had a presidential system of government was the President expected to renounce his party membership and, in any case, even were he forced to do so, he could not give up his personal views. Furthermore it was unrealistic, he argued, to expect that with the party withdrawing from its established functions and undergoing a process of domestic democratisation the President would be bound by party discipline.[25] Another deputy argued that the separation of posts would deny the President the power of the party in this time of crisis.[26] Most deputies did not find these arguments compelling, but they were carried as a result of the manipulation of the proceedings by the chairman: in the vote taken in the Congress, 1,303 deputies supported the view that the President should not hold any other political or state posts. Although this was a majority of those voting (1,974), because Gorbachev was able to have this classed as an amendment to the Constitution it required a two-thirds majority for adoption and was therefore lost.[27]

The law establishing the presidency was adopted on 15 March.[28] The law establishing the presidency restricted occupation of that position to someone between the ages of thirty-five and sixty-five who was not a people's deputy, and limited tenure to two five year terms. The President was to receive a salary only for that position. The President was to be elected on the basis of universal, equal and direct suffrage and by secret ballot in an election in which there was to be no limit on the number of candidates. However the first president was to be elected by the Congress of People's Deputies.

An extensive array of rights, powers and duties was accorded to the President:

a) to act as guarantor of the observance of citizens' rights and liberties and the Constitution and laws;

b) to protect the sovereignty, security and territorial integrity of the USSR and the Union Republics, and to implement the principles of the Soviet national–state structure;

c) to represent the USSR domestically and internationally;

d) to ensure interaction among the higher bodies of state power and administration in the USSR;

e) to present annual reports to the Congress and inform the Supreme Soviet about policy questions;

f) to present nominations for leading posts (including Chairman of the Council of Ministers) to the Supreme Soviet and the Congress, and suggestions for relieving them of their duties;[29]

g) to propose to the Supreme Soviet the resignation of the Council of Ministers and, in agreement with the Chairman of the Council of Ministers, to relieve members of the government of their responsibilities and appoint new ones, with subsequent confirmation by the Supreme Soviet;

h) to sign laws or, within two weeks, to return a law with any objections to the Supreme Soviet for a discussion and vote; if both chambers reaffirmed their original decisions by a two thirds vote, the President must sign the law;

i) to suspend resolutions and orders of the Council of Ministers;
j) to coordinate defence efforts, as Supreme Commander in Chief of the armed forces to appoint and replace the supreme command, to confer the highest military titles, and to appoint judges of military tribunals;
k) to conduct negotiations and sign international treaties, and carry out Soviet diplomatic procedures;
l) to award Soviet orders, medals and titles of honour;
m) to resolve citizenship questions, grant asylum and exercise right of pardon;
n) to proclaim general or partial mobilisation, to proclaim a state of war in the event of attack on the USSR (with immediate submission of this question to the Supreme Soviet for consideration), and to proclaim martial law in specific localities;
o) to introduce a state of emergency at the request or with the consent of the Presidium of the Supreme Soviet or the supreme body of state power of the Union Republic; in the absence of such consent, to introduce a state of emergency with immediate submission of this decision to the Supreme Soviet for ratification by a two-thirds vote of all deputies; in order to ensure the safety of citizens, to introduce temporary presidential rule while preserving the sovereignty and territorial integrity of the Union Republic;
p) to help resolve disputes between the two chambers of the Supreme Soviet and, in the event of failure in this, to propose to the Congress of People's Deputies the election of a new Supreme Soviet;
q) to issue decrees that would have binding force.

The law created two new bodies to assist the President in his work. The Council of the Federation, which was to consist of the highest state official in each Union Republic, was to be concerned with all matters relating to the federation and national questions. The Presidential Council, which was to be appointed by the President (the Chairman of the Council of Ministers was to be a member *ex officio*), was to be his chief executive body. It was to work out measures to implement the basic guidelines of Soviet domestic and foreign policy and to ensure Soviet security. Joint meetings of these bodies could be convened if appropriate. The President could be removed by a vote of two-thirds of the Congress of People's Deputies, but only if the President violated the Constitution or laws. Provision was also made for delegation of the President's responsibilities.

The rights, powers and responsibilities enjoyed by the President were very extensive, but they were less expansive in the law as adopted than had originally been envisaged. Gorbachev had not only to engage in some partisan chairing to get the measures through,[30] but also to make concessions in a number of areas. To calm republican fears, a clause was inserted in the law declaring that 'the institution of the post of president does not change the legal status or entail any restriction on the competence of the union and autonomous republics and Constitution of the USSR'. The President's ability to declare a state of emergency, which in the draft was absolute, was made subject to the agreement of either the relevant republican Supreme Soviet or the all-union Supreme Soviet. The President's ability to appeal to the Congress of People's Deputies in cases when his refusal to sign a law was overturned by a vote of the Supreme Soviet was removed from the draft. The President's power to remove the Chairman of the Supreme Court and to name the membership of the Committee for Constitutional Supervision was also withdrawn because both bodies could have been required to judge the constitutionality or otherwise of presidential actions. The pressures for the President not to be a party leader were resisted, although the provision that the President was to receive a salary only for that position may reflect sensitivity to this.

The changes introduced in March 1990 formally shifted the USSR from a quasi-parliamentary system to a presidential one.[31] Henceforth, the head of state was not to be a member of the legislature, was to have an independent basis of legitimacy through a mode of selection separate from that of the legislature, and was to be assisted chiefly by a body which consisted of his own choices; the Council of Ministers, which was reduced in size by the elimination of many state ministries (see below) and had been playing a more activist role under Ryzhkov, was clearly downgraded as a deliberative organ by the creation of the Presidential Council. The shift to such a system is consistent with the attempt to build a series of checks and balances into the structure of national power. There was a clear attempt in the drafting of the legislation to place checks upon the presidency, and although these may not have been as extensive as in some other presidential systems (such as the American), in constitutional terms they were significant. Personnel nominations and decisions regarding the dismissal of personnel had to be ratified by the Supreme Soviet. Presidential refusal to sign legislation adopted in the Supreme Soviet could be overturned by that body with no constitutional recourse by the President. Proclamation of a state of war was subject to confirmation by the Supreme Soviet, while declaration of a state of emergency was subject to the consent of the republican or all-union Supreme Soviet. Presidentially-invoked dissolution of the Supreme Soviet was subject to agreement by the Congress of People's Deputies, while all presidential actions were subject to oversight by the Committee for Constitutional Supervision.

Nevertheless, there were also elements of the legislation which made presidential powers very wide-ranging indeed. The President could suspend resolutions and orders of the Council of Ministers and could issue decrees possessing binding force without any apparent restriction. He could also proclaim martial law and introduce temporary presidential rule without the sort of restriction imposed upon his ability to introduce a state of emergency.[32] Potentially this enabled the President to exercise a highly authoritarian, personalised style of rule and as long as he did not infringe on the Constitution or existing laws, he was invulnerable to constitutional removal. Even the attempt to shore up the sovereignty of the republics, reflected in the restriction of the introduction of martial law and the clause introduced into the legislation and cited above, could be reduced to nought through the exercise of these powers. The attempt to create checks and balances thus left significant gaps in the buffers created against the exercise of excessive power by the President.

The scope that remained for the exercise of personal power by the President created room for the emergence of a dominating presidential figure. However if a President was to seek to adopt this type of profile, his success in doing so would depend heavily upon the personal authority with which he was invested by the populace at large and by those in the leading state organs. Such authority would be enhanced if conditions were such as to lend strength to the perception that what was needed was a 'strong hand'. But that authority would also depend upon the way in which presidential power was used. A perceived flouting of norms or circumventing of the Constitution would be likely to be less easily accepted than actions which could clearly be seen to be in defence of the 'constitutional order'. Such authority would also appear to be more firmly based when the President had been elected in a competitive election and it is therefore surprising that while the legislation made provision for competitive elections it did not make them mandatory. It declared that 'There is no limit to the number of candidates . . .' For Gorbachev, the lack of popular legitimacy became a major handicap, particularly when he was compared with other leading figures like Russian Supreme Soviet Chairman and then President Yeltsin.[33]

The strengthening of the President's position needs also to be seen in terms of the relationship with the party. The development of an independent presidency was an important step in the attempt to shift power from party to state organs. One of Gorbachev's aims seems to have been to create an activist leadership position based in the state structure to replace the activist role that had formerly been exercised by the General Secretary. Associated with this was an attempt to render the chief state executive independent of party control; Gorbachev sought to safeguard himself against the sort of move in the party that had toppled Khrushchev. While he was Chairman of the Presidium of the Supreme Soviet and Chairman of the Supreme Soviet, Gorbachev remained vulnerable: as a member of the

Congress of People's Deputies only in the capacity of a delegate of the party, the Central Committee could have removed his mandate and thereby terminated his membership of that body. With the establishment of the presidency, this danger was removed. The only way the party could remove him from office legally was if it was able to control two-thirds of the votes in the Congress of People's Deputies and remove him through a vote in that body. With the erosion of the party throughout 1990, this appeared unlikely.

The extension of presidential power

An attempt was made to give a further legislative boost to the presidency in May 1990. Together with passage of a law which provided for the maintenance and service of the President (a taxable monthly salary of 4,000 rubles, residences in Moscow city and province and in the Crimea, transport, protection, expenditure, and retirement privileges),[34] a law was introduced protecting the President's honour and dignity.[35] The law specifically covered public insulting of the President, which was to consist of 'the deliberate humiliation of his honour and dignity, expressed in an improper form', and the slandering of the President, which consisted of 'the dissemination of knowingly false fabrications that defame him'. Speeches critical of the President's action and the policy conducted under his leadership was not covered by this law.[36] This was clearly an attempt to defend the presidency from criticism and thereby shore up the post's prestige and authority, but it did not have this effect: the partisan application of the law and the failure of the courts to convict prominent people charged under the law[37] called the whole exercise into disrepute.

In any event, Gorbachev and those around him soon decided that the powers currently available to the President were insufficient, and in September 1990 extra powers were accorded to that office. A draft law had been presented to the Supreme Soviet on 21 September 1990 and had evoked some reservations on the part of some of the deputies. Some had felt that this was a denial of the role of the Supreme Soviet and a take-over of powers that rightfully belonged to that body. One asked why the President was to be granted additional powers when he did not make adequate use of the ones he already possessed. Others called for the creation of an effective mechanism for ensuring continuing monitoring by the Supreme Soviet of how those powers were exercised. In the Presidium of the Russian Supreme Soviet, the proposal for additional powers for the President was rejected.[38] Despite these reservations, the law was adopted on 25 September.

The law was seen as an extraordinary measure, as its preamble suggests: it was introduced because 'of the complexity of the social and political situation and the need for emergency measures to extricate society from the crisis situation, ensure the changeover to a market economy and strengthen the country's administrative system and law and order . . .'[39] The law then gave the President two specific types of power:

a) Up until 31 March 1992 to issue decrees of a normative nature in accord with the Constitution and to give instructions on questions of property relations, the organisation of the management of the national economy, the budget and financial system, pay and price formation, and the strengthening of law and order. The Supreme Soviet was given overall supervision; if it felt that it was necessary, the Supreme Soviet could establish different rules or recommend to the President that a decision he had made be changed or rescinded.

b) The right to create agencies and other state structures to accelerate the formation of an all-union market, and ensure cooperation for this between the different administrative levels in the country.

The powers accorded to the President were formally limited but in practice quite extensive. Although his powers were to be restricted to facilitating the emergence of the market and maintaining law and order, these aims could be interpreted sufficiently expansively to constitute little real restriction upon the exercise of his power.

The strengthening of the President's powers in September was followed three months later by a reworking of the apparatus around the President in an attempt to provide him with the machinery to play a more active executive role.[40] The chief changes made at this time involved:[41]

1 Creation of a popularly-elected vice-presidency. Nominated for election by the President, the Vice-President was to assist the President in the performance of his duties and take over if through absence or illness the President was unable to carry out his functions.

2 Abolition of the Presidential Council.

3 Its replacement by the Council of the Federation, which gained decision-making powers in place of its former advisory powers. Its brief involved coordination of the activities of the supreme organs of state administration in the Union and the republics, ensuring the observance of the Union Treaty, determination of measures for implementation of state nationality policy, ensuring the participation of the republics in the solution of questions of general union significance, the introduction of measures for the resolution and regulation of inter-national disputes and disagreements. Its members, who were the leaders of the republics, were specifically charged with ensuring the implementation of decisions in their republics. Decisions adopted by a two-thirds majority were to be binding on the President.

4 Establishment of a new Security Council to be concerned with security and military affairs. Members were to be appointed by the President,

having taken into account the views of the Council of the Federation, and approved by the Supreme Soviet.

5 Replacement of the Council of Ministers by a new Cabinet of Ministers whose brief was to cover defence, security, foreign policy, finance, justice, ecology, energy, transport and communications. All of these were to be handled with the agreement of the republics. The Cabinet was to be subordinate to the President, with the office of prime minister effectively downgraded to the status of aide to the President. Members were appointed by the President with the approval of the Supreme Soviet.

The President thus gained a new set of executive organs, one of which reflected the increasing importance of the republics as independent political actors at this time by building the leaderships of the union republics into a central place in the all-union governmental structure. He also gained control over the government through the new Cabinet of Ministers. However, he did not acquire something which all acknowledged was needed in some form or other, a means of ensuring his decrees were implemented.

How did this process of strengthening of the President's powers affect the way that office evolved? By expanding the President's room for legislative action independent (albeit under the monitoring) of the Supreme Soviet, these changes tilted the balance between executive and legislature substantially in favour of the former. Gorbachev made frequent use of his power to issue decrees, introducing measures through this mechanism in a wide range of areas. Economic and law and order issues were prominent.[42] But the exercise of this power encountered two types of limitation, one formal and the other practical. The first, formal, limitation involved questions about the legality of individual actions by the President. Although the Supreme Soviet did not overturn any presidential decrees, the Committee for Constitutional Supervision declared that the President had violated the Constitution when in April 1990 he promulgated a decree transferring control over demonstrations and public events in Moscow away from the city soviet to the Council of Ministers.[43] This was an important decision because it affirmed the principle that the President was not above the law but remained subject to the constitution and the institutions designed to defend it.

The second, practical, limitation was that despite the extensive nature of the President's law-making powers, he possessed little in the way of capacity to ensure that the decrees he proclaimed were actually implemented. This required improvements in the linkages between centre and other levels, and during this time it was these linkages which were becoming increasingly frayed; at the 28th Congress of the party in 1990 one speaker complained about the absence of a system for implementing presidential decisions and raised the possibility of introducing presidential plenipotentiaries at the local level as a solution to this problem.[44] However, the President was given no institutional mechanism for reaching into society independent of the state structure, while that structure itself was becoming increasingly unable to play an effective administrative role. A number of attempts were made to streamline this system. When Gorbachev came to power there had been 109 ministries. In 1985 this number was reduced by the creation of so-called 'super ministries' which united a number of former ministries and state committees into larger ministerial structures. In the following years, as part of the policies of economic decentralisation, the number of ministries was further reduced; between 1986 and 1990 the number of central ministries fell from fifty-five to thirty-seven and state committees from twenty-three to nineteen.[45] Such a dramatic reduction and consequent re-ordering of responsibilities alone would have caused significant disruption to the work patterns and effectiveness of government ministries. The effect of this was exacerbated by the drive for administrative and economic decentralisation, and ultimately independence, by the republics. It was this which destroyed the authority of the central ministries and rendered them totally incapable of carrying out central directives. A streamlining of the decision-making process through the enhancement of presidential power could not overcome this fundamental obstacle to the implementation of central decisions.

One of the pressures leading to the strengthening of the presidency was the perceived paralysis of power within the national political organs. Important here was the perception that the Congress of People's Deputies and the Supreme Soviet were both products of an earlier phase in the course of reform and remained rooted in that phase while the general situation had moved on. They were therefore seen by some to be out of step with the new mood and new needs; the undemocratic nature of their make up, at least in part, was thought to symbolise this. But also important was the view that they were not sufficiently decisive, that they spent far too much time debating issues without taking the sorts of decisions which were necessary to deal with the problems that were emerging. The complaints about 'meeting democracy' and the need for a 'firm hand' were part of this process. But if the hope was that an enhanced presidency could galvanise the legislature into action and unite it behind a vigorous programme in pursuit of agreed aims, it was doomed to disappointment. Despite his undoubted skills as a chairman, Gorbachev was not able to consolidate the legislative chambers behind him and introduce a clear programme of reform. The compromises and retreats evident in the discussion and eventual adoption of an economic reform programme in September 1990 is evidence of this. One reason for this is that Gorbachev himself was ambiguous about policy commitments and failed to give clear and unambiguous leadership. But also important was the release of political energies in the legislative chambers which made them the sort of institutions in which the exercise of such personalised leadership would be very difficult to achieve.

The President's inability to wield presidential influence and thereby assert his authority over the legislature also reflected the stage the process of political reform had reached. The creation of an executive presidency saw the elevation of one people's deputy progressively through chairmanship of a collective leadership (Chairman of the Presidium of the Supreme Soviet) to a position of individual leadership within the space of some eighteen months. That person was not popularly elected at any stage of this process. The President therefore lacked the popular legitimacy that would have gone with direct popular election, and in the eyes of many had even less authority than many ordinary people's deputies who were elected directly by the populace. This may not have mattered had the position of presidency been invested with the sort of aura of office that usually attaches to such positions. However, the office was of such recent origin and the course of its emergence and development subject to sufficient criticism from union republican capitals as to ensure that the aura of office would not immediately attach itself to it. Such a sense of authority, competence and dignity of office could only have developed over time. The office could have become institutionalised in the national power structure if its profile had been clearly defined and its relationships with the other organs of power regularised and stabilised. But such was not to be the case before the abortive coup of August 1991. In the new conditions that prevailed after the coup,[46] the erosion of the position of the centre diminished the stature of the Soviet President; on 30 August the Supreme Soviet voted overwhelmingly to withdraw the emergency powers that had been given to the President in September 1990. With Gorbachev's resignation on 25 December, the post of Soviet President passed into history having had no real chance of proving its worth.

Despite the diminution of the Soviet President, the continuing salience of the presidential model is suggested in the adoption of a presidential system throughout many of the former republics. The most striking case has been that of Boris Yeltsin in Russia. In the attempt to push through radical reform, Yeltsin combined the post of prime minister with the presidency and acquired the right effectively to rule by decree for a period of twelve months. This came under severe criticism, not only because of the policies he was pursuing, but because of the view in the legislature that the system should be parliamentary in type rather than the presidential style of system which Yeltsin preferred. The extent of this disagreement is reflected in the failure of the political authorities to agree upon a new constitution to replace that from the Soviet period. Yeltsin's concentration of power was not replicated in the other republics, and presidents elsewhere sought to rule through the sorts of structures that had characterised the Gorbachev period (see pp. 101–4). Only time will tell whether these attempts to establish a stable form of national leadership will be any more successful than the short-lived Soviet experiment in presidential government.

5   From union to independence

Despite the considerable efforts of Mikhail Gorbachev to hold the country together, in December 1991 the Soviet Union formally dissolved into fifteen independent states. In part this occurred because of the reluctance of Gorbachev and other central authorities to loosen their control over the republics, despite the rapid change in the politics of the republics brought about by the 1990 elections. Gorbachev routinely described leaders and movements in republics that sought independence as 'separatists' who were working against the 'true' interests of their people – ignoring the fact that, in many republics, the drive for independence enjoyed broad popular support. The political future of leaders in these republics would have been jeopardised if they compromised on the secession question. In the end, concessions offered by Gorbachev to preserve the union were inadequate, and the failed coup of August 1991 accelerated the process of disintegration by further discrediting central institutions.

Soviet 'federalism'

The Soviet system, while formally federal in the configuration of fifteen republics, was actually an uneasy combination of an extremely centralised unitary state with some dispersal of power and a federal structure. The federal structure was, even outwardly, incomplete. The lack of true federalism was best exemplified by Russia, by far the largest republic, which had few of the institutions that existed in other republics. A Russian communist party was not created until 1990, and the CPSU central apparatus was responsible for overseeing developments there. Russian ministries were relatively weak appendages of central Soviet ministries.

The elements of tight centralism and a unitary state were brought to the system by a number of institutions. The Communist Party of the Soviet Union, while divided into fourteen republic organisations, retained a centralised structure. Lenin's principle of democratic centralism included the precept that policies adopted by 'higher' organs were binding on 'lower' ones. The CPSU Congress, Central Committee and its Politburo were the party's highest organs, and policy deliberations often were devoted to the behaviour of party organs at the republic level and lower.

The shortcomings of federalism were most apparent in the economy, where effective control and *de jure* ownership of the chief elements of the economy was maintained through the central (*vsesoyuznye*, translated as 'all-union', or simply *soyuznye*, or 'union') ministries and USSR state committees. This system of organising economic activity was a product of the Stalin period that defied all attempts at reform in the pre-Gorbachev period. Central ownership and control was especially prevalent in high priority sectors of the Soviet economy such as heavy industry and the closely related defence industry (approximately 30 per cent of which was located outside Russia), rail, air and sea transportation, power generation, and the extractive industries.[1] As a rule, enterprises in these and other central ministries were the largest and richest in a given city or region.

Individual all-union enterprises in the republics operated quite apart from local and republic administrative systems. Decisions on matters such as housing construction and funding for cultural amenities were often made in Moscow by ministry officials for the benefit of 'their' employees in distant regions. There was very little coordination with local authorities. It also meant that, in practice, huge flows of revenue, taxes, and state expenditures completely bypassed republic and local officials and instead went through all-union institutions. In many republics the 'foreign' character of all-union enterprises was reinforced by the fact that most of the enterprise workforce as well as its managers were Russians or other non-natives who came from outside the republic. Often these employees lived apart from the local population and sent their children to a local network of Russian schools for their education. They generally made no effort to learn the republic's language and showed little interest in local culture.

The extent of central control was greatest in the sensitive areas of defence and internal security. The Soviet military was a highly centralised structure, with a central command in the form of the General Staff that exercised control over all units of the military. Though the heads of regional military commands were represented in republic organs of the communist party and government, they were in no way subordinate to republic officials. Soviet military bases resembled the outposts of an occupying power in their relative isolation from local communities. In the Estonian capital of Tallinn, for example, an entire complex of housing for Soviet military personnel and their families was built without even informing republic or local officials. The KGB, while it had republic-level organisations, was also tightly monitored by the centre and served the centre almost exclusively. The flow of information generated by its vast network of paid and unpaid agents and informers went directly from the republics to the centre. Decisions on personnel changes at the top of the republic division of the KGB were made in Moscow.

In practice, imperfections in the centralising institutions combined with the sheer size and diversity of the country limited the effectiveness of central control. This was a characteristic of the system that also dated back to the Stalin era.[2] While the Politburo could and did intervene to set policy on any question it chose, it could not possibly influence more than a small percentage of these decisions. The source for many of the decisions on issues affecting the republics was the state administrative hierarchy and the economic bureaucracy, which, while concentrated in Moscow, pursued policies that were often uncoordinated and even contradictory. By default, it was often branch (*otraslevye*) interests – not Russian or Soviet interests – that determined policy in republics and other ethnic units. The bulk of decisions on investment, housing and enterprise construction, and social development (including the siting of cultural and pre-school facilities) were made by branch officials.[3]

Limited control over the administration of the economy and society were given over to the republics in the form of republican ministries or jointly controlled union/republican (*soiuzno-respublikanskie*) ministries. These ministries were typically in areas considered of secondary importance in the Soviet economic system – consumer goods, services, education, and health care. Nevertheless, republic-level leaders who were so inclined had considerable power to shape the policies of their republics. The Soviet republics were far from uniform in the way they were governed, and republic leaders could use their ties with the centre to lobby for greater freedom of action. The extent of experimentation or innovation in economic and social policy, widespread even in the Brezhnev years, varied greatly from republic to republic and reflected different political cultures as well as differing styles of leadership.[4]

One of the institutions that played a role in keeping the system together was, of course, the Communist Party. The political changes unleashed by Gorbachev, as we shall see in chapter 7, affected the role of the Communist Party perhaps more than any Soviet institution. The pressures created by democratisation led to increasing differentiation of republic-level communist party organisations. This undermined the potential for the party to play a centralising role, and it did not succeed even as a buffer to reduce the level of conflict between central and republic interests. The first communist party to 'defect' to the side of the nationalists was the Communist Party of Lithuania, which led by Algirdas Brazauskas joined with the rising nationalist movement Sajudis in an attempt to increase its popular stature and preserve its hold on power. 'Perestroika' and 'democratisation' in republican party organisations often meant that the parties attempted to distance themselves from the more conservative central party institutions in Moscow.

Republics vs. the centre

As a result of the elections of 1990, new non-communist republic governments were established in the three Baltic republics as well as in Moldova (Moldavia), Armenia, Georgia, and Russia. Governments of these republics were the most hostile to a continuation of past patterns of relations between Moscow and the republics. Lithuania went the furthest, adopting a declaration of independence in March 1990, at one of the first sessions of the newly elected republican parliament. It was the only republic to claim immediate and complete independence until April 1991, when Georgia adopted its declaration of independence. However, even republican governments that were largely made up of communist *apparatchiki* – Ukraine and Belarus, for example – began to push for greater political autonomy from the centre.

Gorbachev and the leadership in Moscow saw these challenges to central authority as dangerous, and, if not rebuffed decisively, they would result in other republics moving along the same path. The first declaration of sovereignty was actually proclaimed by Estonia, in November 1988, while it was still under the control of a communist government. Gorbachev quickly declared this act unconstitutional and invalid. Gorbachev responded to Lithuania's declaration of independence even more harshly. He condemned the parliament's actions as illegal and imposed a number of sanctions on the republic, including an energy blockade. While the Soviet response did lead Lithuanian leaders to suspend some of their early measures and brought them to the bargaining table, it only strengthened their commitment to achieving complete independence.

In the aftermath of Lithuania's actions, newly elected parliaments in other republics adopted laws on sovereignty in an effort to claim jurisdiction over policy making and natural resources at the republic level.[5] Most of the laws on sovereignty were adopted only after new parliaments had been elected in 1990. The Russian parliament, in June 1990 under the leadership of Boris Yeltsin, was the first of the newly elected parliaments to adopt a declaration on state sovereignty. One of the most radical of the laws on sovereignty was adopted by Ukraine, in July 1990. The Ukrainian declaration included provisions for a separate Ukrainian army and an independent foreign policy.

Efforts to implement these laws on sovereignty were often blocked by the continued role of the ministries and other central institutions. When, for example, the USSR government adopted a resolution on the transfer of a number of all-union enterprises to republic ministries, all-union ministries simply ignored the decision.[6] Most often the disputes were between republic parliaments and central authorities. This so-called 'war of laws' – in essence, jurisdictional disputes in which decisions by 'higher' authorities were not accepted as binding – paralysed policy at all levels of the system in 1990 and 1991.

One would have expected that powerful central institutions such as the Communist Party, the military, the KGB, and central economic ministries would have used all the resources at their disposal to prevent the republics from exercising real power. To an extent this expectation was fulfilled, as central institutions sought to maintain their grip on power. The ability of the centre to influence events in the republics, however, began to erode very quickly over the course of 1990 and 1991. As indicated above, the communist parties at the republic level were torn between carrying out the will of the centre and maintaining their legitimacy within their republics. Other central institutions also began to lose their capacity to prevent the disintegration of the Soviet system.

Republican leaders were not passive observers of this process; many set out to dismantle central institutions as a way to increase their own autonomy. This process progressed perhaps most rapidly in Georgia, under its fervently anticommunist leader Zviad Gamsakhurdia. Well before elections were held in late October 1990, Gamsakhurdia used his prestige as a former dissident and his popularity as the most visible Georgian nationalist to pressure institutions such as the Komsomol and trade unions to sever their ties with Moscow. Oddly enough, the first such action to attract the attention of central authorities was the Georgian decision, forced by Gamsakhurdia, not to allow Georgian teams to participate in football (soccer) matches under the auspices of the Soviet football federation. Once Gamsakhurdia came to power, in November 1990, he worked systematically to deprive central institutions of almost any influence in Georgia – though the Soviet Communist Party and KGB retained some role in Abkhazia and South Ossetia, where local elites sought to use ties with the centre to preserve and extend their own autonomy *vis à vis* Georgia. Gamsakhurdia's pressure on the Georgian KGB, which began even before the elections, in effect brought that institution under Georgian control. Efforts by Gorbachev, Kryuchkov (head of the Soviet KGB), and Boris Pugo (head of the Soviet Ministry of Internal Affairs) to stop Gamsakhurdia from naming his own people to head 'their' ministries in Tbilisi were unsuccessful.[7]

In other republics too the Soviet monopoly on military force ended with the creation of private military formations and republic militias. The initial stages of conflict between Armenia and Azerbaijan over Nagorno-Karabakh in 1988–9 were intensified by military units attached to the Azerbaijani

Popular Front, the Armenian Pan-National Movement, and the competing Armenian National Army. The weapons used by these groups were often obtained from attacks on police stations or Soviet armouries. Gorbachev issued a presidential directive in July 1990 that forbade the creation of armed formations and ordered that their weapons be turned over to Soviet authorities.[8] Like many other presidential orders, this was never implemented. Moldova was the first republic to make the creation of republic military units an element of state policy; in October 1990 the government recruited 'volunteers' to help put down a rebellion by the Gagauz ethnic minority that later became the basis for organising a 'republican guard'.[9] The Georgian government took steps in December 1990 that led to the creation of a 'national guard' that was to form the core of a republican army. Soviet conservatives blamed Vadim Bakatin, then USSR minister of Internal Affairs (MVD), for allowing other republics to form their first military units under the guise of police units.[10]

One of the most emotionally charged issues to arise in relations between republics and central institutions was the conscription of non-Russians to serve in the Soviet military. A number of republican parliaments adopted laws ending the draft on their territory and calling for the return home of their conscripts. The Soviet military was largely powerless to prevent this, despite some efforts in the Baltic to return 'deserters' to their units. The recruitment figures for the Soviet army for the fall of 1990 showed the varying degrees of resistance to central policy in this area: in Georgia only 10 per cent of planned recruits were effectively called up for military service; in Lithuania, 12.5 per cent; in Estonia, 24.5 per cent; in Latvia, 25.3 per cent; in Armenia, 28.1 per cent; and in Moldova, 58.9 per cent. The draft plan fulfilment figure for the USSR as a whole was 78.8 per cent.[11] Other republics, including Ukraine, issued orders in 1991 requiring that their citizens serve only on the republic's territory if drafted.[12]

The Soviet military was surprisingly ineffective at preventing these and other developments that undermined the power of the centre. One important reason was a result of the 9 April 1989 involvement of Soviet military forces in an attempt to disperse a peaceful independence demonstration in the Georgian capital. Twenty people were killed, mostly women and children, and the resulting investigations highlighted the potential dangers involved in the further use of the military to resolve political disputes.

In the aftermath of the Tbilisi events, the Soviet military generally became involved directly only where serious armed conflicts had broken out – and usually only after the violence had run its course. The Baltic republics were an exception to this rule, in that Soviet armed forces – including special divisions, the OMON, attached to the Ministry of the Interior – were used in rather crude attempts to intimidate the local population and republic leaders. The most violent incident in the Baltics was a January 1991 attack on demonstrators by Soviet military units equipped with tanks, with the purpose of seizing the Vilnius television tower. The military interceded in a number of ethnic conflicts in Azerbaijan and Central Asia. The Soviet army became deeply involved in Azerbaijani politics after attacks on Armenians in Baku in January 1990 and also intervened to impose martial law after ethnic explosions in Uzbekistan (Ferghana valley), Kyrgyzstan (Osh province), and Tajikistan (Dushanbe). In these and other republics the Soviet military presence was far from being a stabilising factor. Military units were often the target of attacks by combatants who were seeking weapons and ammunition. In some conflicts, Soviet military personnel engaged in unauthorised sales of weapons to both sides engaged in hostilities. Such as the case in Georgia in late 1991, when heavy equipment such as artillery and armoured personnel carriers were sold to both sides of the escalating conflict between Gamsakhurdia and his opposition.

The outcome of developments in Russia was of crucial importance to any effort to prevent the disintegration of the union, given its size and share of the total population. The election of Boris Yeltsin to the post of chairman of the Russian Supreme Soviet was one of the most important events in the demise of the Soviet system. At the end of October 1990, the Russian parliament adopted a series of measures designed to confront the power of the centre to manage Russian affairs, particularly in the economy. A law on economic sovereignty claimed Russian ownership of its natural resources and the right to regulate foreign exports of its raw materials.[13]

One interesting aspect of the economic interaction of the Soviet republics was the increasingly widespread perception in virtually all republics that one's own republic was being exploited by the other republics, by the centre, or both. The reality is that some republics subsidised other republics. An accurate accounting of the interrepublic balance sheet is impossible, because of the arbitrary character of Soviet prices. Nevertheless, this did not prevent a number of analysts from trying to assess interrepublic trade balances – often in an effort to 'prove' that independence would not be feasible for many republics.[14] There is also the difficult issue of what a republic would have accomplished had it not been cut off from the world economy by Soviet foreign economic policies or if it had not been forced to participate in the internal 'socialist division of labour'. It was the latter policy, for example, that reduced Central Asia to a supplier of cotton and other raw materials to other republics. What was important, however, was not the economic reality but the perception of being exploited that was dominant among elites in every republic, including Russia.

The tendency of ministries to create monopolies in the production of parts and equipment made the economic links between republics extremely prone to disruptions, since a break in supplies meant that there were no or few alternatives. The share of components or other items produced exclusively by one or few enterprises was highest in the machine-tool industry (87 per cent according to one study) but was also substantial in other industries: 47 per cent of items used in the chemical/wood processing industry, and 28 per cent in the steel industry.[15] Just to give one example, a large share of equipment used in oil drilling and refining was produced exclusively in Azerbaijan. Production problems there, caused by civil disturbances, were felt in all oil producing regions of the Soviet Union.

Efforts directed at achieving economic sovereignty at all levels were an important factor in the decline of the power of central economic ministries. The push for economic sovereignty increasingly began to affect the workings of the economy as republic officials began to prevent enterprises from exporting their output to other republics.[16] Supply disruptions led enterprises to pursue barter arrangements in order to continue production. This was the death knell to the power of the central economic agencies responsible for implementing centrally set priorities – the State Planning Commission and the State Committee for Material-Technical Supply (Gosplan and Gossnab). Republics also began to refuse to remit funds for the USSR state budget, which threatened to bankrupt the central budget. In the first quarter of 1991, for example, receipts for the state budget were only one-third the planned amount.[17]

The new central political institutions forged by Gorbachev were no more effective at maintaining control than the old ones. In the USSR Congress of People's Deputies and its Supreme Soviet Gorbachev was able to use his control over party loyalists in the Soviet parliament to achieve an effective majority, aided by a large block of Central Asian deputies who voted as instructed by republic officials. This enabled Gorbachev to manipulate the national legislature on issues concerning the preservation of the union, and undoubtedly contributed to the demise of the union by convincing many republic leaders that their interests would not be reflected in parliamentary decisions adopted at the national level. A glaring example of this was Gorbachev's law on secession, adopted in April 1990. It was described by a number of republic leaders as a 'law against secession' because of the stringent conditions placed on republics that sought to leave the union. In the course of 1990, the more independence-minded republics' parliamentary delegations stopped participating in the work of the Soviet parliament or attended only as observers.

Towards a new union treaty

The state of play of the bargaining taking place between Gorbachev and republic leaders was reflected in a succession of drafts for a new union treaty to replace the agreement of 1922, which was still formally in effect. Five versions of the treaty appeared in major Soviet newspapers on 24 November 1990, 9 March 1991, 27 June 1991, 24 July 1991, and 25 November 1991. Work on the union treaty held up completion of a new Soviet constitution, since the treaty would determine much of the framework that was to be codified in the constitution. Participation in the drafting process was far from universal. Those republics most committed to full and complete independence – Lithuania, Estonia, Latvia, Moldova, Georgia and Armenia – as a rule refused to take part in discussions on the new union agreement. The first, November 1990 version was drafted in much the same way as traditional Soviet legislation, by groups of experts in the context of a lengthy period of controlled 'public discussion' in the mass media, and with significant input from the apparatus of the Communist Party Central Committee.[18] The March 1991 version was initialled by representatives of eight republics, as well as seventeen of twenty autonomous republics (republics created within republics, encompassing concentrated populations of ethnic minorities), but soon it was sharply criticised by Yeltsin and other leaders as a document 'imposed' on them by the centre. In fact, Gorbachev's attempt to involve autonomous regions in the drafting process was a transparent attempt to undermine the authority of republic leaders; leaders of these regions often appealed to the centre to achieve in an attempt to obtain greater independence.[19] As Yeltsin later was to describe the process, 'New drafts of the agreement began to appear one after another. In essence into each of them was dragged the very same model of a Union with a strong Centre. The principle of sovereignty was recognised only as a decorative frill; in fact it was ruthlessly suppressed.'[20]

The six non-participating republics (Estonia, Latvia, Lithuania, Moldova, Georgia, and Armenia) created a short-lived but important coalition to resist pressure from the centre to curb their drives for independence. The group took the name 'Kishinev Forum', since the first meeting took place in Kishinev, the capital of Moldova, in May 1991. Initial steps to create this bloc were taken in March 1991 at the initiative of Moldova.[21] Formally, the group was a coalition of mass movements of the six republics, but since each of the movements was also the dominant force in the republic's parliament, the effort was closely linked to policy. The purpose of the Kishinev Forum was to coordinate actions against the centre, facilitate direct economic ties (though these were hindered by the geographic dispersion of the six republics), and exchange information. The first meeting focused on foreign policy issues. Members called on their parliaments to seek other countries to represent their interests in the United Nations, formally withdrawing that right from the Soviet delegation. In an attempt to assuage international fears that independence for the republics would result in nuclear proliferation, the forum also adopted a declaration that called for the removal of all Soviet nuclear weapons remaining on their territories. At the group's second meeting in July 1991 in Tbilisi, the parties called for the removal of all 'occupation structures (soldiers, the KGB, CPSU, etc.)' from their territories. In a move that confirmed the essentially 'anti-Soviet' orientation of the forum, the organisation dissolved in the aftermath of the August coup.[22]

Gorbachev attempted to apply pressure on these and other republic leaders to sign a new union treaty by holding a national referendum on preserving the union in March 1991. Gorbachev proposed the referendum in December 1990, and the USSR Congress of People's Deputies obliged by quickly passing a Law on Referenda and designating a date for holding this first referendum in Soviet history. The text of the question finally put to voters was highly ambiguous: 'Do you consider it necessary to preserve the Union of Soviet Socialist Republics as a renewed federation of equal, sovereign republics in which the rights and freedoms of people of any nationality will be guaranteed in full measure?' In effect, voters were asked to approve the 'preservation' of something that did not yet exist – 'a renewed federation' – while at the same time being asked to accept the old name (including the word 'socialist') and to endorse a guarantee of minority rights.

The referendum proposal was approved by 76.4 per cent of the voters across the country who participated in the voting (see table 5.1). Negative votes comprised 21.7 per cent of the total. An analysis of the results by region shows that the most significant opposition to the proposition was found in Russian industrial centres, including Sverdlovsk (48 per cent opposed), Moscow (46 per cent), Leningrad (43 per cent), Cheliabinsk (35 per cent), and Volgograd (32 per cent).[23] In a sign of what was to come later, voters in Kiev and the three provinces of Western Ukraine rejected the proposal with solid majorities.

Rather than play into Gorbachev's hands, the parliaments of the six rebellious republics adopted decisions preventing the holding of the referendum on their territory. All six were, for the most part, effective in this effort, despite intimidation from the centre. This in itself was a demonstration of the ability of republics to thwart the will of Moscow, and the centre's unsuccessful effort to bypass the republic leaderships to conduct the referendum only strengthened their commitment to independence. As an alternative to the national referendum, the Baltic republics, Georgia, and Armenia decided to hold their own referenda on independence (see table 5.2). After the failure of the August coup other republics sought to use referenda to ratify and legitimise their own declarations of independence.

While Gorbachev sought to portray the results of the referendum as an endorsement of his views on the preservation of the union, political realities

Table 5.1. *Results of the union referendum, March 1991*

Republic	Registered voters	% turnout	% voting 'yes'	% voting 'no'
USSR total	185,647,355	80.0	76.4	21.7
Turkmenia	1,847,310	97.7	97.9	1.7
Uzbekistan	10,287,938	95.4	93.7	5.2
Tajikistan	2,549,096	94.4	96.2	3.1
Kyrgyzstan	2,341,646	92.9	94.6	4.0
Kazakhstan	9,999,433	88.2	94.1	5.0
Ukraine	37,732,178	83.5	70.2	28.0
Belarus	7,354,796	83.3	82.7	16.1
RSFSR	105,643,364	75.4	71.3	26.4
Azerbaijan	3,866,659	75.1	93.3	5.8

Source: *Pravda*, 27 March 1991.

Table 5.2. *Results of republic referenda on independence, 1991*

Republic	Date	% turnout	% voting yes	% voting no
Lithuania	Feb. 9	84.43	90.47	6.56
Latvia	March 3	87.56	73.68	24.69
Estonia	March 3	82.96	77.73	21.40
Georgia	March 31	90.53	99.08	0.51
Armenia	Sept. 21	95.05	99.31	0.46
Turkmenia	Oct. 26	n.a.	94.1	n.a.
Ukraine	Dec. 1	84.2	90.3	7.6
Azerbaijan	Dec. 29	95.27	99.58	0.24
Uzbekistan	Dec. 29	n.a.	98.2	n.a.

Source: Adapted from Darrell Slider, 'The first Soviet "national" referendum and referenda in the republics: voting on union, sovereignty, and independence', *Journal of Soviet Nationalities* (forthcoming).

finally forced him to compromise with advocates of increasing republic autonomy. Gorbachev began to distance himself from his more conservative appointees in the Soviet government, the officials who would later seek to remove him from power. Yeltsin's authority to champion republic rights was enhanced by his overwhelming election in June to the newly created post of Russian president. Yeltsin's victory occurred in spite of Gorbachev's obvious desire that another of the candidates should win; among those running against Yeltsin were the former Soviet prime minister Nikolai Ryzhkov and Gorbachev's advisor and former interior minister Vadim Bakatin.

It was only in April 1991 that Gorbachev made his first serious attempt to assuage the concerns of republic leaders and find common ground with Yeltsin. On 23 April 1991, the leaders of nine republics and Gorbachev reached a compromise agreement at Novo-Ogarevo, site of a government dacha near Moscow. The autonomous republics that had been drawn into the drafting of the March 1991 draft agreement were now excluded from the process, and the agreement set the stage for the drafts published in June and July. The Novo-Ogarevo agreement, which also came to be known as the 'nine plus one' agreement, appeared to be a breakthrough in creating a new union. It marked the first significant rapprochement between Gorbachev and Yeltsin on issues of republican sovereignty. In a clause of the agreement that brought considerable relief to nonsigners, the republics that did not participate in the new union were to be treated as foreign countries, though without 'most favoured nation' status in trade granted to republics remaining in the union.

The name of the new replacement for the Union of Soviet Socialist Republics was one indicator of the shift in what was acceptable to republic leaders. The name changed in the various drafts from 'Union of Sovereign Soviet Republics' in November 1990 (a name change that was subsequently rejected by the USSR Congress of People's Deputies in December 1990), to 'Union of Sovereign Republics' in March 1991, to 'Union of Sovereign States' in the June, July, and November 1991 drafts. The various drafts left in place a number of central institutions, including an all-union Supreme Soviet, a union president, and national government agencies headed by a prime minister. The relative importance of these institutions and the decision rules that would be applied changed markedly, however, in the direction of greater power to the republics.

The agreement worked out at Novo-Ogarevo was scheduled to be signed on 20 August 1991. Soviet tanks moved into Moscow during the early morning of 19 August. The 19 August announcement of the formation of a State Emergency Committee (*Gosudarstvennyi komitet po chrezvychainomu polozheniiu*) emphasised the need to preserve the 'unity of the Fatherland'.[24] It was clearly the purpose of the plotters to prevent the signing of the treaty. Conservative officials had long signalled their extreme dissatisfaction with the course that Gorbachev had taken on the creation of a new confederation, and they were particularly upset by the concessions Gorbachev had made to republic leaders at Novo-Ogarevo. Of course, the actual impact of the coup was precisely the opposite of what its planners had intended. The coup fully and finally discredited two of the institutions that had been crucial in keeping the union together: the CPSU and the KGB. The apparent complicity of the central Communist Party leadership in the coup led Yeltsin to ban its operations on Russian territory, and property of the Central Committee was taken over by the Russian government. The KGB was initially put in the hands of an outsider, Vadim Bakatin, who set about dismantling the agency and removing a number of top officials. Within months the central operations of the KGB had been absorbed into the Russian security service, while other republics took control of KGB operations on their territory.

The system of governing the country changed dramatically after the coup, with power shifting to the leaders of the republics. In the wake of the coup, republics began to adopt formal declarations of independence and, most importantly, these began to be accepted by the outside world. The first states to adopt such declarations were Estonia and Latvia, thus joining Lithuania. On 28 August 1991, Germany officially recognised Latvia, Lithuania and Estonia. From that point on, any participation by the Baltic states in a common framework with the other Soviet republics was virtually excluded by Baltic leaders. A State Council was created, made up of the remaining republic leaders, which essentially supplanted the most important Soviet legislative and executive bodies. Yeltsin's power in particular was greatly enhanced by the collapse of central institutions and by his ability to determine the most important personnel changes in Soviet institutions resulting from the failure of the coup and the arrest of its leaders.

Negotiations resumed on a possible continuation of the union as republic leaders, with Yeltsin in the forefront, sought to find common ground. A new draft treaty was hammered out in November that would have led to an even looser confederation. The new union would have preserved some vestiges of central authority while changing fundamentally the role of the republics by creating an entity more akin to a confederation than a union. The republics would have complete political sovereignty, would provide representatives to a new Supreme Soviet of the Union, and their leaders would form the central coordinating agency of the new union – the State Council. A key element of the agreement was the parallel effort to preserve a 'common economic space' on the territory of the former union. Ivan Silaev, previously the Russian premier, was placed in charge of these negotiations in September, when he was named chairman of the Interrepublic Economic Committee.[25] In early October a 'Treaty on Economic Community' appeared that was designed to facilitate the preservation of traditional economic ties between the republics.[26]

That the new union treaty represented a significant change from past proposals was indicated by the response of the Armenian leadership, which reversed its previous position and agreed to participate in the new union. The negative economic consequences of independence were an important factor in this decision, as were Armenian wishes to obtain the assistance of other commonwealth members in a favourable resolution of the Nagorno-Karabakh crisis.

Internal political developments in Ukraine, however, ultimately prevented the establishment of a new union. In October 1991 Ukrainian officials indicated that they would not sign the agreement on an economic union. By the time the November 1991 draft union treaty was initialled by seven republics, Ukraine again refused. The Ukrainian referendum on independence, which was coupled with elections that made Kravchuk the republic's president, took place on 1 December 1991. Upon election, Kravchuk made it clear that Ukraine would not be a part of any new union. Yeltsin at that point abandoned his attempts to work with Gorbachev to preserve central authority. Instead, Yeltsin met with the leaders of Ukraine and Belarus and worked out a new framework without a strong centre – and without a president – to be called the Commonwealth of Independent States (abbreviated as CIS, or SNG in Russian, for *Sodruzhestvo nezavisimykh gosudarstv*). By the end of December 1991, the Soviet Union officially ceased to exist.

The Commonwealth of Independent States

The CIS was formed as a result of the agreement signed by the leaders of the three Slavic republics at Brest on 8 December 1991. It was a loose arrangement, one that was outlined in purposely vague language to permit the widest degree of acceptance by other republics. At a decisive follow-up meeting in Alma Ata, capital of Kazakhstan, eight other republics joined including Azerbaijan, Kazakhstan, and the four Central Asian republics as well as long-time holdouts Moldova and Armenia.[27] However, as of late 1992 neither the parliament of Moldova nor of Azerbaijan had ratified the agreement setting up the CIS. Nor were Georgia or the Baltic states in the new Commonwealth. Georgia at the time was in the middle of a violent political struggle that would lead to the overthrow of its president, Zviad Gamsakhurdia. Both sides in the Georgian conflict, however, were opposed in principle to rejoining any reconfigured union.

Once the CIS was formed and the USSR formally disbanded, the republics achieved complete international recognition of their independence that had previously been accorded only to the Baltic states. This included recognition by the United States, which had refrained from taking any steps that could be seen as undermining the union. The Baltic states rejected membership in any association that might reproduce the former union. Instead Lithuania, Latvia, and Estonia sought to regulate and improve relations with Russia and other republics on a bilateral basis. Among the most difficult of the issues raised in these talks was the removal of CIS military forces stationed in the Baltic. Lithuania was the first to come to terms with Moscow, in September 1992, and the withdrawal was to take place by August 1993.

The CIS was purposely limited by its creators to prevent even the appearance of recreating central authority. Its headquarters were placed in Minsk, capital of Belarus, to avoid the inevitable suspicions that would have resulted if Moscow were designated the new 'capital'. The CIS was described in the Alma Ata agreement as 'neither a state nor a supra-state structure'. The work of the CIS was to be carried out, in the words of the agreement, 'in accordance with the principle of equality through coordinating institutions formed on a parity basis'. Decisions in all bodies were to be adopted on the basis of consensus, and any state could refuse to be subject to a decision it did not support.

A Council of Heads of State (designated the 'supreme body' of the Commonwealth) and a Council of Heads of Government (meaning prime ministers) were created as the most important decision-making organs. Soon a 'working group on preparing sessions' for both councils was organised. Councils were also established at the ministerial level for co-ordinating foreign policy, military affairs, energy questions, transportation, customs, and the environment.[28] In March 1992 an Interparliamentary Assembly of CIS State-Participants was also created to coordinate legislative efforts by republican Supreme Soviets. The assembly, made up of delegations of republican parliaments, was to meet no less than twice a year. The first meeting took place in Kyrgyzstan in September 1992, but only Russia, Armenia, Belarus, Kyrgyzstan, Kazakhstan and Tajikistan participated. St Petersburg was chosen as the permanent site for assembly sessions.[29]

The heads of CIS member-states met almost monthly in an attempt to agree on joint efforts and to discuss pressing issues in many spheres.[30] At a meeting of heads of state held in March 1992, for example, republic leaders discussed a common pension policy (Ukraine and Belarus refused to sign, fearing an influx of pensioners from other regions), customs regulations, and energy prices. From the start it was apparent that the CIS was a fragile structure torn by divisions, with the principal fault line between Ukraine and Russia. Conflicts between the two largest CIS members dominated the deliberations of CIS institutions in the early months of their existence, and Azerbaijan and Moldova were reluctant to go along with the other member-states on many issues. In January 1993 seven CIS members finally came to terms on a charter for the organisation. Ukraine and Turkmenistan initially refused to sign, and Azerbaijan and Moldova did not even participate in the discussions; Georgia, as before, remained outside.

There were a number of potentially serious territorial and ethnic disputes that threatened to undermine the Commonwealth. Despite a provision of the CIS agreement that accepted the 'territorial integrity and the inviolability of existing borders' of each of the signatories, there were a number of unresolved conflicts. The most long-standing and serious of these disputes was the open warfare between Armenia and Azerbaijan over the predominantly Armenian territory of Nagorno-Karabakh located with Azerbaijani borders. An armed conflict embroiled Moldavian and Slavic inhabitants of the Trans-Dniester region in Moldova. Also unresolved was a territorial dispute between Russia and Ukraine over the Crimea, a predominantly Russian area that had been ceded to Ukraine by Khrushchev in 1954.

Affirming independence and dividing the spoils

Russia took on the role, for many purposes, of the legal successor state to the Soviet Union. The Soviet seats in the United Nations General Assembly and on the Security Council were taken by Russia.[31] CIS members also agreed that only Russia would continue to have nuclear weapons on its territory, and that strategic armaments in Ukraine, Belarus and Kazakhstan would be removed in the coming years.

One of the most fractious issues to emerge out of the collapse of the Soviet Union was the disposition of its assets. Disputes over precisely how to divide these assets made it increasingly clear that joint activities and cooperation would be very difficult to achieve except on matters of clear mutual interest and benefit. Since most of the property of the former union ministries and the CPSU was on Russian territory, the Russian government was in the best position to take over these holdings and did so – perhaps precipitously in order to avoid claims by other republics. On 19 December 1991, Yeltsin announced that Russia was seizing the Soviet foreign ministry, the KGB, and the Kremlin. Soviet holdings abroad, including embassies and consulates, were taken over by the Russian government – though other republics were promised a share of all-union property abroad and could use Russian facilities for their own diplomatic missions. Other former all-union ministries, their property, and enterprises located on Russian territory were also confiscated by the Russian government.

Most of the institutes of the Soviet Academy of Sciences were on Russian territory, and these too were soon shifted to Russian jurisdiction. The same was true of major universities and other centres of higher education. Russian officials quickly eliminated the special admission quotas for non-Russians that were a major part of Soviet nationality policy, and they began to charge high tuition to non-citizens of Russia who sought to enter Russian universities. Other republics protested that they were being deprived of research and educational facilities which they had helped to create and which were vital for maintaining their scientific capabilities.[32]

The Soviet Union had not only assets but also substantial liabilities.

Pressure from potential Western creditors forced the remnants of the union to agree on responsibility for dividing the former Soviet debt as a precondition for new loans. An agreement was reached on sharing the burden of the Soviet debt in March 1992, after Ukraine withdrew its opposition to an agreement that did not specify the amounts to be repaid by each republic. By September 1992, however, the agreement had broken down and only Russia was making payment on the Soviet debt.

Other economic issues focused on the question of maintaining a common currency and banking system. Control over the money supply at the republic level was seen as an important attribute of national sovereignty, particularly given the level of mistrust over Russia's unilateral decisions on reform adopted in late 1991 and early 1992. Ultimately it was a shortage of rubles and Russia's unwillingness to supply more rubles to the republics that forced republics to introduce their own currencies. Estonia was the first republic to order the printing of its own currency, the *kron*, but it delayed introducing it until June 1992. The *kron* was meant to be freely convertible, backed by Estonian gold reserves that had been kept abroad during the years of Soviet control, and the currency was tied to the value of the German mark. Latvia introduced its own currency, the *rublis*, in May 1992 and made it the only acceptable currency in July. Ukraine was actually the first republic to begin issuing what amounted to a ruble-substitute. In January 1992, Ukraine began distributing so-called 'coupons' that would be used concurrently with the ruble. In March 1992, the Ukrainian parliament voted to replace the ruble entirely in the future, first with coupons and ultimately with its own currency, the *grivnya*. Other republics that had issued coupons by mid-1992 included Lithuania, Moldova, Belarus and Turkmenia. Azerbaijan introduced the *manat* in August 1992, though it would be circulated alongside the ruble and tied to the ruble in value. Lithuania, Uzbekistan and Georgia indicated that they planned to introduce their own currencies at a future date, while the leaders of Belarus and Kazakhstan planned to remain within the 'ruble zone' for the time being. Rapid inflation and concern over fiscal policies in the former Soviet republics led Russia to consider the introduction of a new currency of its own.

Issues surrounding trade, customs, and border crossing also divided the former Soviet republics. To this end, in July 1992 the CIS member-states agreed to set up an Economic Court in Minsk to resolve economic disputes.[33] A subject of particular controversy between Russia and the other states was the price of oil. The former Soviet republics were almost all dependent on Russia for their fuel supplies, and in the past they had received fuel at prices that were only about 30 per cent of world market levels. Russia insisted that its neighbours begin to pay the world price, despite the economic hardship that this would cause. In July 1992 Estonia became the first former Soviet republic to introduce a strict border regime requiring outsiders to obtain visas before entering the country. This led to a number of incidents on Estonia's border to the east as Russians frequently sought to enter without obtaining the proper documentation. When the Baltic states, Georgia, Azerbaijan, and Ukraine refused to enter into a customs agreement with Russia, the Russian government announced that customs stations and border controls would be set up at transit points between these republics and Russia.[34]

The unified command of the CIS army was essentially the last Soviet institution still intact after the breakup of the union. CIS members sought initially to preserve a unified command for the armed forces, in part as a response to international concerns about control over nuclear weapons and in part because the republics had not yet organised their own military units. Yevgenii Shaposhnikov, a Soviet air force general who proved to be a Yeltsin supporter during the failed August coup, was designated head of the Soviet military forces and then head of CIS unified forces. In February and March 1992 eight of eleven CIS member-states agreed to maintain a unified command at least until 1994.[35] Conflicts over preserving a unified military structure for the Commonwealth of Independent States were the result of several factors. Moldova and Azerbaijan refused to participate in the CIS unified military because both faced armed internal conflict from ethnic minorities. Both republics were in the process of creating their own armed forces on the basis of conscripts that would normally be expected to serve in the Commonwealth army. In April 1992 Belarus announced that it also would create its own army, initially of 100,000 men, based on Belarusian draftees serving in the CIS army.[36] Conflicts over the allocation of Soviet military resources led even the Russian government to move away from its commitment to a unified military structure. In March and April 1992 the government of Russia announced steps to create a Russian ministry of defence and that would lead to a separate Russian army of up to 1,250,000 troops based on Soviet army forces recruited from Russia.

The decision by Russia to create its own army was taken in the midst of an acrimonious dispute between Ukraine and Russia over the disposition of the Soviet Black Sea fleet. At one point in the political manoeuvring, in April 1992, both the Russian and Ukrainian leaderships issued orders taking over the entire fleet. A crisis was averted, not through CIS channels, but as a result of bilateral agreements between Yeltsin and Kravchuk. A three-year interim agreement was worked out in August 1992 that removed the fleet from CIS control and established it as a unified Russo-Ukrainian fleet.[37] Georgia, not a CIS member, also claimed a share of the Black Sea fleet but was not included in the initial negotiations. Negotiations also took place on the Caspian Sea fleet, which was to be divided between Russia and Azerbaijan.

Wrangling over the division of resources and the creation of national armies did not preclude agreement on an organisational structure for the unified armed forces in July 1992.[38] Also in July 1992, CIS heads of state agreed to a new role for the CIS military as multinational peace-keeping forces in member-states' internal conflicts. In all cases, the factions involved in the fighting had to agree to CIS intervention. The Trans-Dniester conflict in Moldova was the first to which the CIS 'blue berets' from Russia and Ukraine were sent to separate the warring sides.[39]

Conclusion

The results of the political manoeuvring between Gorbachev and republican leaders were perhaps the most dramatic of the entire period under discussion in this volume. The efforts by central institutions to maintain their power were not simply unsuccessful; they created an atmosphere that made the preservation of the union impossible. At the same time, the political changes in the republics made the push for independence – or at least greater sovereignty – irresistible.

The 'replacement' for the USSR, the Commonwealth of Independent States, represented a structure that was so fragile that its continued existence was in doubt from the beginning. For the foreseeable future, relations between the former Soviet republics will be determined by their bilateral relationships, not by their memberships in the Commonwealth or any other international organisations. Years of subordination to the centre in the context of a unitary, weakly federal system made it difficult for republic leaders to even consider the notion that giving up some sovereignty to pursue common interests might be in the long-term interests of all the former Soviet republics.

6   Patterns of republic and local politics

A major part of the political tumult that shook the Soviet Union in its final years can be attributed to events that occurred at the level of the republics or at even lower levels of the system. In the past, politics at the republic level or lower were always subordinate to political developments at the centre – in particular, changes in the Soviet Communist Party and its leadership, and policies set by the Politburo and within the government bureaucracy.

The major political development of 1990 occurred at the republic level when elections to republic parliaments took place. These elections followed the example of the 1989 national elections to the Congress of People's Deputies, the first in which there was widespread competition for seats. They resulted in what charitably might be called a new dynamism in Soviet politics; to put it another way, they resulted in a rapid escalation of conflict and unpredictability. Much of the instability was the result of protracted jurisdictional struggles between levels of government and between new political institutions at any given level.

New parliaments and leaders in the republics

In all republics except the Russian Federation, there were direct elections in 1990 for deputies to a republican Supreme Soviet (see pp. 31–4). In Russia, the USSR example of a Congress of People's Deputies was replicated, with the Congress in turn electing a Supreme Soviet from among its members. Political changes in the republics paralleled changes brought about at the national level by the March 1989 election of a new parliament. As was true of the USSR Congress of People's Deputies, the new republic parliaments became the most important setting for policy deliberations, though their actual significance depended on the balance of political forces in each republic. In those republics where the parliaments and executive were heavily dominated by the Communist Party, changes in procedures and institutions were often cosmetic. In republics where new, democratic forces were dominant, parliaments became true legislative bodies with an important impact on policy making. Indeed, they typically became involved in a tug of war with executive authority over policymaking.

One of the first truly important changes in republican politics – even in those republics that remained under communist control – was the rise of political movements and parliamentary groupings that opposed the Communist Party. Again, this paralleled a development at the national level discussed in chapter 3, the rise of the Interregional Deputies' Group in the USSR Congress of People's Deputies. In fact, members of this faction who were from the republics later became prominent members of opposition or ruling factions in the new republican parliaments.

As the foregoing indicates, republic parliaments differed greatly in their composition and internal dynamics. One general characteristic that appeared to hold true for most parliaments was the rapidly changing nature of factions and deputy groups. The fact that political competition was still in its infancy meant that very quickly deputy groups began to split apart or lose members. In Moldova, for example, the Moldavian Popular Front was, when the Supreme Soviet began its sessions, the largest deputy group. The Front was largely able to dictate the agenda, and many of the subsequent government appointments reflected its influence. Over time, however, the strategy of the Moldovan Popular Front of pursuing reunification with Romania led a number of deputies to desert its ranks, and efforts to enact land reform meant that it began to lose the support of the group of rural deputies who represented collective and state farms that would be eliminated.[1] As a result, parliamentary deadlocks between these blocs became more frequent. In Lithuania deputies began the practice of walking out before votes on issues that they did not want to come to the floor. Because of this, measures that had majority support were not adopted due to the lack of a quorum.[2]

A much more explosive aspect of the 1990 parliamentary elections and their results was that they soon failed to correspond to a rapidly changing political situation in many republics. In all republics, the political landscape within a year of the elections was markedly different than it had been at the time of the elections. As a rule – and this was especially true in Central Asia – new opposition groups had been too weak at the time of the 1990 elections to mount an effective campaign. In some republics, the communist leaderships either outlawed opposition groups or, as in Belarus, manipulated the elections to undercut the opposition. After the elections new groups emerged and old ones split. In almost all republics, the Communist Party was devastated by the failure of the August 1991 coup and the collapse of the CPSU. The impact of these changes was less immediate in those republics where the Communist Party had retained control of the government.

In this context extraparliamentary pressure became a regular feature of post-Soviet politics in the republics. The streets and squares outside of parliamentary buildings became an important forum for political action as groups that felt disenfranchised sought to demonstrate their popularity through the size and frequency of protests they could organise. Often the protests had as their focus demands that new elections be held. In republics where former communists still dominated parliaments, the opposition constantly pressed demands for new elections with the expectation that elections would give them a hold on power. Demands for new elections were the focus of round-the-clock demonstrations by Islamic and nationalist groups outside the parliament in Dushanbe, capital of Tajikistan, in March-April 1992 and again in late summer 1992. The opposition succeeded in removing Nabiev in September but were themselves ousted from Dushanbe in December 1992 by the former communists. The government promised new elections when the situation 'stabilised', but at the same time set out to destroy the opposition as a political force. In Azerbaijan, in May 1992, just before presidential elections and just after an unsuccessful attempt by the former president to return to power, the old Supreme Soviet was persuaded to hand over its legislative authority to a new body, the national council (*milli meijlis*). Azerbaijani Popular Front members made up over half of this new assembly.[3] In Belarus and Ukraine, petitions were circulated widely to call referenda on electing new parliaments. The Belarusian Popular Front claimed to have gathered almost 100,000 more than the required 350,000 signatures to force a referendum on holding new elections. The authorities disputed the authenticity of many of the signatures and ruled the petition invalid. In any event, conducting a referendum required the approval of the Supreme Soviet – precisely the body that would be disbanded if the referendum passed.[4] Similar demands were often voiced by Rukh in Ukraine. In August 1992, Rukh began the process of gathering signatures to force the authorities to conduct a referendum on dissolving the Supreme Soviet and calling new elections. In part this was a symbolic effort, designed to send a message to the sitting parliament, since the Ukrainian law on referenda required that the petitioners gather three million signatures within a three-month period.[5]

Surprisingly, the first republics to hold elections ahead of their originally scheduled date were republics where the 1990 elections had been among the most emphatic in rejecting the Communist Party in favour of radical nationalist movements. Elections for new parliaments in what were now post-Soviet republics were first held in Estonia, Lithuania, and Georgia. The Estonian elections, which took place in September 1992, were marked by a striking change in the electorate: only citizens of Estonia were allowed to vote, and Russians who were relatively recent arrivals to the republic were to be granted citizenship only two years after application and only if they showed a basic competence in the Estonian language. The Lithuanian elections were held in October 1992, when they returned the former communists – now the Democratic Labour Party – to power. The elections in Georgia were motivated by a quite different set of factors. In October 1990, a narrow coalition of parties led by the dissident Zviad Gamsakhurdia won a clear majority in parliament. The extraparliamentary opposition to Gamsakhurdia was joined after August 1991 by the Georgian national guard, and much of the urban intelligentsia. Attempts to use parliamentary channels to limit Gamsakhurdia's power or force him to resign as president were ineffective; only a few of his supporters in parliament defected to the opposition. When government troops apparently fired on demonstrators in December 1991, the opposition resorted to a massive military attack to oust Gamsakhurdia, and a Military Council ruled briefly after taking power in January 1992. Its successor, an appointed legislative body called the State Council (soon headed by the former Soviet foreign minister, Eduard Shevardnadze), scheduled elections to a new parliament in an attempt to legitimise the new regime. Because of the circumstances of Gamsakhurdia's removal from power, however, it was a foregone conclusion that many of his supporters would boycott the elections that were held in October 1992. Thus, the result was a new, extraparliamentary opposition made up of Gamsakhurdia supporters.

In Russia, where communists elected in 1990 often voted as a bloc to obstruct the radical reforms pushed by Boris Yeltsin, there were frequent calls for new elections. The leading reformist coalition, Democratic Russia, initiated a petition drive in order to force a referendum on disbanding the Russian republic's Congress of People's Deputies and direct elections for a new Supreme Soviet. At one point, this demand was supported by Yeltsin. By September 1992, however, Yeltsin dropped this challenge to the legitimacy of parliament, perhaps when it became clear that a new parliament might be as conservative as the old one.[6]

At the first sessions of republican parliaments, deputies chose the top leader of the republic, at first designated the chairman of the Supreme Soviet. Most often on the recommendation of the newly elected chairman, the parliament also voted for a prime minister, who would serve as chairman of the Council of Ministers. This post was particularly important in light of the economic crisis facing all republics, and because of the implications of reform for the ministries and state committees that had previously managed the economy. At the same time, the division of responsibilities between the chairman of the parliament and the head of government were unclear and led to political infighting.

The deepening economic crisis, parliamentary deadlocks, and confrontations with what remained of central Soviet authority led most republic leaders to seek additional powers. They followed Gorbachev's lead by creating a new office, that of president of the republic. In order to enhance the authority of the presidency, they chose a path that Gorbachev had avoided – direct popular elections. Thus, a new series of elections were held, mostly in 1991, for the post of president in all republics except the Baltic states and Belarus. In late 1990 an election for president of Turkmenistan was held, and the other republics followed over the course of 1991: Georgia in May, Russia in June, Azerbaijan in September, Kyrgyzstan and Armenia in October, and Ukraine, Uzbekistan, Tajikistan, Kazakhstan and Moldova all in December. In Belarus and the Baltic, the top leadership post continued to be chairman of the Supreme Soviet, though leaders in these republics also favoured a presidential system. Vytautas Landsbergis in Lithuania sought to use a referendum to create the post of president in May 1992, but a low turnout invalidated the results. Elections for president were held in February 1993 which returned to power the former communist leader, Algirdas Brazauskas. In September 1992, Estonia created the post of president and combined elections for the new post with parliamentary elections. The law included an unusual provision that allowed the new parliament to elect a president in the event that none of the candidates received over 50 per cent of the vote in the first round of balloting. In Belarus, Supreme Soviet Chairman Shushkevich won parliamentary approval for a new constitution in February 1993 that introduced the post of president.

Usually the laws passed by parliaments for presidential nomination and election were weighted heavily in favour of the current president or head of the republic parliament. The election date was often set a few weeks into the future – giving the opposition little time to put forward a candidate, much less mount an effective campaign. In a number of republics – Moldova, Turkmenistan, Azerbaijan, Kyrgyzstan and Kazakhstan – the republic's leader ran unopposed. In addition, in 1991 the media in most republics were either still under the effective control either of the communist party or the parliamentary leadership, and in some republics these were the same people.[7] Newspapers of opposition groups generally could be read only by a small portion of the electorate in urban areas, and the opposition received little coverage on television in most republics. As a result, even in republics where there were apparently strong opposition challengers for the post, the vote received by the president far exceeded that of his closest competitor. Among those with the largest margins of victory were Nazarbayev of Kazakhstan with almost 99 per cent of the vote, Snegur (Moldova) and Mutalibov (Azerbaijan) – 98 per cent of the vote, Akayev (Kyrgyzstan) – 95 per cent, Gamsakhurdia (Georgia) – 86 per cent, Karimov (Uzbekistan) – 86 per cent, and Ter-Petrosian (Armenia) – 83 per cent. In some of these cases, particularly in Azerbaijan and Central Asia, opposition leaders charged that the elections or their results had been manipulated by the leadership to insure victories for the incumbent.

In several republics presidents ran against relatively strong opposition candidates and won by smaller margins. Leonid Kravchuk won in Ukraine in December 1991, with almost 62 per cent, against Viacheslav Chornovil, a popular dissident and political figure from western Ukraine who had served time in Soviet prisons for his nationalist activities. Boris Yeltsin won the Russian presidency in June 1991 with over 57 per cent of the vote, while the second leading vote-getter of the five candidates, former Soviet prime minister Nikolai Ryzhkov, received only 17 per cent of the vote.

Elections and large margins of victory were no guarantee of legitimacy and political stability, however, which was their intention. Two of the seemingly most popular of the newly elected presidents were thrown out of office within months of the elections: Gamsakhurdia of Georgia in January 1992 and Mutalibov of Azerbaijan in March 1992. Zviad Gamsakhurdia's excessive caution at the time of the August coup in Moscow lost him the support of most of the Georgian national guard. At the same time, Gamsakhurdia's increasingly dictatorial actions – caused in part by his interpretation of the election results as a mandate to take direct personal control over policy – caused a rapid erosion of his popularity, particularly in Tbilisi, the Georgian capital. Violent attacks on demonstrators led the opposition to unite and use its military forces to attack Gamsakhurdia, who had taken refuge with several thousand of his supporters in the parliament building. After weeks of fighting, Gamsakhurdia fled the republic. The opposition leaders ultimately invited Eduard Shevardnadze to return to Georgia and serve as chairman of an appointed pseudo-parliament, the State Council. Gamsakhurdia's successors discussed abolishing the post of president (which Gamsakhurdia still claimed was his) and returning to parliamentary rule. Less than six weeks prior to the October 1992 elections, the State Council adopted an unusual decision making the post of speaker of the parliament one that would be elected by the population on the day of the parliamentary elections. Shevardnadze, who ran uncontested, was elected by a 96 per cent landslide.[8]

In Azerbaijan, Ayaz Mutalibov was the victim of popular outrage over the government's inadequate response to the massacre of Azeri civilians by Armenian forces in the village of Khodzhaly. Massive demonstrations outside parliament led deputies to demand his resignation. Mutalibov ultimately complied, but later attempted to stage a coup in May 1992, evidently in order to preempt new presidential elections. His supporters were soon defeated, however. New elections for president were held in June 1992, and the chairman of the Azerbaijan Popular Front, Abulfez Elchibei, won with around 60 per cent of the vote.[9]

The Tajik president, Rakhmon Nabiev, had been elected in November 1991 with over 58 per cent of the vote in an election marred by charges of massive vote fraud. Nabiev, like Gamsakhurdia and Mutalibov, was ousted at gunpoint. An anti-communist coalition of Islamic rebels (aided also by Tajiks from Afghanistan), secular democratic reformers, and clans from regions that considered themselves neglected under Nabiev took over Dushanbe, the Tajik capital. Nabiev was forced to resign after being captured at the airport before he could escape in September 1992. In December 1992 the former communists, aided by forces from Uzbekistan, fought their way back to power. Imamali Rakhmonov was designated chairman of the parliament, and the presidency was abolished.

Another feature of republic-level politics that contributed to conflict and instability was uncertainty over the constitutional roles of the government and the prime minister. The Council of Ministers, following previous Soviet practice, was the principal coordinating organ for the government bureaucracy at the republic level. In many republics this organ was later replaced by a somewhat reduced Cabinet of Ministers. This reorganisation often accompanied the shift to presidential rule and paralleled changes at the centre which increased the role of the president in overseeing the government.

The introduction of the office of president called into question the need for the traditional post of prime minister. Partly as a result of this, there were relatively frequent conflicts between presidents or chairmen of the Supreme Soviet and their prime ministers. Such conflicts led to the prime minister's resignation after less than a year of office in Armenia (Manukian), Lithuania (Prunskiene), Moldova (Druk), and Georgia (Sigua). In all four cases the former prime ministers subsequently became leading critics of the government in power.[10] In the Russian republic, while there was no apparent conflict between Boris Yeltsin and his prime minister, Ivan Silaev, in the aftermath of the August coup Yeltsin took over the responsibilities of prime minister himself 'for the period of economic reform'. Only under pressure from the Congress of People's Deputies in April 1992 did Yeltsin agree to name a prime minister at a later date.[11]

Conflict also resulted from the struggle between the legislature and the executive over control over the government and government policy. With the infusion of new power to parliaments came the problem of defining the limits of legislative authority. The writing of a new Russian constitution over the course of 1992 encountered difficulties in this area, as Yeltsin pushed for a draft that would have enhanced the office of president and given him broad powers to shape the Russian government that were claimed by the Congress of People's Deputies and its Supreme Soviet. An object of particular struggle in 1992 was the central bank of the Russian Federation. The central bank was formally and practically subordinate to the parliament, and government officials complained that its policies after July 1992 ran counter to government policy and IMF recommendations, thus threatening Yeltsin's reform programme.

In Belarus, constant infighting over executive authority led parliament to approve in April 1992 the formation of a separate, new body, the Anticrisis Committee, headed by the prime minister, Viacheslav Kebich. The agreement setting up the chief organ of the committee, the Executive Council, gave it in some cases broader powers than those held by the Supreme Soviet and the government.[12]

Changes in local government

Competitive elections to local soviets – in cities, provinces, and districts – also took place in 1990. The vast number of candidates and races makes the study of these elections very difficult. Despite severe organisational difficulties, loosely organised democratic forces captured a number of important city soviets, including some of the most important cities in the Russian republic – Moscow, Leningrad, and Sverdlovsk.[13] Once the soviets had been elected, the continued existence of old institutional structures, both within the soviets and outside them, became a source of conflict. The old system of local government had been designed less to govern than to provide an instrument for administration guided by the local organs of the communist party. It was the communist party at the province, city and district level that served as the chief coordinating agency.[14]

The USSR Supreme Soviet adopted a new law on local soviets in April 1990 entitled 'On General Principles of Local Self-Management and Local Economy in the USSR'. As was true of many pieces of legislation adopted in the waning days of central Soviet authority, few officials at any level took it seriously. Republic parliaments naturally saw the system of local rule as their concern, and in fact the Soviet law gave them substantial powers to define the competence of local soviets.[15] In practice, the press of other crises delayed the adoption of laws on local administration, and local soviets were often left to solve their internal problems on their own.

Attempts by newly elected soviets to infuse the old structures with a new meaning – an effort encapsulated by the democrats' resurrection of Lenin's slogan 'All power to the soviets!' – quickly led to new conflicts. This was even true where a majority of the deputies were democrats or communists. The communist party often was unable to control deputies who were party members, and in many regions the local communist party was ineffective in forming links with communist deputies in the soviets. As a rule, most communist deputies did not become members of a communist party group in the soviets, and party discipline hardly existed. In April 1991 the CPSU Central Committee issued a resolution 'on the work of communists in soviets of people's deputies' that contained a thorough critique of the role of party groups in republic parliaments and local soviets.[16] The absence of political parties other than the Communist Party at the time of the elections meant that deputy groups or coalitions were fragile and shifting, and rarely was there a consistent majority among the deputies. Frequently major policy questions were put on hold because of the inability of the soviets to achieve a consensus.

As was true at the republic level, the elections of top officials by province and city level soviets confirmed the extent to which, in some regions, a political revolution had occurred. Radicals succeeded in taking the top posts in a number of important local soviets. Two of the leading members of the USSR Congress of People's Deputies Interregional Group, the economist Gavriil Popov and the legal scholar Anatolii Sobchak, were chosen to be chairmen of the Moscow and Leningrad city soviets respectively. The leading Ukrainian dissident from the 1960s, Viacheslav Chornovil, was elected chairman of the L'viv soviet. Valentin Fedorov, a Moscow economist who in the past had suggested creating a free economic zone on Sakhalin Island in the Soviet Far East, was invited to run for the Sakhalin provincial soviet and then was elected its chairman.

At the same time, in many areas of the Soviet Union the Communist Party retained its role of dominance, at least until the failed coup of August 1991. In regional soviets in the Russian republic, the most typical outcome was that a majority of seats were won by candidates supported by the local Communist Party. As a result, the new chairmen of regional soviets were often conservative *apparatchiki*. In part this electoral result occurred because districts were used that vastly underrepresented urban voters.[17] Interestingly, surveys showed a wide variation by republic in the degree of popular confidence in local authorities. A spring 1992 survey in three republics found the lowest levels of support in Ukraine: 59 per cent indicated that they completely lacked confidence in local government, while only 3 per cent trusted them totally. Similarly, in Armenia 54 per cent lacked confidence while only 1 per cent completely trusted the authorities. In Kazakhstan, on the other hand, polls indicated divided opinions: 21 per cent had total confidence in local authorities while 24 per cent completely lacked confidence in local organs of power.[18]

In a number of republic-level parliaments opposition and centrist deputies waged a struggle against the Communist Party apparatus in their midst by forbidding heads of soviets from simultaneously serving as first secretary of the Communist Party at that level. The Russian Congress of People's Deputies adopted such a decision in June 1990, though its legality was contested by Gorbachev and the centre.[19] The decision by Russia and other republics forced party leaders to make a choice based on their beliefs about the future prospects of each institution of power. A number of first secretaries resigned from their party posts in order to accept the chairmanship of the soviet at the corresponding level.[20] In other cases the party leader was reluctant to make the leap from the party to the soviet when forced to choose. The overwhelming majority of soviet chairmen, however, remained members of the Communist Party until the failed coup of August 1991, and most were members of the bureau of the regional or city party committee. The flow of party leaders from district and province committees into executive positions in the soviet apparatus after the August coup provided perhaps the strongest evidence that the dismantling of Russian communist party structures was complete.[21]

A second line of attack against the party was undertaken in several republics to undermine and destroy the old institutional basis for party control. These measures were taken under the label 'depoliticisation'. Its purpose was to expel Communist Party organisations from schools, law enforcement agencies, the courts, and enterprises. The first republic to begin to reduce the party's role was Lithuania, in March 1990, and soon similar steps were underway in Estonia, Armenia, and Georgia. Yeltsin's depoliticisation began in July 1991 with a decree that no political parties should be allowed to organise at the workplace or in government institutions.[22]

The failure of the August 1991 coup created an extraordinary opportunity for some republic leaders to remove the Communist Party as an organised opposition. The Communist Party was effectively dismantled in Russia, the Baltic republics, Moldova, Georgia, and Armenia. In all these republics, party properties – often including extensive publishing facilities – were confiscated by the government. In republics where the Communist Party was essentially still the ruling party in August 1991 – in Azerbaijan, Kazakhstan and the Central Asian republics – it reappeared under a new name though with the same officials and structures that operated much as before, at least for the time being. Similarly, in Ukraine and Belarus the top officials in the republic government, most members of parliament, and the heads of local government remained former communists.

In Russia, there were few cases where the regional soviet elected in 1990 was dominated by radicals. Even in Moscow and Leningrad, centres of radical political organisation, the rural regional soviets comprising the territory outside of these cities were relatively conservative. One of the exceptions was the Volgograd regional soviet. Elected chairman of the soviet was Valerii Makharadze, a former factory director who ran on a radical programme of economic and administrative reform.[23] Makharadze attempted a conciliatory approach to the Communist Party, which retained significant power in the province. He effectively won the support of local Communist Party organs by organising what was essentially a 'round table' arrangement that gave all participants a role in forming government structures.[24]

One problem was the size of the councils, a holdover from the previous system of soviets which attempted to demonstrate through sheer numbers the democratic nature of the soviet structure. The size of soviets, and the fact that their members were not deputies full time, meant that little actual deliberation could take place at their sessions. Experiments on streamlining the soviets took place in Arkhangelsk and Vologda in early 1991. All soviets at the city and district level in Arkhangelsk were combined in a 'city assembly' which in turn elected a 'small soviet' (*malyi sovet*) made up of twelve deputies from the city soviet and five from each district. In Vologda, the 200 deputies in the current soviet decided to elect a small soviet of eleven deputies that was then given a large share of the policymaking power of the full soviet. The full soviet, in turn, preserved its right to select the chairman and his deputies, approve other administrative appointments, and monitor budgetary allocations.[25] In July 1991 Yeltsin issued an order that 'small soviets' be created that were approximately one-tenth the size of the existing soviets. An unfortunate consequence of this, from the standpoint of political and economic reform, was that in many provinces pro-reform forces were too weak to be represented on the new organ.[26]

Another holdover from the past system was the division between the representative legislative bodies (the soviets) and executive power (the *ispolkom*, or executive committee). Traditionally the executive agencies of the local soviets, the *ispolkom* and its departments, had primarily an economic function and were in part subordinate to the bureaucracy at higher levels. In the words of one soviet chairman, they served as the 'weak tentacles of the Council of Ministers'.[27] Another feature of the old system was that the Communist Party exercised significant influence over the departments of the *ispolkom*, including the selection of personnel to head these departments.[28] In most parts of the country at the time of the 1990 elections, the Communist Party apparatus remained in place and preserved its ties to the government bureaucracy at the local level. Government agencies that were legally subordinate to the soviet at first often continued to look to the local party leadership for direction, bypassing the newly elected leaders. Sobchak complained, for example, about the continuing flow of information and reports from Leningrad state officials to Boris Gidaspov, the Leningrad party leader, while he was left in the dark.[29]

In the past, the *ispolkom* dominated the soviet and the chairman of the *ispolkom* was the most important local government official. With the shift to an emphasis on the soviets themselves, the relationship was reversed. A new chairman of the soviet was elected who was supposed to be the most powerful local official. The position of chairman of the *ispolkom* remained separate at the provincial level in most republics, creating a division of responsibilities essentially parallel to that between chairman of the Supreme

Soviet and prime minister at the republic level. The chairman of the soviet would, as a rule, recommend a candidate for the post of chairman of the executive committee, who would be directly responsible for supervising departments of local government. Unclear, however, were the relative roles that would be played by the soviets and the *ispolkom* in making state policy. In Ivanovo, for example, growing conflicts between the city soviet and *ispolkom* led the chairman of the *ispolkom* to resign.[30] Members of local soviets often complained that the *ispolkom* usurped their legislative function, and decided important policy questions the way they had in the past – on their own.[31] Most often it appeared that the result of such disagreements over function was paralysis. In Belarus, Turkmenia and Ukraine the conflict was avoided in at least some provinces by retaining the old system of one person simultaneously holding the posts of chairman of the province soviet and chairman of the *ispolkom*.[32]

In the aftermath of the 1990 elections, problems encountered with the new system of dual (and sometimes duelling) chairmen gave birth to significant administrative experimentation in several republics. Institutional changes were enacted that were designed at times to strengthen soviets *vis à vis* the executive and at times to weaken them. In Russia in 1990 and 1991 there were a number of attempts to return to past practices and combine the highest posts of legislative and executive power. One of the first such 'experiments' took place in a district in Yaroslavl' province, in September 1990.[33] Yeltsin himself proposed that such an experiment be applied in his home province of Sverdlovsk in July 1990 – a restructuring in which the chairman of the regional soviet would take over the role of chairman of the *ispolkom*. The soviet rejected the proposal, but decided instead to place the chairman of the soviet above two deputies, one representing the executive and one representing the legislature.[34] A similar restructuring was endorsed by the Volgograd regional soviet for lower level soviets. The new structure put the soviet chairman on top, with a first deputy chairman as chairman of the *ispolkom* and a deputy chairman with responsibilities including 'the work of the soviets, deputies, and standing commissions'.[35] In Kyrgyzstan, a change in the regulations governing local soviets adopted by the republic parliament in February 1991 introduced changes designed to strengthen soviet control over the *ispolkom*. The first soviet to implement these measures was the Osh regional soviet, which replaced its executive organs with four deputy chairmen and a new presidium of 11 persons which was to serve as the chief organ of executive power in place of a separate *ispolkom*. New departments were formed and the apparatus was reduced in size by 40 per cent.[36]

A number of the chairmen of city soviets very soon became advocates of strengthening the executive by cutting the tie of dependence on the soviet and giving the chief executive greater control over policy implementation. Gavriil Popov, chairman of the Moscow soviet, became the most visible spokesman for this change. In a widely discussed brochure named after Lenin's famous polemic *What is to be done?*, Popov put forward the goal of 'desovietisation' which would give most power of policy initiation to the mayor and his subordinates in the executive.[37] The new post of 'mayor' (*mer* in Russian) was officially created in Moscow, Leningrad and one or two smaller cities as a result of elections that took place in June 1991.[38] It was a step that paralleled the shift from chairman of the republic Supreme Soviet to republic president. The new mayors, popularly elected, sought a mandate to increase their own powers at the expense of the soviets, both at the city level, and over district soviets within the city. The extent of the conflict was apparent in Moscow when Popov resigned his mayoral post in June 1992. The Moscow soviet refused to recognise the legitimacy of his successor, vice-mayor Yuri Luzhkov, and set new elections for chief of the city administration in December. There were other cases where local soviets took the initiative to remove their chairmen or *ispolkom* chairmen, events that were unheard of in the past. In Voronezh, for example, when the city soviet discovered in mid-1990 that its chairman and the chairman of the *ispolkom* had for years violated laws on housing and registration of residence, it voted to remove them from office.[39]

Vertical relations between soviets[40]

One of the most common patterns in the newly independent republics was the struggle over jurisdiction over policy, a struggle that paralleled disputes between Gorbachev and the republics during the 'war of laws'. As in this earlier struggle, the jurisdictional issues were aggravated greatly by political and ethnic disputes. Elections played an important role in creating new conflicts between republics and lower-level soviets, between province bodies and city soviets, and between city and borough soviets. The common pattern in the local elections of a conservative regional soviet and radical city soviet led to inevitable conflicts. In Russia, where the Yeltsin government was committed to reform, this led to conflicts on two levels: between reformist republic officials and conservative provincial leaders, and between conservative provincial leaders and reformist city governments.

The Soviet system gave preeminence to authorities at the province level, and their attempts to preserve this role against both republic and city officials became a source of tension. Province officials often maintained control over important levers of power. They were able to determine the content of many local newspapers, for example. Food distribution in particular was dependent on actions by regional officials who maintained control over the agricultural supply system. The catastrophic food situation in many Soviet cities resulted from a breakdown in this system and the refusal of province leaders to cooperate with urban soviets. One example of the kind of conflicts that could emerge was the dispute between the Russian government and Tomsk region over the issue of privatisation. When Yeltsin issued a decree outlining the basic steps that would be required for privatisation of the Russian republic's holdings in each region, the Tomsk regional soviet passed a resolution declaring Yeltsin's decree invalid on Tomsk soil and replaced it with their own guidelines. The government responded with threats to stop the transfer of Russian property to the control of local officials.[41] Another example of conflict, this time between city and regional officials, was Riazan', in the Russian republic. The radical leader of the Riazan' city soviet, Valerii Riumin, complained that province soviet officials, all prominent communist leaders, were sabotaging decisions adopted by the city soviet by declaring them illegal and by stimulating conflict (through party-controlled newspapers) between borough soviets and the city soviet. Riumin also accused the regional soviet of confiscating city property and municipal service departments, thereby depriving the city of budget sources.[42] When the regional soviet attempted to conscript city workers and public transportation for the harvest, the city soviet responded by ordering all party employees into the fields, including all regional party chauffeurs. The regional soviet chairmen, L. Khitrun, at one session described Riumin – a decorated veteran of the war in Afghanistan – as 'inadequate not only morally, but genetically'.[43] Regional television, under the control of the party, refused to allow Riumin to appear in front of the camera because of his views.[44]

One way that cities attempted to overcome the power of the regions was to forge new horizontal ties and form groups that could lobby for their interests. One of the first such organisations was the Association of Siberian Cities, founded before the elections in January 1988 under the auspices of economists and sociologists at the Siberian division of the Academy of Sciences.[45] The Russian cities of Moscow, Leningrad, Sverdlovsk, Omsk, Irkutsk, Saransk, and Riazan' joined together in mid-1990 to form the Association of Democratic Cities of Russia.[46] A similar organization united the Ukrainian cities of Kiev, Rovno, Lutsk, Zhitomir, Sumy, Khar'kov and Donetsk.[47] In March 1991, representatives from 57 Russian cities met to form a new union of Russian cities. Valerii Riumin, the radical soviet chairman from Riazan', was elected president.[48]

Another common pattern was the effort by republic leaders to create new structures to monitor local implementation of republic policy. This process began first in republics that had elected reform governments. Leaders sought to overcome resistance to their policies at lower levels, particularly in soviets that continued to be controlled by the Communist Party and its apparatus.

The most radical steps to increase the authority of republican leaders over local decision making were taken in Georgia, under the anti-communist and increasingly authoritarian rule of Zviad Gamsakhurdia. In late January 1991 Gamsakhurdia appointed prefects to bring localities under the control of republic officials.[49] The continued role of local communist leaders, often operating in conjunction with key figures in the underground economy, led Gamsakhurdia to attempt to take over completely the power exercised by local leaders. In the law on the prefect, it was stated that 'the prefect is the highest official of the district or city' and that he 'directs economic and sociocultural development on the territory under his jurisdiction'. The prefects were appointed directly by Gamsakhurdia, were accountable first of all to him, and could be dismissed by him.[50] Additionally, local soviets in Georgia were replaced by a new representative body with reduced powers, called *sakrebulebi*, from the Georgian word for 'meeting'. The powers of these assemblies were poorly defined, but it was clear that their role would be much diminished as the power of officials at the republic level increased. Only the deputy chosen to lead the assembly would be released from his or her other duties, for example. All other members would continue to work full-time at their regular jobs.[51] Elections to the *sakrebulo* were held at the end of March 1991, but their diminished role made the outcome of electoral competition less significant. In another move that undermined local powers, a law adopted in September 1991 created the post of mayor of Tbilisi, but instead of making that post popularly elected, the mayor of Tbilisi was to be directly appointed by the republic's president.[52] Once Gamsakhurdia was driven from office at the beginning of 1992 the institution of prefects was one of the first to be dismantled, though the unstable political environment in many regions led the new government to create a similar post in the form of an appointed 'chief of administration'.

In Moldova a law was proposed that also introduced a prefect system. After lengthy debates, the general outlines of the law were passed in June 1991, which included provisions that would strengthen the role of Moldova's president at the expense of local authorities while giving them new budgetary powers.[53] The final version of the law, which was accompanied by a radical reorganisation of the administrative districts, gave the president the right to appoint mayors and prefects who were nominated by councils at the municipality and district level. The president could remove these officials at his discretion if they 'violate the constitution and laws of the republic of Moldova or do not perform their functions'.[54]

Given the sheer size of the Russian republic, it was inevitable that the issue of central control over the provinces would arise. Yeltsin first began to create a system for controlling the work of regional soviets in the context of land reform, a policy that was being systematically undermined by conservative leaders at the regional level. After the August coup, Yeltsin took the offensive against his opponents both by suspending the activities of the Russian Communist Party and by sending 'representatives of the president' to the provinces. In the words of the decree, the representatives were named in order to 'coordinate the activities of organs of executive authority of the RSFSR, *krais* and regions'. By November 1991, sixty-two had been appointed, encompassing all *krais* and regions as well as other administrative units such as Moscow and Leningrad.[55] The representatives selected by Yeltsin were a diverse group. The largest contingent was made up of officials from national, republic and local soviets – twenty-four of fifty-one on whom information was available. Nine held posts at enterprises or farms, and seven were scholars or journalists. Half were deputies to the Russian Congress of People's Deputies, and of these most were from the radical wing of the body of deputies.[56] Yeltsin chose Valerii Makharadze, the innovative Volgograd soviet chairman mentioned above, to oversee and coordinate political developments in the regions. In the past, the USSR procuracy was assigned the role of contesting decisions by local soviets that conflicted with existing legislation. This role was retained by the procuracy in Russia and other republics. The Russian procuracy contested approximately 8,000 laws or other decisions adopted by local government organs in the twelve months ending in mid-1992.[57]

At the same time that presidential representatives were being appointed in the Russian republic, officials in each province were designated 'chiefs of administration'. This official was also named by Yeltsin, and at first it often was someone other than the current head of the local government. This process led to conflicts with conservative regional soviets, including those of Ulianovsk, Cheliabinsk (where Yeltsin chose the head of the city soviet), Khabarovsk, and Krasnodar. In each of these cases, the province soviet sought to have Yeltsin's choice replaced by the current head of the province soviet.[58] Yeltsin's original plan was to have these officials, along with chiefs of administration who would be designated at lower levels (down to the district), stand for election in December 1991. This would couple his power of appointment with an element of democracy in the process of selecting local leaders, and also introduce direct popular elections for all positions at lower levels.[59] But in the face of a growing economic crisis, Yeltsin reversed himself and won the agreement of the parliament to put off all elections until December 1992 at the earliest. (He later agreed to postpone the elections even further in the interests of political stability.) At the same time, Yeltsin agreed that – unlike his earlier appointments – newly designated chiefs of administration must be approved by the corresponding soviets and members of the RSFSR parliament from that territory.[60] In September 1992 Yeltsin compromised further and agreed that heads of administration at the city level should be named, not by the Kremlin, but by provincial chiefs of administration to whom they would be subordinate.[61]

In Kyrgyzstan, instead of a prefect system the reform-minded president, Askar Akaev, sought changes in the draft law on local self-management that would allow him the power to approve or veto the choice of chairman of soviets at the local level. In this way, he explained, chairmen of soviets would play a dual role – embodying local self-management and representing state authority. Rather than give province-level chairmen the right to approve district and city chairmen, Akaev argued that 'in the existing Constitution, the chairman of the regional soviet is himself approved by the president. Therefore he could approve chairmen of lower soviets only with the agreement and at the direction of the president. Why do we need such complications? Would it not be simpler to give this right to the president?' Akaev also asked for the right to remove chairmen of lower-level soviets. All these measures were designed to 'guarantee a strengthening of state discipline and order in our republic'.[62]

By early 1992 the notion that it was necessary to create a new hierarchy to establish control over policy at the local level had spread to virtually all republics. This was true even where both the republic's leadership was made up of former *apparatchiki*. In Kazakhstan, Nursultan Nazarbayev created a system of vertical power which in essence replaced the executive committees of local soviets with appointed 'district administrators'. Approximately 40 per cent of the former chairmen of local soviets were replaced in the process.[63] In Ukraine, Leonid Kravchuk appointed 'representatives' who in effect became the most powerful officials in the regions. Most of those appointed had reputations as moderate reformers and centrists.[64]

At the level of city administration, there were attempts by city soviets and their leaders to eliminate borough soviets completely. In Kishinev, the capital of Moldova, such a measure was adopted and sent to the republic parliament for approval.[65] The leaders of Moscow and Leningrad submitted plans to the Russian parliament for approval that would reduce significantly the number of administrative units in the city.[66] In Moscow, this was accompanied by a prefect system made up of officials appointed directly by the mayor.[67]

The most violent conflicts between levels of soviets occurred when there was an ethnic, separatist component to the disputes. The existence of numerous concentrated populations of ethnic minorities within republics set the stage for frequent confrontations between soviets at the republic and local level. Here a distinction can be made between legally elected bodies that were 'captured' by local elites, and what might be termed 'local initiative' elections that were not authorised by republic officials. In the latter case, these elections often preceded attempts by ethnic territories to secede from the republic. There were many parallels between the struggle of these republics and the republics of the former Soviet Union that had sought complete independence. All these entities, for example, declared the sovereign right to dispose of their own natural resources. One important difference between the nationalist-reformist leaders of the recalcitrant Soviet republics, however, was that, on the whole, leaders of the Russian autonomies tended to be more conservative, communist *apparatchiki* who retained power even after the dissolution of the Communist Party. They sought to use independence as a way to limit and control the process of economic reform, land reform and privatisation on their territories.

Among the most serious disputes of this kind were those arising in the Narva soviet in Estonia, the Daugavpils soviet in Latvia, the Polish district soviets of Lithuania, the Slavic and Gagauz enclaves in Moldova, the autonomous regions within Georgia of South Ossetia and Abkhazia, and Nagorno-Karabakh within Azerbaijan. In most of these cases republic governments either prevented the holding of local elections in these regions or invalidated the results of elections held at local initiative. In Nagorno-Karabakh in 1990, for example, Azeri officials delayed local elections, then declared that efforts by the Karabakh Movement to organise elections to district and province soviets in October 1990 were illegal.[68]

In Russia, during the drafting process for a new constitution in March and April 1992, attention turned to local soviets and their relationship to the republic's government. The result was a new law 'On the *krai*, regional soviet of people's deputies and *krai*, regional administration'.[69] In Russia the situation was much more complicated than in other republics because of the large number of ethnically based administrative units that sought to retain their autonomy and special status within or outside the Russian Federation. Many declared themselves 'republics' and sought virtual independence from Russia. Among the most recalcitrant of the republics within the federation were the Chechen republic, Tatarstan and Bashkorto-stan (formerly Bashkiria). The first major confrontation between the Yeltsin government and a breakaway province occurred when the president of the Chechen republic, Djokhar Dudaev, declared independence from Russia after he was elected in September 1991. A half-hearted military operation to reassert Russian control was an embarrassing failure.

In an attempt to head off additional problems within Russia, work on negotiating a new federation treaty was intensified; sporadic talks had been under way for almost two years. A final version was signed by representatives of the supreme soviets of eighteen republics within the Russian

Federation in March 1992. The talks were held without the participation of Tatarstan (whose representatives attended the talks but were not authorised to sign any agreement) and the Chechen republic.[70] The new treaty would serve as a basis for relevant sections of the outline of a new constitution for Russia approved in April 1992. The treaty set out in very general terms the rights and obligations of federal and regional entities. How the agreement was applied in the practice of federal/republic relations would determine whether the Russian Federation would follow the same path as the USSR, or whether promises of political and economic autonomy would satisfy local elites.[71]

Conclusion

Most of what has occurred in the area of republic and local politics cannot be described appropriately as political reform, but rather as crisis management. Leaders at the republic and local level were confronted by a rapidly changing political situation in the midst of a profound economic crisis. This affected virtually all republic political institutions – parliaments, the governmental structure, the offices of president and prime minsiter – as well as local politics. The conflicts between different levels of legislative and executive authority became a distinguishing feature of politics and a major source of instability. An additional complication in many republics was created by the rise of nationalism, often countered by ethnic self-assertion by minorities at the local level.

Beyond the parallels and patterns that come from the transition away from a communist political system, the impact of independence was to strip away the superficial uniformity that was a product of being part of a unitary state. The future will undoubtedly bring even greater diversity – and considerable adversity – to the political life of the fifteen former Soviet republics.

7 The withering away of the party

The six and a half years between the launching of the reform programme in April 1985 and the aftermath of the abortive coup of August 1991 have seen the CPSU transformed from the dominant institution within the political system to one which has been denied a place in the post-coup political arrangements. From the outset until he quit the party on 24 August, Gorbachev had publicly assumed that the party would maintain its leadership in society. With the assistance of reformist allies in the party's ranks, Gorbachev imposed upon that organisation a series of reforms designed to achieve this end. The effect of these changes was not what the reformers had hoped, and their failure was part of the party's more general failure to adjust to forces over which it had no control. This failure to adjust was a significant factor in the party's ultimate demise.

From traditional campaign to democratisation

From the outset, Gorbachev and those around him recognised that part of the problem which they had inherited from the 'time of stagnation' lay in the party. The Communist Party had become lax, with many of its leading positions at all levels filled by people who were more concerned with a comfortable life than with struggling for the construction of socialism. There was a general malaise within the party, as the years of a comfortable existence under the 'stability of cadres' policy of the Brezhnev administration encouraged responsible party officials to be little concerned with high levels of performance in their official functions. Symbolic of this was the corruption evident in some parts of the country, particularly Central Asia. One of the major sources of this was the way in which power was structured at many levels of the party. Despite the plethora of rules, regulations, directives and decisions relating to the conduct of intra-party life, that life was in practice only weakly structured by official normative principles. In many parts of the party, particularly at the lower levels, power was highly personalised, resting on the party first secretary and a clique of supporters who ruled their region like a medieval fief. This sort of system had emerged in the period immediately following the October revolution and had become institutionalised as the normal method whereby the party functioned.[1] The essence of such 'family group' control was the informal political machine whose aim was the maintenance of control over the local area and which sought to implement central decisions in such a way as not to shake that control. The accountability of the lower level leading groups to the centre was thus mediated through a concern for their own best interests. The Brezhnevian 'stability of cadres' policy well served this type of power structure because of the autonomy it granted to local leaders.

The lower levels of responsiveness of the party as a whole to central commands inherent in this structure was a matter of concern to the new reformist leadership.[2] They recognised that the simple replacement of individual responsible officials, while itself necessary, was insufficient to overcome this problem. What was needed was a new organisational culture in the party, the generation of a regime of party life which would embed a system of values in the party inconsistent with continuing family group control. Initially the development of such a culture was seen as coming about through the re-emphasis of traditional themes of party life. Four were particularly significant:

1. The concern for increased *trebovatel'nost'* (demandingness), for ensuring higher standards of performance on the part of party leaders. These leaders were expected to work hard, to be dedicated to their jobs and to set the highest standards of performance upon which others could model themselves. Tasks had to be approached in new and innovative ways, with leaders showing dedication and initiative rather than waiting for instructions from above as they sought to overcome the problems with which they were faced.[3] This was essentially a focus upon individual attitudes, a call for the psychological restructuring of cadres in the spirit of the times. Just as power was personalised, this emphasis saw the solution to lie in the changing personal attitudes of party leaders.

2. The mobilisation of the populace into political life. The principal element of this was to be the opening up of the party's operations to public gaze and, in such things as the evaluation of the qualifications of a would-be party member for entry to the party,[4] participation in its work by non-party members.

3. Criticism – self-criticism. This was meant to ensure that all party organs not only continually evaluated the quality of their own work, but also made judgements about how satisfactorily party bodies above (and below) them were performing their tasks. The intention was to ensure that the sharp edge of external criticism prevented abuses.

4. Collectivism in leadership. The leadership of all party bodies was to be collective in nature, although this was not to weaken the personal responsi-

bility of each individual for the implementation of their own duties and commissions.[5]

The reassertion of these traditional themes was designed to combat family group control by a combination of changing personal attitudes and encouraging a more critical atmosphere in the party. These measures were seen as constituting a strengthening of democracy in the party, with democratisation the organisational culture that was to overcome the deficiencies inherent in family group control. In the initial stages of reform, therefore, Gorbachev saw democracy in terms of the extension of existing principles and the changing of personal attitudes, not of structural changes to the party itself. But attitudes could not be changed in isolation from structures. Although at one stage in 1985 Gorbachev seems to have supported a maximum tenure in one post of ten years for party secretaries,[6] it was not until the beginning of 1987 that he made a major drive for structural change in the party.

Gorbachev's speech to the thrice postponed Central Committee plenum in January 1987[7] was a landmark in the process of party reform because it combined a continued emphasis upon attitudinal change with the first major proposals for structural reform. The early part of Gorbachev's speech contained a stinging attack upon the deficiencies in the way in which the party had worked in the immediate past. Among the charges flung at the party were conservatism and inertia, toadyism and personal adulation, intolerance of criticism, ambition and careerism, administration by decree, permissiveness, mutual cover-ups, departmentalism, parochialism, nationalism, a weakening of the role of party meetings and elective bodies, embezzlement, bribery, report-padding and violation of discipline. In the field of personnel management he criticised the underestimation of the importance of political and theoretical training in the selection, placement and distribution of personnel, the absence of a regularised pattern of personnel turnover, and the filling of offices with those unfit to do so. The key to overcoming these deficiencies was greater democratisation. Gorbachev argued that many proposals had been forthcoming regarding the formation of leading party bodies, and that these proposals could be summarised in two points:

1 In the election of secretaries of party bureaux and committees in the party branches or PPOs, full scope must be given to the views of all communists.

2 Secretaries, including first secretaries, of district, area, city, regional and territorial party committees and the central committees of union republican parties[8] should be elected by secret ballot at plenary sessions of the respective committees. While this was the long-established position in the party Rules, what was new was Gorbachev's declaration that

members of the committee should have the right to enter any number of candidates in the voting list.

The summary of proposals given by Gorbachev was an important step in the direction of democratisation. Both proposals emphasised accountability, the former by focusing on the breadth of opinion necessary for the filling of responsible office, the second by opening the way for multi-candidate competitive elections. Moreover, there was provision for those candidates to be chosen by the immediate electorate rather than being handed down through the *nomenklatura* mechanism from above. But the effect of this was immediately qualified by the injunction that the decisions of higher bodies were to remain binding on lower bodies.

Gorbachev's speech also criticised the Central Committee and its *modus operandi*. Too often important issues were not discussed in this forum, where meetings were often brief and formal and where many members were unable to participate effectively. There was, therefore, a need for a fresh influx of new forces into this body (and the Politburo), although continuity of leadership needed to be maintained. The answer to overcoming these deficiencies, and therefore the way in which democratisation was perceived in this context, was through raising the role of elective bodies generally. According to the General Secretary, there had been excessive growth in the role of executive bodies at the expense of elected organs. While plena may have been held regularly, their work was often excessively formalised, or only secondary measures or measures which had already been decided were brought up for discussion. This resulted in a lack of proper control over executive organs and their leaders, who often saw elective bodies purely as nuisances. This view, declared Gorbachev, was also sometimes present in the relationship between committee members and the permanent staff. Executive organs must not be allowed to supplant elective organs or to dominate them.

Gorbachev's speech to the plenum was a major challenge to existing practice in the party. He had called for a much more vigorous electoral process characterised by multi-candidate elections, the conscious participation of all party members in the discussion of candidates, and the strengthening of elected bodies at the expense of executive organs and of the apparatus. But the plenum as a whole did not take up this challenge, at least not in the specific forms enunciated by Gorbachev. The resolution of the plenum[9] acknowledged the need to democratise the work of party organs, to democratise party elections, to open up the work of party bodies to the gaze of all, to strengthen the accountability of elected and appointed leaders, to further develop criticism and self-criticism, to ensure that elected organs were characterised by full collectivism, equality and freedom of discussion, and to exercise control over executive organs and the work of the apparatus.

The plenum thus supported the general thrust of Gorbachev's comments, but without setting in place specific provisions which would have given that thrust effective content, in particular multi-candidate elections.

Gorbachev's drive for democratisation through structural reform elicited signs of major opposition within the party to his reform plans. The postponement of the plenum and that meeting's failure to endorse his specific proposals reflected this opposition. So too did the failure of the party leadership to press for democratisation through specific measures in the months following the plenum. However, at this time, the impetus for democratisation in the party came from below in the form of multi-candidate elections for party secretaries. The first occurred in February 1987 in Izhmorskii district, Kemerovo region, and was widely publicised in the press.[10] This was followed by a string of multi-candidate secret ballot elections to fill party posts, with some 120 secretaries of district party committees being elected in this way.[11] This experiment, while important in maintaining the momentum for democratisation, was strictly limited in scope: during this period most positions that were filled were done so in the traditional way, none of the competitive elections was for posts higher than the city level, and even in those competitive elections candidates were nominated from above rather than the voters being able to nominate anyone they chose.

At the June 1987 plenum where Gorbachev pressed the need for democratisation and openness in party work,[12] the convocation of the 19th Conference of the CPSU was announced. This would be the first party conference since February 1941, and therefore was to be an event of some importance in party life. Furthermore it was explicitly charged with, *inter alia*, introducing 'measures for the further democratisation of the life of the party and society'.[13] Delegates were to be elected by secret ballot at party plena, although there was no mention of competition being mandatory, and the conference was to be preceded by a wide-ranging party debate.

The debate which characterised the pages of the party press in the period leading up to the conference was wide-ranging in the issues it raised. There were calls for the party to stand aside from the direct management of economic affairs and leave these to state organs, thereby raising the issue of the party's place in Soviet society. Multi-candidate elections for all positions in the party, limited tenure for all elected posts, mandatory turnover levels, age limits for responsible officials, a more active role for the Central Committee and greater openness of its plena, the election of the General Secretary by an electorate other than the CC, a reduction in the size of the party apparatus, the abolition of party privileges and criticism of the *nomenklatura* for the way it rendered officials free from notions of accountability were among the most important issues aired in this debate. The criticism of the established patterns of party life was significant at this time. It was clearly stimulated by some of the speeches by Gorbachev. But important too were the general campaign for glasnost which was unrolling in the press at this time and resentment at the treatment of Boris Yeltsin. The way in which he was dismissed first from the Politburo and then from the position of first secretary of the Moscow city party committee was reminiscent of the crude power politics of the past and seemed to directly contradict the new style of party life which Gorbachev had espoused. Yeltsin's treatment had a radicalising effect on many people, including party members.

The election of conference delegates also stimulated the pressures for democratisation in the party. Formally the nomination of candidate delegates lay with the PPO and work collectives, with these nominations being approved by city and district party organisations before being voted on at the regional and sometimes district level. Candidates thus had to go through a sieve before reaching the stage of the ballot, and this sieve was composed of the traditional power wielders in the apparatus. In many areas local authorities used this tactic to weed out undesirable candidates. However, in contrast to earlier elections inside the party, such tactics often evoked loud and public protest. Charges of ballot-rigging appeared and the press published a series of reports of popular discontent at the activities of some local authorities. In Sakhalin the undemocratic selection of candidates was condemned by a public meeting which attracted some 4,800 people, a development which resulted in the sacking of the regional party first secretary. In Omsk a meeting of some 8,000 people criticised the way local party leaders had pressed the candidacy of their own people without consulting the public, while in Yaroslavl' public protests led to the withdrawal of a former regional leader who had been chosen by the local party leadership as a delegate. In Moscow, there was a small public demonstration in favour of 'honest elections' while public action forced the rejection of Yuri Afanas'ev as a delegate to be overturned.[14] The publication of such instances of the defeat of so-called '*apparat* games' heightened popular expectations about the Conference and strengthened the feeling that this would be an event at which there would be a major trial of strength between reformers and conservatives. This perception had also been stimulated by the mounting conservative attack on reformist policies during the first half of 1988, symbolised most clearly by the notorious Andreeva letter of March 1988 (see below, p. 206).[15]

When the Conference opened on 28 June, the agenda had been set on a reformist course. The Theses for the Conference published at the end of May[16] contained many elements central to the task of democratising the party including the radical restructuring of the PPOs, competitive secret ballot elections with nominations possible from the floor, elected office to be filled for a maximum of two terms except in exceptional cases when a third term would be possible, the accountability of party functionaries to elected party bodies, increased activity by elected organs, the collective principle in the CC, provision for the partial replacement of CC members between congresses, freedom of debate to be followed by concerted action after a majority decision has been made, and the life of party organisations to be characterised by openness, debate, criticism and self-criticism, comradeship, discipline, collectivism and personal responsibility. In addition, the Theses called for a strict demarcation of functions between party and state organs and the concentration of control and auditing work within the party in one organ. In his address to the Conference Gorbachev discussed all of these points, and made a strong argument for the change of the party's organisational culture and its operating conventions.[17] His speech was reflected in many of its essentials in the decisions of the Conference (see below).

But the importance of the Conference for the course of democratisation in the party is not to be found only in its decisions. The conduct of the Conference itself was an important stimulant. The lifeless, stylised atmosphere that had characterised most party gatherings since 1925 was absent. A real process of debate occurred, with speakers addressing themselves to the key questions of the day, raising such sensitive topics as the privileges enjoyed by responsible officials, criticising contemporary leaders for their failings, and even calling for the removal of individual members of the leading group. Much of the Conference proceedings were presented live on television, thereby providing a model of the type of organisational culture which Gorbachev wished to see structuring party life in the future. But the Conference also showed the mounting sense of unease felt by conservative elements in the party at the course reform was taking.

The decisions of the Conference provided a significant stimulus to reform of the party, both in terms of its place in the society and in its domestic operating procedures and power structure. In his speech Gorbachev had called for a radical reform of the political system involving the reanimation of the soviets, a new national political structure, and a clear demaracation between party and state functions. The clearly expressed aim was to withdraw the party from the direct management of the day-to-day affairs of the state, to pass the responsibility for these over to the soviets, and to encourage the party to exercise its leading role through political means rather than administrative *fiat*. The plenary assemblies of the soviets were to be revived so they could play a more important role than the executive organs, and one means of achieving this was to be the combination of the position of party first secretary with that of chairman of the soviet. This proposal potentially placed the party first secretary in an interesting position. Once elected as party leader, the secretary would be nominated for the post of chairman of the soviet. If that person failed to be elected, in Gorbachev's words, 'the party committee and the communists will obviously have to draw the necessary conclusions'. This proposal seemed to place the party leader in the position of having to have his position ratified by the people through the deputies to the soviet, and thereby cast into question the right of the party to choose its own leaders. The proposal also directly contradicted the desire for a separation between party and state.

In the six months following the Conference, the main recommendations relating to the party's position in the political system were given a constitutional grounding. Following a month of public discussion, constitutional amendments were adopted by the Supreme Soviet on 1 December 1988.[18] Among other things, these provided for a new national power structure consisting of a Congress of People's Deputies and Supreme Soviet (see chapter 3). Measures were also adopted to revive the soviets at all levels, but no formal provision was made specifying that the party leader should also be chairman of the soviet. Rather than a formal rule, this was envisaged as an informal convention. Thus by the end of the year, a new soviet structure had been introduced, at least on paper, which was to have important implications for the future of the party.

The conference resolution on democratisation of the party also introduced measures of great importance for the structuring of internal party life. As well as calling for the reanimation of the PPOs and of elected bodies more generally, the resolution called for the Central Committee to exercise closer supervision over the Politburo, for the establishment of commissions to involve Central Committee members more continuously in its work, the publication of stenographic reports of plena, and the possibility of the replacement of up to 20 per cent of the membership of the CC by party conferences convened midway between congresses. Personnel policy was to be updated and based on a democratic approach and elections, which were to be characterised by more candidates than there were positions to be filled and secret ballot. This was associated with a rejection of the traditional *nomenklatura* approach: 'The formalistic approach to the selection and placement of key personnel, an approach based on sticking to a rigid list of approved cadres, is losing its effectiveness.' Elected office-holders were to be restricted to two five-year terms, with no provision for a third term, while lower party organs were allowed to suggest candidates for higher office. A new combined control and auditing apparatus was to be established, and the resolution declared that the party apparatus was to be strictly subordinate to elected organs, was to be reduced in size, and should operate more efficiently.

The decisions of the 19th Conference posed a major challenge to the position of the apparatus and the way it exercised power through the *nomenklatura* system. This challenge was given substance through the implementation of these measures in the months following the Conference. New regulations for the conduct of party elections were introduced in August.[19] While these regulations provided for the election of all leading party organs up to and including the CC by secret ballot following wide discussion of each candidate individually and limited tenure of elected office to two terms, they only provided for 'the possibility' of more candidates than there were seats on the ballot paper. Thus multi-candidate competitive elections, while desirable, were not mandatory. Furthermore the new regulations made decisions in the discussion and nomination phases subject to open voting and made provision for cooptation onto elected organs either on the recommendation or with the agreement of higher standing bodies. Clearly, the regulations had sufficient loopholes in them to enable local leaders to avoid real competition and continue to operate through the old methods if they wished.

During the autumn major changes were also introduced into the party apparatus. At a Politburo meeting on 8 September, the decision was taken to establish six CC commissions.[20] Although the commissions were not finally established until the November 1988 plenum,[21] from September the Secretariat seems effectively to have been abolished. Six commissions were established: party construction and cadre policy, ideology, social-economic policy, agrarian policy, international policy and legal policy. They were specifically designed to involve members of the CC more continually in party affairs and thereby to enhance the participation of those people in the party's policy-making. The organisational work for the commissions was to be undertaken principally by the departments of the CC, which were to be reduced in number from twenty-two to nine and to have their staff cut by 40 per cent.[22] Significantly for the avowed aim of withdrawing from the day-to-day work of the state, most of the CC departments dealing with economic matters were abolished. Much fuller stenographic reports of party meetings and CC plena began to appear and a new journal, *Izvestiia TsK KPSS*, which contained much fuller information about the party's internal affairs, began publication in January 1989.

Despite reservations within the apparatus, pressure for multi-candidate elections was maintained. While acknowledging that this principle had been 'taking a long time to become established' in the party, the official line remained one of advocating this as the most appropriate means of handling cadre questions.[23] Although neither Gorbachev in his address to the February 1990 plenum nor the CC in the Draft Platform adopted at that plenum[24] advocated competitive elections in principle, Gorbachev did talk about the need for the accountability of elected organs and the increased influence of the rank-and-file upon those organs, and the CC Platform advocated contested elections in two specific cases: the election by all communists of delegates to conferences and congresses[25] and the direct election of party first secretaries by the plenary meetings, congresses and conferences. The draft Rules presented to the March plenum entrenched choice in elections to party office and the two specific cases contained in the CC Draft Platform.[26] By emphasising the role of the party rank-and-file and plenary assemblies in the election of party offices, these proposals clearly were directed against the traditional power axis of the party, the *nomenklatura*. That this was a major intention of the democratisation of the party electoral process was openly stated in the Soviet press.[27] The declarations by the CC Commission on Party Construction and Cadre Policy that the so-called records and monitoring *nomenklatura* located in the apparatus of party committees was to be abolished[28] and by Ukrainian First Secretary Ivashko that the old methods of cadre work had been eliminated[29] reinforce this view.

The party in a new power structure

The changes to the central party apparatus engendered significant resentment within the party. Indeed, the radicalisation of the programme of political reform at the 19th Conference had stimulated a strengthening of opposition. This was reinforced by the difficulties the party encountered in the elections to the Congress of People's Deputies in March 1989. At the January plenum (as we have seen) the CC had approved a list of 100 candidates for the 100 seats the party had allotted to it under the constitutional amendments adopted the previous month, hardly setting a positive example of an organisation devoted to the principle of competition in elections. Even the major spokesman for this principle, General Secretary Gorbachev, refused to face the electors and was to be found in this list. The plenum also adopted an election manifesto upon which its candidates were meant to stand in the coming electoral contest. When the votes were counted, they showed substantial voter disillusionment with the traditional style of party candidate. Although some 88 per cent of the delegates elected to the Congress were party members and many prominent party figures were successfully returned to the new legislature, the most striking feature of the election was the defeat of many local party and state leaders and the triumphant return of Boris Yeltsin (see pp. 27–28). The shock created by these results was great, and the mood it engendered is well reflected in the statement by Kemerovo first secretary Mel'nikov that following this election, no party official in the region was willing to stand for election to the local soviets because it appeared certain that they would be defeated.[30] The new political arrangements introduced at Gorbachev's behest had clearly created a situation that was profoundly disturbing to many within the party by enabling the extent of popular disillusionment with it to become evident. The fears of these people were not assuaged by the performance of the new state organs.

Both new bodies, the Congress of People's Deputies and the new style Supreme Soviet, were dominated by party members. But their style of operation was very different from that of their predecessors. In both assemblies the government came under withering criticism as delegates used the opportunity they provided to attack past performance and perceived current deficiencies. In particular they became the scene of nationalist complaints. The refusal to be a mere rubber stamp of government and party policy is best reflected in the difficulties Prime Minister Ryzhkov had in gaining Supreme Soviet ratification of his government. The decline in party control is also clear in the establishment in July 1989 of the Inter-Regional Group of Deputies, a radical caucus of deputies (including Boris Yeltsin) which sought consistently to adopt a radical line on government policy. These developments signified the breakdown of party discipline, the inability of the party leadership to ensure that all of the party members who were deputies adhered to the central party line. Despite the attempt to formulate a doctrine that would give deputies some independence while ensuring obedience to the party line on issues of principle,[31] the erosion of the notion of party discipline was impossible to hide, and with it the myth of a monolithic party evaporated.

Important too was the way in which the new legislative organs, and in particular the Supreme Soviet and the array of specialised committees and commissions it generated, expanded to fill the governmental vacuum. Like all new institutions, the Supreme Soviet adopted an expansive view of its rights, powers and responsibilities. This was associated with an apparent decline in the activity of leading party bodies and in particular in their involvement in governmental affairs. By 1989 the Politburo had ceased to meet on a regular basis,[32] and does not seem to have been closely concerned with many major issues of government policy; at least according to one member, there was no discussion in the Politburo of such an important issue as the government's measures for the transition to a regulated market economy.[33] The Secretariat effectively ceased to function and the new CC commissions were largely inactive.[34] Although the CC met on more occasions in 1989 than in any earlier year of Gorbachev's rule,[35] more than half of those meetings were related to the need for the party to formalise its position on matters coming before the Congress of People's Deputies or Supreme Soviet, and all meetings were of short duration. Furthermore the

CC's ability to generate the sort of moral authority which would have enabled it to exercise effective leadership was undermined by the continuing pattern of unanimous voting despite open disagreements over the matters under discussion. The complaints that were frequently made in the press about an absence of leadership from leading party organs[36] was accurate.

As the state sector became more active, at least at the centre, the party organs appear to have become less concerned with matters of state. In accord with the decision of the 19th Conference, a demarcation was occurring between party and state organs with the latter becoming much more autonomous than had hitherto been the case. The withdrawal of the party from state, and particularly economic, matters was a cause of concern among some circles within the party. This combined with a worry among many who had made their careers in the party apparatus that that apparatus was now becoming sidelined; the effect of the changes initiated at the Conference was to emasculate the central apparatus and, by so doing, severely reduce the power traditionally exercised by those who worked in the party apparatus. Genuine concern for the fate of the party and the country was thereby given a tangible edge by the threat to job security that the changes involved. Such concern was vividly reflected in a robust exchange of opinions between Gorbachev and party leaders in July 1989,[37] and through the process of continuing debate and criticism within party ranks in the two years between that meeting and the coup.[38] In this period, cause for concern about the fate of the party mounted.

The difficulties experienced by the party in the election to the Congress of People's Deputies had been particularly marked in the Baltic states, where well-developed national front movements had played a major role in the election. In all three states it was now these national fronts which set the political agenda. The emergence of such informal political groups and their growing strength, which was to be reflected in the elections to republican and local soviets in early 1990, plus the withdrawal of the party from the direct administration of state affairs, raised acutely the question of the party's leading role. This had been an article of faith for many years and was firmly rooted in Article 6 of the 1977 Constitution. Party leaders continued to maintain the importance of the party's leading role, even if they also argued that this should be sustained not through the administrative practices characteristic of the past, but by political means. The party should exercise influence through prestigious party members, by working for the support of the people, gaining a majority in the legislative organs and thereby being able to implement its policies. The party had to earn its leading role through the trust it gained as a result of its performance.[39] This implied that the party was not the only possible repository of the people's trust and, intellectually, conceded the principle that other parties should be permitted. However party leaders were reluctant to concede this point in practice. Throughout most of 1989, the party leadership rejected a multi-party system as inappropriate for the Soviet Union. But this position began to change, principally under the impact of events in Lithuania and particularly the way in which the party in that republic was in danger of becoming politically irrelevant to the course of republican politics. In December 1989 Gorbachev acknowledged that Article 6 of the Constitution might not be essential;[40] two months later at the February 1990 CC plenum, it was decided to remove the party's political monopoly from the Constitution.[41] This was done by formal amendment of the Constitution in early March. The new provision opened the way for a multi-party system, and although party leaders continued to argue that the party was the necessary leader to ensure the success of perestroika, the ending of the official ban on opposition parties clearly heralded a significant change in the position of the party, especially in the context of the low level electoral support it enjoyed.

Despite the overwhelming support expressed in the CC for the abolition of the party's constitutionally entrenched leading role, those who were concerned about the way in which the party was being sidelined were not pleased by this move. Nevertheless, they swallowed their reservations and voted for the change. Their concerns were not eased by alterations to the state structure in March and to the party's leading organs at the 28th Congress in July. In March the Congress of People's Deputies established a new executive presidency with wide-ranging powers[42] and elected Gorbachev to it.[43] The executive presidency, a post without precedent in Soviet history, concentrated potentially enormous power in the hands of the president (see chapter 4). It also provided Gorbachev with a powerful institutional basis independent of the party. In the three months following its creation, Gorbachev adopted a higher profile as President than as General Secretary, and the Presidential Council was more prominent than the leading party organs. Increasingly the party was being pushed to the side by the enhanced state organs.

Having established a powerful institutional position at the apex of the state structure, attention was now turned to the leading organs of the party. Changes to these organs had been foreshadowed earlier in the year when the draft Programme and Rules were adopted for party-wide discussion at the February and March plena.[44] Not all the changes foreshadowed were finally adopted at the 28th Congress, but those that were significantly altered the contours of elite party organs. The most important change was the transformation of the membership, and therefore the nature, of the Politburo. Candidate membership was abolished, but more importantly, the Politburo membership was changed. The General Secretary and the newly-created post of Deputy General Secretary were *ex officio* members. So too were the fifteen leaders of the republican communist parties. In addition, the CC was to elect a number of members; at the 28th Congress, seven people were elected. Three aspects of this membership are significant. First, because of the large number of *ex officio* members, none of whom were to be chosen by the CC, the notion of Politburo responsibility to the CC was severely weakened. Second, because of the republican responsibilities of two-thirds of the membership, the Politburo was prevented from meeting on a weekly basis as its predecessor had normally done; it was reduced to a monthly timetable. In any case, the republican concerns of most of its members limited its capacity to exercise effective overview of national affairs. Third, the overlap between the Politburo and the leading state organs, and in particular the Presidential Council, was minimal. Only the General Secretary and his deputy were also members of this body. These changes thus prevented the Politburo from having any sustained involvement in state affairs. The new relationship with the Presidential Council reflected the desire for institutional demarcation between state and party.

The relative infrequency with which the Politburo was to meet meant that the day-to-day affairs of the party came increasingly under the supervision of the revamped Secretariat. The Secretariat was to consist of eighteen people: the General Secretary and his deputy, eleven CC secretaries and five 'members of the Secretariat' elected by the CC. Of the eleven secretaries, all were accorded specific spheres of competence except for Boris Gidaspov, the first secretary in Leningrad. Five of the CC secretaries (in addition to the General Secretary and his deputy) were also members of the Politburo; of the other 'members', three were workers or farmers and two local party secretaries. The Secretariat was to meet weekly, and the bulk of the work and the power would be in the hands of the CC secretaries; the five other members were justified as representatives of the population, but their precise function was uncertain. It is unlikely that they could contribute much to the smooth and orderly functioning of the Secretariat as an administrative machine. The commissions and departments established in 1988 were replaced by a new and expanded set of both bodies, and although these embraced a broader range of policy areas than those they replaced, they did not suggest a more intrusive role by central party organs in state affairs.[45] The size of the CC apparatus was also reduced.[46]

The Congress also changed the way the General Secretary was to be chosen and created the post of Deputy General Secretary. Both posts were to be filled by direct secret ballot in the congress, thereby liberating both positions from responsibility to the CC. The new deputy position was to be responsible for the supervision of the work of the Secretariat and the CC commissions and departments and chair Politburo sessions when the General Secretary was unavailable.

These changes significantly affected the ability of the leading party organs to play a major role outside the party itself. The Politburo would meet sufficiently infrequently and had insufficient overlap with government bodies to be able to play a major part in the daily course of policy-making. However both the CC commissions and the Secretariat were more active and did give the central apparatus a focus which it had lost after September 1988. The responsibilities of the CC secretaries suggest that it was principally concerned with party affairs, although the presence of secretaries for international affairs, agriculture, defence industry, nationalities and women does mean that there was at least some residual interest in these areas of policy. The establishment of the post of Deputy General Secretary effectively freed the General Secretary from the day-to-day grind of party matters and enabled Gorbachev to devote more of his time to state affairs; it thereby also increased the flow of power and authority in that direction. The changes at the Congress further enhanced the power of the state organs at the expense of those of the party, and thus the aims of the reformers to extricate the party from daily management of the society. But these changes to the central organs were occurring in a party structure that was falling apart.

A fracturing party

The difficulties experienced in many of the republics in 1989–90, and in particular those of the Baltic region, because of the strengthening of the nationalist sentiments generated pressures within the party structure as well.[47] Republican party leaderships struggled to maintain authority among the local populations who increasingly looked to the popular fronts as genuine voices of local nationalism. In contrast, the local communist parties were seen as Moscow's arm in the republic. Local party leaders were aware of the dangers posed to their positions by such a development, and as early as July 1989 calls were being made for the federalisation of the party.[48] The hope was that such a development would enable the republican parties to generate their own policies, structures and practices which would be more suitable for local conditions. The response of the central leadership was to reaffirm the validity of the unitary principle in party organisation, but also to recognise the need for greater autonomy on the part of the republican parties. The form that it was suggested this might take was for the regional and republican parties to draw up their own 'socio-economic action programmes', although these had to be consistent with the Programme of the CPSU. But under pressure from local nationalism and with the approach of elections to republican and local soviets early in 1990, this concession was insufficient for some republican party leaders and on 21 December 1989 the Lithuanian party declared itself organisationally independent of the CPSU.

This step was soon followed by the Latvian and Estonian parties.[49] Although these parties split between pro- and anti-Moscow wings, the reality was clear: the party was fracturing along national lines.

Further evidence of this was provided by events surrounding the Russian communists. There had for a long time been a sentiment among communists of the RSFSR that that republic should have its own party organisation independent of the central party organs and apparatus. This became even stronger as nationalist pressures across the country began to mount and as the reform programme embraced notions of republican political autonomy and *khozraschet* or financial self-sufficiency. Furthermore conservative elements in the party, which as the founding congress of the Russian party in June 1990 demonstrated dominated leading positions in the party in Russia, saw the creation of a powerful Russian party as a potential counter to the reformist elements in the central leadership. Such a feeling could only have been strengthened by the election of Boris Yeltsin as Chairman of the Supreme Soviet of the RSFSR at the end of May 1990. In any event, pressures for a separate party organisation mounted throughout the second half of 1989. The leadership's response was the establishment of the Russian Bureau of the CC at the December 1989 CC plenum.[50] Such a half measure had no chance of succeeding. It had already failed under Khrushchev,[51] it worked inefficiently, and once the new state structure for the Russian Republic had been established following the March 1990 elections, the only way the CPSU could hope to compete was through a party which had its attention concentrated solely upon Russian affairs. As a result, at the February 1990 plenum, the CC foreshadowed the convocation of a republican party conference prior to the 28th Congress to discuss the question of the development of the party in the RSFSR.[52]

Through a combination of initiative from the regions, particularly Leningrad, and activity from the centre, the Russian party conference was convened in Moscow on 19 June. The conference transformed itself into a congress, formally established the Communist Party of the RSFSR, and elected a conservative party leader from Krasnodar, Ivan Polozkov, as its first secretary. This creation of an autonomous Russian party raised two interesting questions, which could not immediately be answered. The first had immediate political implications and concerned the effect upon reform a conservative Russian party would have. Given that it covered most of the USSR, if it chose to attempt to block the reform process this could have significant implications for the success of the central party leadership's policies. The second question concerns the role of the central party organs. If responsibility for republican affairs was devolved to republican parties, what would be left for the central party organs to do? While it was not clear what the answer to these questions was thought to be, Gorbachev recognised the dangers. This is shown by his desire to have the Russian party share apparatus and premises with the central organs of the party.

An attempt was made at the 28th Congress to systematise the relationship between central and republican parties and to boost the status and importance of the latter. While rejecting pressures for the federalisation of the party in favour of a party with a common programme and statute, the Congress adopted a new set of party Rules[53] which declared the republican parties to be autonomous and empowered them to compile their own programmatic and normative documents on the basis of the principles of the Programme and Rules of the CPSU. Republican parties were given the right to decide organisational, financial, personnel, publishing and other matters, to pursue party policy in the areas of state construction and the social, economic and cultural development of their republics, and to maintain ties with other parties and social movements, including foreign ones. Republican party first secretaries were made *ex officio* members of the Politburo and a mechanism was established to enable republican parties to dispute decisions of central bodies which they believed to infringe their interests. Finally the convocation of an extraordinary CPSU congress required the support of at least three republican parties, while the decisions of such a congress were to be binding only if a majority of republican parties were represented at it. These were significant changes and substantially increased the standing of the republican parties. Even so, the only chance the central leadership had of holding the line against the formal federalisation of the party was if in practice the remaining restrictions posed by the need to adhere to the CPSU Programme and Rules were interpreted very liberally. But given the continuing strength of nationalist feeling, the Lithuanian solution of creating a completely independent national party would be the only viable option for local communists if they wished to play a part in the new political conditions. The same problem of adherence to orthodoxy applied in the question of democratic centralism and fractions.

The recognition of a diversity of interests in society and the corollary of a diversity of views to give expression to those interests was worked out institutionally in the society through the emergence of a range of informal groups. But the party's abnegation of a monopolistic orthodoxy on ideas in the society had direct implications inside the party as well: if the party was not the sole bearer of truth in the society, then neither was the party leadership the source of truth within the party. Other views were legitimate, and clearly the only way of resolving which of the competing positions was correct was through the direct and open clash of opinions. This logic, stemming from developments in the society at large, was reinforced by three developments in the party. First, the provision for multi-candidate competitive elections made little sense unless the candidates were able to openly disagree over issues and to present different programmes to the electors. Second, the experience of some party member delegates to the new state legislative organs in criticising authoritative party positions without suffering party discipline showed that the line against the pluralisation of opinion in the party had become untenable. Third, in the debate over federalisation of the party, the Lithuanian party had clearly differed from the central party authorities and yet was still considered (at least until 21 December 1989) an integral part of the party. Indeed the later provision for regional and republican parties to design their own programmatic documents was formal recognition of the right of party organisations to hold different views, albeit within limits. This sort of development undermined the monolithic ethos associated with the banning of fractions and the meaning of democratic centralism that had emerged in the 1920s and remained into the 1980s to shape party life.

By early 1990 it was clear that the traditional understanding of these concepts was subject to serious revision. At the February 1990 plenum Gorbachev declared that the renovation of the party implied 'the rethinking of the principle of democratic centralism, with the accent on democratism and the power of the party masses'.[54] The CC Draft Platform accepted that fundamental for the renewal of the party was, *inter alia*, 'pluralism of opinions, freedom of criticism, diversity of approaches and platforms . . . and the minority's right to uphold its views subject to mandatory fulfilment of decisions made by the majority'. But the renewal of democratic centralism along these lines was explicitly seen as designed to forestall 'the formation of fractions with their own internal organisation and discipline'.[55] An important development in legitimising the pluralisation of opinion was the emergence of the first open fractions in the party since the 1920s, the Democratic Platform and the Marxist Platform. Both groups were formally created in early 1990,[56] and both possessed organisational structures and policy positions, even if these were weakly developed. The Theses of both Platforms were published in the press as part of the discussion preceding the 28th Congress.[57] But what was important was that the Theses were presented as the considered views of an established fractional grouping in the party, an action which implicitly legalised the sort of organised group the revision of democratic centralism was meant to forestall. This view was not, however, universally acknowledged within the party leadership; on 11 April 1990 a call was issued under the imprimatur of the Central Committee for the expulsion of Democratic Platform members from the party.[58]

The debate in the party on this issue leading up to the Congress turned on the question of whether organised fractions should be permitted in the party or not. All sides accepted that there must be some way of protecting minority viewpoints in the party, of ensuring that those whose point of view did not prevail in the course of party debate were able to maintain that view and even continue to press it while at the same time falling in behind the decision taken and helping to implement it. The question was how this was to be achieved. The Democratic Platform, whose main focus of concern was with internal party affairs, believed that the only way a full pluralisation of opinion could be realised was through the formal legalisation of fractions. However, the tide of opinion in the party, at least as reflected in the press, was against this view. The result was the ambiguous measures ratified at the 28th Congress. While the new Rules retained the principle of democratic centralism, the five supplementary points which had defined its meaning in the party Rules adopted in 1986 were omitted. The precise meaning of the principle was thereby left uncertain. Fractions remained formally banned, but there was to be full freedom of discussion including the right to present platforms. But in practice this was an impossible position to sustain, as some official speakers acknowledged.[59] The emergence of platforms encouraged the development of organisational structures to advance those platforms, with the result that fractions would be the inevitable result. By failing to recognise this and to legalise fractions, the party not only lost the Democratic Platform (whose leaders announced their departure from the party at the 28th Congress), but it ensured that this would remain a continuing issue in party life. Furthermore as the need to compete with other parties sharpened intra-party debate on policy questions, the prohibition on organising in support of policy views became unnecessarily restrictive.

This question of increased autonomy inside the party, reflected in the issue of the status of the republican parties and the question of fractions, was also raised in terms of lower level party organisations more generally. In particular, the status of the primary party organisations came under debate. Reflecting concern with the widespread disillusionment among party rank-and-file,[60] there was a consensus in the party that the PPOs had to be more active. The suggested means of bringing this about were various, but essentially they amounted to increasing the financial autonomy of PPOs and allowing them to organise their party structures and methods of work in ways which they believed best suited local conditions. The centre was no longer to impose a standardised set of structures and processes upon lower level organs; the latter were to generate their own, albeit within the broad principles that structured the party as a whole.

The increased autonomy granted to lower level party organs was a recognition of the parlous state the party was in within the society as a whole. The elections to republican and local soviets in early 1990 had further eroded the party's capacity to play a dominant role in the country's life. The only way it could hope to maintain its position was through increased flexibility on the part of party bodies in adjusting to different and changing local conditions. But its capacity to do this was severely limited by its own internal difficulties. The divisions within the leadership had become more marked as the reform programme was radicalised, with the result that no consistent policy line was forthcoming from this source. A clear indication of this was the failure on the part of the 28th Congress to agree on the text of a new party Programme despite the fact that discussions had been under way on a draft since March. This lack of leadership was a common criticism by conservative elements at the time. The Politburo was accused of having 'lagged behind the development of events, most of all in the democratisation of the party, and often took decisions only under pressure of public opinion'.[61] In more colourful language, a speaker at the Russian party congress declared 'Instead of strengthening all links of the party, of defining its strategy and tactics in answer to the given political moment, the leadership of the CPSU devoted itself to a position of defencelessly sitting in the trenches under the massed fire of quickly-organising anti-socialist forces'.[62] The opposition reflected in such statements occurred at all levels of the structure and was reflected in foot-dragging and the sabotage of measures and attempts by authorities in some areas to maintain their grip and continue rule in the former fashion.[63] This sort of attitude prevented the party from thinking its way through the problems and coming up with creative solutions, and while such a positive approach may have been evident in some party members, it was not true of the organisation as a whole. The party's inability to act as a committed and united body clearly limited its capacity to meet the challenges which faced it.

A further aspect of the difficulties the party faced in responding to these challenges lay in the widespread demoralisation affecting party ranks. The clearest evidence of this was the shrinkage of the party. Initially recruitment rates lagged; by 1988 the rate of increase of the party had dropped to 0.08 per cent a year compared with a level of 1.7 per cent earlier in the decade, with recruitment levels in some areas dropping as much as half.[64] But more telling was the emergence of a phenomenon virtually unknown in the post-war period, the exodus of members from the party. The numbers of people leaving increased by more than 38 per cent in 1988 compared with 1987,[65] while in the eighteen months prior to July 1991, 4.2 million members had left the party.[66] Party speakers bemoaned the losses among the symbolically important proletariat, but inferential evidence suggests that depletion rates among the intelligentsia were also significant. But disillusionment was reflected not only in party membership levels.[67] The results of surveys published in the press showed the low standing of the party in many party members' eyes. A survey administered in mid-May 1990 showed that only 17 per cent of party member respondents believed the party could regain its authority through perestroika and the achievement of its ends.[68] Another survey later the same month showed that only 27 per cent of respondents believed that the CC was functioning better than it had been six months earlier; with regard to party bodies much closer to the individual members, the district and city committees, only 14 per cent believed their performance had improved.[69] Some 53 per cent of people surveyed believed that the party was no longer the leading political force in the country,[70] while in another survey 80.7 per cent of people believed the party's prestige had declined over the last two–three years and only 18.8 per cent said they would vote for it if a multi-party system had been in existence.[71] According to one speaker at the Moscow party conference in June 1990, the party was so discredited that in the elections, candidates 'forget' to mention that they were party members.[72] By mid-1990, the extent of demoralisation in the party was a matter of major concern to leading party figures.

The party's ability to respond to the challenges confronting it was also hindered by the difficulties it was experiencing in the material sphere. The party was the largest property owner in the USSR, possessing office buildings, residential accommodation, hotels, sanatoria, holiday accommodation, printing presses and vehicles in all parts of the country. Increasingly, challenges were mounted to the party's continued possession of this property; for example, in Yaroslavl' the city soviet demanded that various buildings currently in party hands be handed over to the soviet, in Donetsk a strike committee meeting called for the nationalisation of party property,[73] in Ternopol' party property was nationalised,[74] while in Primorskii *krai* the local party committee handed some facilities over to the community in an attempt to head off growing demands.[75] Despite a presidential decree[76] designed in part to protect the property of public organisations like the CPSU, the legal basis upon which much party property rested was uncertain. In many cases it amounted to little more than simple possession, but even when there was a form of legal title, this may not have been consistent with the emerging legal structures throughout the country. In Jurmala in Latvia, for example, state arbitration declared that the city party committee had to vacate its premises because the Communist Party of Latvia could not prove the building was party property.[77] But even if, in such an uncertain legal environment, such property could indisputably have been proved to belong to the party, it would not have been the unalloyed asset it once was. Such property was to be subject to taxation and, if some were to get their way, such taxes would have been backdated. In addition, the party's revenues were much reduced, principally as a result of falling membership, reduced levels of membership dues,[78] reduced circulation of party publications[79] and the loss of the state subsidy the party had enjoyed since 1917. Party income was reported to be down by about 60 per cent in

1990 compared with 1989,[80] and by mid-1991 the party was reported to have a budget deficit of 1.1 billion rubles, five times the shortfall of 1990.[81] The continued existence of the party as a viable entity was clearly under threat.

In the face of this serious erosion of its basis, in the twelve months following the 28th Congress the party was able to do little to strengthen its position. It continued to splinter with the emergence of a range of new groups within its ranks, including the conservative Communist Initiative Movement, Yedinstvo and the Bolshevik Platform, and the more liberal Democratic Party of Communists of Russia headed by Russian Vice-President Alexander Rutskoi. Despite the loss of prominent reformists immediately following the 28th Congress (and early in 1991) fierce debates and disputes continued to wrack party ranks, reflecting in particular a reluctance to accept the need to operate in new ways in the new conditions.[82] But the main blow against the party prior to the abortive coup occurred in July 1991 with Russian President Yeltsin's decree banning the activity of political parties and organisations in state bodies, soviets and state enterprises in the RSFSR.[83] If implemented fully, this would have eliminated the workplace control the party traditionally had exercised throughout Russia.

Despite opposing the move,[84] the party seemed resigned to carrying out this decree; indeed, in many workplaces throughout the country, party organisations had already been disbanded. But the full implementation of this decree was overrun by the coup and its aftermath. The collapse of the coup led to the formal elimination of the party: on 22 August party head-quarters in Moscow and Leningrad were seized and sealed, and on the following day Yeltsin signed a decree temporarily suspending the activities of the Russian Communist Party on the territory of the RSFSR. On 24 August Gorbachev formally quit the party, nationalised party property, called for the dissolution of the CC, and banned party cells in the military and security structures. Party assets were frozen and property and offices seized or sealed. Similar measures were taken in other republics. On 29 August the Supreme Soviet adopted a resolution suspending the activities of the CPSU across the country, freezing the party's financial assets, instructing the Minister of Internal Affairs to ensure the safety of the party's archives, and ordering an investigation of its actions during the coup. On 6 November, Yeltsin signed a decree finally banning the party in Russia.[85] These measures seem to have delivered the *coup de grace* to an already badly haemorrhaging body.

These measures, plus the outflow of members following the coup, crip-pled the party's capacity to play a major role in political life. In many parts of the country it splintered, with the splinters calling themselves political parties and espousing a range of views. In Russia some tried to keep the party going, challenging the legality of its banning in the Constitutional Court and convening a rump CC plenum and congress in early 1993. However these were minor affairs and, a year after its suspension, the party remained a minor player on the political scene. But this does not mean that in all parts of the country there has been a major change in the way politics is structured. It is by no means clear that the measures Gorbachev introduced to combat family groups were successful. Throughout large parts of the country, particularly in Central Asia, the Caucasus and rural areas of Russia and Ukraine, the informal political machines which had formerly run the local areas through the party have continued to exist. To the extent that such control remains unshaken, the old rules of the political game remain in force. The passing of the party does not, therefore, inevitably mean the elimination of the kind of political culture within which it had operated; nor of political parties that, like the CPSU, claim to operate in the interests of the proletariat.

8 The emergence of competitive politics

One of the most important aspects of the changes that occurred in the USSR since 1985 was the breakdown in the monolithic nature of politics. This was reflected in the increasing pluralisation of politics in the party discussed in the previous chapter, but its most striking manifestation was the proliferation of politically-active groups outside the party. An important, although by no means only, element of this was the hesitant approach to a multi-party system.

The essential prerequisite for this development was the breakdown of the rationale for single party rule. Although not all realised it at the time, the intellectual rationale for single party rule was undermined by the shift in views that occurred under Andropov. Fundamental to this was the acknowledgement that interests in Soviet society were not always compatible. Before Andropov, officially it had been assumed that, although the society consisted of a wide diversity of interests, all of those interests were basically compatible. It was this assumption that was at the heart of the Khrushchevian notion of the all-people's state and of the view that the party united within itself the most advanced and conscious part of the working class, collective farm peasantry and the intelligentsia. During the early part of the 1980s, this assumption came under challenge in a form which impressed itself upon the political leadership. The Novosibirsk Report by Tatiana Zaslavskaia,[1] as we have seen (p. 2), argued that Soviet society was characterised by a diversity of groups pursuing different interests. Zaslavskaia was primarily concerned with the interests of 'socio-economic groups',[2] which were conceived in hierarchical or 'vertically aligned' terms with conflicts of interest between the different levels, workers and foremen, foremen and the chiefs of enterprises, and chiefs of enterprises and administrators in the ministries. While this focus upon the productive process was traditional, Zaslavskaia's emphasis upon the clash of interests and the satisfaction of one interest only at the expense of the others was not. The references to 'antagonistic social groups' and even to 'class groups' under socialism, with the clear picture of a plurality of conflicting interests in

140

socialist society, punctured the official picture of a harmonious and integrated society.

Recognition of the disharmony of interests in the society was a crucial step in justifying the emergence of alternative modes of political activity. Although Zaslavskaia's analysis was traditional in its focus upon groups in the production process, by giving conflicting group interests a central place in that analysis she established the principle that analysis of such interests was essential to an understanding of contemporary social processes. Furthermore, logically this type of analysis could not stop with groups rooted in the production process; once group interests were conceded in principle, the line could not be drawn at those with an economic basis alone. In this way, group analysis was legitimated as a mode of social analysis. That this did not remain restricted to the academic authors of the document is suggested by the status of that document itself, a discussion paper which seems to have been fed into considerations about economic reform at the highest level, and by Zaslavskaia's later role as an economic adviser to Gorbachev. More broadly, it is reflected in the terms in which much of the debate and discussion in subsequent years was conducted.

The political implications of the acknowledgement of conflicting interests were significant. Most importantly, by recognising that interests were not compatible, the role attributed to a monolithic, united communist party of representing the interests of all society was rendered logically impossible. If the party had to remain cohesive and united around a common set of principles and interests, it could not represent the diversity of conflicting interests that were now acknowledged to exist within the society. Recognition of the party's inability to represent society as a whole logically meant that the way was cleared for the emergence of new bodies which could take up this diversity of interests and represent them in the political sphere. Official acceptance of the notion of 'socialist pluralism'[3] and the formal rejection of the constitutional entrenchment of the party's leading role reflected acknowledgement of this. These constituted official recognition of the right to independent organisation and activity within Soviet society.

But the emergence of independent organisations did not wait for formal acknowledgement that they had a right to exist. Such groups forced themselves onto the public scene, stimulated by the freer atmosphere under the Gorbachev leadership and by two aspects of the policies that came to be associated with the reform process. The first of these was the drive to harness the energy, enthusiasm and commitment of those at lower levels of Soviet society. The initial emphasis upon acceleration in the economy relied very heavily upon inputs of effort from the factory floor. Workers were called upon not only to bend their backs to achieve economic improvement, but to become increasingly aware of the performance of their manaagers and to respond to this when it was considered deficient. They were thus being asked to use their initiative, to take up independent positions and to exert pressure upon the authorities when they believed their interests and concerns (albeit defined in terms of general economic improvement) were not being accommodated. Criticism of the authorities, also reflected in the later revisions to electoral procedures, was thus encouraged as a central component of the reform process. This encouraged independent organisation.

The second aspect of the reform process was glasnost. Particularly influential in this regard was the course of historical investigation. Legitimised by Gorbachev's injunction that the 'blank spots' of Soviet history should be eliminated,[4] historians began to investigate what were previously prohibited areas of concern. The effect of this was to undermine any claim the party may have had to universal wisdom in its guidance of the regime and its development. Indeed, for many the moral authority of the party was undermined by the revelations about many of the darker chapters of Soviet history, and with this went the party's claim for primacy with regard to the ability to guide the society into the communist future. With its authority thus in question, the grounds upon which the continuing denial of the right of others to organise to pursue their interests were untenable.

But the importance of glasnost lay not only in the puncturing of the party's claims for infallibility. It was also important because of the injustices of the past which it brought to light and the stimulus this gave to the emergence of a public, even mass-based, form of political activity. Although not the first case of mass political disturbance,[5] the demonstration by the Crimean Tatars in Moscow in spring and summer 1987 was of particular importance. This demonstration, in Red Square, was not forcibly broken up, was given some coverage in the press, and resulted in the establishment of a commission headed by Andrei Gromyko to investigate their grievances. This implied that public demonstration was a legitimate mode of political activity, a legitimacy later grounded in a series of regulations designed to provide a legal basis for (and to restrict) this.[6] Furthermore this also created the precedent that people and groups who felt aggrieved at their treatment at the hands of the Moscow authorities could take to the streets to object to that treatment, even when the cause of their concern lay some time in the past. Following the example of the Crimean Tatars, groups across the country adopted the public demonstration as a method of expressing their views. By 1989 nationalist groups in particular were using this weapon on a large scale to press their cases.

The mass public demonstration became a potent form of protest, but it could only be effective in stimulating the development of a genuine competitive politics if some forms of organisational structures either arose out of or were strengthened by this public activity. The consolidation of such organisations did occur, with the popular fronts the best examples of this. These will be discussed below. Also significant were the informal groups more broadly conceived.

Informal groups

These were voluntary associations which sprang up, principally in cities, across the length and breadth of the country.[7] They began to emerge on a major scale in 1986–87, with *Pravda* in February 1988 estimating their number to be 30,000; by February 1989 the estimate had grown to more than 60,000.[8] However their roots lay in the Brezhnev period, with the emergence of various groups around particular issues, usually of an environmentalist or conservation nature. With the increased scope for popular activity evident in the second half of the 1980s, such group activity expanded significantly. Despite a measure of hostility from some official quarters, particularly at local levels, the range of informal groups expanded rapidly and their activities became more diverse. With the increased politicisation of society in 1988 and 1989, informal groups with a more explicitly political orientation became more prominent.[9]

The one common feature shared by all the informals is that they were to be found outside the traditional Soviet establishment; while many possessed personal links with that establishment, they emerged more from within society than as a result of formal initiatives from above. They were not mobilisational vehicles to be used by the authorities, but the mechanisms whereby groups of citizens sought to advance and defend their interests. This essential purpose was the commonality of these groups, while in terms of complexity of organisational structure, size and nature of membership, specific aims and methods adopted to pursue those aims, the groups varied enormously. Three broad categories of groups can be identified.[10]

The first type of group is that specifically designed to pursue the immediate personal interests of its members. Some of these were related to the members' hobbies or cultural interests – rock music, poetry, art, a healthy lifestyle and film clubs are examples of this sort. But others were linked with more direct material interests. Examples of this type of group include associations for defence of the rights of the disabled and groups of Afghan veterans. But even such organisations often were not without broader political ramifications. For example, the Initiative Group for the Defence of the Rights of Invalids (IGZPI) formed in Moscow was established under the aegis of the Moscow Helsinki Group and drew its intellectual sustenance from the commitment to human rights that was fundamental to that group. Similarly groups of Afghan veterans came together to assist one another in the often difficult transition back into civilian life, but their objectives soon became more expansive. Salang, the association of Afghantsy established in Latvia in April 1987, included among its aims 'the military-patriotic and international education of the youth (and) the struggle with negative phenomena in Soviet society'.[11] Such sentiments were often behind the reports of vigilante type actions taken by groups of Afghan veterans at different times in various parts of the Soviet Union.

The broader perspective that this type of outlook implies obscures the lines between the first type of informal group and the second, that which pursued an issue of more general popular interest. The range of such groups is enormous. Some were of merely local relevance, such as that seeking to change the name of the city from Zhdanov to Mariupol'. Others sought to advance general group interests; temperance societies, such as the Avrora club in Vladivostok and the Feniks club in Kazan', and pacifist groups such as Trust (Doverie) and Free Initiative (Svobodnaia Initsiativa), both of which actually date from 1982, in Moscow, together with the Lithuanian Pacifist Movement in Kapsukas, Lithuania are examples of this type. Some of these interests were of all-Union, and potentially political, significance.

One example of this type of concern was environmentalism. With their roots in the environmental activism that emerged during the Brezhnev period in some parts of the country, with the campaign to save Lake Baikal probably the most important aspect of this, a plethora of environmental or green groups emerged right across the Soviet Union. They appeared in the countryside, in small towns and in large cities. The Chernobyl disaster was an important factor both in stimulating environmental awareness and encouraging people to organise over environmental issues – the Kiev-based Noosfera is an example of such a body. Others emerged to combat specific local environmental problems, such as Ecology and Public Opinion in Pavlodar in Kazakhstan, which was formed in the course of protests against the construction of chemical factories and the Irkutsk-based Baikal Movement, which was originally concerned with the fate of Lake Baikal but then moved on to embrace the wider issues of environmentalism and development. This sort of concern clearly called into question the main thrust of governmental economic policy and the history of environmental degradation inherited from the recent past. This widening of concern was reflected in the tendency of many environmental groups to create linkages beyond their immediate locations. One pattern was for the affiliates of a group to be established in neighbouring areas: for example, groups of the Vladivostok-based Society of Ecological Action were established in Arsen'ev, Nakhodka, Dal'negorsk, Ussuriisk, Dal'nerechensk and Roshino. Another pattern was for the creation of a union designed to act as an umbrella for groups with such concerns; the Social-Ecological Union established in August 1987, with 140 groups from nine cities as members in 1989, is an example of this type. There was also an affiliate of Greenpeace in Ukraine.

The main forms of activity of the environmental groups were the organisation of meetings, demonstrations and petitions. Their aim was to raise popular awareness of environmental problems and to bring pressure to bear on the authorities in regard to these issues. However their longer-term importance may lie in the salience of environmental issues in a society that has suffered the extent of environmental degradation experienced in the Soviet Union. The green movement, and expansion of green consciousness, may be a potent foundation for political mobilisation in the future, just as it has been elsewhere in the former communist world.

Trade unions were another form of this type of organisation, seeking to unite workers across enterprises in defence of their rights. Some of these organisations dated back into the Brezhnev period: Free Trade Unions in Donetsk and led by Vladimir Klebanov following his release from a psychiatric institution in 1987 was founded in 1977 while the Moscow-based Free General Workers' Association (Svobodnoe Mezhprofessional'noe Ob"edinenie Trudiashchikhsia – SMOT) was established in 1978. All of the unofficial trade union organisations sought to provide an organisational umbrella for enterprise based groups which sought not only an expansion of workers' rights within the factory, but also the protection of their socio-economic interests during the proposed transition to a market-based economy and the actual economic difficulties experienced at this time. Organisation at the workplace, involving meetings, industrial activity and leafletting, was supplemented by some publishing activity: SMOT published a guide to informal groups in the USSR[12] while the Leningrad-based For the Democratisation of Trade Unions published a monthly magazine (entitled *Rubikon*). These organisations were really something of a hybrid between the clubs typical of the perestroika period and more broadly-based trade unions. Nevertheless, with the official trade union structure in difficulties as a result of its loss of authority, these organisations were well-placed to pick up the support of disaffected Soviet workers. Their potential in this regard was evident in the way in which in the miners' strike of summer 1989, independent pit-based trade union organs emerged and exercised real authority in the coal fields.

Another form of this type of informal group was that which sought to provide a means of defence for the ordinary citizen. At one level were those groups which emphasised the protection of human rights. Many of these, like the Initiative Group for the Rights of Man and Humanitarian Assistance in Voronezh, openly associated themselves with the Helsinki Declaration and used this as the legal basis upon which to press for the observance of human rights in the USSR. At another level were those groups which sought to offer legal assistance to citizens who fell foul of the law. The Committee of Social Defence (Komitet Sotsial'noi Zashchity) in Moscow, which was linked with SMOT and was represented in various cities, was an instance of this sort of organisation. A variant of this was organisations designed to look after the interests of those who had been politically detained. The Lvov-based Ukrainian Committee for Defence of the Politically Detained (Ukrainskii Komitet Zashchity Politzakliuchennykh) was one example of this.

A broader focus was to be found in one of the most important of the informal groups of this type, Memorial. The beginning of Memorial was action taken by a group of people who sought, through gathering signatures on a petition, to gain the erection of a memorial to the victims of Stalinist repression. By the time of the 19th Conference of the party in mid-1988, this effort had gained sufficient momentum to encourage that gathering, on Gorbachev's initiative, to approve of the construction of such a memorial. Shortly after, the body came officially into existence with the founding of the Memorial Society under the sponsorship of the USSR Unions of Cinema and Theatre Workers, Architects, Artists, and Designers, the magazine *Ogonek* and the newspaper *Literaturnaia gazeta*.[13] Memorial sought to maintain the pressure for the establishment of a centre to remember the victims of the Stalin era, both through the construction of a suitable memorial and through the gathering together of documentary materials relating to this period. By sponsoring meetings and encouraging both research and writing, Memorial sought to achieve its aims. But by far the most important step in its campaign was the so-called Week of Conscience held in November 1988. This was a public exhibition of designs for the proposed memorial complex, and constituted an important opportunity for all of those who had suffered either directly or indirectly under Stalinist repression to gather together, exchange information and give one another emotional support.[14]

Analogues of Memorial were established in many parts of the country,[15] but there does not appear to have been a significant linkage between these organisations. Nevertheless in those areas where the society was established, it pressed for the memory of those who had suffered under Stalin. Many of these groups sought to publish regular magazines, although the frequency with which they appeared is not clear. The impact of Memorial was important for the unrolling of the anti-Stalinism campaign and for propelling the discussion of Stalinism to the forefront of the reform process. Without such a discussion, the course of reform would have been significantly inhibited, and it is probable that without Memorial, that discussion would itself have been more restricted than it was to be in practice. Furthermore by projecting its appeal to the ordinary people in the street, Memorial rooted the re-evaluation of Stalinism in the populace as a whole and thereby ensured that it could not easily be dismissed by its undoubted foes.

Another form of this type of group was the patriotic society, which sought to unite people on the basis of feeling for their country. The stirrings of this sort of group can be seen in the growth under Brezhnev of a strong sentiment of Russian national feeling, reflected in the emergence of such groups as the All-Russian Society for the Preservation of Ancient Monuments in 1966. Indeed, Russian nationalists were prominent in the mobilisation of forces against the plans to divert some of the north-flowing Siberian rivers to provide irrigation for the monocultures of Central Asia during the last years of Brezhnev and the Andropov and Chernenko inter-regna. Their opposition was based in part on the destructive effect this project would have on parts of the traditional heartland of Russian culture. This linkage between ecological concerns and national sentiment was carried forward into the outlook of many of the patriotic groups that emerged during perestroika. The linkage had two strands. The first was the way in which environmental degradation can adversely affect the monuments and symbols of the culture; dirty factories and the pollution they produce can have a dire effect on the fabric of old buildings, as many Russian cities can attest. This concern was reflected in the description of the aims of one such group, Motherland (Rodina) in Cheliabinsk: 'It speaks out for the closure of ecologically hostile enterprises, for the protection of monuments.'[16] The second strand of the linkage reflects the place in national identity held by the natural environment. Among Russians in particular there is a very strong attachment to 'the Russian land', with both its wide expanses and its birch forests, an almost mystical link between nature and person. While this is evoked most fervently by avid patriots like Solzhenitsyn, it has some resonance with all Russians. Patriotism, love of country, has thus become closely associated with environmental concern; 'questions of ecology and culture'[17] are the staple fare of many patriotic groups.

The environment is not the only well-spring of patriotism. Religion has also been important, and this too is reflected in the outlook of some of the informal groups that arose during perestroika. For some, the linkage seems to have been one of cultural symbols, as relfected in the name of one such group in Kuibyshev (Samara): Za vosstanovlenie khramov (For the restoration of places of worship). Others, such as Vozrozhdenie (Rebirth) in Nizhnii Tagil, sought to restore the life of the religious community around the cathedral. But for others, what was important was the role religious values play in the regeneration of the national spirit and the definition of national identity and purpose. This orientation was clearly reflected in the aim of the Christian Patriotic Union in Moscow: 'the rebirth of the national self-consciousness of the Russian people on the basis of Orthodoxy.'[18] Unfortunately, the emphasis upon national self-consciousness has at times overflowed into a form of national exclusiveness. There may be a hint of this in one of the aims of the Moscow-based Rossiiskoe obshchestvo spravedlivosti (Russian society for justice), 'the granting to the peoples of Russia of equal rights with the peoples of the other republics of the USSR'.[19] But it has clearly been evident in the activities of Pamiat', an organisation with affiliates throughout the Soviet Union,[20] which has projected a rapid Russian chauvinism combined with virulent anti-semitism. Popular demonstrations, including physical violence to individual Jews and damage to Jewish property, have been a common form of activity encouraged by this organisation.

The reassertion of national identity has also been important in the non-Russian parts of the USSR. Sometimes this has been associated with an emphasis upon religion, where that religion was seen as part of the national identity and thereby as setting the people apart from the Russians.[21] More usually, the orientation of these groups has been towards fostering the development of the national culture, perhaps through the sponsoring of libraries and cultural centres, and through encouraging the use of those languages at the expense of Russian. In some cases, most particularly the Baltic republics, Belarus and Moldova, such groups were significant factors in the drive to reassert the primacy of the national language over Russian in dealings in the republic. The prominent role played by such groups in language issues, and the clear political ramifications of such issues, demonstrates the porous nature of the boundary between the second type of group, that pursuing issues of a general character, and the third type, which had specific political aims from the outset.

In broad terms, the politically oriented groups can be divided into two types, the national or popular fronts, and the more narrowly 'ideological' groups. This distinction is not clearly defined, and is least appropriate in Russia where the move for increased national autonomy or national independence, which became the focus of popular front activity in the non-Russian republics, was less easy to sustain, with the result that ideology was likely to be more significant than it would otherwise have been. In the non-Russian republics, the aim of increased autonomy/independence meant that ideological differences were less salient; political activists tended to subordinate such differences in the interests of the higher goal. In such cases, the front really was a broad-based umbrella group in which individual differences were forgotten in the interests of unity the better to achieve the ultimate aim.

Popular fronts

The popular fronts first emerged during 1988, mainly in the middle of the year or in the second half, following the 19th Party Conference. The main stimulus for their emergence was the party conference, and in particular the struggle between pro- and anti-perestroika forces that was being conducted in the leadup to the conference, at that assembly and in its aftermath. This origin is reflected in the names adopted by many of the fronts or by the committees that were formed to organise the fronts: Popular Front for Perestroika (Kostroma), Popular Front for Revolutionary Perestroika (Cheliabinsk), Initiative Group for the Popular Front for Perestroika (Vinnitsa), the Moldovan Democratic Movement in Support of Perestroika and Initiative Committee for the Establishment of a Popular Front in Support of Perestroika (L'vov) were typical of the names used. The front was seen as an umbrella organisation designed to mobilise and unite forces in society in support of perestroika to counteract the opposition from within the political apparatus. The first aim of the Estonian Popular Front was declared to be: 'with the assistance of the masses of people, who have joined together to support the CPSU's policy of restructuring, to stop any attempt to retard the process of democratization and development of openness in the Estonian SSR; to be a social guarantor of the renewal of society'.[22] The Front proposed to play an important role in actually implementing the changes in society which is beleved perestroika implied. It did not, there-fore, see itself purely as a subordinate, supportive body, but as a movement which could independently hasten the changes that were seen as necessary.

The political crisis which spawned the popular fronts, a crisis whose importance at the time was interpreted principally in terms of the struggle for the election of reformist conference delegates, was crucial because it legitimised independent socio-political organisation and the appeal to it in the course of political struggle. It thereby expanded the political arena and the number of actors who could play a part in it. The politicisation of society that this involved began processes which were to lead to the radicalisation of Soviet politics generally and of the positions taken up by many of the popular fronts, particularly in the non-Russian republics.

The emergence of the popular fronts was not always an easy process. By 1988 it was widely recognised among unofficial politically aware circles that a new form of organisational vehicle was necessary if the informal groups were to have a major impact upon the course of events. The informals largely retained their club-like appearance, with all of the limitations that implied: restricted membership and limited vision. They needed to be able to expand their membership, and with this their policy focus, but in order to achieve this they had to enlarge their organisational infrastructure. The most expeditious means of doing this was to unite existing groups around a common programme.[23] In the non-Russian republics, the focus of such a programme initially was the assertion of national autonomy within a confederated USSR, although this often soon gave way to demands for full independence: one of the aims of the Estonian Popular Front was 'to make the Popular Front a true mouthpiece of the will of the Estonian People, while recognizing the right of the people to self-determination'.[24] This aim was sufficient to weld together the different groups and enable them to forget their differences.

The most significant front movements emerged in the Baltic republics. The Estonian Popular Front had first emerged in June 1988[25] and held its official founding congress in October, at which it adopted a charter of aims and principles of organisational structure. In Latvia an initiative group consisting of representatives of labour collectives and social and religious groups was formed in June which convened a constituent congress in October at which the Latvian Popular Front was created. This congress adopted a programme and organisational rules, and elected a leadership. In Lithuania an initiative group was formed in June and this convened a congress in November at which Sajudis, or to give it its formal title the Lithuanian General Movement for Perestroika, was launched. The congress adopted a programme and organisational rules for the movement, and elected a leadership.[26] The fronts grew rapidly: by October 1988 more than 1,500 support groups had registered as participants in the Estonian Popular Front, while by February 1989 the Latvian Popular Front united nearly 230,000 people and Sajudis nearly 180,000 people.[27]

The strength and importance of the Popular Fronts expanded significantly over the eighteen months following their formation. This was in part a natural function of the way these bodies seemed to embody the aspirations for national independence which had long been just below the surface of the population. They also gained assistance from sympathisers within the official governmental and administrative apparatus, a factor which was very important because it meant that the official hostility encountered elsewhere was qualified somewhat by this more supportive approach. But also important in the rise of these movements was the erosion of the authority of the Communist Party, as reflected in the election to the Congress of People's Deputies in March 1989. The rejection of many leading party figures at the polls, including the decimation of the official leadership of Leningrad, laid bare the limits of the party's authority throughout the country. More specifically, in the Baltic republics the popular fronts worked actively during the election campaign, with the result that when the votes were counted, front representatives dominated the delegates returned to the Congress; party members who gained election were largely only those who had gained front support.

Following these successes, the fronts continued to gather strength, principally through spearheading the drive for independence which became such an important feature of the radicalisation of Soviet politics during 1989–90. Local support groups were established, the front's message continued to be projected through their newspapers and the newsletters of local groups, and the three fronts sought to coordinate their activities through their own centre, the Baltic Council. The strength of their position was clearly demonstrated by the results of the republican elections in February-March 1990: in all three republics, the popular fronts formed governments, even if in Estonia reliance had to be had on allies. As the issue of independence became more prominent during the following months and pressure from Moscow increased on the Baltic governments following their respective declarations of independence, the positions of the popular fronts, legitimised by their governing roles, were strengthened.

In the Baltic republics, the popular fronts were thus able to rise to a position of dominance. Swept along by the pressure for national independence, pressure to which they contributed significantly, and exploiting the weak domestic roots of communist party authority, they became the leading political organisations in their respective republics.[28] Their dominance was shown not only in the governing positions they were able to achieve, but in the way in which their actions were instrumental in producing splits in the republican communist parties in late 1989-early 1990. The momentum of the drive for independence plus the pressures imposed upon them from outside the republics were important factors in helping to maintain the unity of the popular front coalitions. Similar factors were also at work in some of the other republics; Moldova, Belarus and Ukraine all experienced powerful nationally-based front movements.[29] But where such factors were absent, most particularly in Russia, the efforts to construct a powerful popular front movement have been less successful.

At the same time that popular fronts began to emerge in the Baltic republics, initiative groups were formed in many parts of Russia, including Kostroma, Pskov, Rybinsk, Yaroslavl', Sverdlovsk, Stavropol', Chelyabinsk, Moscow, Leningrad, Irkutsk, and Kazan'.[30] Despite the clear agreement by many of the politically active in the cities of Russia about the utility of the popular front form of organisation, no effective nationwide popular front along Baltic lines emerged. In part this was a problem of size, scale, and consequently logistics and communications. But also important was the diversity of views shared by those participating in the movements to form popular fronts and the absence of the welding effect of external challenges and overriding aims such as those which operated in the Baltic region.

Although the extent of the diversity of views has not always been as great as it was among those seeking to form the Moscow Popular Front,[31] the experience of Moscow was not unique.[32] In June 1988 a meeting of independent socialist groups met to discuss the forthcoming party conference. Eighteen of these groups decided to band together to form a temporary Organising Committee for the Popular Front. In the following months, other groups joined the Committee, bringing its number to thirty by February 1989.[33] However the discussions designed to work out a programme and rules for the Front were characterised by numerous ideological and political differences between the member groups. In the words of one participant, Boris Kagarlitsky: 'Although a majority of the committee's members viewed the new organization as a broad association of left-wing forces under the slogans of self-management and democratic socialism, a minority dreamt of a "union of all democrats irrespective of ideological differences". The principled differences between these two tendencies on the most important questions of the development of the social movement had always existed . . . As soon as normal work commenced in the organizing committee, the differences immediately came to the surface.'[34] Clearly there were ideological differences between the various groups involved in the Front, but there was also tension as a result of the 'personal ambitions of the leaders of the movement',[35] particularly over whether the Front should function as an umbrella organisation for the individual groups or clubs, or whether they should submerge their individual identities in a much tighter organised structure. Despite the disagreement and debate, agreement was reached on a draft programme, and the foundation conference of the Front was held on 20 May 1989. Although it too was the scene of considerable argument and dispute, from its proceedings the Moscow Popular Front officially emerged.

The course of development of the Moscow Popular Front had been marked by considerable doctrinal debate and argument. It has nevertheless been able to expand its popular support in the capital and its members played a part in the 1989 elections; one member, future deputy mayor of Moscow Sergei Stankevich, even gained election to the Congress of People's Deputies.[36] However it could not become the force in the capital that its counterparts in the Baltic were able to be. In part this was because of the greater hostility shown towards it by the city authorities during 1988–9. But also important was the diversity of views within the Moscow political spectrum. This was reflected not only within the ranks of the Popular Front movement itself, but also in the range of political groups that emerged to challenge the Front for popular support.

Nascent political parties

Politically oriented groups had emerged in many areas during 1988, reflecting the conviction shared by many of the need to mobilise to defend perestroika. It was this conviction which mobilised many of the formerly apolitical associations and discussion clubs into continuing political activity. The names of many of these organisations, such as Committee to Aid Perestroika (Krasnoiarsk), Democratic Initiative (Magadan), Moscow Tribune and Elections 89 all suggest an overt political activism that was previously less apparent. Such activism included the sponsoring of broad-based discussion, participation in electoral activity and organisation of demonstrations. Some, recognising the limitations imposed by their size, tried to organise into broader associations, like the Federation of Socialist Clubs. This included such groups as Commune, Civic Dignity, Alliance, Che Guevara, Socialist Initiative, Social Democrats and the anarcho-syndicalists. Despite such umbrella organisations, these groups remained essentially small clubs.

But alongside these emerged a variety of groups which conceived of themselves not as informal organisations or political discussion clubs, but as political parties.[37] Reflecting the diversity of views in the society, these parties adopted positions that stretched right across the political spectrum. This can be illustrated by a survey of some of the parties emerging at the end of the 1980s.

1. The Democratic Union was founded in May 1988.[38] There has been much uncertainty about whether this should be classed as a political party or as an informal group umbrella organisation seeking to unite all democratic forces under its aegis. However according to a handbook of informal groups, it considered itself an opposition party and possessed such 'party attributes' as 'congresses, party cards, a programme, records, rules, declarations, announcements, fractions and candidate status.'[39] The Union had affiliates throughout the Soviet Union, but it is not clear how closely these were linked. At the time of its foundation it supported what would be considered traditional liberal positions in the West, including a multi-party system, a mixed economy, the rule of law and respect for human rights. It rejected any cooperation with or continuing role for the CPSU and, because of its refusal to acknowledge that the Soviet regime had any legitimacy at all, declined to participate in the electoral process.[40] The main form of its activity seems to have been popular demonstrations, and it was a major competitor of the more socialist-inclined Popular Front in Moscow.[41]

2. The Christian Democratic Union was established in August 1989.[42] At its foundation formally it stood for a parliamentary democracy, multi-party system, separation of powers, free elections, a mixed economy, self-

determination, and a peaceful non-expansive foreign policy. The party established strong links with the broader Christian Democratic movement in Europe, but also sought to build links with other democratic parties in the country.

3. The Russian Christian Democratic Movement was founded in March 1990. Formally it supported the same sort of democratic agenda[43] as the Christian Democratic Union, but it seems to have favoured a larger role for the church in society. It sought to expand its links with democratic forces in Soviet society, and thus decided at its second congress in October 1990 to join 'Democratic Russia' (see below).

4. The Union of Constitutional Democrats announced its creation in October 1989 and held its first congress in May 1990. It claimed to be the continuation of the pre-revolutionary Kadets[44] and emphasised the rule of law and human rights, an active and educated citizenry, a democratic political system and a mixed economy.[45] The Union seems to have had close links with the Democratic Union.[46]

5. The Orthodox Constitutional Monarchist Party of Russia was founded at a conference in May 1990. The party sought restoration of the monarchy through the election of a member of the Romanov dynasty by a Zemskii *sobor* or Assembly of the Land, the preservation of the Russian empire and return of the land to the peasants. It sought the rejection of all of the alien distortions introduced into society by the Bolsheviks and the restoration of the pre-1917 order, including the dominating role of the church.[47] The party will accept only Orthodox Christians as members and seems to have had close links with the Orthodox Church.

6. The Social Democratic Party of Russia held its first congress in May 1990 and its second in October. The party programme worked out through discussions at these congresses borrowed significantly from abroad and, reflecting the contemporary domestic situation, emphasised the problems, especially for workers, involved in the transition to a market economy. Many party members reject Marxism. The party has sought to establish close links with the Social Democratic movement abroad and, through joining 'Democratic Russia', the democratic forces in the USSR.[48]

7. The Democratic Party of Russia held its founding congress in June 1990. Formed principally by people who left the CPSU, the party took up an explicitly anti-communist position. It supported a market economy based on private property and the convocation of a constituent assembly which would make a clean break with the Soviet past and establish a 'sovereign Democratic Republic of Russia'.[49] The party saw its task to be to consolidate all democratic forces in Russia with a view to assisting in the transition from a single-party to a multi-party democratic system. Its organisational structure was therefore very loose, and in April 1990 it split.[50]

8. The Socialist Party held its founding congress in June 1990.[51] While maintaining a commitment to socialism, the party recognised the need for a mixed economy, but emphasised the importance of workers' control and of guarantees for the workers during the transition towards the market. The party sought to maintain strong links with socialist forces both inside and outside the USSR.

9. The Republican Party of Russia was established at a founding congress in November 1990. The impetus came from members of the former Democratic Platform in the CPSU, the leader of which announced their departure from the party following the 28th Congress in July. The party, which had branches in many parts of the country, advocated a mixed economy, political pluralism and guarantees of social and political rights. At the founding congress, there was a strong sentiment favouring a merger with the Social Democratic Party of Russia.[52]

This survey of some of the parties that emerged in Russia gives some idea of the range of different views represented on the new political scene. But this constitutes only a fraction of the party groups that announced their existence towards the end of the 1980s and the early 1990s (see table 8.1). Independence parties emerged in most republics, green parties have been common, in Moslem areas there have been parties explicitly associating themselves with Islam, while Christian Democratic and Social Democratic parties have emerged in many republics.[53] But does the existence of this multitude of parties reflect the emergence of a multi-party system?

A multi-party system?

The legal basis for a multi-party system was not created until 1990 when two crucial measures were introduced. The first was the March elimination of the Communist Party's monopoly from Article 6 from the Constitution. This article had enshrined the party's dominant position in all walks of Soviet life, and it was replaced by a provision which declared: 'The Communist Party of the Soviet Union, other political parties, as well as trade union, youth, and other public organisations and mass movements participate in shaping the policies of the Soviet state and in running state and public affairs through their representatives elected to the soviets of people's deputies and in other ways.'[54] This legalised the principle of non-communist parties. The second measure was the Law on Public Associations adopted in October.[55] This law established the mechanism whereby political parties and other organisations could gain the status of juridical persons, thereby enabling them legally to engage in such activities essential to their purposes as conclusion of contracts with printing houses, rental of premises, acquisition of copying equipment, opening of bank accounts,

Table 8.1. *Political parties in the Russian Federation, 1992*

Date of regn	Name of party	No. of members at regn
14 March 1991	Democratic Party of Russia	28,608
	Social-Democratic Party of the Russian Federation	5,089
	Republican Party of the Russian Federation	over 5,000
12 April 1991	Peasant Party of Russia	2,143
6 June 1991	Russian Christian Democratic Movement Party	6,027
18 Sept. 1991	People's Party of Free Russia	5,233
25 Sept. 1991	Russian Christian-Democratic Party	2,356
	People's Party of Russia	1,318
	Constitutional-Democratic Party	2,079
4 Nov. 1991	Russian Bourgeois-Democratic Party	1,771
19 Nov. 1991	Russian Party of Democratic Transition	637
21 Nov. 1991	Socialist Workers' Party	2,500
9 Dec. 1991	Russian Party of Free Labour	1,734
	Russian Christian-Democratic Union	1,395
9 Jan. 1992	Russian Communist Workers' Party	over 6,000
15 Jan. 1992	Conservative Party	1,399
	Party of Constitutional Democrats of the Russian Federation	660
	National-Republican Party of Russia	5,037
23 Jan. 1992	European Liberal-Democratic Party	5,890
17 Jan. 1992	Free Democratic Party of Russia	1,696
20 Feb. 1992	'New Left' Political Party	115
10 March 1992	Republican Humanitarian Party	139
12 March 1992	Russian Social-Liberal Party	348
19 March 1992	Russian Party of Communists	over 2,900
25 June 1992	Party of Economic Freedom	662

Source: Argumenty i fakty, 1992, no. 24, p. 8.

possession of foreign currency, and operation of their own newspapers. All public associations had to be registered. To gain registration, an organisation had to present its statutes, minutes of its founding meeting, details of its aims, and the names and addresses of members of its executive for scrutiny by the relevant authority. For registration at the all-union level, an organisation needed 5,000 members. Registration could be refused if an association's statutes were at variance with the provisions of the law. In practice, registration proceeded slowly;[56] by August 1991 only the CPSU and the Liberal Democratic Party had gained registration at the all-union level. Many people were suspicious that the party apparatus was using this as a means of hindering the emergence of viable political parties. However it is not clear that the failure to register has substantially hindered any particular group in pursuing its political aims.

The legalisation of political parties and the removal of the Communist Party's monopoly alone were insufficient to produce a workable party system. The parties themselves had to develop as coherent institutional structures but, at least in the early stages, they were little different from the informal groups. In essence, the difference between these two types of organisation rested in the more general political conditions and the need to come to grips with them. The informal groups emerged when the principle of the leading role of the Communist Party remained intact. This dictated a political strategy of discussion and popular mobilisation in an attempt both to raise political consciousness and to place pressure upon the ruling party. The notion of the club, which was at the heart of many of the informal groups, was appropriate for this task, at least in the early stages. However with the erosion of the party's authority becoming clear from early 1989, political activists no longer had to think purely in terms of placing pressure on the communist rulers; the replacement of them was now on the political agenda. A broader organisation was needed for the displacement of the communist rulers.

The party form was seen as the most appropriate vehicle for this because it accorded with the democratic sensitivities, and the corresponding principle of the replacement of leaders through the electoral process, that were central to the expressed outlook of much of the informal movement. In some cases, voters' associations acted as a form of halfway house toward the creation of parties. In the leadup to the 1990 elections (and therefore before a multi-party system was rendered possible by the modification of Article 6 of the Soviet Constitution) many organisations sought to establish independent voters' clubs, gain official registration and nominate their own candidates. In the autumn of 1989, a number of these clubs came together to form the Moscow Association of Voters which published its own information bulletin and sought to organise the campaigns of the democratic candidates in the city. In the short term, then, the parties did not develop as radically different organisations from the informal groups that were their precursors. For this to occur, a genuine multi-party system had to emerge, and this required the parties to develop the organisational capacity to operate effectively in the three arenas of which such a system would consist, grassroots organisation in the streets, in electoral competition, and in the legislative chamber.

The parties have differed significantly among themselves. The size and nature of memberships and support groups are uncertain, although most leading figures seem to have come from the intelligentsia; Nikolai Travkin of the Democratic Party of Russia, an engineer and construction manager, is one exception to this rule. Most leading figures also seem to have spent some time in the CPSU in earlier years, some in full-time positions in the apparatus. Given the role the CPSU played for so long as the only vehicle for political activity on the part of those with political interests, this pedigree should not be surprising. Information on the membership is impressionistic and contradictory. The size of the parties has tended to be small,[57] perhaps reflecting the disillusionment with party activity stemming from popular experience of the CPSU. One observer believes that the parties draw their memberships principally from the intelligentsia, a belief which is consistent with the view that although there are parties which are oriented toward certain economic interests, the linkages between material interest and party affiliation are really quite weak.[58] However the co-operatives have been reported to be a source of support for the Constitutional Democrats, while professionals, cooperative members, entrepreneurs and businessmen are said to support the Free Labour Party.[59] Figures cited for the Democratic Union suggest that 30 per cent of its members are blue-collar workers, 28 per cent white-collar workers, 20 per cent students, 2 per cent peasants and 20 per cent others.[60] Such information is too sketchy to reach reliable conclusions about the social basis of the parties' existence. But if the view that they are principally the vehicles for political activity by the intelligentsia is correct, the social basis of party political activity is very narrow.

The organisational resources available to the parties has varied significantly. Some, like the Christian Democrats and Social Democrats, would be likely to secure financial and material assistance from allies abroad, even though the Law on Public Associations specifically forbade this.[61] Others have been able to gain access to resources generated from within the USSR. The Russian Christian Democratic Movement has gained funds through the operations of cooperatives, publications and trade, chiefly through the activities of one of its principals, Viktor Aksiuchits, while the Democratic Party of Russia was given office space by the soviet in the Oktiabr'skii district in Moscow. The Social Democrats have relied upon membership dues, the sale of publications and some income from the cooperative sector.[62] Despite problems in gaining access to printing facilities and paper supplies, many parties have been able to publish their own newspapers. These have appeared with different degrees of regularity, have often been poorly reproduced and have not been available through the regular newspaper outlets. Print runs are clearly insufficient to sustain an organisation with national aspirations, and the distribution system is inadequate.[63] Although many parties claimed to have branches spread across the country, the paucity of resources and the inadequate communications infrastructure has severely restricted their capacity to generate a coherent national party structure to rival that formerly possessed by the CPSU. The creation of a nation-wide organisational structure was also hampered by the increasing stridency of independence sentiments in the republics, by frequent disagreements within the parties over organisational matters,[64] and by the propensity to devote greater attention to debating ideological questions rather than building an effective party structure.

Despite the attention devoted to ideological questions, another problem these parties have faced in developing as coherent and powerful entities has been the lack of distinctiveness of the programmes many of them espoused. A glance at the short descriptions of the outlooks of many of the parties given above will show that there has been significant commonality within the range from right-wing monarchist to socialist.[65] A large number of parties have labelled themselves 'democratic', supported parliamentary democracy and a multi-party system, a market-based economy and the elimination of the communist system. However, few have developed the sort of highly-detailed specific legislative programmes that would provide a real guide to their intentions were they to gain control of government. This means that ideological and policy differences have shaded into one another, and that the basis of partisan affiliation has often been more personalistic than ideological.

Leaders have played a significant role in the emergence of the parties and the definition of their outlooks. Although none of the main groupings of deputies in the country's legislative chambers,[66] such as the liberal Inter-Regional Group of Deputies[67] and the conservative Soiuz group, acted as the nucleus for a political party, it is striking how many of the leading figures in the parties were people's deputies either at the national or republican level.[68] The importance of membership of the legislature has lain not in the ability of these people to emerge as parliamentary leaders, because there has been no party system emerging clearly in the legislative chambers, but in the opportunity that such membership gave them to emerge as national figures.[69] This combination of similar ideological positions and often strong leader personalities has constituted a danger for the development of strong parties. Where parties are clearly ideologically different, unification is not on the agenda and the parties and their leaders can concentrate on pursuing their policies. Where the parties are not clearly distinguished, pressures for unification will inevitably increase, and where strong personalities are involved, there will be a reluctance to accept a subordinate position. The result is likely to be heightened conflict, ostensibly focused upon ideological nuances. Such conflict has been responsible for the splitting of many parties[70] and the debilitation of the democratic movement in general.

In the early stages of their emergence, the parties also had to contend with some opposition on the part of the CPSU and its apparatus. Publicly, the communist party's attitude to the informals, and later the parties, was ambiguous: support for the contribution they were making to perestroika and glasnost along with criticism for what were perceived to be unacceptable activities. At various times such activities were deemed to include overt criticism of the system under the guise of democracy, criticism of the CPSU and its leaders, and organised opposition.[71] This sort of stance, positive but critical, reflects less a clearly formulated policy towards informal groups than the tensions within the party regarding the whole process of perestroika, with the more conservative elements taking a more negative line towards the informals.[72] Initially, too, it was hoped that the informals could be kept under control; the fostering of the popular fronts was clearly designed to provide a framework within which the activities of the informal groups could be encapsulated and contained.[73] With the modification of Article 6 and the consequent acceptance of a multi-party system, the CPSU's formal position became one of seeking cooperation and dialogue with those organisations whose aims were not incompatible with its own; special sections were to be established in party organisations to facilitate such contacts.[74]

But despite this formal acknowledgement of the need for cooperation, at a practical level the new parties were often confronted with opposition on the part of party officials. In some areas party officials used the power they possessed over registration and access to facilities such as premises and printing equipment to frustrate the activities of the emerging parties. Party leaders also tried to hinder the development of new parties by such measures as infiltration of existing organisations, fostering alternative groups to oppose those they perceive to be a challenge,[75] attacks in the media and the forcible break up of meetings. But the main tactic seems to have been one of encouraging party members to join informal groups to render them more sympathetic to the party, the establishment of discussion clubs to maintain a dialogue between the groups and the party,[76] and the mounting of greater efforts on the part of the party to understand the groups.[77] Clearly the emergence of powerful new parties has been hindered by a reluctance on the part of sections of the CPSU to see its traditional position challenged.

But part of the problem of the weakness of the emergent parties has been the absence of a clearly defined arena, with rules to structure interaction within which the parties could develop. There has as yet been no effective multi-party system through the operation of which partisan strengths could be measured and the prize of government attained. It is through competition in such an arena that parties are forced to work out their programmes and positions, make adjustments according to electoral contingencies, and build up their support among the populace. The key to this is the emergence of a truly competitive electoral system which, through the regular competition for votes, enables parties to develop their structures and regularise their processes. While two sets of elections have been held across the country since the beginning of 1989, for the national Congress of People's Deputies and for the republican assemblies, in neither did the individual parties have the time to prepare well-considered campaigns. Nor was there the basic infrastructure necessary to create the conditions for adequate competition: such things as access to printing facilities and the media, difficulties placed in the way of party candidates by local electoral officials, a lack of cooperation by some local authorities (which controlled meeting venues), and the inability of parties to gain registration and thereby to legally campaign for office ensured that party competition was partial and unsatisfactory.

Despite such problems, non-CPSU candidates were widely successful. But the results, at least in the Russian Federation and Georgia, reflect the problem of size faced by the parties. In elections in both republics, majorities were gained not by any single party but by blocs of parties. In Moscow, in the 1990 elections, the Democratic Russia bloc, which united a number of the democratic parties (including the Democratic Party of Russia, the Social Democratic Party, the Russian Christian Democratic Movement, the Democratic Platform of the CPSU, and various non-party social-political associations like Memorial and the writers' club Aprel'[78]), won fifty-five of the sixty-five seats allotted to the Moscow area in the RSFSR Congress of People's Deputies and 263 of the 465 seats in the Moscow city soviet. Democratic Russia was not a party, but a bloc of parties, something like the popular fronts. In the words of one observer in July 1990: 'It is very amorphous, very diffuse and doesn't have any unified directing organs. But nonetheless it represents a distinct political reality. It doesn't have a formal organisational structure, but it does have leaders. And even though there are programmatic differences within it, Democratic Russia does have a common orientation and common postulates.'[79] The success of Democratic Russia shows that the multitude of small, ideologically similar parties need to combine if they are to have a major impact on the course of events. Similarly in Georgia, victory in the 1990 election went to the Round Table, a coalition of seven groups: the Helsinki Union, the Society of St Ilia the Righteous, the Merab Kostava Society, the Union of Georgian Traditionalists, the Popular Front Radical Union, the Liberal Democratic Union and the National Christian Party.[80] Clearly no single group was strong enough to win a majority alone. Recognition of the weakness resulting from the small size of the parties may be reflected in the moves to systematise Democratic Russia through greater rigour about its programme and the establishment of continuing organs.[81] It is also reflected in the fact that, apart from the CPSU, the main opposition to Democratic Russia was the conservative Bloc of Russian Public-Patriotic Movements.

The lesson of these two elections is clear: no party was able in its present state to attain the sort of majority which would deliver stable government following a free and fair election. Through the development of electoral alliances, like Democratic Russia and Round Table, and through conferences of like-minded groups designed to bring about greater unanimity of outlook and structure,[82] the multitude of parties may be able to sort themselves out into fewer, larger, more effective party structures. Without this, a multi-party system would only generate instability and continued conflict.

The third arena crucial for the development of a viable multi-party system, the legislative arena, was also weak in the USSR. Although new legislative organs had been established at the all-union and republican levels, and while these acted as major fora for criticism of the government, they did not act as the incubators of effective parliamentary parties. The electoral unity created by adherence to organisations like Democratic Russia was rarely carried into the chamber, with deputies often preferring to unite along regional rather than policy lines. Furthermore with the emergence of presidential rule and the expansion of presidential powers, legislatures lost their role as generators of a legislative programme and were reduced to a mainly reactive role, responding to the initiatives of the president. As a result there was no pressure on individual groups within the legislature to formulate clear and consistent policy positions. Nor were there effective rules of procedure and standing orders for the structuring of activity within the legislature which could facilitate the emergence of coherent parliamentary party structures. The legislative arena was therefore not a positive force for the emergence of a viable multi-party system.

The dramatic changes brought to what was then the Soviet Union by the August 1991 coup had implications for the emergence of multi-party competition. Territorial disintegration changed the arena within which individual parties sought to act and gave a boost to those which sought to associate themselves with nationalist goals. It also made the former republican legislative arenas more prominent and banished the former all-union structure of legislative deliberation. The collapse of the CPSU removed a major barrier to effective party development and competition, although it also removed one of the key sources of unity for other partisan groups, opposition to communist dominance; this was one factor in the splits in Democratic Russia in early 1992.[83] The collapse of the CPSU also led to the emergence of a number of newer party groups as the old party structure spawned many splinter organisations bearing new names but often the old faces. However in the larger former republics, particularly Russia, the collapse of the all-union framework did not make the generation of a national party organisation significantly easier; problems of distance, communications and logistics remained. Nor, given the continued primacy of presidential rule, albeit challenged by pressures for enhanced parliamentary power from within the Russian legislature, did it lead to the increased authority and effectiveness of legislative organs. Indeed, with many of these retaining substantial communist representation, they were increasingly widely seen as being irrelevant to current problems and in need of substantial renewal.

The key to the emergence of a viable multi-party system is the generation by those parties of a national structure that can sustain regular electoral competition, generate meaningful policies and sustain parliamentary representatives. What is also needed is a political system in which such parties can play a positive role. They must be able to perform in the streets, in electoral competition and in the legislative arena. This requires major organisational improvements in the parties themselves and the generation of new, effective constitutional structures that can gain the confidence of the populace. This in turn makes it likely that the development of a truly competitive political system will depend upon the resolution of the other crises that wracked the states that had formerly constituted the Soviet Union in the early 1990s.

9   The politics of economic interests

An important characteristic of the transition from Soviet to post-Soviet politics has been the rise of new types of interest groups that have sought to influence the political process – in particular, policies connected with economic reform. This, together with the slow rise of political parties, represents an important stage in the democratic development of the republics that formerly made up the Soviet Union. Newly created business associations as well as new and reconfigured trade unions are the most important of these groups. The new structures can be viewed in contradictory ways. On the one hand, interest groups are an integral part of civil society, and economic interests should have the same rights to organise as any other group in society. Through these groups, economic forces that are vital to the development of a market economy and a democratic polity are represented in the policymaking process. On the other hand, economic interest groups pose a danger to new democratic institutions because of the potential influence of money, the ability to organise strikes, and the use of other methods to insure favourable treatment.

In the Soviet period, certain branches of the economy had powerful spokesmen in top decision-making bodies in both the Communist Party and the government. The interests of heavy industry and, in particular, military industry had long been dominant at all levels of policy making. There was necessarily a role for such groups as industrial managers, collective farm chairmen, and the trade unions in economic policy making, and they accumulated a great deal of power at the local level by virtue of their control over material resources.

The primary weakness in the past of institutions that could have performed the role of interest groups was that they lacked independence from the Communist Party. They often did not have separate organisational structures that would allow them to coalesce and advance group interests. Leaders of the trade unions, professional groups, and other organisations were appointed through the party *nomenklatura*. While unions and other groups did much more than perform the function of so-called 'transmission belts' – meaning the relaying of centrally determined policies to different

164

sectors of society – party control placed limits on the expression of group interests.[1]

As the locus of policymaking shifted away from the Communist Party and toward legislatures, city councils, and other elected bodies, economic interests began to organise in ways that would permit them to influence policy decisions. This chapter will focus on two groups that have been most successful in these efforts – industrialists and entrepreneurs.

Industrialists

It would be misleading to argue that enterprise managers represented a coherent interest group in the context of the radical transformation underway in the late Soviet and early post-Soviet period; in fact there were sharp divisions among business interests and managers. The most significant division was between so-called 'industrialists' (*promyshlenniki*) and 'entrepreneurs' (*predprinimateli*), though the terms were not always applied consistently. By industrialists were meant the managers of what remained of state-owned enterprises. Many of these managers were openly opposed to the type of liberal economic reform advanced by Yeltsin's reform government headed in 1992 by the economist Yegor Gaidar and endorsed by the International Monetary Fund. Industrialists, used to working under the conditions of a centrally managed economy, sought a continuation of important elements of the Soviet economy: the state-managed supply system and government subsidies or easy credit not connected with performance. They opposed new laws that would require enterprises to be profitable or declare themselves bankrupt. Government, in their view, should play an active role in setting priorities and give favoured treatment to those sectors. Conservative industrialists also opposed privatisation except for those forms that would allow them a considerable role, preferably by granting management a controlling share of stocks. They generally opposed Yeltsin's use of privatisation vouchers as a strategy for creating new owners of the means of production.

Industrialists had a built-in political advantage in that many of their number had been elected to the USSR Congress of People's Deputies in 1989 and to republic parliaments and local soviets in 1990. They were able to use this representation to engage in direct lobbying for their interests. A group of around 215 deputies in the Soviet parliament formed the 'Scientific-Industrial Group', one of the largest and most cohesive blocs in the Soviet parliament. It was chiefly responsible, for example, for drafting the 1990 Soviet law on entrepreneurial activity.[2] Managers of enterprises made up a substantial share of the body of deputies in republican parliaments as well; of deputies chosen in the 1990 elections, managers comprised around 21 per cent in Russia, 13 per cent in Ukraine, 22 per cent in Kyrgyzstan, 25 per cent in Georgia and Moldova, and 39 per cent in Tajikistan.[3] At the local level, managers were even better represented in certain cities and provinces. During the 1990 election in the central Russian region of Perm', for example, enterprise managers and other members of the economic elite aggressively sought and obtained the status of the political elite.[4]

In the Russian Congress of People's Deputies a group of about seventy-two deputies, mostly managers of state enterprises, formed the Industrial Union (*Promyshlennyi Soiuz*), one of the largest such groups in the Russian parliament.[5] It was generally acknowledged that the most effective lobby in the Russian parliament was the industrial lobby. In late 1992 deputies from the Industrial Union fraction were successful in getting the state bank, which was subordinate to the parliament and not part of the government, to extend new credits to state enterprises that were already heavily in debt. Industrialists and union leaders who were deputies frequently worked together in the Russian parliament to lobby for their interests, both in floor debates, parliamentary commissions, and in the corridors. Managers and labour leaders, for example, helped draft and make changes in the March 1992 Law on Collective Agreements, a basic element of labour law that defines relations between management and an enterprise's employees.

Industrialists organised a number of extra-parliamentary associations to advance their interests in the late Soviet and early post-Soviet period. The president of one of the most conservative of these groups, A. Tiziakov of the Association of State Enterprises and Associations in Industry, Construction, Transportation, and Communications, joined leaders of the State Emergency Committee which attempted the coup of August 1991.[6]

By far the largest and most powerful of the associations of industrialists in the Soviet period was the Scientific-Industrial Union (*Nauchno-promyshlennyi soiuz* or *NPS*) headed by Arkadii Vol'sky. Vol'sky was previously chief of the Machine-Building Department in the CPSU Central Committee, and he spent most of his career in the party apparatus – including service as an economic adviser to Andropov.[7] The NPS was formed on the initiative of twenty-four deputies in the USSR Congress of People's Deputies in May 1990, who saw the need for increased horizontal ties between enterprises as the system of ministries began to fall apart. The close links between the NPS and the Soviet government were underscored when Vol'sky organised an 'All-Union Congress of Directors' in March 1991 that was attended by over 1,300 managers from all branches of the economy. Among those who participated in the work of the congress were Gorbachev and Prime Minister Valentin Pavlov.[8] The large number of state enterprises included in Vol'sky's organisation, estimated to control approximately

65 per cent of total Soviet manufacturing output, made it a powerful lobbying force both in the parliament and in government circles. By September 1991 the NPS had as members over 1,500 large state enterprises and had a staff of over 100.[9] After the collapse of the Soviet Union, the association was reorganized as the Russian Union of Industrialists and Entrepreneurs (*RSPP* is its Russian acronym). The NPS and RSPP included directors mostly of large state enterprises, with many from the military-industrial complex. Vol'sky later claimed, however, that defence industry directors joined in large numbers only after the August 1991 coup and Tiziakov's arrest.[10] The RSPP also became a sponsor of two influential newspapers that had previously been organs of the CPSU Central Committee: *Workers' Tribune (Rabochaia tribuna)* and *Economics and Life (Ekonomika i zhizn')*.

Vol'sky and other leaders of the NPS/RSPP insisted, somewhat disingenuously, that their organisation was purely economic and had no political role. In order to work more openly for a political programme, Vol'sky organised a political party, called the 'All-Russian Union "Renewal"' (*Vserossiiskii soiuz 'Obnovlenie'*) in late May 1992.[11] The goal of the organisers – who included a number of parliamentary leaders – was to create a new mass party that would attract not just enterprise directors, but also labour collectives and local administrative authorities. Vol'sky's deputy Alexander Vladislavlev, another of the party's leaders, claimed that Renewal also sought to represent the interests of entrepreneurs, though in an interview, he could do no better than describe Vol'sky as 'very tolerant toward business'.[12] The most important goal of the party in the short run was to provide industrialists with a mechanism for creating a shadow government. Ultimately, Vol'sky and Vladislavlev sought negotiations with Yeltsin that would place Renewal candidates in the government.[13] The Russian democratic movement viewed the Renewal party with suspicion, and one liberal commentator charged that it represented 'in essence, a neo-conservative attempt to preserve a model of an ineffective economy and an entire social-hierarchical system that inevitably would be destroyed under conditions of radical reforms'.[14]

Almost simultaneously with the formation of the Renewal party, on 21 May 1992, Vol'sky grouped around his party a new political coalition called the Civic Union (*Grazhdanskii soiuz*). Two of the other parties that joined the group included the People's Party of Free Russia headed by Yeltsin's vice-president, Alexander Rutskoi, and the Russian Democratic Party headed by Nikolai Travkin.[15] The Civic Union soon emerged as an opposition coalition that endorsed a 'correction' in the Russian government's reform programmes that would substantially meet the demands of enterprise directors. The Civic Union's 'Alternative Programme' was presented in the form of a 200-page document worked out by economists at the

Russian Academy of Sciences Institute for Economic Forecasting under the direction of Yuri Yeremenko. In September and October 1992 leaders of the Civic Union attempted to use their influence in the Russian parliament to force Yeltsin to change basic elements of his economic policy and replace a number of the more radical supporters of reform in his cabinet with representatives of the Civic Union.[16]

The Civic Union's programme represented a point-by-point critique of Gaidar's strategy for economic reform. Gaidar's programme called for a freeing of prices, including prices for fuel, rapid privatisation through the creation of joint-stock companies and the issuing of privatisation vouchers to the population, tight monetary policy, as well as greater financial and economic discipline for enterprises. This latter policy was designed to penalise enterprises that were slow to adjust to market conditions; enterprises that did not make a profit would be declared bankrupt. If implemented fully and rapidly, the government programme would represent the kind of 'shock therapy' applied in Poland, and would result in numerous plant closings and a rise in unemployment. Needless to say, almost all of the above policies were anathema to the industrial lobby. Gaidar's policies were equated with 'deindustrialisation of the country'. Government would play a much more active role in managing the economy and the investment process, providing credits to the most promising sectors and enterprises. Prices for many items would be stabilised through state subsidies, and wages would be indexed to adjust for inflation. In general, the programme was designed to preserve much of the existing system of central economic management while ignoring the potential problem of hyperinflation that would seem to follow from the fiscal side of the alternative programme.[17]

Of particular interest to industrialists was the question of privatisation of enterprises, a policy that represented a threat as well as a potential opportunity to managers of state enterprises. A number of potential methods of privatisation were under consideration from 1988 through 1992, including a variety of methods that would involve the issuing of stock. One method would be to give stock in an enterprise only to its employees. In theory, turning over factories to the workers would undermine the role of managers. But if management itself received a large share of stock, it could be in a position to retain effective control over the enterprise. To lobby for this type of privatisation, Arkadii Vol'sky's RSPP helped organise the Association of Enterprises with Employee Ownership in March 1992. The president of the association was Alexander Mironov, director of the Moscow Ventilator Plant, a state enterprise that was one of the first to privatise by way of issuing stock. Among the members of the association's board of directors was Vladislavlev, Vol'sky's deputy in the RSPP.[18] The Gaidar government's issuing of privatisation vouchers to the entire Russian population beginning in October 1992 was faulted both for being too ambitious and for placing too many restrictions on the use of the vouchers. The Civic Union's alternative programme called for a temporary halt to privatisation of large state enterprises, with a long period of experimentation to determine the pluses and minuses of various privatisation schemes in different sectors of the economy. At most the number of enterprises to undergo immediate privatisation would be a few hundred, and it should take place only through a case-by-case approach. Thus, the state sector would remain dominant for the foreseeable future.[19]

In other republics, too, industrialists organised to further their political and economic interests, sometimes on the basis of what had been republican branches of Vol'sky's Scientific-Industrial Union. In Kazakhstan the president of the country, Nursultan Nazarbaev, took steps to organise the industrialists, forming what appeared to be an officially sanctioned interest group. In August 1992, Nazarbaev arranged for the organising committee to meet at his official residence, and in September he presided over the first congress of the new Union of Industrialists and Entrepreneurs of Kazakhstan (SPPK). The first vice-premier of Nazarbaev's government was elected president of the organisation, and the managers of the republic's largest industrial enterprises comprised its leadership. There was speculation that Nazarbaev intended to use the organisation as his new power base in post-Soviet Kazakhstan.[20] These steps foreshadowed a privatisation programme in Kazakhstan that appeared to give the cohort of current enterprise directors a dominant role. In Belarus, managers of the largest industrial enterprises united in the Belarusian Scientific-Production Association. This association served as the basis for a party of industrialists, formed in October 1992 in Belarus and named the Belarusian Scientific-Production Congress.[21]

Links between industrialists in different republics were facilitated by the International Congress of Industrialists and Entrepreneurs. Founded in February 1992 in Moscow, the Congress was essentially a reforming of the old Scientific-Industrial Union, and it naturally chose Arkadii Vol'sky as its chairman and coordinator. By October 1992 its members included not just industrialists from all republics in the former Soviet Union but also from Bulgaria, Hungary, Poland, and Czechoslovakia. The group called on the governments of the Commonwealth of Independent States to take more decisive measures to ease trade ties among the former republics and former CMEA states.[22]

Entrepreneurs

Entrepreneurs represented the new economic structures that were created as a consequence of economic reform and changes in the structure of ownership: cooperatives, private enterprises, leased enterprises, joint ventures, commercial banks, and stock and commodities markets. Entrepreneurs favoured, in general, more radical and consistently pro-market economic policies. Since entrepreneurs had enormous liquid assets at their disposal they stood to benefit from rapid privatisation that would allow open bidding for state property rather than one allowing shares to be sold exclusively to enterprise employees.

A variety of organisations arose to represent the interests of these new forms of economic activity. One of the first groups of this type to be created was the Association of Joint Ventures (enterprises with some degree of foreign participation), formed in 1988. The Association's chairman from the beginning was Lev Vainberg. Another influential organisation representing new commercial interests was the Interregional Union for Stock Exchanges and Trade, headed by Konstantin Zatulin. Also falling into this category was the Russian Union of Private Property-Owners, whose president was V. Shchekochikhin. The well-known economist, Pavel Bunich, was selected to head the Union of Lease-Holders and Entrepreneurs. Perhaps the most significant of the early groups representing entrepreneurs, however, were formed by chairmen of cooperatives. Cooperatives, which began to be formed in 1987–88, were the pioneers of the new Soviet private sector. As such, they acted as a lightening rod for attacks by the Communist Party, the ministries, local mafias, and a population that had been well indoctrinated in the evils of private ownership.[23] To defend their interests, chairmen of cooperatives began to create organisations at the local, republic and national level. These generally arose from the grassroots, without the involvement of the Communist Party or government officials who tended to be viewed as the enemy by chairmen of cooperatives. Leaders of these movements came together in July 1989 and founded the USSR Union of Associated Cooperatives (*Soiuz ob"edinennykh kooperativov*). The assembled delegates chose as their president Vladimir Tikhonov, a well-known free-market economist. The purpose of the national organisation was to affect policy at the centre.

Entrepreneurs set up or attempted to set up their own independent associations in many of the former Soviet republics, both at the national and local level. Associations of cooperatives were established at the republican level in 1988 and 1989. In republics where economic reform was actively resisted by governments in power, entrepreneurs were often a centre of opposition activities. In Belarus, the Union of Entrepreneurs of the Republic of Belarus and other business organisations met in June 1992 and declared their republic inhospitable for business. The vice-president of the Union complained that the parliament, dominated by the Communist Party, needed lessons from 'a good kindergarten teacher' to understand some basic economic truths.[24] In the self-proclaimed independent republic of Tatarstan, the Union of Entrepreneurs of Tatarstan also declared their republic inhospitable for business as a consequence of the government's efforts to separate from Russia.[25] Businessmen in Kazakhstan formed a Congress of Entrepreneurs in November 1991 with the purpose of presenting their views to the president, parliament and government of the republic. Another organisation was created in June 1992, the League for the Defence and Support of Entrepreneurs, to counter Nazarbaev's formation of a state-controlled business association.[26] In Uzbekistan entrepreneurs met in June 1992 and created a new movement of businessmen in order to express their opposition to bureaucratic restrictions on economic freedom and entrepreneurship.[27] In Ukraine, the largest group of entrepreneurs was the Congress of Business Circles, headed by the founder of the Ukrainian Stock Exchange, Valerii Babich.[28]

Links were established between entrepreneurs across republic boundaries similar to those established by industrialists. Again, the purpose was to attempt to solve trade problems that arose in the wake of the collapse of the Soviet Union. A group of businessmen, bankers and stock brokers from the former Soviet republics met in Minsk in April 1992 and signed an 'anticrisis agreement' designed to facilitate economic links between the republics and establish some stability in currency operations involving the ruble.[29] The Ukrainian Congress of Business Circles organised an International Congress of Entrepreneurs in June 1992 to both support economic reintegration and help encourage a dominant role for private ownership in the new states.[30]

Entrepreneurs, like the industrialists, sought to have a direct impact on policy by electing their members to parliaments and local soviets. They were much less successful in this effort, however, than the industrialists. Efforts by cooperatives to gain representation in the March 1989 USSR Congress of People's Deputies under the quota for representatives of organisations were rebuffed with the explanation that no organisation of cooperatives was truly national in scope. One of the reasons that Tikhonov was chosen to head the new national union in July 1989 was that he already was a highly visible deputy to the USSR parliament. The controversial vice-president of the Union of Associated Cooperatives (SOK), Artem Tarasov, had been narrowly defeated in the 1989 popular elections but was later elected to the Russian parliament.[31] Only a handful of entrepreneurs, however, were elected to republic parliaments in 1990.

In the absence of effective political parties, business interests sought to create their own parties in an attempt to find a more effective means to exert influence on the political process. A number of attempts were made by leaders of the cooperative movement to set up a 'party of free labour' without much success. The most significant organisation to emerge from the entrepreneurial stratum was the Party of Economic Freedom (*Partiia ekonomicheskoi svobody*). It was founded by Konstantin Borovoi, the well-known head of the Russian commodity exchange, which had been in operation since late 1990.[32] The party, which held its organisational conference in May 1992, was officially registered with the Russian Ministry of Justice in June and listed as having 662 members. Joining Borovoi as co-chairman of the new party was another prominent entrepreneur, Sviatoslav Fedorov. Even in the communist period, Fedorov, an eye surgeon, showed his entrepreneurial prowess as the originator of the technique of radial keratotomy to correct vision problems. Fedorov ultimately built up a network of affiliated hospitals and clinics across the country (and abroad) that performed these operations for a profit. When, in 1992, Coca-Cola decided to open its first operations in Russia, Fedorov was taken on as a partner. While Borovoi and Fedorov were two of the richest businessmen in Russia, Borovoi viewed the party as 'not a club of millionaires, but a union of citizens'. He also expected to set up a 'highly professional and well paid apparatus and structure across the entire country'.[33] Borovoi resigned his post in the commodity exchange in order to devote all his efforts to party activities. It was reported that he contributed 50 million rubles of his own money to the party's coffers.[34]

The programme of the Party of Economic Freedom emphasised free market principles and a reduction in the state sector. Compared to the industrialists, entrepreneurs were more supportive of the Gaidar programme, particularly its emphasis on financial stabilisation and balancing the state budget. Nevertheless, Borovoi's party was critical of the consequences of the reforms as they were being implemented. The party programme attributed many of the problems to the fact that reform was taking place in the context of an economy dominated by monopolies that were a legacy of the Soviet period. The party also strongly criticised the role of the state bank in expanding credit and allowing state enterprises to accumulate extensive debts. Enterprises in the defence industry were singled out in particular as 'the chief "black holes" of our economy'. The Economic Freedom Party complained that tax policies placed an unfair burden on the private sector, particularly in trade and banking.[35]

On the issue of privatisation, Borovoi's party favoured a rapid acceleration of this process. According to Fedorov, the process could be accomplished 'in the course of a year'. The method favoured by the party for large state enterprises was the selling of stock to all who wished to purchase it. This of course would allow participation by private entrepreneurs in the process of privatising state concerns. In particular, Borovoi argued that the private sector should be permitted to take over factories in the military-industrial complex. Somewhat surprisingly, the Economic Freedom Party also saw a beneficial role for privatisation by the current enterprise directors, despite the past difficulties entrepreneurs have had in dealing with this stratum. In their view, industrialists should have a stake in the process of reform, and a programme allowing management buy-outs would provide this. At the same time, Borovoi spoke out against privatisation by the former Communist Party apparatus and the bureaucracy.[36]

While more conservative industrial groups had a strong lobby in the Russian parliament, Borovoi's group was sufficiently dissatisfied with the antireform direction of the Supreme Soviet and Congress of People's Deputies that in September 1992 it called for a referendum to dissolve the parliament and convene a new constitutional assembly.[37]

Entrepreneurs sought to organise political parties in other republics of the former Soviet Union. A party similar in emphasis to Borovoi's was created in April 1992 in Ukraine. The Liberal Party of Ukraine held its organisational congress in the Donbas region, and it sought to unite businessmen and farmers on a programme of market reform. In October 1992 the party created a shadow cabinet to express its discontent with the Ukrainian government's continued reliance on the state sector.[38] Another Ukrainian party, New Ukraine, was created in June in Kiev, and it joined together liberal political figures and entrepreneurs.[39] Private entrepreneurs in Kyrgyzstan formed their own party in an attempt to support the market reform policies of President Askar Akaev.[40]

Industrialists and entrepreneurs were united on several issues, however, which permitted some degree of collaboration in lobbying efforts. Issues determining the business climate, including in particular tax policy, affected both state enterprises and private entrepreneurs. Both groups also were united in their opposition to political instability, strikes, and conflicts between executive and legislative authority. Borovoi and Vol'sky in July 1992 announced that they would work together on these and other matters through a newly created Council of Constructive Forces (*Sovet konstruktivnykh sil*), despite their differences on other programmatic issues. The Council also included a number of other political parties and labour unions who agreed to participate in an on-going, round-table forum.[41]

Government and representation of economic interests

Efforts by business interests to lobby government had their origins in 1988–9. Attempts by conservatives in the Ministry of Finance to assess prohibitively high taxes on income by members of cooperatives led to an outpouring of protests by chairmen of cooperatives. The result was that, in July 1988, for the first time in the history of the USSR Supreme Soviet, legislation proposed by the government was defeated. When in 1989 the power to set tax rates for cooperatives was shifted to the republic level, unions and associations of cooperatives frequently became involved in the legislative process – with the greatest impact in Latvia, Lithuania, and Belarus.[42] The Union of Associated Cooperatives (SOK) began the first, coordinated national lobbying effort on behalf of Soviet entrepreneurs at the end of 1989. By 1990, this effort included a sophisticated strategy of assigning lobbyists to individual government ministers.[43]

The political leadership both in the Soviet and post-Soviet period sought to institutionalise such contacts. In July 1990, for example, the USSR Council of Ministers adopted a resolution that gave the Scientific-Industrial Union, the Union of Associated Cooperatives and associations representing other economic interests the right to attend all sessions of the Council of Ministers, its presidium, and other government bodies.[44] Political leaders in the executive sought to coopt industrialists and entrepreneurs by creating 'councils of entrepreneurs' at many levels. In theory such organs would give industrialists and entrepreneurs direct access at the very top of the political system. The first such council was created in late 1990 and attached to the office of the Chairman of the USSR Council of Ministers. It comprised only industrialists and was called the Council of Managers of State Enterprises, Associations and Organisations.[45] In October 1991, Gorbachev created a Council on Entrepreneurship attached to the office of president. Its members included both industrialists and entrepreneurs. A. Vladislavlev of the Scientific-Industrial Union was named chairman, and Borovoi, Tikhonov, and Bunich were among its members.[46]

Many of the same entrepreneurs selected by Gorbachev were carried over into a council of the same name set up by the Russian president, Boris Yeltsin, in March 1992.[47] It too was supposed to involve businessmen in the process of working out reforms and was also chaired by Vladislavlev. The actual impact of this council was doubtful, however. In the first seven months of its existence the Russian Council on Entrepreneurship never met with Yeltsin, and its recommendations were usually ignored by Yeltsin's staff. According to one of its members, the council 'never found its place in the structures of power' and 'did not generate nor defend the corporate interest of entrepreneurs'.[48] In November 1992 the presidential council was abolished and reconfigurated as the Council on Industrial Policy. Attached to the Russian government, the Council was designed to provide input from industrialists and entrepreneurs to ministers who would also sit on the Council. The Council was supposed to take part in both drafting decrees on the economy and in evaluating government policies. Yeltsin also tapped prominent entrepreneurs to serve in his personal council of advisers. Among business leaders serving as advisers to Yeltsin in 1992 were Pavel

Bunich, head of the Union of Entrepreneurs and Leaseholders, Sviatoslav Fedorov, co-chairman of the Party of Economic Freedom (along with Borovoi), and Vladimir Tikhonov, head of the Union of Associated Co-operatives.[49]

The progressive mayor of Moscow, Gavriil Popov, who held that office from 1990 until his resignation in May 1992, took the first steps toward creating a council of entrepreneurs in November 1991, though a functioning council was only set up in February 1992. Named chairman of the council was M. V. Masarsky, president of the Association of Enterprise Managers.[50] Apparently the first such council to be formed at the province level was in the oil-rich Tiumen' region. The head of the province administration hoped that the council would be able to attract more capital to the region in order to avert threatened strikes by oil workers.[51]

In other republics too, councils of entrepreneurs and industrialists were set up by the top leadership. In Kazakhstan in early 1991, President Nazarbaev created a Higher Economic Council that took part in the preparation of economic legislation and included among its members enterprise managers.[52] The Moldovan president, Mircea Snegur, formed a Council of Entrepreneurs in February 1992. Its purpose was to allow managers some input on economic policies, including government support of enterprises.[53] In Tajikistan, then president Nabiev created a Consultative Council made up of 'entrepreneurs and leaseholders' attached to the Cabinet of Ministers.[54]

The most direct attempt to include the interests of industrialists in the policymaking process took the form of new appointments to government posts. In Russia in June 1992, Vladimir Shumeiko, a former enterprise director from Krasnodar who had been elected to parliament in 1990, was named first deputy prime minister. Shumeiko had been close to Vol'sky and was one of the members of the group that organised the industrialist party Renewal. Georgii Khizha, former director of a large defence plant and deputy mayor of St Petersburg, was named a deputy prime minister in June 1992. Khizha also previously served as chairman of the Leningrad Association of Industrial Enterprises. In addition, another former enterprise director and government official, Viktor Chernomyrdin, was named vice-premier for energy questions.[55] Shumeiko and Khizha both had the reputation of being supporters of market reforms, but it was clear that both brought the perspective of the industrialist lobby to the highest level of the Russian government. As Khizha said in one interview, 'I am a dedicated supporter of the market – precisely because I represent the interests of Russia's big industry'.[56] Many questioned the ability of Shumeiko and Khizha to work with the more radically free-market prime minister Yegor Gaidar, and industrialists lobbied to have Gaidar replaced by one of their number. In December 1992 the Russian parliament rejected Gaidar and chose Chernomyrdin as the new prime minister.

In several other republics in the course of 1992, new prime ministers were named who were drawn from the ranks of industrialists. In Armenia, Khosrov Arutiunian was appointed prime minister in July 1992. Arutiunian had been director of a relatively small textile plant and had developed a reputation as a centrist in the Armenian parliament. In February 1993 Arutiunian was forced to resign when he publicly opposed the government's new economic programme.[57] In Ukraine, another former enterprise director was chosen prime minister in October 1992 after a vote of no confidence in Vitold Fokin, who had been prime minister since the communist period. Leonid Kuchma filled one of the highest posts on the Communist Party *nomenklatura*, that of director of the former Soviet Union's largest rocket manufacturing plant, 'Yuzhmash', in Dnepropetrovsk. Kuchma was put forward by the powerful industrialist faction in the Ukrainian parliament. True to his origins, Kuchma called for a cautious reform strategy that would preserve the powers of large state-owned enterprises.[58]

Yet another channel for the involvement of business interests in the Russian government was the 'trilateral commission'. Made up of industrialists and entrepreneurs, representatives of trade unions, and the government, the commission attempted to regulate social and labour relations in a type of 'social partnership'.[59] Meetings were chaired by top government officials, including the head of Yeltsin's staff, Gennadii Burbulis, and then Labour Minister Alexander Shokhin. A participant in the meetings reported that the chief disputes in these talks were usually between labour and government, with industrialists acting as a mediating force.[60] The Russian government viewed the official union as illegitimate; in the words of the deputy minister of labour it was 'not a trade union, but debris from the totalitarian system'.[61] The new independent trade unions, on the other hand, often sided with the government.

The extent to which lobbying efforts have changed legislation or affected government decisions is difficult to measure. By its nature, lobbying is a process largely hidden from public scrutiny, and the participants often have an interest in keeping their activities secret. The willingness of participants to engage in threats and other forms of pressure was clear, however. In an August 1990 interview, for example, Arkadii Vol'sky indicated that his Scientific-Industrial Union would, if necessary, 'apply pressure (I do not fear this word) during the drafting and adoption of basic laws which concern the interests of industrialists'.[62]

The role of industrialists and entrepreneurs brought a new set of challenges to Soviet and post-Soviet politics. The rise of parliaments as real legislative bodies meant inevitably that special interests would attempt to lobby for beneficial treatment in legislation and administrative decisions. The frustration felt by Soviet conservatives over the apparent strength of parliamentary support for cooperatives in early 1990 led Ivan Polozkov and several others to claim that cooperatives had 'bought' deputies and paid for favourable media accounts of their activities.[63] These were the first such charges of unethical lobbying tactics. Since lobbying was a new phenomenon in Soviet politics, no law existed on lobbyists that would limit or regulate their activities. No procedures existed, for example, for registering lobbyists or accounting for their use of funds.[64] There were also no restrictions on the 'outside' activities of members of parliament. In April 1992 it was revealed that fifty-five deputies in the Russian parliament were 'employees of commercial structures' – presumably newly hired – who acted as lobbyists for these interests.[65]

The succession of different governments in the USSR and Russia has been marked by wide variation in the willingness of policymakers to listen to the concerns of businessmen. According to one participant in these efforts, Lev Vainberg, chairman of the Association of Joint Ventures, the Soviet government under Prime Minister Ryzhov was, paradoxically, the most attentive to the interests of entrepreneurs.[66] Industrialists and entrepreneurs alike were upset by the post-August 1991 Yeltsin government headed by Gaidar, and both groups complained that the Russian economic reforms were worked out and adopted without their participation.[67] Ultimately, the fact that government depends on the actions of leading managers in the state and emerging private sectors to make reforms work insures that industrialists and entrepreneurs will enjoy regular access to top policymakers.

10   Public opinion and the political process

A measure of how much Soviet politics changed in the critical period from 1988 to 1991 was the increasing importance of public opinion. Popular attitudes were reflected, of course, in the local and national elections and in the national and republican referenda that are discussed elsewhere in this volume. The national, republic and local elections were, at best, highly imperfect snapshots of public opinion that was rapidly shifting. More systematic monitoring of public opinion was another innovation of the Gorbachev period, and this chapter focuses on both the study of public opinion and how public opinion changed in the period under review.

Glasnost and the changing Soviet media

Gorbachev's emphasis on increasing openness or glasnost in the media was perhaps the single most important factor in changing and mobilising Soviet public opinion. The more open discussion of social problems, particularly from 1987 on, was one of Gorbachev's first political reforms. In the past, journalists' roles were heavily linked to supporting the status quo and its ideology as directed by the Communist Party apparatus that controlled their activities.[1] None the less, many journalists were strong supporters of reform, and with the shift in policy under Gorbachev, they were given much greater freedom to explore areas that had been off-limits in the past.[2]

At first there were significant limits to glasnost. Gorbachev assigned Yegor Ligachev the role of Central Committee secretary for ideology until at least April 1988, and Ligachev objected to press material that would undermine the role of the party; though he was unable to exercise prior censorship, Ligachev often attempted to cajole or intimidate editors of the more liberal publications. Gorbachev himself often took this approach to limit criticism of party leaders and his policies. In fact, it was a relatively small segment of the media that took on the role of crusaders for perestroika – publications such as *Moscow News*, *Ogonek*, and *Argumenty i fakty*. The circulation of many of these newspapers and journals fell well below demand for them; the shortage of paper was given as one explanation for

178

this, and the archaic and centrally controlled distribution system meant that most were difficult to obtain outside Moscow, Leningrad, and a few other large cities.

The process of breaking past limitations on political discourse was accelerated greatly in 1989 with the election of the new national parliament, the Congress of People's Deputies. Debates and proceedings of the first sessions of the parliament were broadcast live to the nation. Opposition deputies, most of whom joined the Inter-Regional Deputies' Group led by Andrei Sakharov, Boris Yeltsin, and others, quickly became the focus of national attention when they spoke openly and critically on themes and issues that had only been partially uncovered by glasnost in the media. The threat Gorbachev and party leaders perceived from the Inter-Regional Group led them to block efforts by the opposition to publish its own newspaper.[3]

Television was particularly important in its impact on public opinion because of its mass audience extending across the entire Soviet Union.[4] Glasnost soon spread to television, and several important television broadcasts – such as *Vzgliad* (Viewpoint), and *Prozhektor perestroiki* (Perestroika Spotlight) – were among the most popular on Soviet television. The most widely watched programme, *Vremia* (Time), the nightly news broadcast, was somewhat less affected by glasnost, but it too became more objective and critical. This changed after November 1990, when Leonid Kravchenko was appointed by Gorbachev as chairman of the State Broadcasting Company (Gosteleradio); tight control over central television was reestablished.[5] Kravchenko arranged for the cancellation of *Vzgliad* in December 1990, despite its popularity, and also limited the appearances of controversial (meaning opposition) political figures. By that point, however, it was too late to reverse the substantial shift in urban public opinion in support of radical reform.[6]

The dissolution of the CPSU after the failure of the August 1991 coup led to major changes in the media. Soon after the coup, Kravchenko was replaced as head of central television and radio by the liberal editor of *Moscow News*, Yegor Iakovlev. Before the coup most newspapers and publishing houses were still owned and controlled by the Communist Party at various levels. Changes in ownership of the media began with *Moscow News*, which reorganised itself as an independent paper with several sponsors and a number of prominent shareholders. After the coup other newspapers, including the daily of the Communist Party Central Committee, *Pravda*, proclaimed that it had cut its ties to the party and become independent, though it and other papers apparently continued to enjoy the support of former party members and successor organisations.[7]

There was a proliferation of new newspapers in 1990 and 1991, including the influential *Nezavisimaia gazeta* (Independent Newspaper). Other new papers, such as *Rossiiskaia gazeta* in Russia, were founded as press organs of the now independent republic parliaments. The increasingly high cost of newsprint as the newspaper and publishing industry shifted to market principles caused serious difficulties, particularly for large-circulation papers. At the same time, efforts by newly independent governments to maintain control over the mass media remained a serious problem. Television and the leading wire service, ITAR-TASS, remained under state control, as did the distribution network for most newspapers.[8] Russian government subsidies for some of the largest circulation newspapers continued in 1992. According to one account, over 300 periodicals received some support from the state budget, with the largest subsidies granted directly by parliament for the former official papers of the labour unions and the communist youth league, *Trud* and *Komsomol'skaia pravda*, respectively.[9]

The study of public opinion

The systematic study of public opinion began to increase well before the rise to power of Mikhail Gorbachev. Many Communist Party organisations began to seek input from sociologists for their decisions in the 1970s and early 1980s, though the role of these sociological investigations was often quite narrow. In 1985 it was reported that there were over 150 sociological laboratories, groups, departments or councils attached to party committees plus around sixty research units made up of volunteers. In addition higher educational institutions and the Academy of Sciences reportedly had another 220 groups with a sociological focus.[10]

Even quite conservative political leaders attempted to coopt the use of public opinion studies. Konstantin Chernenko was the first top party official to propose the creation of a national centre for public opinion research, in a speech given as ideological secretary while Andropov was General Secretary, in 1983.[11] Ultimately, however, it was reform-minded communist leaders who found in sociologists natural allies, while other local party officials tended to dismiss sociological research as a potentially dangerous instrument for evaluating their performance. One of the highest ranked party leaders to expand the use of public opinion was Eduard Shevardnadze, who, before becoming Gorbachev's foreign minister, was party first secretary in Georgia from 1972 to 1985. In 1975 Shevardnadze established a Centre for the Study of Public Opinion attached to the Central Committee of the Georgian communist party, and he frequently cited its results to justify popular and reformist policies.[12]

The first 'national' centres for public opinion research set up in the mid-1980s had a definite conservative slant, a reflection of years of inhibited development. A centre was organised in late 1985 at the Institute of Sociological Research (later renamed the Institute of Sociology) under the direction of Viktor Britvin, a scholar who had previously specialised in social problems at the workplace.[13] Another relatively conservative polling group, the Sociological Research Centre (*Tsentr sotsiologicheskikh issledovanii*), was created at the Central Committee's own Academy of Social Sciences. The centre attached to the Institute of Sociological Research worked closely with the newspapers *Sovetskaia Rossiia* and *Izvestiia,* sometimes surveying readers or summarising letters to the editor. The Institute of Sociological Research still suffered from the effects of the purge of prominent specialists that took place in the early 1970s.[14] Early studies were limited in scope; and these limits were often self-imposed by conservative sociologists who had survived the purge. In early 1988, for example, when the *New York Times* and CBS News attempted to commission a study on Soviet public opinion through the institute, researchers rejected a number of proposed questions, including one about the relative popularity of top political figures.[15] It was not until 1990 that polls measuring the popularity of top leaders became acceptable.

Clearly, a completely new research organisation would be needed to overcome past inertia, and the Central Committee and Council of Ministers in July 1987 decided to create the All-Union Centre for Public Opinion Research (VTsIOM, to use its Russian acronym). Many months passed before VTsIOM was finally organised, however. The centre was not created under the auspices of the Academy of Sciences, but instead was attached to the national trade union council and the State Committee for Labour and Social Questions.[16] When VTsIOM was finally opened at the end of March 1988, the prominent reformist sociologist Tatiana Zaslavskaia was named as its director.[17] Zaslavskaia was one of the most innovative Soviet sociologists; she spent the period of stagnation – as the Brezhnev era came to be known – at the Siberian branch of the USSR Academy of Science in Novosibirsk. She was chosen president of the Soviet Sociological Association in late 1986. In a February 1987 *Pravda* article entitled 'Perestroika and Sociology', Zaslavskaia was highly critical of the state of Soviet social science and urged a major programme to expand and upgrade the training of professional sociologists.[18] Zaslavskaia's own scholarly efforts were directed above all at presenting a more complex picture of Soviet society by exposing the diversity of social groups and interests.[19] She brought to the newly formed research centre a number of leading reform-oriented sociologists, many of whose careers had suffered during the Brezhnev period. Among these were Boris Grushin, a deputy director and author of one of the first comprehensive studies on Soviet public opinion, Valerii Rutgaizer, also a deputy director of VTsIOM, Yuri Levada, and Leonid Sedov.

Glasnost in the area of politics and public opinion data was only partial in

1988, and this affected the work of VTsIOM. Early studies were limited in scope to fairly specific issues of state policy: the first polls measured attitudes toward the election of managerial personnel, newspaper subscriptions, leasing of enterprises, and school reform. Only seven polls had been conducted by VTsIOM by the end of 1988. These first efforts had a very limited geographical reach, and could hardly be called 'national'. The first poll, on electing managers, was conducted in only three cities. The last poll conducted in 1988, an 'omnibus' poll touching on many different themes, encompassed seven regions in three republics.[20] The pace of polling increased dramatically in the years that followed, and what was reported to be the first 'national' poll was conducted in 1989.

Zaslavskaia set out to create a nationwide network of pollsters; already in March 1988 she announced that twenty-five divisions of VTsIOM were to be set up in the capitals of the republics and in major industrial centres.[21] By late 1989 regional affiliates of VTsIOM had been established in Leningrad, Gor'ky, Saratov, Perm', Novosibirsk, Krasnoiarsk, Magadan, Stavropol' (all in the Russian republic), Kiev, L'vov, Dnepropetrovsk (all in Ukraine), as well as in the capital cities of Moldova, Belarus, Latvia, Lithuania, Estonia, Azerbaijan, Georgia, Kazakhstan, Kyrgyzstan, Uzbekistan, and Turkmenistan. By mid-1991 the number of regional divisions had reportedly reached thirty-six, of which fifteen were in the Russian republic.[22] A number of problems were encountered in this process of creating a national network, not the least of which was the lack of trained sociologists. Conducting surveys was made more difficult by the fact that it was impossible to use telephone interviews in a country were telephones were so unevenly distributed. Perhaps only in Moscow was the percentage of telephone ownership large enough (about two-thirds of all households) to permit a representative sample of the population.

Methodological shortcomings diminished the reliability of the VTsIOM results that were reported, and the margins of error in some of the studies (rarely provided with the research results) were very large indeed.[23] Given the extreme diversity within the boundaries of the former USSR, attempts by VTsIOM and other polling organisations to achieve a 'national' sample were probably misdirected. The size of typical samples from each region was extremely small, and simply adding them together did not solve the very serious problem of representativeness. Furthermore, extreme regional variation resulted in mean values that reflected very little of the political realities of the country. More useful would have been an effort to obtain larger samples in various republics and provinces and then use the results to show regional differences and/or similarities. By instead collecting small samples widely dispersed across the country, the polling data undoubtedly understated the weaknesses of the regime and its policies – particularly in the republics most energised by nationalism. In fact, few surveys conducted by VTsIOM or other polling organisations focused on regional differences in results, and most polls overrepresented Russians at the expense of other nationalities. Another flaw of most surveys was that urban respondents were vastly overrepresented. In general, the distribution of sociologists and related institutes strongly favoured research in urban areas to the exclusion of rural areas and in large cities to the exclusion of small ones. Because of its accessibility, Moscow was by far the most frequently surveyed region in the country.

Very few polls were presented in ways that would show differences in responses by age, sex, nationality or social group. Instead, only overall percentages were reported. Usually the size of the sample was indicated, but the degree of representativeness or margin of error was not.[24] Another shortcoming, from the standpoint of charting changes in public opinion over time, was a lack in consistency in the wording of survey questions, even in those surveys carried out at different times by the same organisation. This, of course, complicates the creation of a time series, since responses to somewhat different questions may not be comparable.

Despite the reformist bias of many of the top researchers at the Centre, surveys were often commissioned by the government. In 1989 VTsIOM was commissioned by Leonid Abalkin, then chairman of the State Commission on Economic Reform, to study public opinion on economic issues and the possible social consequences of the transition to a market economy.[25] In mid-1990 the reform commission created a Sociological Council to coordinate such studies and review policy recommendations in light of their results.[26] The Russian Supreme Soviet established its own Sub-committee on Studying Public Opinion in 1991.[27] With the erosion of budgetary funding for social science research after the end of Soviet socialism, many polling organisations (including VTsIOM, renamed the All-Russian Centre for the Study of Public Opinion) expanded their activities to include market surveys or other commercially valuable data. In addition, a large number of private polling organisations arose that conducted polls commissioned by television, newspapers or Western organisations.[28]

Changing political values

One element of Gorbachev's strategy for political reform was to use public support for change as a lever to reform the Communist Party and undermine the opponents of reform. At the same time, however, he sought to use public opinion as a stabilising factor to reign in attempts at more radical transformation. One of the reasons Gorbachev failed in this strategy was that he misread the rapid shifts in public opinion away from support for central institutions and gradual, limited reform. The demise of the Soviet Union was in part the unanticipated result of a rapid decline in the authority of central institutions of power, including the authority of the Communist Party, the Soviet government, and of Gorbachev. The Communist Party did not reform itself as many had hoped, and support for radical changes in the political and economic system increased dramatically as economic conditions worsened. This process occurred most rapidly in places where economic issues were reinforced (and often overshadowed) by nationalism – particularly in republics on the periphery of the Soviet Union. Voters in the Baltic states, Georgia, Armenia, and Moldova elected parliaments in 1990 that played a key role in undermining attempts to preserve the Soviet Union.

The crucial element of glasnost in the media, the first of Gorbachev's political reforms, was itself a political issue. A poll conducted in late 1988 found that 95 per cent of the Soviet public favoured expanding glasnost. When the question was formulated in terms of setting boundaries to glasnost, 65 per cent opposed all limitations, while 32 per cent agreed with the statement that 'one should be free to say anything which does not run counter to socialist principles'. Three per cent would permit only viewpoints 'completely in accord with the CPSU official line'.[29] Another survey conducted at the end of 1990 – a time when Gorbachev was again seeking to rein in the media – there was a somewhat greater percentage, 37 per cent, favouring limits on glasnost, while 43 per cent still opposed any limits. While a 1989 survey found that only 13 per cent of the respondents felt glasnost had gone too far, by late 1990 their number had increased to 28 per cent.[30]

At the beginning of perestroika, many of the elements of the Soviet ideology which had for so long dominated the mass media, continued to affect mass opinion. Opposition to political pluralism, meaning the end of the political monopoly of the Communist Party and the rise of a multi-party system, was widespread. A poll conducted among Muscovites in early 1988, for example, found that 51 per cent agreed (while 28 per cent disagreed) with the statement that 'A one-party system in the USSR promotes the development of democracy'. For all age groups, the percentage agreeing with this statement exceeded those disagreeing, though older respondents supported that position more consistently than younger ones. However, there was widespread support, 77 per cent in favour and 4 per cent opposed, for the more limited pluralism of electoral competition. This support for multi-candidate elections was strong among all age groups.[31]

Shifting political allegiances moved dramatically in the direction of support for proponents of reform. This trend had only begun in March 1989, the time of the national elections to the Congress of People's Deputies, but even then it had embraced the Baltic republics and many of the major cities in the European part of the USSR. By February 1990, just before the start of most of the republic parliamentary elections of 1990, a national poll asked which political orientation respondents would like to achieve a majority in the new parliaments. The largest number, 39 per cent, hoped for a victory by proponents of 'radical democratic reforms'. Another 23 per cent wanted supporters of 'gradual transformations' in power, while 22 per cent supported a victory by those who would impose order with 'harsh measures'.[32] A different survey conducted at about the same time found that, in response to the question 'What is your attitude toward new democratic movements (popular fronts and other "informal" socio-political organisations)?', over 65 per cent 'support the ideas of some of them' while about 32 per cent did not support their ideas.[33]

Concurrently, support for the Communist Party was rapidly declining. In the early years of Gorbachev's ascendency direct questions about attitudes towards the party and its monopoly on power were not possible. Indirect evidence of the declining authority of the party was collected nonetheless. In one study conducted by the Central Committee's Academy of Social Sciences in 1986, 1988 and 1989 respondents were asked if they had noted any improvement in party work, or in the day-to-day operations of the party. Those answering 'yes' declined from 26 per cent in June 1986 to 16 per cent in February 1988 and 11 per cent in February 1989.[34] As glasnost expanded it became possible to ask more frank questions about the party. A poll conducted in March 1989 found that 23 per cent completely distrusted the Communist Party, and by February 1990 this group had increased to 35 per cent. In the latter survey almost 90 per cent agreed with the statement that the party had made mistakes that had hindered the country's development, and 60 per cent agreed at least in part that the CPSU had lead the country down the wrong path.[35] After the August coup, when the CPSU was disbanded for its role in those events, few mourned its passing. A VTsIOM poll conducted in December 1991 found that only 6 per cent in Russia, 3 per cent in Ukraine, and 9 per cent in the Central Asian republics (plus Kazakhstan and Azerbaijan) were saddened that the party was no more.[36]

The survey results summarised in table 10.1 show that, in addition to the Communist Party, almost all central institutions of power suffered an erosion of trust between 1989 and 1991. Similar findings of low confidence in central political institutions were obtained in a joint American-Soviet survey conducted in May and June 1990.[37] Another survey commissioned by the US Information Agency obtained results in August 1990 that corresponded closely to those presented here.[38] In contrast to central institutions, popular support of republican parliaments increased in the period after the

Table 10.1. *Percentage expressing complete confidence or a complete lack of confidence in political institutions*

	Mar. 1989	Aug. 1989	Dec. 1989	Mar. 1990	July 1990	Oct. 1990	Dec. 1990	Oct. 1991	Jan. 1992
	USSR	USSR	USSR	USSR	USSR	USSR	USSR	Russ.	Russ.
CPSU									
yes	38	22	27	16	14	11	7	n.a.	4
no	n.a.	n.a.	24	36	38	52	50	n.a.	56
Army/Military									
yes	n.a.	n.a.	44	35	35	36	41	56	45
no	n.a.	n.a.	14	23	16	19	13	36	6
USSR Council of Ministers (in 1991–2, the USSR State Council)									
yes	28	14	34	23	20	15	n.a.	15	5
no	n.a.	n.a.	11	23	20	38	n.a.	28	25
KGB									
yes	n.a.	n.a.	38	32	24	29	n.a.	n.a.	15
no	n.a.	n.a.	15	22	18	24	n.a.	n.a.	24
USSR Supreme Soviet									
yes	43	32	45	34	32	24	18	n.a.	3
no	n.a.	n.a.	7	15	14	22	24	n.a.	37
Respondent's republican parliament									
yes	n.a.	n.a.	27	23	40	40	n.a.	48	13
no	n.a.	n.a.	14	21	11	14	n.a.	43	18
Local soviet									
yes	18	16	16	14	21	18	n.a.	17	10
no	n.a.	n.a.	31	40	25	29	n.a.	73	36
News media									
yes	39	30	36	37	34	35	n.a.	30	19
no	n.a.	n.a.	9	15	13	11	n.a.	62	12
Trade unions									
yes	20	n.a.	21	n.a.	n.a.	n.a.	n.a.	25	n.a.
no	22	n.a.	26	n.a.	n.a.	n.a.	n.a.	66	n.a.

Sources: March 1989, August 1989, December 1989, March 1990 – *Moscow News*, 3–10 June 1990, p. 9; July 1990 – *Izvestiia*, 29 November 1990. October and December 1990 – *Nezavisimaia gazeta*, 24 January 1991. Trade union data – *Trud*, 26 October 1990. All of the above studies were carried out by VTsIOM, using a national sample. Additional unpublished data, including the January 1992 survey data (N = 1,990), were provided to the author by VTsIOM. October 1991 – *Rossiiskaya gazeta*, 24 October 1991. Centre for Comparative Social Research, N = 1,434, conducted in 22 regions of the federation. The latter survey was worded slightly differently to permit only two responses, while VTsIOM surveys allowed for more ambiguous responses.

1990 elections, and it was these bodies that played a major role in initiating the end of Soviet rule by pushing for sovereignty and independence.

In light of these findings, it is not surprising that an effort to seize power undertaken by the vice president, head of the Soviet government, and leaders of the Soviet military and KGB with the tacit support of the apparatus of the Communist Party was greeted less than enthusiastically. After the fact, a December 1991 survey in the Russian republic found that only 13 per cent would like to have seen the leaders of the August coup in power, while 61 per cent were opposed.[39] The army, the one central institution which commanded widespread trust, also suffered a decline in the course of 1991. Additional survey results from March, July, and September 1991 showed a drop in those responding that the army fully deserved the people's trust, from 45 per cent in March to 34 per cent in July and, finally, 25 per cent in September. Those expressing a complete lack of trust rose from 10 per cent in March to 16 per cent in July and then fell to 8 per cent in September, after the coup was over and the military leadership had been changed.[40]

Another series of polls conducted periodically by VTsIOM in 1990 and 1991 saw a sharp and fairly steady decline in confidence toward what the survey termed 'the country's leadership' (rukovodstvo strany), headed at the time by Gorbachev. At the beginning of 1990, 65 per cent expressed trust (completely or basically) in the leadership while 23 per cent did not. By July corresponding figures were 45 per cent and 38 per cent, and by the end of 1990 only 32 per cent trusted the leadership, while 54 per cent did not.[41] By July 1991, the month before the coup, confidence in the leadership remained at virtually the same level: 31 per cent trusted the leadership while 53 per cent did not. Just after the coup, in September, there was a brief increase in trust (37 per cent), but by October the results were virtually the same as those obtained in July.[42] One direct political consequence of this trend in 1990–1 was that it eliminated for Gorbachev the option of making the Soviet presidency an elected post. An elected president would have had increased legitimacy and would have helped to justify the shift to a stronger executive. Gorbachev had reason to worry, however, that a presidential race would attract a formidable opponent, perhaps Boris Yeltsin (though he consistently denied any interest in the post) or Anatolii Sobchak, then mayor of Leningrad. Until 1990–1, pollsters still were either prevented from, or were reluctant to, pose direct questions about the popularity of political personalities. There seemed to be a particular reluctance to report results on the relative popularity of Gorbachev and Yeltsin. Zaslavskaia subsequently reported that the highest measured approval rating for Gorbachev was 62 per cent and that it fell to 20 per cent by early 1991.[43] As for Yeltsin, it is easy to lose sight of the fact that until his selection as chairman of the Russian Supreme Soviet in mid-1990, Yeltsin was treated as a non-person in the official media. Nevertheless, or perhaps because of this official disdain, Yeltsin emerged as the most popular political figure in the country.

These changes in public confidence in the leadership and political institutions occurred against a backdrop of an increasingly serious economic crisis. When in early 1989 Muscovites were asked how their lives had changed in the past three years – a period meant to coincide roughly with the beginning of the Gorbachev's rule – only 24 per cent felt their situation had worsened, while 37 per cent saw some improvement and 33 per cent detected no change.[44] By late 1989/early 1990 polls indicated increasing dissatisfaction with changes in the economy and the impact on their lives. In Moscow 37 per cent expressed complete dissatisfaction with changes in their personal well-being over the past four years. Corresponding data from Kiev, L'vov, and Tashkent showed complete dissatisfaction on the part of 38 per cent, 45 per cent, and 34 per cent respectively.[45] A national survey conducted in summer 1990 found that 7 per cent felt their lives had improved under Gorbachev, 22 per cent saw no change, while 57 per cent thought that their situation had deteriorated.[46] In December 1990, another survey found that the overwhelming majority of the population, 88 per cent, felt that they were worse off than in the mid-1980s. Only 8 per cent believed that their personal situation had improved over that period.[47] Similarly bleak figures were obtained from surveys conducted in Russia after the end of the Soviet Union. When respondents were asked to assess their personal situation in April and June 1992, the percentage answering 'good' dropped from 13 per cent to 8 per cent and 'bearable' dropped from 63 per cent to 53 per cent; those responding 'bad' increased from 15 per cent to 31 per cent, and 'unbearable' from 3 per cent to 8 per cent.[48] A similar survey in September 1992 found that 11 per cent considered that they lived 'well' (including 1 per cent that responded 'very well'), 51 per cent responded 'average', and 37 per cent responded with either 'bad' (28 per cent) or 'very bad' (9 per cent). More negative attitudes were expressed, as one would expect, by those whose incomes lagged most, pensioners and soldiers, as well as workers.[49]

Support for reform and reformers

The lack of significant progress on economic reforms during the Gorbachev era left a full agenda for republic leaders in the post-Soviet republics. The success or failure of any reform effort would necessarily be linked to the level of popular support for that policy. In the Russian republic in particular, there was a substantial increase in the frequency of public opinion surveys on political and economic issues. The potential effect of worsening economic conditions on popular support for reform became one of the major policy questions of the post-Soviet period. In evaluating these figures, it would be incorrect to identify negative estimations of one's personal well-being with opposition to reform. When respondents in August 1992 were asked about whether they thought that economic reforms should continue or whether they should be stopped, 53 per cent expressed support for a continuation while only 20 per cent wanted an end to reform. In other words, many respondents who were unhappy with their present situation believed that further reforms would improve matters.[50]

When attitudes toward particular reforms are examined, rather than 'reform' in the abstract, the situation becomes more complicated. Survey results showed considerable opposition to important elements of any reform package, and it is clear that attitudes to reforms varied considerably over time and by region. A June 1990 survey singled out the issue of market-based pricing – prices based on supply and demand, that most people correctly interpreted would mean higher prices – as the main element of the transition to the market. The survey found that the largest number of respondents in all republics, though by a very narrow margin in Estonia, favoured a continuation of stable, government-set prices for all goods. (See table 10.2.) The largest percentage of respondents favouring state pricing (44 per cent or over) were in Central Asia, Azerbaijan, Belarus, Ukraine, Georgia, Russia and Kazakhstan. Hostility toward the freezing of prices continued after this became the first element of reform introduced by the Russian government. An April 1992 survey in Russia found that 49 per cent did not support market-based prices, while only 22 per cent did.[51]

The most important of the reforms, and the one that most went against the grain of decades of indoctrination, was the shift from state to private ownership. The first manifestation of legal private enterprises in the Soviet Union, the cooperative movement, met with considerable popular resistance in 1988–9. A national survey conducted in late 1989, for example, found that almost half of all respondents disapproved of the new businesses while only 25 per cent approved.[52] Attitudes toward private ownership were changing quickly, however. Another survey conducted six months later, in June 1990, found that 54 per cent of all respondents were willing to work for a private employer, while only 27 per cent categorically refused.[53] A December 1990 poll found that 44 per cent favoured the continued development of privately owned enterprises, while 26 per cent opposed this phenomenon.[54] A later survey in Russia found nearly identical figures in April 1992 – 47 per cent favoured privatising state property, and 23 per cent did not support this policy.[55]

One of the last surveys to include all republics found significant regional differences in public opinion on the privatisation issue. (See table 10.2.) The survey, conducted in October 1990, found that the opponents of private ownership of enterprises exceeded supporters in the Central Asian

Table 10.2. *Attitudes toward price formation, June 1990 (percentages)*

Republic	Market prices for all goods	State should set all prices	State should set some prices
Estonia	25	26	40
Armenia	15	40	20
Latvia	9	26	9
Georgia	9	47	19
Moldova	7	39	32
Ukraine	6	48	6
Uzbekistan	6	49	29
Azerbaijan	5	53	12
Russia	4	45	31
Kazakhstan	4	34	4
Belarus	4	49	28
Kyrgyzstan	4	44	32
Tajikistan	3	68	16
Turkmenistan	3	56	18

Source: Vestnik statistiki, 1991, no. 2, pp. 61–2. The survey was performed by USSR Goskomstat in all republics except Lithuania; (N = 30,000. Not included in this table are those who did not answer or who responded with 'difficult to say'.

republics, Azerbaijan, Russia, Belarus, and Moldova. The greatest support for privatisation of enterprises was found in the Baltic republics and Armenia. There was a slight preponderance of support for private ownership in Ukraine, Georgia and Kazakhstan.

An additional feature of attitudes toward reform was that, in general, younger respondents were more enthusiastic about reforms than older respondents. Those over age sixty were most likely to oppose reform policies in favour of a return to the old system.[56] In attitudes toward privatisation reported in table 10.3, this pattern was true in all republics except Estonia and Lithuania, where the pre-Soviet generation still remembered when private ownership was the norm, and the older generation supported this aspect of economic reform even more than young people.[57]

In one important respect, trends in public opinion in the immediate post-Soviet period continued the pattern noted above for the last years of Soviet power – a marked decline in the level of confidence in the institutions of government. This was in part a result of a deterioration in the economy that took the form of rapidly rising prices and increasing unemployment. In late June 1992 a poll taken in Russia found that Yeltsin's government, headed at the time by Yegor Gaidar, was 'fully' trusted by only 4 per cent of the respondents (down from 6 per cent in February), while 24 per cent 'basically' trusted the government. Those with sceptical attitudes included

Table 10.3. *Attitudes toward private ownership of enterprises, October 1990* *(percentages)*

Republic	Support	Oppose	Hard to say
Estonia	52	26	22
Armenia	50	24	26
Latvia	48	33	19
Lithuania	44	31	25
Ukraine	39	35	27
Tajikistan	35	41	24
Georgia	33	30	37
Kazakhstan	32	29	39
Belarus	31	38	32
Uzbekistan	31	42	27
Moldova	26	31	43
Russia	26	35	39
Kyrgyzstan	26	41	34
Azerbaijan	17	36	48
Turkmenistan	11	36	53

Source: USSR State Committee on Statistics, Bureau of Sociological Research, reported in Darrell Slider, Vladimir Magun, and Vladimir Gimpel'son, 'Public opinion on privatization: republic differences', *Soviet Economy*, vol. 7, no. 3 (July–September 1991), p. 258; N = 3,466.

42 per cent who trusted the regime 'not much' and 26 per cent (up from 21 per cent in February) who distrusted the regime completely. Support for the government was highest among students, specialists, and private entrepreneurs.[58]

The level of support in Russia for politicians who advocated rapid political and economic reform was also questionable, particularly outside the major urban centres. A mid-1992 poll found that only 14 per cent of respondents favoured the 'democrats' (21 per cent in Moscow and large cities versus 5 per cent in small towns), 5 per cent still supported communists (13 per cent in small towns and only 1 per cent in Moscow), while 50 per cent would prefer 'experienced managers (*praktiki* and *khoziaistvenniki*) without consideration of their political preferences'.[59] Such polls undoubtedly raised questions in Yeltsin's Kremlin about the wisdom of pushing for early elections to parliament. In September 1992, perhaps on the basis of such polling data, Yeltsin declared that he would not challenge the right of the current Russian Congress of People's Deputies to serve out its term. Another factor in the changing political situation in Russia was the decline in Yeltsin's popularity, though he continued to be immensely popular. One survey conducted in mid-1992 showed Yeltsin trailing another political figure for the first time since he had been elected Russian president. Yeltsin's vice president, former army colonel Alexander Rutskoi, appealed to Russian nationalism with his outspoken criticism of the leaders of neighbouring republics and his support for Russians and other ethnic minorities now outside Russia's borders. The survey found that 28 per cent of the respondents completely trusted Rutskoi, while 24 per cent gave the same evaluation of Yeltsin. Fewer (19 per cent) distrusted Rutskoi than Yeltsin (32 per cent), while the percentage of those who partially trusted each was roughly the same (36 per cent for Rutskoi and 33 per cent for Yeltsin).[60] In other polls in the post-Soviet period, however, Yeltsin remained much more popular than any other Russian political figure.

The last years of the Soviet Union and the beginning of the post-Soviet period in Russia and the other republics were marked by the increased importance of public opinion in policy making. Political leaders, understanding the importance of popular support and in the context of new elections, began to pay much more attention to surveys of public opinion. It is clear that both Gorbachev and Yeltsin decided key issues of political strategy on the basis of their interpretations of prevailing popular moods.

11 Letters and political communication

Gorbachev made frequent reference to opinion polls during his period of office, particularly during the last months of his Presidency. Discussing the attempted coup with newspaper editors in September 1991, for instance, he noted that 40 per cent of the public at large – according to the polls – had supported it.[1] Speaking to *Literaturnaia gazeta* on the eve of his resignation, Gorbachev insisted that there was a popular desire to preserve some form of union: the 'latest opinion polls' showed that more people were in favour of the union than during the March 1991 referendum, when the principle of federation had been supported by a 76 per cent majority.[2] And yet throughout the Gorbachev years, and before them, there was another way in which leadership and society were connected, and through which public opinion could express itself: letters, above all to the press.[3] Letters were certainly unrepresentative of the wider society: for a start, they over-represented pensioners, the better educated and urban areas.[4] Letters, at the same time, reached party and government offices, as well as the press, in enormous numbers. How, pollsters were asked, could their samples of a thousand or two compare with the millions of communications that reached decisionmakers more directly?[5] Letters, equally, allowed members of the public to express themselves in their own words, without the mediation of interviewers: and it was this direct expression of opinion in which party and state officials were most interested throughout the Gorbachev period, rather than statistical summaries.[6] Later still, letters were one of the 'seven channels' through which President Yeltsin kept in touch with the popular mood in Russia.[7]

Writing letters: from the revolution to Gorbachev

Although an official emphasis upon 'work with letters' dates back no further than the 1960s, the attempts made by Soviet writers to establish its Leninist origins are not completely without foundation. Even before the revolution the Bolshevik paper *Vpered*, published in Geneva, received about 300 letters a month, an unusually large postbag for the time.[8] After the revolution such

193

popular contacts developed further. Leading political figures such as President Kalinin travelled widely about the country, giving speeches and receiving the comments and complaints of citizens (the train in which Kalinin undertook these journeys, the 'October Revolution', was called 'Soviet power on wheels').[9] Complaints or queries could also be addressed to the Presidium of the Central Executive Committee (VTsIK), the legislative body elected by the Congress of Soviets, and many of them reached the attention of Lenin, who as chairman of the Council of People's Commissars was answerable to VTsIK. The central office of the Council of People's Commissars received about 10,000 letters of this kind a year, many of which were reportedly taken into account in the elaboration of government decrees and instructions, and citizens could also address themselves to the reception offices of the Communist Party Central Committee.[10] Lenin's own postbag was itself a substantial one, including many that directly challenged official policies.[11]

During the 1920s and 1930s, as the emphasis of party and state policy shifted from discovering what popular preferences might be to mobilising the masses towards the achievement of objectives that had already been centrally determined, 'work with letters' began to receive rather less attention. The soviets lost most of whatever democratic content they had originally possessed; newspapers devoted more space to record-breaking economic achievements than to the legitimate complaints of citizens; and the style of party leadership became increasingly remote and hierarchical. The Stalin Constitution, published in draft for national discussion, involved nearly forty million members of the public, who among them suggested over 40,000 changes.[12] The new family legislation of 1936, however, was a better indicator of the use that was made of communications from ordinary citizens at this time. A sharply retrogressive measure, it was intended to strengthen marriage and (among other things) outlawed abortion. A few letters appeared pointing out that 'lack of living space' was often the real problem; but the published correspondence as a whole, together with the editorial coverage, was overwhelmingly favourable. It later emerged that the great majority of letters had in fact opposed the new law but that only a few had been allowed into print, while every single communication in favour had been published. 'The Boss says we must have more children' was the simple explanation.[13]

A serious degree of attention to the oral and written communications of the public is in fact for the most part a development of rather later years, of the post-Stalin and even post-Khrushchev period.[14] The first clear sign of a change in official policy was a Central Committee decree of August 1967, 'On the improvement of work on the consideration of letters and the organisation of the reception of toilers', and it is from the adoption of this resolution that the more recent emphasis upon communications from the public may be said to date. Letters, the resolution pointed out, were 'one of the main forms of strengthening and broadening the link between party and people, of the participation of the population in the conduct of state affairs, a means for the expression of public opinion, [and] a source of information on the life of the country'. Party, state and public bodies were urged to analyse and discuss such communications more frequently, newspapers were urged to publish them more often, and in all cases the matters raised, 'as a rule', were to be dealt with not later than a month after the receipt of the communication concerned.[15] The following year the first comprehensive all-union legal provision for these activities was made in a decree of the Presidium of the USSR Supreme Soviet, and a decree was adopted on the same date establishing procedures for the consideration of letters by deputies to the USSR Supreme Soviet.[16]

Somewhat later, in April 1976, the Central Committee adopted an additional resolution on the subject, 'On the further improvement of work with letters of the toilers in the light of the decisions of the 25th Congress of the CPSU'. There were still occasions when an 'inattentive, indifferent attitude' was taken towards the proposals, requests and complaints of the public, the resolution noted. It urged party, state and public bodies to take communications of this kind into consideration more frequently in their day-to-day activity, checking that they were being dealt with properly and discussing them at party bureau and ministerial collegium meetings, and dealing severely with those who were guilty of excessive delay or negligence in this connection.[17] The new Soviet Constitution, adopted in 1977, gave additional backing to these principles. Article 49, in particular, established the right of all citizens to submit proposals and criticisms to state and public bodies, which were obliged to respond to them within specified time limits, and Article 58 gave citizens the right to lodge complaints against the actions of officials and prescribed how they were to be considered. Both of these provisions had previously been embodied in legislation but neither had been included in the Constitution, the 'basic law' of the Soviet state.[18]

Finally, in 1980, the Presidium of the USSR Supreme Soviet adopted revised and expanded versions of its decrees of 1968, strengthening both of them, at least in wording. The decree on the consideration of the proposals, declarations and complaints of citizens now referred specifically to the right of citizens to 'criticise shortcomings' in the work of state and public bodies and to 'lodge complaints against the actions of officials, state and public bodies', and the decree on the consideration of letters by Supreme Soviet deputies now made reference to the right of deputies to participate themselves in the resolution of the matters at issue. Dissatisfied citizens could appeal, if they wished, to a higher instance, and if there was any violation of established procedures, or any attempt to victimise those who had spoken out of turn, the officials concerned could – in serious cases – be subject to criminal prosecution.[19] Speaking at the Presidium session at which the first of these two decrees was adopted, Brezhnev emphasised the importance of ensuring that every Soviet citizen felt certain that any well-founded proposal, declaration or complaint he might make would be carefully examined and that an appropriate course of action would be adopted. 'The maximum of sensitivity, the maximum of attention, the maximum of concern for people – that is what the party demands from our institutions and officials', the Soviet President told the meeting.[20]

He had always made a point, Brezhnev explained in his memoirs, of examining not only his official papers but also the letters that came from ordinary people all over the country.[21] Up to 2,000 of them arrived every day; and it was impossible to read them without emotion, raising as they did all kinds of public as well as private concerns. If letters to local party and state committees were included and those that appeared in the press, it was a 'unique phenomenon, characteristic only of our Soviet way of life'. Brezhnev asked for negative letters as well as positive ones, and although he could scarcely go through his post himself he was 'systematically' briefed on its changing content. The most interesting letters were put aside to be read and re-read; other members of the Politburo and Secretariat were regularly briefed in the same way, and the most important communications of this kind were considered at their meetings and in the preparation of laws and decrees.[22] Konstantin Chernenko, earlier a Brezhnev aide, laid a similar emphasis upon letters during his own General Secretaryship and quoted them directly at meetings of the Central Committee.[23]

There was certainly a substantial flow of letters to party and state, as to other institutions, during the Brezhnev years. Just over two million letters reached the Central Committee between 1971 and 1975; more than three million were received between 1976 and 1980, and nearly 100,000 citizens addressed themselves directly to the Central Committee offices.[24] During the same period some nine million letters had been received by local party bodies, and as many as six million members of the public had made their concerns known in person.[25] In order to handle this substantial flow of communications the Central Committee established a Letters Department in 1978, headed by B. P. Iakovlev, a member (from 1981) of the Central Auditing Commission. Many of the letters he received, Iakovlev reported the following year, required no particular reply: such as the letter from I. Mukhin, a captain in the Vladivostok fleet, who wrote in to our 'leader and wise mentor' to tell him that his ship had 'fulfilled the ninth five year plan with honour', or the letter from I. Il'in of Archangel who thanked Brezhnev for his memoirs and his 'measureless contribution to the cause of world peace'.[26] Many more letters, however, were concerned with the ordinary concerns of Soviet life: pensions, retail trade, the telephone system, labour law, and – more often than anything else – housing.[27] Concerns of this kind also predominated in letters to local and higher levels of government.[28]

Very much greater numbers of letters were received, during the Brezhnev and subsequent years, by the local and national press. The average annual postbag of central dailies like *Pravda* and *Trud* was about half a million or more in the early 1980s, generally about twice the level of correspondence they had received in the 1950s, and the total postbag of the central press alone was an estimated 60–70 million a year.[29] About half of the letters of this period contained complaints of various kinds: in *Izvestiia*, for instance, 19 per cent of the letters that were received raised housing issues of various kinds, 13 per cent were about social security, 12 per cent were on legal questions, 6.5 per cent dealt with transport, and between 4 and 5 per cent respectively dealt with family matters, health and leisure. The Moscow evening paper reported a similar picture.[30] Increasingly, it appeared, the flow of letters dealt with national or global concerns, and contained proposals rather than criticisms; but there was still a mass of complaints about the low quality of consumer goods, delays in the postal service, shortages of medicine and other practical matters.[31] Up to 5 per cent of the letters received by a national daily at this time were published in its pages; the others were analysed and statistical breakdowns sent to party, state and other bodies. In a few cases the newspaper department – typically the paper's largest – was able to detail a member of its own staff to examine the matter at first hand.[32]

The letters that were selected for publication were not necessarily a representative sample of the letters that a newspaper had received. In Taganrog, for instance, 26 per cent of all the letters that were published in the local paper dealt with industry and construction, although these accounted for only 14 per cent of all the letters the paper had received. By contrast, only 3 per cent of the letters that were printed dealt with transport and communications, although these accounted for a much larger proportion (10 per cent) of all the letters that had been received. Retail trade and catering (4 and 12 per cent respectively), public services and town planning (5 and 20 per cent respectively) and housing (1 and 5 per cent respectively) were similarly underrepresented. More generally, some 69 per cent of the letters the paper printed were mainly or entirely favourable in character, although these accounted for only 25 per cent of the letters the paper had received; while negative or hostile letters accounted for 67 per cent of the letters the paper had received but for only 8 per cent of the letters it had published.[33] The letters that were printed in other papers on the proposal to divert the Siberian rivers could 'hardly be called a discussion' so much did the '"exchange"of opinion move in a single direction'.[34] Letters, in some cases, were actually written by members of the newspaper's own staff, and it was certainly a general practice to edit all communications of this kind and modify them stylistically.[35]

The discussion that took place of the draft 1977 Constitution reflected both the strengths and weaknesses of exercises of this kind during the Brezhnev years. More than 140 million citizens were reported to have taken part in the discussion, or more than four-fifths of all adults; a display of popular activism on this scale, Brezhnev told the Supreme Soviet, was historically unprecedented. About one and a half million meetings of various kinds had been organised for discussion of the draft, together with a further 450,000 party meetings at which a total of three million members and others had been in attendance. More than two million deputies had considered the draft at meetings of their local soviet, and letters had arrived in an 'unending flow' from ordinary citizens. All of these letters and other communications, Brezhnev suggested, had shown that a 'new person' had come into being, one who identified the state's interests as his own; the people as a whole had been the 'real creator' of the new constitution.[36] Only much later did it emerge that the letters actually received from ordinary citizens had included sharp criticisms of the electoral system, attacks on Article 6 (which institutionalised the Communist Party's leading role), and inquiries about Brezhnev's two Hero of the Soviet Union awards, conferred thirteen years after hostilities had formally concluded.[37]

Letters in the Gorbachev era

Gorbachev had referred to glasnost, and the need to secure the widest popular awareness of the reasons for their successes and failures, in an article he published in the journal *Don* as early as 1974.[38] He expressed similar concerns in an article on 'work with letters' in the party organisational journal in 1975. There were numerous references, in the article, to the practices that had been adopted in Stavropol itself under Gorbachev's first secretaryship. As soon as the mail arrived at party headquarters it was read and entered into a set of record cards. A 'significant proportion' of the letters were reported upon immediately to the *kraikom* secretaries, who then decided what further action should be taken. More than half of the mail was dealt with by party officials directly; local secretaries were informed once a month about the number of letters that had been received, and once every three months about the issues that had been raised and the manner in which they had been considered. Housing issues were raised most frequently of all, and also violations of the labour law; local citizens could also call into the *kraikom*'s reception office, or write to *Stavropol'skaia pravda* (which prepared monthly analyses of its letters for party officials).[39]

Gorbachev made frequent references to letters after he had been elected General Secretary, sometimes quoting from them directly. There was the sad case of comrade Mashinaia of Perm', which he mentioned in a speech in Tol'iatti in April 1986. Mrs Mashinaia had brought a television set, made at the 'Ekran' factory in Kuibyshev, which had worked for just fifteen minutes. It later turned out that the whole delivery of televisions from the same source had been defective. In fact, about a quarter of the enterprise's entire production had needed repair. How could anyone be satisfied with workmanship of this character?[40] The careless use of bread was raised by two villagers from the Krasnoiarsk territory, Ivanov and Mangalov. Bread, they wrote, was life itself, the wealth and strength of the Motherland; but how wastefully it was used! As a correspondent from Moscow pointed out, nobody was starving; would it not be better to use the bread that was being wasted in restaurants and cafeterias as cattle feed?[41] In another speech Gorbachev mentioned a letter from a comrade Dmitriev, who lived in the town of Kakhovka. Dmitriev was sure that 'sabotage' was taking place in the Urakine; macaroni, cakes and sweets, matches and soap were all disappearing from the shelves, and the bread that was being baked was uneatable. For all these shortcomings, Dmitriev told Gorbachev, the blame was being thrown on perestroika. Nor, added Gorbachev, were letters of this kind coming only from the Ukraine.[42]

Gorbachev made particularly frequent use of letters to justify the policies he was recommending to the Central Committee. In April 1985, for instance, he mentioned that party members had been asking why officials held the same posts for years on end,[43] and in January 1987 he quoted the views of ordinary citizens in support of his programme of democratisation.[44] In June 1987 he referred again to letters when he addressed the Central Committee on the question of economic reform. People wrote in, he told the Central Committee, to say that they were in favour of perestroika, but that they saw no changes in their own immediate environment. The Politburo could not ignore a situation of this kind, and it had been discussed many times in preparation for the plenum.[45] Gorbachev was asked, during a visit to Leningrad in October 1987, if letters from ordinary people actually reached him. Yes, they did, he replied; he tried to read as many of them as possible, and took many home with him for further study.[46] Gorbachev referred to the 'wonderful' letters that were appearing in the Soviet press in his book *Perestroika*. Letters and direct communications of other kinds from citizens, he noted, were 'the major "feedback" linking the Soviet leadership with the masses', and they were discussed at regular intervals within the Politburo.[47]

Gorbachev received up to 40,000 letters a month after his accession as General Secretary, and over 400,000 in 1985 alone.[48] The letters covered all kinds of subjects. 'Perestroika is what the people long for. Do not stray from the path you have chosen, do not retreat', wrote A. Lavrik of the Amur region. 'If there is a return to the past then better the hangman's noose', thought L. Sheveleva of Bratsk. 'Please take care of your health: the battle is just starting', warned E. Glushkov of Iuzhno-Sakhalinsk. 'It is clear to everyone how much of your energy, time, intellectual strength and health is being consumed by the colossal, inhuman burden you have brought down upon yourself', wrote K. Lasta of Leningrad. 'Perhaps it will be a little easier for you if you know that the huge mass of ordinary people are entirely behind you, that they admire you and support you.' Z. Potop was 'endlessly proud' of Gorbachev as he observed the President's activities abroad; ordinary people would be 'ready to give up everything and to live on bread and water if only we can preserve the peace'. An engineer in the Novolipetsk metallurgical works, O. Iurkina, had called her second son Mikhail Sergeevich; from the first year of perestroika she had been his 'ardent supporter'.[49]

A substantial part of Gorbachev's postbag came from abroad, particularly from Germany, Sweden and the USA.[50] Letters to Soviet leaders from foreign correspondents had become a tradition at least as early as 1982, when a ten-year old American, Samantha Smith, wrote to congratulate Yuri Andropov on his appointment and to express concern about the prospect of a nuclear war.[51] Gorbachev himself made extensive use of his foreign correspondence during visits abroad. In Geneva in 1985, at the first Soviet–US summit, he told a press conference he had been 'greatly impressed' by the letters he had received from children, veterans and others in foreign countries.[52] In Washington for the summit in December 1987 he told NBC he had received 80,000 letters that year from ordinary Americans, quite apart from the number that had been sent to the Soviet Embassy, and quoted directly from a letter written to him by seventeen-year old Emily Holders: if the family of man did not learn to live together, she had told the Soviet leader, they would surely die together.[53] These and other letters of their kind, he added, had helped him understand the American people better, and had made clear their concern for a better and peaceful world and for better relations between their two countries in particular.[54]

Gorbachev received letters from businessmen, Nobel Prizewinners, writers and government ministers. Paul McCartney wrote to suggest the issue of a special album of rock and roll tunes; a Japanese student wrote to say 'I love you, and USSR', and he was invested with honorary membership of the Pumpkin Club and the Cousteau Society.[55] Americans wrote to defend the Strategic Defense Initiative – a programme from which both sides could benefit – and to suggest that the Soviet leader test his popularity in the United States with an opinion poll ('a time-honored method here'). There were proposals to build a bridge from Alaska to Siberia ('we could then visit friends of ours on both sides'), and requests for quite specific assistance in completing college assignments; even offers to take the whole Gorbachev family to Disneyland.[56] At least one foreign letter appears to have some influence upon the Soviet leader: a letter from Gene La Roque, a retired Rear Admiral of the US Navy, in which he suggested that the Soviet Union stop the testing of nuclear devices on or before 6 August, adding that the United States might be persuaded to follow suit. Shortly after Gorbachev's accession the Presidium of the USSR Supreme Soviet announced that it would enter into a unilateral moratorium to stop the Soviet testing programme, explaining that La Roque in his letter had 'appealed for a declared moratorium on the testing of all nuclear weapons from 6 August 1985 – the 40th anniversary of the atomic bombardment of Hiroshima. The Soviet Union welcomed this initiative and announced its willingness to take this step of goodwill'.[57]

The changes that took place in Soviet public life over the years of perestroika had a considerable impact upon the flow of communications to party, state and press from the mass public. As state institutions grew in authority, the number of letters to the Supreme Soviet increased: from 203,581 in 1985 up to 869,934 in 1989, the year in which the Supreme Soviet was reconstructed as the country's first-ever working parliament.[58] By 1990 some of this enthusiasm had evaporated, yet the Supreme Soviet still received 678,000 written and verbal communications from the ordinary public and in addition entertained a further 52,000 citizens in person.[59] The Communist Party, by contrast, lost ground substantially. Some three million letters were addressed to the Central Committee between 1976 and 1981, 3.5 million between 1981 and 1986, and 3.8 million between the 27th Congress in 1986 and the 28th, in July 1990.[60] Subsequently, however, there was a decline, and the number of members that addressed themselves personally to party headquarters fell more sharply still, from 26,650 in 1989 to 13,288 in 1990.[61] Letters none the less remained a vital source of information for leading officials at all levels: more important communications of this kind were reported upon daily to the General Secretary and other members of the Secretariat, and over the inter-congress period more than 100 analyses of current issues based on letters and other communications were prepared for the Politburo.[62]

Letters, in the early 1990s, were still predominantly to the press rather than to party, state or other bodies. Almost half (48 per cent) of those who addressed themselves in this way to the authorities in 1990 wrote to the newspapers; the executive committees of local soviets came second (29 per cent), and then party, trade union and Komsomol committees (21 per cent).[63] Among the newspapers themselves *Pravda*, up to 1991, was still the organ of the CPSU and the single most authoritative Soviet publication. Its letters department, about 100 strong, was at this time the paper's largest, handling up to 2,000 letters every working day.[64] *Pravda* played a particularly prominent role in the discussion that took place about the strategy of perestroika: more space was given over to letters than ever before, they often appeared on the front page, and new rubrics appeared such as 'Your position on perestroika', 'Life as it really is' and (from 1991) 'Cri de coeur'. *Pravda*'s editorial policy remained relatively orthodox; its editor was criticised in person at the 19th Party Conference (he was replaced in 1989), the paper was briefly suspended after the attempted coup, and in 1992 it began to experience commercial difficulties and breaks in publication. At the same time it remained the paper in which the party conducted most of its open self-examination, and it was in *Pravda* that the single most sensational publication of the early perestroika years appeared, a digest of letters on privilege under the title 'Cleansing' (*Ochishchenie*).[65]

Pravda's circulation none the less declined steadily from the late 1980s, and so too did the stream of letters it received. In 1981 there had been 514,000, and in 1986, another Congress year, there were 622,044. In 1988, also a busy year for party policymaking, the flow of correspondence had increased to 672,000.[66] By 1989, however, with the party's public standing and the paper's own circulation both in decline, *Pravda*'s postbag was down to 473,201, and by 1992 it had fallen to less than 100,000.[67] Other established papers, among them *Izvestiia*, also saw a fall in their postbag in the late 1980s and early 1990s. There were 520,000 letters to *Izvestiia* in 1981; in 1990, fewer than 300,000; in 1991, just 110,000.[68] The trade union paper *Trud* fared rather better, with 415,000 correspondents in 1981 and 475,000 in 1989.[69] Much of the decline in letters to the central press was in any case compensated for by an increase in the postbag of newer, often livelier competitors. The popular weekly *Argumenty i fakty*, for instance, increased its postbag from 54,000 in 1987 to over half a million in 1990; in 1979, its first year of publication, it had just thirty-five correspondents.[70] Another radical weekly, *Ogonek*, had a postbag of 12,000 a day in 1986 but had reached about 200,000 by 1990,[71] while the youth weekly *Sobesednik*, founded in 1984, had 20,000 letters in that year but 42,000 by 1988.[72] Letters to the central radio and television service, 2.3 million in 1979, were up to 3.5 million by the end of the 1980s.[73]

Letters to the press in the Gorbachev years were still marked by a number of characteristic failings. As a Kiev historian pointed out, there was still the 'fatal practice' by which journalists wrote the letters and then signed them with readers' names, particularly when 'responses' to particular publications were needed.[74] All that was genuine, complained a reader from Kyrgyzstan, was the signature at the end.[75] In Kursk, the local paper organised letters in support of the August coup in this way; and in the

Central Committee itself, letters from 'honest Communists' complaining about the reform process were kept on file in the Secretariat.[76] Some editors, however, forbade practices of this kind;[77] and it was equally the case that fewer letters than ever before were anonymous. As *Sobesednik*'s letters editor pointed out, the stream of communications of this kind had 'almost dried up', and students and young specialists were now quite prepared to put their name to letters that were openly critical of the authorities.[78] There were also more responses to other letters than ever before: *Sobesednik* had more than 1,800 commentaries on a letter written by 'Natasha', a young woman from an affluent family who had become a drug addict and then abandoned her child, and *Pravda* had its largest response to a letter from a mother who was attempting to bring up five young children in difficult circumstances.[79]

The letters: themes and issues

What did the letters of perestroika suggest about the popular mood? There were, of course, the statutory plaudits for the party's bold and far-seeing strategy. A teacher from northern Kazakhstan, for instance, wanted *Pravda* to know that perestroika had reached the state farm on which he worked; more houses were being built, there were fewer drunks about, and the hairdresser was even paying them a regular visit.[80] Workers from the industrial town of Cherepovets reported that labour turnover had been reduced.[81] An employee from an engineering factory in Simferopol wrote in to say that the suggestions he had made in a letter concerning the Law on the State Enterprise, adopted in June 1987, had been incorporated into the final draft. 'Even now', he wrote, 'I still find it difficult to contain my feelings'.[82] There were compliments for the Soviet health service and its personnel, and praise for the housing officials that had helped a reader obtain a new flat.[83] And there was certainly no lack of goodwill, at least in the early years of perestroika. Tell Gorbachev, wrote I. Goncharov from the Tatar republic, that 'all the working class' as well as 'honest' members of the scientific and technical intelligentsia were in favour of the course he was pursuing.[84] 'We are all very satisfied with M. S. Gorbachev and our government', wrote another reader as the General Secretary set off for the Washington summit at the end of 1987.[85]

The new openness, however, also allowed a much wider range of short-comings to be discussed, some of them of fairly long standing but others more directly connected with perestroika. The shortage of sugar was an example of the second of these, stemming as it did from the anti-alcoholism campaign that had been launched in 1985. As A. Shuliachenko reported from the Kiev region, in order to discourage moonshiners it had been decided that sugar would be sold locally only between 4 and 5 pm. The queues were 'kilometres long'.[86] Another reader, also from the Ukraine, reported that in his local area every shop had been given a limited amount of sugar to sell; people were queueing overnight, and if all the family were working they got none at all.[87] The shortage of drink on sale through the usual channels, until the policy was relaxed somewhat in 1988, also caused a great increase in the price of *samogon* or home brew. As a letter from a group of collective farmers in the Voronezh region reported, *samogon* had actually become more expensive than the real thing: 70 rubles was being asked for a three-litre bottle. They could provide a list of the moonshiners if requested, but asked not to be named as 'perestroika hasn't reached us yet'.[88]

The shift of emphasis from state to private and cooperative trade also had unfortunate consequences, if readers' letters were any guide. Shops, for instance, arbitrarily increased their prices three or four times.[89] Tea became more difficult to obtain, in part because of restrictions on the sale of alcohol, and so did sugar; in December 1990 *Pravda*'s correspondents had still nothing to drink their tea with but coupons.[90] Coupons were in themselves no solution: they got lost, the ration they provided was in any case insufficient, and with a single coupon for a pair of shoes every eighteen months should they buy summer or winter ones?[91] There were shortages of butter and milk, and bread was rarely available.[92] Another correspondent had found it difficult to obtain a pair of socks that would fit him, and 'without socks I can't participate in perestroika'.[93] As another correspondent told the Central Committee, you couldn't put statistics on your feet.[94] And where had matches disappeared to?[95] The situation in health care, the most important of the public services, was 'catastrophic'.[96] A seventy-nine-year old pensioner from Sverdlovsk, for instance, had been waiting four months for some medicine for her headache; never in her lifetime had there been such a lack.[97] It was worse still for invalids, who were just 'buried alive'.[98] An increasing number of appeals were sent to the Central Committee, which had to point out that it was 'not a department store'.[99]

Older problems also persisted, among them the range and quality of consumer goods. Children's shoes, for instance, gave out after ten days.[100] One of *Izvestiia*'s correspondents had taken delivery of a Zhiguli after years of waiting; but it broke down straight away and there were no spare parts.[101] A distraught pensioner, V. Grybina of Vladivostok, wrote to complain about the reliability of Soviet televisions. There had been no perestroika at all in matters of this kind, she told *Pravda*. The first television she had bought, at a cost of 300 rubles, quickly broke down; so did the second, approved by the state quality control commission, on which she had lavished the 200 rubles she had managed to save from her pension. 'Now I sit and cry', wrote Mrs Grybina; 'where am I to get the money to buy a third television?'[102] Aeroflot had increased its prices but reduced its services; railway carriages were dirty and poorly maintained.[103] Other correspondents complained of delays in the mail,[104] of shortages of newspapers at retail kiosks, of overcrowding and delays on public transport, of the lack of children's clothes (from a mother of eleven), and of food queues as long as they had been during the war.[105]

There were, of course, some improvements to report, but they were often cosmetic. A worker from Kuibyshev, for instance, wrote to *Pravda* that he had popped into his workshop canteen after he had returned from holidays. He hardly knew it – it had been reconstructed just like a restaurant! The comfortable oval tables beside the buffet, the panels on the walls, the cleanliness – nothing like it had ever been seen before. Then he had a look at the menu – it was no different. It emerged that 'there were changes on the outside, but inside all remained the same'.[106] Other writers reported that the new electoral arrangements for the selection of leading personnel had often been used to eliminate trouble-makers and to replace them with clients of the director.[107] Virtually all of *Pravda*'s correspondents were 'for' perestroika; the trouble was that it had led to little but words, while local conditions had hardly been affected. As a blacksmith from Kuibyshev told the paper, perestroika reminded him of a storm in a forest: 'there is a lot of noise at the top, but down below hardly a puff of wind'.[108] Local officials, it emerged, had responded to the challenge of perestroika in all kinds of ways. Some ignored it, and others passed resolutions about it; still others, more inventive, set up commissions on perestroika and organised campaigns about it with targets that were noisily overfulfilled.[109] One of *Pravda*'s correspondents, a practising Catholic from Lithuania, was so impressed by the resistance Gorbachev was confronting that she prayed for him at Mass every Sunday, since in his own way he was helping to save the world from its sins.[110]

Readers and correspondents, by the late 1980s, were raising still more serious questions about the nature of perestroika itself. A mother in Minsk, for instance, wrote to complain about the lack of positive values on which she could raise her three children. She herself had grown up with socialism as her ideal and purpose in life. But now, with glasnost and unrestrained criticism of all aspects of the society, the socialist ideal was becoming discredited. Her own faith was wavering, while her children were swamped by a flood of negative information that denigrated everything. How could young people grow up in conditions of 'total criticism', in a society where 'nothing was sacred'?[111] Or there was Sergei Slipkov of the Krasnoiarsk territory, who wrote in to the youth newspaper *Komsomol'skaia pravda*. 'I'm seventeen', he began. 'I've read *Children of the Arbat* and newspaper and magazine articles about the repressions, about the persecution of Zoshchenko and Akhmatova, about Lysenko's hold over science, and life seems a nightmare to me. There's nothing ahead. I used to believe we'd overcome all hardships, for our history has been so heroic. I no longer do. How do I regain my faith?' (the paper had no obvious answer).[112] Or there was Yuri Kotov from Mogilev, a thirty-two-year old who had 'originally believed in the illusion of perestroika'. But what was actually happening was some sort of nightmare, not just because of shortages, but because of the complete unpredictability of the future. How could he find himself in the new world of 'fixers' and shameless political operators?[113] Others were confused by the changes in terminology. What was 'real socialism', for a start, asked I. Koniakhin of Gorky; did this mean there could be 'unreal socialism', or a socialism that was neither real nor unreal?[114]

Many, in these circumstances, called more or less openly for a return to the past. A letter from Leningrad chemistry lecturer Nina Andreeva to *Sovetskaia Rossiia* in March 1988, widely described as an 'anti-perestroika manifesto', was the most celebrated of these communications; she later emerged as the head of a hard-line grouping which denounced Gorbachev for his 'revisionism'.[115] Why was the whole of the Soviet past being denigrated, wrote Lev Zhdanov, a party member from Voroshilovgrad? Why were the works of counter-revolutionary generals like Denikin being prepared for a wide readership, while the writings of Molotov, Malenkov and others were unobtainable?[116] A party member from the Rostov region was concerned that he had found nothing in favour of socialism throughout 1989. 'You call this pluralism? It's just a series of own goals'.[117] 'In the past the press wrote that everything was alright in this country and that everything abroad was wrong. Now it's the other way round: . . . is that reality?' asked Arnold Korolenko from Khar'kov.[118] 'Bring back Stalin', urged V. Kravchenko of Khar'kov; at least there had been order and discipline – what, by contrast, had democracy done for them?[119] Many were simply bewildered by the changes through which they were living. 'Who am I?', asked one of *Izvestiia*'s readers; 'a citizen of the former Soviet Union? Or a citizen of a single economic space?'[120] *Argumenty i fakty* had a similar letter from 'Confused' of Moscow in late 1991: what was the name of the country in which he lived? The paper suggested 'Take any three letters from the alphabet and you have the answer'.[121]

There was still support for Gorbachev, in the darkening world of the early 1990s, though less so than ever before. A veteran from Archangel, for instance, wrote in to *Pravda* to let him know of his support for the 'wise foreign policy' that was being followed by the Soviet government 'and especially by President M. S. Gorbachev'.[122] A Moscow translator, Sergei Svetushkin, pointed out that daily life had become more lively and that international tensions had been reduced under his skilful administration.[123] A group of veterans thought he deserved 'sharp criticism', but he should still be retained for the moment in the positions he occupied. Another letter, written in the late spring of 1991, thought Gorbachev was pursuing a 'purgatorial but still a correct path'.[124] The post that reached the Central Committee in the early 1990s, however, became increasingly critical of Gorbachev and of the party leadership as a whole. Letters were uncompromising in their demands and in their criticisms; there were more and more letters from the poor, and more that expressed openly anticommunist sentiments. A few expressed pride that they were joining the CPSU in the difficult circumstances of 1990, but many more enclosed their party cards, and there were calls for Gorbachev to resign and for an emergency party congress to be convened.[125] Why, correspondents wanted to know, were things going from bad to worse?[126]

There were still more categorical opinions. Perestroika, in the view of a correspondent from L'vov, was the 'worst they had had to live through since the war (and for that matter in peacetime and because of the actions of our own government)'. Not a single foreign enemy had brought the USSR so much suffering as perestroika, wrote a further correspondent. What had perestroika produced for ordinary people? 'Mass unemployment and rationing system.' For another of *Pravda*'s letter-writers, perestroika had led to 'empty shelves in the shops, price rises, the collapse of the union, banditism, violence, hooliganism, interethnic conflict, the disintegration of the CPSU and the collapse of the socialist community'.[127] For some it was a 'nightmare', or as another letter put it, 'Only in hell could you have a life like this'.[128] Conclusions of this kind were supported by the steadly increasing proportion of those who were prepared to say, when asked by pollsters, that they would have opposed perestroika if they had known to what it was going to lead. In 1990 supporters and opponents were equally divided, with a third in favour and a third against. By September 1991, however, 23 per cent of those who were asked said they would still have supported perestroika but twice as many (52 per cent) said they would have opposed it.[129]

Letters and policy formation

Letters, throughout the Soviet period, have been one among a number of mechanisms in which the authorities have interacted with the wider society. Election campaigns, even of the traditional kind, have offered opportunities for popular influence through comments on ballot papers, complaints to candidates and canvassers, and threats not to vote.[130] There were further opportunities through the party, Komsomol and trade union movement, and through nominally independent bodies such as the people's control committees.[131] The authorities, for their part, have always had other means of assessing public opinion, including surveys (as we have seen in chapter

10) and the questions put to lecturers and propagandists by their audiences. Questions put to Soviet lecturers by foreign tourists were also studied, to assist in the presentation of counterpropaganda, as were indicators such as the turnover of political literature in public libraries, church attendance and levels of crime.[132] A particularly important role has always been played by the KGB, represented (after 1973) within the Politburo, directly responsible for official policy towards dissidents and the counterculture, and the centre of a nationwide intelligence and reporting network.[133]

Within this complex of communication, letters have always had a particular role to perform. The first of these is what has been called an 'ombudsman' function, the righting of a wrong or the correction of a particular instance of maladministration. There was the case of comrade K. from the village of Artem in the Donetsk region, who complained to his local soviet about shortcomings in the organisation of retail trade in his village. He received no satisfactory response and thereupon approached *Izvestiia*, which was able to extract an assurance from the regional soviet that the necessary action would be taken. The paper was similarly able to secure a resumption of the water supply in a district of the Ternopol' region in the Ukraine.[134] Another family was able to secure the two roomed flat to which they were entitled after *Pravda* had taken up their case; and a place was found in an old folks' home for an elderly man from Cheliabinsk.[135] Letters could also lead to reprimands and even prison sentences for those responsible if the facts that had been quoted were confirmed by subsequent investigation; the trade union paper *Trud* was particularly successful in securing the sanctioning or dismissal of factory executives who had violated the labour code.[136] More positively, individual communications have sometimes made a direct input into legislation: the law on labour collectives of 1983, for instance, incorporated ten published and three unpublished proposals from ordinary citizens into its final text.[137]

Letters began to play a more substantial role, during the 1980s and 1990s, in shaping the policy agenda. The 'food programme' launched in 1982, for instance, appears to have been influenced, at least in part, by the fact that the Central Committee was 'deluged' with letters about the subject, many of them in blunt terms and about half of them unsigned, complaining of the discrepancy between promises of a better future and the steadily deteriorating reality.[138] The adoption of measures against corruption during the Andropov years was also prompted, at least in part, by letters of concern from ordinary citizens to the Central Committee and Presidium of the USSR Supreme Soviet. The very first Politburo meeting to be reported in the press, in December 1982, heard that while there was 'unanimous support' for the party's foreign and domestic policy, the letters had contained a series of suggestions for improving labour discipline, reducing waste, allocating housing more equitably and minimising other violations of legality and justice. The letters were described as a 'mandate from working people to party and state agencies', and the issues they raised were to be 'carefully examined and resolved'.[139] The strengthening of law and order was similarly presented as a response to pressure from citizens in Gorky, who had been afraid to walk the streets at night.[140]

Letters began to play a more direct part in agenda-setting under Gorbachev, who circulated digests of them to party meetings for this purpose. Before the crucial Central Committee meeting on democratisation in January 1987, for instance, Gorbachev circulated copies of letters of complaint from ordinary citizens about the party bureaucracy together with a draft of his own speech.[141] All the delegates of the 19th Party Conference in the summer of 1988 were given summaries of the letters that had been reaching the Central Committee; they suggested that a wider range of political forces should be persuaded to support perestroika, that the 1987 Law on the State Enterprise was being sabotaged by ministries and Gosplan, that price reform should be more thoroughly considered, that priority should be given to food and housing, and that democratisation should be extended and accelerated (it could 'hardly be considered normal', for instance, that there had never been a referendum in seventy years of Soviet rule).[142] Participants in the February 1988 Central Committee meeting were given a review of letters of a similar kind on the reform of secondary and higher education.[143] Reviews of this kind appear first to have been carried out for the June 1986 Central Committee plenum; they were also carried out in advance of the Russian party conference and the 28th Party Congress in 1990.[144]

Letters of this kind could obviously be used in a manipulative way, selected and presented so as to facilitate leadership objectives. Letters, however, could relate to each other, in the form of a continuing correspondence on issues of topical concern, and in ways that often took them beyond the framework of official thinking. The first articles on prostitution, for instance, in the summer of 1986, focused on 'nocturnal butterflies' whose clients were Westerners. After further discussion in the press, however, including letters from some of the females concerned, it began to be accepted that paid sex with foreigners were simply a small part of a substantial social phenomenon. The tone of the letters, meanwhile, changed from moral indignation to sympathy with the victims of the social conditions that had given rise to prostitution and often forced desperate women on to the streets.[145] There were even some readers that astonished the journalists concerned by calling for legalised brothels:

The postbox sometimes takes us aback [wrote the letters editor of *Sobesednik*]. Many readers talk of the need . . . to open brothels. When I saw that for the first time I thought the reader must be a crank. Yet several dozen more letters like that then landed on my desk![146]

Another paper, *Studencheskii meridian*, had more than 2,000 letters in response to an article about a youth who was gaoled for eight years for killing a young punk.[147]

Letters, moreover, were sometimes able to raise issues that were on the very margin of the publicly acceptable. The issue of privilege was one of these. *Pravda*'s review of letters, 'Cleansing', referred to an 'immobile, inert and viscous "party-administrative stratum"' that had formed between the party and the working class, and pointed out that social inequalities had been widened by 'all kinds of special canteens, special shops, special hospitals and so forth'.[148] A letter in *Argumenty i fakty* raised similar issues. Why, asked a group of building workers, were they being asked to construct a block of exclusive flats for party officials, with a day-care centre, 'state of the art design, improved interior layout and the highest quality materials'? Three apartment buildings had been pulled down to make room for it, and the former tenants had been moved to the outskirts of town (it was this letter, rather than the revelation that Sakharov was a more popular parliamentarian, that so angered Gorbachev he sought to remove the paper's editor).[149] Why should party officials enjoy special privileges, such as better apartments, a better food supply, better hospital care and even (asked a war and labour veteran) better cemeteries?[150] And why had a seven-storied palace been built for the regional party committee in Gorky within sight of a wooden, delapidated hospital for sick children and in a district that still lacked its own bathhouse?[151]

Letters could also raise all kinds of personal questions. For instance (in *Argumenty i fakty*):

I am writing to you for the second time. My brother is 13. He engages in onanism. Is it dangerous for his health, and if so, how can it be combatted? I beg you, answer, because I'm worried for my brother, and he's too ashamed to go to the doctor.'[152]

The paper – in the early 1990s, the world's best-selling publication of its kind – was also asked how much it cost to engage the services of a prostitute. No more than a glass of port wine, it reported, on Komsomol Square, where three of Moscow's main stations were located, but up to $300 in an Intourist hotel, and rather more for special services (foreigners apparently thought these charges rather high).[153] And it was again to the press that ordinary Russians turned to find out – for instance – if they could take a dog on the underground, if they could buy a place in a graveyard with their privatisation voucher, if the Russian government had an astrological service and if the presidents of the CIS states had been born under a particular sign of the zodiac.[154]

The opportunities for political action clearly widened during the later Gorbachev years, still more so after communist rule had ended. Letter-writing, however, still retained a significant place among the repertoire of political activity that was available to ordinary citizens. In 1989, for instance, the most widespread form of political participation was associated with new social movements, meetings and demonstrations (14 per cent); but in second place came collective appeals and protests, and in fourth place, after party and trade union meetings but ahead of strikes, individual appeals to newspapers or to party and state bodies.[155] In 1992, in a Russian poll, meetings and demonstrations were the form of unofficial action most widely cited; but 'letters to party and state bodies' were also important, after strikes and shopfloor discussion but ahead of hunger strikes and armed resistance.[156] Only one person in ten, at the same time, has ever written a letter to a newspaper;[157] and letter-writers are known to be unrepresentative of the wider population – they are disproportionately male, better educated than the average, and more often pensioners than their share of the total population would suggest.[158]

It may be best, in the end, to regard letters as a form of evidence that is valid in its own terms and indicative of at least a segment of opinion although not necessarily an accurate guide to the wider society. What, for instance, have children been making of the country's economic difficulties? Nine-year old Anastasia of Irkutsk, at least, was sufficiently concerned to write to *Argumenty i fakty* about it: please, she asked, make sure that Father Christmas visited their flat on New Year's Eve, rather than Ded Moroz, as Ded Moroz (the Russian equivalent) was 'suffering from a shortage of presents'.[159] And how were the elderly adapting to the transition to market relations? *Pravda*'s correspondents, again, may not have been representative, but they were certainly indicative of a significant section of the over-sixties. Mrs Saveleva of Taldy-Kurgan, for instance, had eaten up the money she had saved for a decent funeral and was concerned she might be interred without a coffin. Or there was Nektarii Fomin of Yekaterinburg, a war and labour veteran, who spent 'whole days' standing in line to redeem his scanty ration cards. There was 'virtually nothing in the stores', 'no clothes at all' and 'no medicine'. Old people who had lived sixty or seventy years, he thought, should be 'given a painless injection and sent on to the next world'.[160] And what about the victory of democracy in August 1991? Perhaps in Moscow and St Petersburg, wrote V. Beloboky, but in Bashkiria the only change was that prices were going up even faster. In Cherepovets, according to another writer, the local 'totalitarian regime' had remained, and 'even strengthened itself'.[161] Polls provide us with a picture of the distribution of opinion; evidence of this kind helps us to understand its qualitative and more personal dimensions.

12 The Soviet transition and 'democracy from above'

The changes which have transformed Soviet and now post-Soviet life in the period since 1985 have been as wide ranging and important as those that shaped the structure of Soviet society at the end of the 1920s and early 1930s. As Gorbachev and others have acknowledged, this constitutes a veritable revolution.[1] Some would argue that this was a 'revolution from above', although this is a designation which Gorbachev disputed.[2] As earlier chapters have shown, there has been significant impetus from below in the course of the changes, and this has not just been of a mobilisational kind; political forces stemming from society as a whole have been important in shaping the contours of change and providing much of the impetus for its development. Nevertheless, the role played by the political elite has been substantial both in initiating the changes and in giving them their flavour. An important aspect of this was the attempt to construct an institutional and regulatory framework for perestroika. Indeed, it is no exaggeration to talk about an attempt at revolution by legal fiat as the central authorities sought to set in place a panoply of laws designed to restrict some developments and to foster others. The central strand of this was the process of democratisation and the attempt to promote and structure this through legislative enactment. It was this official attempt to consolidate democratisation that is meant by the term 'democracy from above'.

Law and democracy

A central element of the process of reform as it unwound during 1988 was Gorbachev's avowed aim of establishing a 'socialist law-governed state'.[3] This aim was endorsed by the 19th Conference of the party in June–July 1988 and subsequently elaborated through the press.[4] The attempt to implement such an aim meant the generation of a vast array of legal enactments covering virtually all aspects of life, and the effort to enshrine the main principles of perestroika in the legal superstructure of the state. In this sense, the Gorbachev leadership sought to construct a legal framework within which perestroika could be encapsulated and thereby define the contours of that reform through legal statute. The essence of the socialist law-governed state lay in the primacy of law, its supremacy in all spheres of life. The supremacy of the law means that all are subject to it, including both state and citizenry, and that it is therefore perceived as a power independent of the governors. It sets limits on both government and individuals, and thereby constitutes an important mechanism for defending individuals against that government. Law would thus be invested with normative authority rather than having the purely instrumental nature that characterised it throughout Soviet history.

But the notion of a law-governed state is not necessarily democratic: a government and populace may both have their actions structured by law without the relationship between the two being of a kind we would regard as democratic. For this type of relationship to exist, what is important is the content of the laws. Those laws must establish the responsibility and accountability of the government to the populace, and they must enshrine the sorts of rights and freedoms of citizens, with corresponding limits on government, which empower them to play an active and dominant part in a democratic political process. If the substance of the law in a law-governed state achieves these two aims, the attempt to create such a state is part of the process of democratisation. In the Soviet Union under Gorbachev, the attempt was made to invest the law with these qualities.

In order to facilitate the emergence of democracy, action was necessary in two political arenas. The first was the formal institutional arena, and involved the structuring of an institutional framework which entrenched the desired notions of accountability and responsibility into the formal political institutions. The second was the public arena and involves what has been called 'restructuring public space'.[5] What this means is the creation of an arena within which autonomous political activity may legitimately be pursued. Any attempt at democratisation which did not embrace both arenas would be bound to fail: it would lead either to the existence of formal democratic institutions which lacked real substance, or the emergence of a politics of the streets which had no institutional manifestation in the formal political structure.

In the institutional arena, the attempt to consolidate governmental accountability involved the shifting of governmental authority from the non-accountable section of the politico-administrative structure to the accountable, and strengthening the mechanism through which account-ability could be exercised. Although advocated earlier, it was not until the 19th Conference that major steps were made to bring this to fruition. There were two aspects. The first involved the withdrawal of the party from a direct administrative role in the Soviet polity, reflected in the call for the party to exercise 'political' rather than administrative leadership. To facilitate this shift in the party's function, some restructuring of party organs was carried out and, in March 1990, the constitutional enshrinement of party dominance was abolished. In practice, this process was more difficult to achieve than the simple adoption of constitutional amendments. In part this was because of the extent of opposition to this process from inside the party, but it also reflects the belief that the party would be able to maintain its dominance even in the absence of its former administrative control. This assumption of continuing party dominance in part undercut the attempt to shift power from the publicly unaccountable party.

The second aspect was to build up accountable bodies of state power. This was to be achieved through new electoral arrangements and a new state structure consisting of the Congress of People's Deputies and its standing parliament, the Supreme Soviet.[6] Designed to replace the old Supreme Soviet, these bodies did emerge as vigorous debating fora and were not the tame creatures of the party the former legislative organs had been. However there were also severe deficiencies in their democratic livery. The law governing elections to the Congress of People's Deputies did not make competitive elections mandatory, reserved a third of the seats for representatives of non-popularly elected public organisations, and left excessive power in the hands of local authorities in determining who could stand for election and who could not. In the chamber, a large number of delegates continued to look to the party for guidance, while the chairman was often able to manipulate proceedings to get his way over the wishes of many of the delegates. The Supreme Soviet was not directly elected by the people but was elected by the Congress of People's Deputies, so its democratic character was even more in question. Although these are serious reservations about the democratic nature of these bodies, the development of these institutions was a step closer to notions of popular accountability on the part of the government.

Enshrining rights and freedoms

In the public arena, the attempt to achieve democratisation through the socialist law-governed state was evident in the attempt legislatively to create room within which autonomous citizen activity could be conducted. This took the form of enshrining in legislation various rights and freedoms fundamental to a democratic system. A survey of the post-1985 Soviet record shows that a wide array of such measures was introduced. Fundamental to such a process is the introduction of measures designed to enable citizens to think as they wish and believe what they wish. Recognition of this is reflected in the discussion that surrounded the drafting of a law on freedom of conscience during 1989,[7] and the ultimate adoption of such a law by the Supreme Soviet on 1 October 1990.[8] However, as the emphasis of this law suggests, freedom of conscience was interpreted overwhelmingly in religious terms; the new law is actually entitled a Law on Freedom of Conscience and Religious Organisations, and most of the text is devoted to those organisations and their legal standing. This means that the applicability of the law is more restricted than it need be. The absence of any provision in the law for conscientious objection from military service is perhaps the clearest example of its limited scope.[9] Certainly official Soviet acceptance of the need to bring its domestic legislation into harmony with international norms, conventions and obligations on human rights[10] implied a generalised commitment broader than that expressed in the Law on Freedom of Conscience and Religious Organisations, but this would be more soundly based were such a commitment to the general principle clearly espoused in this legislation.

A right to freedom of belief means little if it is not accompanied by a right publicly to espouse that belief. In effect, this means freedom of speech. A considerable step forward was made with the adoption of a Law on the Press on 12 June 1990.[11] Following considerable debate, this law formally abolished pre-publication censorship (except for matters of state security)[12] and allowed any organisation[13] or individual to start a publication. The grounds upon which registration enabling publication could be denied were strictly limited: calls for the overthrow of or change in the existing political system by force, propaganda of war or of racial, national and religious intolerance, pornography or disclosure of state secrets. The law also made it mandatory for government departments to answer questions directed to them by newspapers and gave the journalists the right to refuse to write what their editors dictated; the law did, however, give proprietors potentially significant editorial control. Through its provisions, this law appears to have created a framework within which an independent media could develop, although it did not grapple with two major inhibitions on this: the virtual monopoly enjoyed at that time by the CPSU over publishing facilities in the Soviet Union, and the strict control exercised by party and government over the distribution of paper. The law could also not prevent the exercise of pressure upon media outlets, such as the ousting of the independent Interfax news agency from its temporary premises in January 1991. Nor should it be seen as a sufficient guarantee of freedom of speech, as shown by the detention of Democratic Union activist Valeriia Novodvorskaia in September 1990 under the provisions of the law against the slander of the president.[14] Nevertheless, in terms of giving an independent media a legal basis upon which it could rest, this law was a significant innovation.[15]

An independent media was important because it provided the opportunity for individuals and groups which were not part of the traditional political establishment to express their views and thereby to seek the support of their fellow citizens. It also meant that there were now alternative, legal, avenues through which people could gain information and thereby acquire the sort of knowledge which would enable them to pass judgement upon the performance of the authorities. The already critical public could thereby have their critical stance much more solidly based than when they were forced to rely upon official media or rumour for information. But the press was not the only vehicle through which non-official views could be expressed. In June 1987, a Law on Nationwide Discussion[16] was introduced, providing a formal mechanism for popular involvement in the drafting of legislation, although this law did not make referenda mandatory on all major issues of contention. The concern to tap into public opinion is also evident in the establishment in early 1988 of the All-Union Centre for the Study of Public Opinion on Socio-Economic Problems,[17] a body designed to elicit public views on social and economic issues (see pp. 181–3). But if what was required was an informed, active citizenry, more than just the legislation of independent channels of information and expression was required. Also important was the right of organisation and activity.

The right to hold public demonstrations has existed for some time, although formally they had to be registered with the appropriate authorities before being held. Such a regulation clearly provided scope for the authorities to ban specific demonstrations by refusing them registration, a practice to which resort was had on a number of occasions;[18] in September 1988 a nation-wide ban was imposed on 'anti-Soviet' demonstrations. However the frequency with which demonstrations occurred suggests that in practice such restrictions were not a major problem. Nevertheless, the requirement for prior registration was in principle a significant limit on free assembly, particularly when the conditions under which the right to deny registration were not clearly spelled out but were instead covered by vague catch-all phrases like 'public security'. Much here depended upon the room for interpretation available to those in control of the registration process.

More important is the question of strikes, because this involves not only considerations of the more extended disruption of public life and of economic production, but also acts of opposition by that class which the party traditionally claimed to represent. Following debate, and under the direct influence of the miners' strike in the summer of 1989, the Supreme Soviet adopted a 'Law on the Order of Solving Collective Labour Disputes (Conflicts)'.[19] While this law legalised strike activity, it did so under restrictive conditions. Indeed, the law was explicitly designed to establish a procedure for working out labour disputes before they culminated in a strike. A complicated procedure of discussion, conciliation and arbitration had to be gone through before workers were legally permitted to indulge in strike activity to press their grievances. Furthermore the legislation gave the All-Union and republican supreme soviets or their presidia the right to suspend or postpone a strike for two months and banned strikes that were linked with demands for the violent overthrow or alteration of the Soviet state and social system or demands which violated national or racial equality. In addition strikes were prohibited in transport, communications, electric power, government administration, military production, defence and law enforcement, when they posed a threat to the lives and health of people and in continuous-process industries. Although these restrictions were significant, the legislation did at least recognise that strike activity was a legitimate form for workers to use to press for alleviation of their grievances. However, specific limitations on strike activity were introduced by the authorities at different times; for example, on 16 May 1991 Gorbachev introduced a decree banning strikes in key industries such as energy, coal, oil, gas, chemicals, petrochemicals, metallurgy and railways.[20]

Another important aspect of this law was that it gave the right to any group of workers to form their own collective, or union, and establish a strike committee. But it did not address the problem of what the rights and responsibilities of trade unions should be. This question was currently under discussion in the form of a draft law on the rights of trade unions.[21] The draft was sponsored by the official trade union structure and was an attempt to strengthen that structure in the face of the challenges confronting it by the growing alienation of the workforce. When the final version of the law was passed by the Supreme Soviet on 10 December 1990,[22] it created a framework for the emergence of unions which were organisationally and financially independent of state, political and economic organs. Legally they retained a significant role in enterprise life. What the law did not specify was how the inevitable conflict between the established trade union structure and the new trade unions that were emerging would be resolved. Despite this ambiguity, a legal structure providing for independent unions and strikes was put in place.

More broadly, the right of free organisation was enshrined in the 'Law on Public Associations' adopted by the Supreme Soviet on 9 October 1990.[23] This legislation was meant to cover the activity of all public associations except cooperatives, religious organisations and local government organs; paradoxically it therefore also covered trade unions. It provided a legal framework for the emergence of a multi-party system, and was therefore a key element in the aim of establishing a democratic society. Parties were all guaranteed equal status, and financial support from the government at any level was denied. Registration of parties could be refused only if certain technical aspects of the law were breached (such as the principles of their formation – see Article 4), if they aimed either to change the constitutional order or violate the territorial unity of the USSR by force, or advocated war or hatred. Political parties were permitted to participate in election campaigns, play a part in the soviets and help form governments, as well as publish newspapers and espouse their views. Unlike the other kinds of associations covered by this legislation, parties were forbidden to receive financial assistance from abroad. The law thus gave the necessary legal basis for parties to participate actively in the election campaigns for the soviets, and provided the essential foundation for independent political organisation in Soviet society.

All of these individual pieces of legislation introduced specific rights and freedoms essential to the process of democratisation. Their import was brought together and codified by the Declaration of Human Rights and Liberties adopted by the Congress of People's Deputies on 5 September 1991.[24] This declaration laid down the general principles underpinning much of the earlier legislation and the process of democratisation as well as pushing this further in some areas than it had gone previously. The declaration did not give a definition of human rights, preferring to list guarantees in specific areas. Among these were freedom of expression and belief, the rights to demonstrate, to privacy, to ownership, to work, to movement and residence,[25] to organise, to a sufficient and adequate standard of living, to secrecy of communication and to be defended by the law. As a general statement of principles this summarised the sphere of autonomous activity which the state recognised needed to be established for a democratic society to flourish.

These pieces of legislation were explicitly designed to make it possible for Soviet citizens to indulge in the type of activity previously denied them. The sphere of acceptable activity was thus expanded while that which was the preserve solely of the state contracted. A similar process of the expansion of space for individual activity, with political consequences, occurred as a result of measures which were designed to improve economic performance. Although the government's record in designing a consistent and effective economic policy was poor, there was a general trend in the direction of a loosening of central control in the economy. While this was reflected most strongly in the rhetoric of reform at the end of the 1980s, it was also clearly evident in many of the legislative measures which were introduced.[26] The effect of this was to increase the scope for individual and private initiative, most particularly in the emergence of non-state economic actors like the cooperatives and private entrepreneurs.

The emergence of such actors had an important effect: the creation of an economic sphere largely independent of state control buttressed the growing constraints upon state action as a whole and strengthened the emergence of a legitimate social sphere. The importance of the ability of such actors to conduct their economic affairs in partial independence from the old central control apparatus (although independence would be partial until the system operated totally on market principles[27]) lay not just in the shaping of the economy, but also in the structuring of political life. Because they were not dependent upon state managers or other authorities for their livelihoods, they were able to pursue their activities without concern for the need to satisfy such state-based authority figures. Moreover by operating independently, they were much better able than people working within the established system to amass the kind of economic resources which could give them the capacity for independent action.[28] Such resources could be mobilised for all sorts of political activity, including subsidisation of publi- cations and nascent political parties and for exerting influence on the authorities. While this remained in its early stages prior to the coup, the beginnings of an economically independent sector of society introduced a new factor into the Soviet political scene and an extra buttress against the extension and use of state power. It also called into question the utility of much of the earlier legislation on workplace democracy introduced by the Gorbachev leadership to apply in state enterprises. The emergence and activity of these independent forces was substantially facilitated by the economic reform measures translated into law by the Gorbachev leadership.

Limits on state power

The Gorbachev leadership also introduced a series of measures which were explicitly designed to limit the arbitrary exercise of state power. The effort to shift power and authority away from the party and into the soviets and the state structure noted above was one aspect of this. The desire to create a system in which governmental arbitrariness was limited is also reflected in the attitude to the constitution. In 1988, 1989 and 1990, extensive amend- ments were made to that document. The scale of the changes introduced in these amendments is staggering and far exceeds changes introduced through the amendment process during any earlier period of Soviet history. The scope and speed of these changes and the ease with which they were introduced reflects the fact that the constitution was not superior law; it could be changed by the legislature alone. This means that the capacity of the constitution effectively to bind the government was limited because the latter could, if it felt unduly restricted by that document, change it by virtue of its control in the legislature. But what is interesting about the 1988–90 constitutional changes is that even though the authorities could have ignored that written document and changed the formal structure of govern- ment at will, they believed the document to be sufficiently important that it should be amended to reflect the changing institutional reality. While this may appear to be mere window dressing (and the cavalier treatment accorded the formal tenets of the constitution in the aftermath of the coup supports such an interpretation), it is consistent with the aim of establishing a law-based state: unless constitution and formal structure were in accord, the former could not hope to generate any normative authority. Despite the means whereby they could be brought about, the constitutional changes therefore suggest a commitment to government limited by superior law. Paradoxically, the actions of the coup leaders in August 1991 may also reflect the entrenchment in Soviet norms of the principle of adherence to the law: they sought to justify their action by reference to the Constitution and its provision for the transfer of power from an ailing president to the vice-president.[29]

Of more immediate consequence has been the Committee for Constitutional Supervision established by the USSR Congress of People's Deputies in December 1989. The Committee was foreshadowed at the 19th Conference of the party in 1988, with its brief said to be ensuring that republican constitutions and the laws of both the all-union and republican governments conformed to the tenets of the USSR Constitution.[30] However following opposition from some of the republican leaders who feared that such a body would block their moves towards independence, when the Committee was created its sphere of concern was restricted to all-union legislation; it was not given oversight of republican legislation. The Committee was also not given the power to annul unconstitutional legislation. It was empowered to suspend a law for three months and inform the law-making body of its decision, but if the latter refused to repeal the offending legislation, and it was not overridden by the Congress of People's Deputies, the law was to remain in force. Despite these limitations the Committee exercised its authority on a number of occasions, including the suspension of both legislative and presidential measures.[31] While such an organisation clearly needed expanded powers to act as an effective constitutional watchdog, it was an important development in the attempt to construct a law-governed state.

So too was the introduction of a mechanism for handling citizens' complaints against those in authority. In June 1987 a new law on appealing officials' actions[32] gave citizens the right of legal redress against the violation of their rights by public authorities. Although there were specified exceptions when this law could not apply, this mechanism for appeal against official action constituted, in principle, a popular check on the activity of the bureaucracy and a means for the citizenry to defend itself against the state.

Another aspect of the defence of the citizenry against the state, and an essential prerequisite to a law-governed state, is a judicial system independent from political pressure. Only such independence can enable it to defend the citizen from unlawful governmental activity. Some steps were made in this direction, with the decision that trial by jury would be instituted, even if only for those accused of offences punishable by up to fifteen years imprisonment or by death, judges would be elected by higher soviets for a ten rather than five year period, and courts were called upon to abide by the Constitution. In addition, defence lawyers were to be able to begin work on a defendant's case as soon as charges were brought to bear instead of having to wait until the prosecution had prepared the case. These were important measures, strengthening the position of the accused. The elimination of Articles 70 and 190 of the RSFSR criminal code, the catch-all provisions which were used widely prior to 1985 to charge dissidents, was also an important step in this regard.[33] But to really change the situation the legal profession itself needed to become independent and depoliticised, and while moves were begun in this direction, only a beginning was made prior to the coup.

The question raised by this attempt to proceed to democratisation and a law-based society through the construction of a regulative framework is how successful such an endeavour can be. This raises the issue of the transition from authoritarian to democratic rule. Such a transformation can be accomplished successfully, culminating in the emergence of a democratic system. This has been the experience of post-war Japan and Germany and of some of the states of South America, although there were considerable differences between these cases and the Soviet Union. In South America the democracy achieved was often of an institutional form without the major social changes that would have given it real meaning; the same broad groups retained power following regime transformation, while the role of the people underwent little change from the earlier authoritarian structure.[34] This means that while the new democracies were characterised by institutional changes, these were not always accompanied by the emergence of an organised and active citizenry determined to play a continuing role in political affairs.

It has been this revolution in public expectations and the determination not to be excluded from political life which has been largely missing in the South American cases but which was evident in the successful transitions in Greece and Spain, and in the unfinished 'transitions' in Eastern Europe and the Soviet Union. The case of Japan and Germany, in both of which democratic systems seem to have become solidly rooted, also differ significantly from the Soviet Union because of the presence in both the former of an occupying power. The democratic systems were established under pressure, principally from the United States. As such, they were introduced by people who had a clear idea of the sort of system they wished to see established and, because of the destruction of much of the infrastructures of these two societies, they were not confronted with entrenched opposition and institutional inertia which could not be overcome. This situation clearly contrasts with that in the Soviet Union, where the extent of opposition to such a transition remained powerful and where there was no single force like that of the allied powers to enforce its will.

The essence of the transition from a highly centralised authoritarian to a more decentralised, democratic structure is the dismantling of the administrative apparatus and its replacement by a structure more attuned to democratic principles while at the same time ensuring that society does not descend into chaos. In more precise institutional terms, in the Soviet Union it has meant the withdrawal of the communist party structure from a direct role in all aspects of life and the dismantling of the command-administrative apparatus to create room for the expansion of the competence and activity of the state organs and the emergence of new vehicles of popular activity. This has implied the replacement of an established set of operating principles and conventions, of ways of getting things done, by a new but as yet untried and not fully formulated set of principles. The withdrawal of an existing structure, and one which was still operating in a moderately effective fashion at least in its capacity to maintain public order, and their replacement by new ones creates great potential for disruption. Not only must new governors get used to functioning in an environment in which the procedures are uncertain, but many of the control mechanisms which ensured some semblance of procedure cease to apply. New governors, uncertain ground rules and the release of institutional and popular political pressure makes for a potentially unstable mix, as many of the regions of the USSR found. The consequent disorderly nature of the process creates pressure for the reassertion of firm control (the so-called 'firm hand'), and yet it has been the destruction of the mechanism whereby this could be achieved which has helped to create the disorder in the first place.

As well as this problem of the uncertainty of the conditions and the consequent increase in pressure for a reassertion of central control, the weakening of the control apparatus creates further problems for the aim of introducing democratisation through legal means. One aspect of this is the proliferation within the political structure of actors with their own particular agendas and, often, with the political position and resources to press those agendas. The clearest manifestation of this is the way in which the ethos of unity, and therefore the propensity to keep policy disagreements behind closed doors, was destroyed. A cacophony of voices, platforms and positions characterised the discussion of the course of reform. An essential component of democratisation is disagreement, and therefore those supporting the thrust of the changes could hardly suppress opposition and dissent without destroying the moral heart of the programme they espoused.

The emergence of public debate meant that every stage of the reform process was beset by bitter arguments and debates, with an ever-increasing circle of participants. As the programme was radicalised, uncertainty about its course and consequences multiplied, and more segments of the politico-administrative structure and of the population at large were mobilised into the debate. Decision-makers, themselves often uncertain about aspects of the policies they were pursuing and lacking a clear overall vision of what they hoped to achieve, found themselves under unprecedented attack and were forced to defend themselves in ways which they had not had to do in the past. Furthermore the strength of the opposition, particularly in a context of some uncertainty on the part of the reformers, was on many issues sufficient to ensure that the measures that were introduced were almost lowest common denominator decisions, measures which may have been consistent with the reform programme but which because of the need to pacify all sides were limited in their effect. Some of the individual measures discussed above may fit into this category. The strength of opposition was also often sufficient to lead to the introduction of measures which actually contradicted and set back the process of change, such as the decision of the Supreme Soviet in January 1991 to take measures to 'ensure objectivity' in reporting. The strength of opposition allied to their own lack of clear vision was thus sufficient to prevent the reformers from enunciating and setting in place a coherent programme of change. Instead, that programme was subject to setbacks, diversions and zig-zags as decision-makers sought to deal with the uncertainty and opposition within the ranks of the politically active.

This problem of decision-making was exacerbated by the uncertainty created at the apex of the political system by the rapid institutional changes that characterised life at the top. The withdrawal of the party from day-to-day decision-making and the generation of a range of new bodies designed to take decisions created considerable ambiguity. For example, the Congress of People's Deputies, Supreme Soviet, Council of Ministers, Presidency, Presidential Council (which was displaced by the Cabinet of Ministers in December 1990, within nine months of its establishment) and Council of the Federation were all new organs established in the eighteen months from the beginning of 1989. The precise functions and inter-relationships between these bodies were not clearly worked out before they were established, and were formally changed on a number of occasions soon after their creation. The result was considerable confusion and jockeying for position as the different institutions sought to establish for themselves a meaningful place in the political structure. Clear and consistent decision-making was continually frustrated by the institutional uncertainty that existed among the top organs.

Beside the problems in the decision-making process was a significant decline in the capacity of central decision-makers to enforce implementation of their decisions. In practical terms, this meant an increased propensity on the part of those who oppose the reforms to take active steps to subvert those measures. A continual complaint within reform circles was about the way in which 'the bureaucracy' was dragging its feet in implementing changes, was distorting the intent of some measures and was completely undermining others. While this complaint in part reflects unrealistic expectations about what is possible and within what timetable, it also recognises the reality. Sections within the commanding structures of the society did work to blunt the sharp end of reform, using their positions and the power they possessed over policy implemementation to hinder the unrolling of the reform process. Many within the government ministries, fearing for their positions and often really believing that the proposed measures were not the correct ones, acted this way. Sections within the security and military apparatuses were similarly motivated. So too were wide ranks of responsible officials in the party structure. This was evident long before the abortive coup of August 1991. Such a development was a feature of Soviet politics since the foundation of the regime, but what made the contemporary situation different from most of that which went before is the scale on which it was occurring and the reduced capacity of the centre to prevent it. The centre's inability to ensure implementation constituted a real problem for any reform programme premised upon legal enactments by that centre.

Another problem, although in the sense of the loss of central control it is but one aspect of the last, is the growth of regionalism. During 1990, and in particular in its second half, the established territorial power structure was overthrown. All union republics, and many of the smaller territorial units issued declarations of sovereignty which asserted the supremacy of local laws over those adopted in the capital. In effect, this meant that all-union laws would be considered binding only if local legislatures assented to them. This position, by denying the sovereignty of the all-union capital and the laws adopted by the all-union government, negated the strategy of structuring the reform process by legal enactment. If there was disagreement about who had the power to pass laws and what jurisdiction they would have, there was no basis for the sort of commonality upon which the move to a law-based state must rest. While competing sovereignties remained unresolved, agreement on which laws would lie at the basis of the state could not be reached.[35]

The problem of competing sovereignties, and the implications it had for the territorial integrity of the Soviet Union, strengthened the calls for a 'firm hand' noted above. The clear threat to the continued territorial integrity of the Soviet Union that was posed by the actions of many republican leaderships during 1990 strengthened the view that what was needed was a reassertion of firm control from the centre. Such a sentiment was behind the support many gave for the expansion of presidential powers in the second half of 1990. It was also evident in statements by military and KGB leaders at this time, particularly some of those Russian officers stationed in the Baltic, and in the vociferous campaigns emanating from many so-called 'patriotic' groups within Russia. It was also reflected in the public appeal issued by those who conducted the coup. At one level this reflects the continuing commitment to the notion of an imperial Soviet Union. But at another it is a clear illustration of the difficulties in democratising a multi-ethnic society. As soon as authoritarian controls are loosened, those ethnic groups which have been dissatisfied with their lot will use the new conditions to press for a remedying of their complaints. Usually this can only be done by the granting of independence, particularly if that group has felt particularly suppressed for a long period of time. Such pressures may generate opposing pressures from the centre and from within the non-indigenous populations of those areas demanding independence. The drive for democratisation in a multi-ethnic state thus leads to ethnic conflict, if not through force of arms, at least at the political and rhetorical levels. The Soviet Union experienced such conflict at all levels, even before the spate of independence declarations which followed the coup's collapse.

Culture and transition

The reliance upon law-making to bring about the transition to a democratic, law-based state is a process fraught with contradiction. The adoption of laws is clearly an essential part of the process of democratisation. These are needed to provide some guidance and structuring to the emergent political processes and to give legal guarantees to the rights and freedoms that are part of a democratic structure. But also essential to a democratic system is a culture, or set of values. Political scientists have been trying to define what a democratic culture is like for a long time. At minimum it must include an active and participant citizenry along with a recognition of what are appropriate forms of behaviour and what are not. This means that there must be, formally undefined but generally acknowledged, limits to behaviour. Those defeated at elections, for example, must know that such defeat is not to be met by administrative manipulation to maintain their positions or force of arms to reverse the verdict. Such a culture can develop only if the citizenry participates, and not only when the new system is established but during the process of its establishment as well. To rely purely upon legislative *fiat* to introduce the new order is to perpetuate the sort of political culture that is characteristic of authoritarian regimes. It is the sort of culture which must be overcome.

The record of the Gorbachev leadership in stimulating popular involvement in the process of change is a positive one. The populace was widely encouraged to play an active part in the process. Indeed, one of the early tactics of the group around Gorbachev was to mobilise the populace in an attempt to bring pressure to bear upon more conservative opponents in the apparatus. The policy of glasnost and the support, albeit not always unambiguous, given to informal groups constitute further forms of encouragement of popular involvement and interest. The question is whether the basis existed within the society for this sort of participation to blossom into that which would constitute a firm foundation for a democratic order. Was there within the society the roots of a culture which would be favourably disposed to the process of democratisation and a law-based state? One way in which this question has often been approached has been through the notion of civil society.

Civil society has become an important concept among Western students of the Soviet Union (and Eastern Europe) who are attempting to understand developments in those countries.[36] It is also a concept that was mobilised into debate in the Soviet Union.[37] However, the use which is made of this concept is not always as judicious as it should be. There has been a tendency on the part of many to see civil society purely in terms of the emergence of groups and organisations among the populace which are based upon commonalities of interest and which are independent of the state. In this view, what is important is the non-state nature of the social groups. Clearly this is an essential characteristic of a civil society, but alone it is insufficient. If all that was required was the presence of non-state organisations, a society in which a variety of non-state armed groups dominated public life, like the Lebanon throughout much of the 1980s, could be classed as a civil society. The notion of civil society also implies the acceptance of some rules of behaviour, both by governmental authorities and by the citizens and their groups. The governmental authorities must recognise that there are limits to the intrusiveness of their power and to their appropriate sphere of competence. They must acknowledge that the citizen-based groups have a legitimate right to independent activity, including the protection of the citizens from inappropriate governmental interference. They must also recognise that, in conducting governmental relations with the populace, the procedures which have been formulated to guide governmental activity must be followed. The law must have normative authority.

Simultaneously, social groups must recognise that the government has a legitimate role to play in structuring public life. They must recognise that there are limits to their own activities which, if breached, makes governmental action against them legitimate. They must recognise that there are processes and procedures which must be followed in the structuring of their relations among themselves, their relations with the government, and their pursuit of what they perceive to be their interests. This means that there must be recognition of a sense of restraint; the end does not justify any means, and the means must be kept in accord with the basic rules of the game. Civil society, therefore, means not just the existence of independent groups, but the recognition by all players that they are partners and that there are certain defined arenas of activity within which they should not participate. While there may not be complete consensus about the precise location of the boundary between the governmental and group arenas, there will nevertheless be a general consensus about the contours of both arenas. It is recognition of this, and the sense of constraint that goes with it, that is essential for the emergence of civil society. The question is whether such a civil society was emerging in the Soviet Union and the post-Soviet successor states.

At one level the answer to this must be no. With the collapse of the territorial integrity of the country and the drive by various republics to leave the federation and establish independent states, the notion of a single society is hard to sustain. It may be that civil societies are emerging in the individual republics, but these should not arbitrarily be aggregated into a single civil society for the whole of the former union. The comments that follow, while general, relate principally to Russia.

Many have argued that the bases for a civil society emerged in Russia prior to 1985. Geoffrey Hosking has argued that the traditional peasant community may be a useful basis upon which notions of collective organisation in defence of one's interests could develop.[38] Others have argued that in the post-war period the society became much more the source of innovation and initiative, and this was reflected in the range of unsanctioned activity which emerged during the Brezhnev period: informal groups and the dissident movement in particular were important here.[39] But the existence of such groups can only establish one of the essential elements of a civil society. Nothing has been said about the recognition of autonomous spheres of activity or of the sense of restraint essential for such a society to develop.

On the side of the governmental authorities, the range of legislation discussed above suggests that there was at least a formal recognition of the existence of such a sphere and acknowledgement of the need to buttress it by legislative enactment. But at the practical level, the situation remained ambiguous. Prior to the coup, the refusal to abolish party organs in places of work (particularly in the military and security spheres), the reluctance on the part of communist party first secretaries to relinquish the dominant role the party played in the economy, the barriers placed in the way of the functioning of many of the informal groups by local authorities, some of the repressive actions undertaken by the coercive arms of the state, and the veiled warnings from some military quarters about the need for firm control, all reflect a less than total commitment to the withdrawal of the political authorities from the public sphere. The limitations and restrictions in the individual measures noted above may also reflect this concern. One of the main strands of the tug of war within the regime over the course of reform has been this aspect of the degree to which society should be liberated from the direct and immediate control of the state.

The ambiguity in the official sphere has been mirrored in a similar ambivalence in the public sphere where the citizen-based groups are to be found. While the mainstream of these groups acknowledged the need for the rule of law and therefore for a government which had legitimate functions to perform in society, there were also trends which placed political qualifications upon recognition of such a boundary. Two main kinds of qualification exist. The first is reflected in the principle that the legitimacy of the government depends upon its political coloration. More specifically, any government in which communists remained the dominant element possessed no legitimacy and had no right to enforce any rules or play any part in society's life. As a corollary, any kind of action was acceptable if it would rid the society of such a government.[40] The second type of qualification relates to the period of transition and the difficulties this involves. The principle embodied in this argument is that the boundary between the autonomous spheres should temporarily be removed. The danger of instability during the transition, of unregulated conflict between the emergent interests and groups, means that democratic processes should temporarily be suspended while a firm hand guides the society towards a situation when democratic processes would be more appropriate.[41] These two sorts of sentiment, which have not been confined to unimportant fringe groups, suggest that at least among some of the groups there remained only a qualified acceptance of the role of government in a civil society.

Turning to the rules of the game, there was some ambiguity here too. This ambiguity results principally from the circumstances under which the transition was taking place. Most importantly, the newly emerging political groups were operating in a legal vacuum until October 1990. With no clear legislative guidelines to structure their activity, no legislative defence against governmental suppression and not even a stable political arena within which they had an obvious role, there was no basis upon which widely accepted rules of the game could emerge. The inexperience of the political activists reinforced the effect of the absence of external structuring mechanisms to create a politics of the informal groups which was *ad hoc* and idiosyncratic. This should be remedied by the emergence of a genuine multi-party competitive system (which would constitute the arena which is currently lacking), but until this happens the progress towards acceptance of rules of the game involving a sense of restraint will be slow.

What this means is that 'democracy from above' and the move to a law-based state through legislative enactment cannot succeed without the development of an appropriate culture within the society as a whole. Not only must the old formal structures be eliminated, but the old patterns of thought and the informal structures of power must be superseded by a new culture of politics. Such a culture must recognise the legitimacy of certain sorts of governmental activity and acknowledge the legitimacy of only some sorts of political activity on the part of independent political actors. Such a culture cannot emerge through legislative *fiat*. Certainly enlightened despotism may facilitate this process, but such a course makes ultimate success contingent upon the will and perceptions of the despot. Historically this has been the Russian way. But historically Russia has not been very successful in nurturing the sort of culture appropriate to a civil society or a democratic political system. Such a culture can only develop as a powerful entity if it does so through its own means. It must be self-propelled, although a sympathetic state can facilitate its development through appropriate legislative initiatives. Some would argue that Gorbachev was genuinely trying to achieve this. It is on the ability of the new political authorities to realise this aim, plus the capacity for learning on the part of all political actors, that the success of such an endeavour will depend.

Notes

1 BEYOND MARXISM

1 As Alain Besançon has put it, ideology '*is* the Soviet regime itself' (*The Intellectual Origins of Leninism* (Oxford: Blackwell, 1981), p. 4).

2 A. F. Losev, *Dialektika mifa* (Moscow: Nauka, 1930), p. 147.

3 See respectively Bertram Wolfe, *An Ideology in Power* (London: Allen and Unwin, 1969), and Mikhail Geller and Aleksandr Nekrich, *Utopiia u vlasti*, 2nd edn (London: Overseas Publication Exchange, 1986).

4 See, for instance, Stephen White and Alex Pravda, eds., *Ideology and Soviet Politics* (London: Macmillan, 1988), and Archie Brown, 'Ideology and political culture', in Seweryn Bialer, ed., *Politics, Society and Nationality inside Gorbachev's Russia* (Boulder, CO: Westview, 1989), pp. 1–40.

5 See M. N. Marchenko and I. N. Rozhko, *Demokratiia v SSSR. Fakty i domysli* (Moscow: Mysl', 1988), pp. 164–6.

6 Georgii Arbatov, *Zatianuvsheesia vyzdorovlenie* (Moscow: Mezhdunarodye otnosheniia, 1991), pp. 172–3, and similarly in *Vestnik Akademii Nauk SSSR*, 1991, no. 3, p. 6.

7 See AS 5042, August 1983: translated with a commentary by Philip Hanson in *Survey*, vol. 28, no. 1 (Spring 1984), pp. 83–108.

8 Stephen F. Cohen and Katrina van den Heuvel, *Voices of Glasnost* (New York: Norton, 1989), pp. 117–19.

9 M. S. Gorbachev, *Izbrannye rechi i stat'i*, 7 vols. (Moscow: Izdatel'stvo politicheskoi literatury, 1987–90), II, p. 129. For some of what follows I have drawn upon Stephen White, *Gorbachev and After*, 3rd edn (Cambridge and New York: Cambridge University Press, 1992).

10 *Ibid.*, pp. 152–73, esp. pp. 153–67.

11 Texts of all of these editions are conveniently available in *Programmy i ustavy KPSS* (Moscow: Izdatel'stvo politicheskoi literatury, 1969).

12 *Programmy i ustavy*, pp. 131, 135. Khrushchev's own comments on the draft were generally more cautious than those of the working group which had been established in 1958: see *Voprosy istorii KPSS*, 1991, no. 8, pp. 3–8.

13 See V. S. Semenov, 'Uchenie o razvitom sotsializme i ego pererastanii v kommunizm', *Voprosy filosofii*, 1980, no. 7, p. 10.

14 *XXVI s"ezd Kommunisticheskoi partii Sovetskogo Soiuza 23 fevralia–3 marta 1981 goda. Stenograficheskii otchet*, 3 vols. (Moscow: Politizdat, 1981), I, pp. 97–8.

15 *Pravda*, 16 June 1983 (Andropov) and 26 April 1984 (Chernenko).

16 Gorbachev, *Izbrannye rechi i stat'i*, III, p. 275. The draft appeared in *Izvestiia*, 26 October 1985. For leadership opinion, see Vadim Pechenev, *Gorbachev: K vershinam vlasti* (Moscow: Gospodin narod, 1991), pp. 21–2.

17 Pechenev, *Gorbachev*, p. 22.

18 For the 1961 Programme, see *Programmy i ustavy*, pp. 63–224; the 1986 Programme is in *Materialy XXVII s"ezd KPSS* (Moscow: Politizdat, 1986), pp. 121–87. An English translation and discussion is available in Stephen White, *Soviet Communism: Programme and Rules* (London: Routledge, 1989).

19 *Materialy XXVII s"ezda*, p. 122.

20 *Kommunist*, 1986, no. 16, p. 80; Pechenev, *Gorbachev*, p. 64.

21 *Materialy XXVII s"ezda*, p. 122; for the references in the draft, see *Kommunist*, 1985, no. 16, pp. 4 and 9.

22 Gorbachev, *Izbrannye rechi i stat'i*, IV, p. 110.

23 *Programma KPSS (novaia redaktsiia)*. *Proekt* (Moscow: Pravda, 1985), p. 31.

24 Gorbachev, *Izbrannye rechi i stat'i*, VI, pp. 395–7.

25 M. S. Gorbachev, *Perestroika raboty partii – vazhneishaia kliuchevaia zadacha dnia* (Moscow: Politizdat, 1989), pp. 30–1.

26 *Pravda*, 26 November 1989; also in *Kommunist*, 1989, no. 18, pp. 3–20.

27 *Pravda*, 15 July 1990; also in *Materialy XXVIII s"ezda KPSS* (Moscow: Politizdat, 1990), pp. 77–98.

28 *Materialy XXVIII s"ezda*, p. 4.

29 *Ibid.*, p. 62.

30 *Pravda*, 26 October 1990; *Kommunist*, 1989, no. 18, p. 4.

31 *Materialy XXVIII s"ezda*, pp. 35, 36, 53.

32 See, for instance, Alla Nazimova and Viktor Sheinis in V. I. Mukomel', ed., *Demograficheskii diagnoz* (Moscow: Progress, 1989), p. 675, and Volkov and Krasin in *Kommunist*, 1990, no. 7, p. 15.

33 *Pravda*, 27 July 1991 (Gidaspov) and *Izvestiia*, 8 August 1991 (Tishkov).

34 For the text, see *Pravda*, 8 August 1991, and *Kommunist*, 1991, no. 12, pp. 3–15.

35 *Pravda*, 26 July 1991.

36 As late as 1989 pluralism could be described as a concept derived from 'bourgeois politology' which obscured the 'presence under capitalism of antagonistic class interests [and] the domination of a monopoly capital in political life' (*Kratkii politicheskii slovar'*, 6th edn (Moscow: Politizdat, 1989), p. 420).

37 Iu. V. Andropov, *Izbrannye rechi i stat'i*, 2nd edn (Moscow: Politizdat, 1983), pp. 194–5.

38 Gorbachev, *Izbrannye rechi i stat'i*, V, p. 219.

39 *Ibid.*, p. 300, and *Pravda*, 30 September 1987.

40 Gorbachev, *Izbrannye rechi i stat'i*, VI, pp. 61, 205, 212.

41 *Ibid.*, pp. 342, 393, 401, 411.

42 *Ibid.*, p. 442.

43 *Ibid.*, VII, p. 228.

44 *Ibid.*, pp. 588–9, 591; *Materialy plenuma TsK KPSS 5–7 fevralia 1990 g.* (Moscow: Politizdat, 1990), p. 10; and (for party theorists) *Dialog*, 1990, no. 7, p. 59. On these and related issues, see Archie Brown, ed., *New Thinking in Soviet Politics* (London: Macmillan, 1992).

45 *Kommunist*, 1991, no. 12, p. 10.

46 *Literaturnaia gazeta*, 20 April 1988, p. 2, and in Burlatsky, *Novoe myshlenie*, 2nd edn (Moscow: Politizdat, 1989), pp. 324–45.

47 *Izvestiia*, 16 February 1988. Kurashvili wrote similarly in *Argumenty i fakty*, 1988, no. 26, in *Moscow News*, 5 June 1988, and in *Sovetskaia molodezh'*, 27 April 1988.

48 *Sovetskoe gosudarstvo i pravo*, 1989, no. 8, pp. 99–110; similarly in Iu. M. Baturin, ed., *Pul's reform* (Moscow: Progress, 1989), pp. 62–6.

49 Boris P. Kurashvili, *Strana na rasput'e* (Moscow: Iuridicheskaia literatura, 1990), p. 55 and elsewhere.

50 On these writings, see White and Pravda, eds., *Ideology and Soviet Politics*, pp. 14–16.

51 Anatolii Butenko, *Vlast' naroda posredstvom samogo naroda* (Moscow: Mysl', 1988), pp. 168, 144, 173.

52 *Pravda*, 8 August 1989.

53 See 'Problemy razrabotki kontseptsii sovremennogo sotsializma', *Voprosy filosofii*, 1988, no. 11, pp. 31–71.

54 Hayek's *Road to Serfdom* was published in *Voprosy filosofii*, 1990, nos. 10 and 11, and in *Novyi mir*, 1991, nos. 7 and 8; his *Poverty of Historicism* was in *Voprosy filosofii*, 1992, no. 8. He was described as the 'idol' of economic oppositionists in *Pravda*, 6 June 1990.

55 *Pravda*, 14 July 1989, and 16 July 1989. A more orthodox statement was G. L. Smirnov et al., *Ocherki teorii sotsializma* (Moscow: Politizdat, 1989); S. Platonov's posthumous *Posle kommunizma* (Moscow: Molodaia gvardiia, 1990) was also influential.

56 *Kommunist*, 1989, no. 13, pp. 3–24.

57 *Pravda*, 19 August 1990.

58 *Kommunist*, 1991, no. 1, pp. 18–29.

59 *Dialog*, 1990, no. 9, pp. 56–64. Alekseev's views were set out at greater length in his *Pered vyborom*, 2nd edn (Moscow: Iuridicheskaia literatura, 1990).

60 *Kommunist*, 1991, no. 4, pp. 18–31, and 5, pp. 16–30.

61 Iu. Afanas'ev, ed. *Inogo ne dano* (Moscow: Progress, 1988), pp. 551–2.

62 The terms are drawn respectively from Alexander Tsipko in A. A. Protashchik, ed., *Cherez ternii* (Moscow: Progress, 1990), p. 66; Alexander Iakovlev in *Muki prochetniia bytiia* (Moscow: Novosti, 1991), p. 199; Anatolii Butenko in *Sovetskoe gosudarstvo i pravo*, 1992, no. 4, p. 78; and H. Diligentsky in *Mirovaia ekonomika i mezhdunarodnye otnosheniia*, 1989, no. 12, p. 82.

63 See the discussion in *Pravda*, 21 January 1990.

64 *Nauka i zhizn'*, 1988, nos. 11 and 12, and 1989, nos. 1 and 2. Tsipko's views also appeared in (for instance) *Voprosy ekonomiki*, 1990, no. 12; *Novyi mir*, 1990, no. 4; and *Vestnik MGU*, series 12, 1990, no. 2. For a collection of his writings, see Tsipko, *Nasilie lzhi, ili kak zabliudilsia prizrak* (Moscow: Molodaia gvardiia, 1990).

65 *Novyi mir*, 1989, no. 2, pp. 204–38; an earlier article appeared in *ibid.*, 1987, no. 11, pp. 150–88.

66 *Novyi mir*, 1988, no. 5, pp. 162–89.

67 *Kommunist*, 1989, no. 11, pp. 34–5.

68 *Soviet Weekly*, 4 November 1989.

69 See V. E. Guliev, ed., *Politicheskaia reforma: tseli, protivorechiia, etapy* (Moscow: Institute of State and Law, 1990), pp. 26–30.

70 *Kommunist*, 1991, no. 4, p. 29.
71 *Pravda*, 30 April 1992.
72 *Voprosy ekonomiki*, 1989, no. 2, pp. 3–12.
73 A. N. Iaklovlev, *Realizm – zemlia perestroiki* (Moscow: Politizdat, 1990), pp. 459–76.
74 Iakovkev, *Muki*, p. 89.
75 *Ibid.*, pp. 145–6.
76 *Ibid.*, pp. 113–25, and *Realizm*, pp. 486–505.
77 *Kuranty*, 17 December 1991, p. 4; and *Svobodnaia mysl'*, 1992, no. 7, pp. 93–9. See further Iakovlev, *Predislovie, Obval, Posleslovie* (Moscow: Novosti, 1992).
78 *Obshchestvennoe mnenie v tsifrakh*, 1991, no. 13, p. 12.
79 *Izvestiia*, 29 April 1992.
80 *Literaturnaia gazeta*, 1990, no. 38, pp. 3–6.
81 See for instance Mark Deich and Leonid Zhuravlev, *Pamiat'. Kak ona est'* (Moscow: Tsunami, 1991).
82 For some of these titles see *Glasgow Herald*, 26 November 1990, and *Izvestiia*, 10 March 1992.
83 *Izvestiia*, 24 March 1992.
84 *Voenno-istoricheskii zhurnal*, 1990, no. 11, pp. 35–8; *Novaia i noveishaia istoriia*, 1992, no. 5, pp. 189–231.
85 *Izvestiia*, 3 February 1992.
86 *Argumenty i fakti*, 1991, no. 11, p. 6.
87 *Moskovskie novosti*, 1991, no. 12, p. 7. Levels of dissatisfaction, 20 per cent in the early 1980s, were now running at 80 per cent or more: *Pravda*, 30 May 1992.
88 *Sotsiologicheskie issledovaniia*, 1991, no. 8, p. 14; *Mir mnenii i mneniia o mire*, 1992, no. 5, p. 8.
89 *Obshchestvennoe mnenie v tsifrakh*, 1990, no. 16, pp. 19–21; similarly in *Moskovskie novosti*, 1990, no. 44, pp. 8–9.
90 *Izvestiia*, 24 April 1991.
91 Times Mirror Center for The People and the Press, Washington DC, 1991, typescript, pp. 256–7.
92 *Svobodnaia mysl'*, 1991, no. 7, p. 4.
93 *Mir mnenii i mneniia o mire*, 1992, no. 9, p. 6; similarly in *Moskovskaia pravda*, 24 September 1992.
94 *Obshchestvennoe mnenie v tsifrakh*, 1990, no. 16, p. 20.
95 *Pravda*, 3 January 1991 (more positive evaluation); *Izvestiia TsK KPSS*, 1990, no. 4, pp. 191–3 (priests); *Argumenty i fakty*, 1990, no. 46, pp. 6–7 (Tsar's family).
96 *Moskovskie novosti*, 1990, no. 49, p. 9.
97 *Argumenty i fakty*, 1991, no. 39, p. 1. On the reassessment of Lenin see John Gooding, 'Lenin in Soviet politics, 1985–91', *Soviet Studies*, vol. 44, no. 3 (1992), pp. 403–22.
98 VTsIOM, *Data Express*, 21 August 1991, p. 2.
99 *Ibid.*, pp. 3, 2.
100 *Izvestiia*, 26 August 1991 and 24 August 1991.
101 Glasnost was particularly popular and a substantial majority (60 as against 12 per cent) favoured its further extension: *Narodnyi deputat*, 1991, no. 9, p. 54.
102 *Data Express*, 21 August 1991, p. 4.
103 *Izvestiia*, 20 September 1991.

104 *Ibid.*, 15 June 1992, and *Pravda*, 26 October 1991.
105 *Izvestiia*, 23 March 1992.
106 *Ibid.*, 6 April 1992.
108 *Nezavisimaia gazeta*, 29 July 1992.
109 *Moskovskie novosti*, 1991, no. 38, p. 5.
110 *Argumenty i fakty*, 1991, no. 30, p. 5.
111 *Obshchestvennoe mnenie v tsifrakh*, 1990, no. 2, p. 11.
112 *Trud*, 11 January 1992.
113 *Izvestiia*, 2 March 1992.
114 *Moskovskie novosti*, 1992, no. 4, p. 19.
115 These data, from the 'Russians between state and market' survey, appear by courtesy of Yevgenii Tikhomirov and Professor Richard Rose.
116 Richard Rose, 'Russia between state and market', mimeo., May 1992; a fuller statement is available in Rose, *Russia at the Start of the Longest Journey* (University of Strathclyde, Glasgow: Centre for the Study of Public Policy, 1992).

2 REFORMING THE ELECTORAL SYSTEM

1 For a discussion of electoral practices before the Gorbachev era, see, for instance, George B. Carson, *Electoral Practices in the USSR* (London: Atlantic Press, 1956); Max E. Mote, *Soviet Local and Republican Elections* (Stanford CA: Hoover, 1965); Theodore H. Friedgut, *Political Participation in the USSR* (Princeton NJ: Princeton University Press, 1979); and Ronald J. Hill, *Soviet Politics, Political Science and Reform* (Oxford: Martin Robertson, 1980).
2 See Stephen White, *Political Culture and Soviet Politics* (New York: St Martin's, 1980), ch. 2.
3 See, for instance, William G. Rosenberg, 'The Russian Municipal Duma Elections of 1917', *Soviet Studies*, vol. 21, no. 2 (October 1969), pp. 131–63.
4 I. V. Stalin, *Sochineniia* 13 (16) vols. (Stanford: Hoover Institution, 1967), I (14), p. 130.
5 John Maynard, *The Russian Peasant*, 2 vols. (London: Gollancz, 1942), II, p. 438.
6 See Stephen White, 'Reforming the electoral system', in Walter Joyce et al., eds., *Gorbachev and Gorbachevism* (London: Cass, 1989), pp. 3–6.
7 *Izvestiia*, 13 July 1992. For the term 'acclamatory elections', see W. J. M. Mackenzie, *Free Elections* (London: Allen and Unwin, 1958).
8 *Materialy XXVII s"ezda KPSS* (Moscow: Politizdat, 1987), p. 22.
9 *Vizit General'nogo sekretaria TsK KPSS v Pol'skuiu Narodnuiu Respubliku* (Moscow: Politizdat, 1988), p. 15.
10 *Materialy XXVII s"ezda*, pp. 56, 100, 140, 159.
11 On this discussion and electoral reform more generally, see White, 'Reforming the electoral system', pp. 1–17; Georg Brunner, 'Elections in the Soviet Union', in Robert Furtak, ed., *Elections in Socialist States* (Hemel Hempstead: Harvester Wheatsheaf, 1990); Michael E. Urban, *More Power to the Soviets* (Aldershot: Elgar, 1990); and Viktor Danilenko, 'Electoral reform', in Robert T. Huber and Donald R. Kelley, eds., *Perestroika-Era Politics* (Armonk NY: Sharpe, 1991).

12 See Stephen White, 'Noncompetitive elections and national politics: the USSR Supreme Soviet elections of 1984', *Electoral Studies*, vol. 4, no. 3 (1985), p. 222.

13 *Izvestiia*, 5 July 1986.

14 *Izvestiia*, 10 February 1987.

15 *Sovetskoe gosudarstvo i pravo*, 1987, no. 4, p. 5.

16 *Ibid.*

17 *Izvestiia*, 10 February 1987.

18 *Pravda*, 7 March 1984.

19 Arkhiv Samizdata AS 5112, 1983.

20 *Pravda*, 5 March 1989.

21 *Izvestiia*, 29 April 1988.

22 See Rasma Karklins, 'Soviet elections revisited: voter abstention in comparative perspective', *American Political Science Review*, vol. 80, no. 2 (June 1986), p. 451; similarly Victor Zaslavsky and Robert J. Brym, 'The functions of elections in the USSR', *Soviet Studies*, vol. 30, no. 3 (July 1978), pp. 363, 366.

23 *Izvestiia*, 5 March 1990.

24 *Materialy XIX Vsesoiuznoi konferentsii KPSS* (Moscow: Politizdat, 1988), p. 37.

25 *Materialy plenuma TsK KPSS 27–28 ianvaria 1987 goda* (Moscow: Politizdat, 1987), pp. 24–30, 72.

26 *Izvestiia*, 7 July 1987.

27 White 'Reforming', pp. 9–13. See also Jeffrey Hahn, 'An experiment in competition: the 1987 elections to the local soviets', *Slavic Review*, vol. 47, no. 2 (Fall 1988), pp. 434–48. The results were reported in *Vedomosti Verkhovnogo Soveta SSSR*, 1987, no. 26, pp. 500–5.

28 *Materialy XIX konferentsii*, pp. 47–8.

29 *Pravda*, 2 July 1988.

30 *Materialy XIX konferentsii*, p. 120. For the Theses, see *Tezisy TsK KPSS k XIX Vsesoiuznoi partiinoi konferentsii* (Moscow: Politizdat, 1988), p. 21.

31 *Sovetskoe gosudarstvo i pravo*, 1988, no. 6, p. 59; *Izvestiia*, 26 October 1988.

32 For the draft law see *Pravda*, 23 October 1988; for the text of the law as adopted, see *Zakon SSSR o vyborakh narodnykh deputatov SSSR* (Moscow: Izvestiia, 1988).

33 Several accounts are now available: see V. S. Komarovsky, ed., *Vremia vybora* (Moscow: Politizdat, 1989); Max E. Mote, 'Electing the USSR Congress of People's Deputies', *Problems of Communism*, vol. 38, no. 6 (November–December 1989), pp. 51–6; V. A. Kolosov et al., *Vesna 89. Geografiia i anatomiia parlamentskikh vyborov* (Moscow: Progress, 1990); Vladimir N. Brovkin, 'The making of elections to the Congress of People's Deputies (CPD) in March 1989', *Russian Review*, vol. 49, no. 4 (October 1990), pp. 417–42; Peter Lentini, 'Reforming the electoral system: the 1989 elections to the USSR Congress of People's Deputies', *Journal of Communist Studies*, vol. 7, no. 1 (March 1991), pp. 69–94; and Stephen White, 'The Soviet elections of 1989: from acclamation to limited choice', *Coexistence*, vol. 28, no. 4 (December 1991), pp. 513–39.

34 *Izvestiia*, 22 November 1988.

35 *Izvestiia*, 11 February 1989; *Pravda*, 27 February 1989. *Sovetskoe gosudarstvo i pravo*, 1989, no. 7, p. 16, also mentioned the Tomsk region.

36 *Pravda*, 17 January 1989.

37 *Kommunist*, 1989, no. 17, p. 31.

38 *Materialy plenuma TsK KPSS 10 ianvaria 1989 goda* (Moscow: Politizdat, 1989), pp. 13–14, 16–29.
39 *Pravda*, 22 January 1989.
40 *Literaturnaia gazeta*, 29 March 1989, p. 1.
41 *Izvestiia*, 21 January 1989; *Soviet Weekly*, 11 February 1989, p. 4.
42 *Izvestiia*, 7 February 1989.
43 *Pravda*, 21 March 1989.
44 *Izvestiia*, 28 January 1989.
45 *Novoe vremia*, 1989, no. 5, p. 25.
46 *Izvestiia*, 19 January 1989; *Soviet Weekly*, 18 March 1989, p. 15.
47 Anatolii Sobchak, *Khozhdenie vo vlast'*, 2nd edn (Moscow: Novosti, 1991), pp. 13–20.
48 *Ibid.*, pp. 20–6.
49 *Sovetskaia Estoniia*, 19 February 1989.
50 *Izvestiia*, 23 February 1989; *The Independent* (London), 13 March 1989.
51 *Pravda*, 17 March 1989; *Izvestiia TsK KPSS*, 1989, no. 2, pp. 209–87.
52 *Sovetskaia Estoniia*, 19 February 1989.
53 *Pravda*, 28 March 1989.
54 *Sovetskaia kul'tura*, 28 March 1989.
55 *Izvestiia*, 5 April 1989.
56 Susan Richards, *Epics of Everyday Life* (Harmondsworth: Penguin, 1991), p. 152.
57 *Izvestiia*, 5 April 1989.
58 *Pravda*, 1 April 1989; *Izvestiia*, 1 April 1989; *Izvestiia*, 30 March 1989.
59 *Argumenty i fakty*, 1989, no. 21, p. 8; a full list of all the deputies elected appeared in *Izvestiia*, 5 April 1989.
60 *Soviet Weekly*, 11 October 1990, p. 7.
61 *Sovety narodnykh deputatov*, 1989, no. 5, pp. 11–13. A defence was also offered by V. Guliev in *Kommunist*, 1989, no. 18, pp. 43–4.
62 See for instance *Sovety narodnykh deputatov*, 1989, no. 11, p. 62. S. Avak'ian took the same view in *Vestnik MGU: Pravo*, 1989, no. 6, p. 9.
63 *Obshchestvennoe mnenie v tsifrakh*, no. 2 (September 1989), pp. 4–8. In a separate poll sponsored by *Sovetskaia Rossiia* and the Institute of Sociology of the USSR Academy of Sciences, 45 per cent were opposed to selection conferences: *Sovetskoe gosudarstvo i pravo*, 1990, no. 6, p. 34. A Moscow poll reported in *Sotsiologicheskie issledovaniia*, 1989, no. 5, p. 34, found 46 per cent opposed and 20 per cent in favour.
64 *Izvestiia*, 24 October 1989.
65 *Ibid.*, 17 December 1989; the text of the legislation is in *ibid.*, 23 December 1989.
66 *Ibid.*, 7 March 1990 and 15 February 1990.
67 *Moscow News*, 1989, no. 45, p. 10.
68 *Izvestiia*, 17 December 1989.
69 An 'elector's calendar' appeared in *Pravda*, 4 December 1989. On these elections, see Darrell Slider and Rein Taagepera, 'The Soviet Union' and 'The Baltic states', *Electoral Studies*, vol. 9, no. 4 (December 1990), pp. 295–302 and 303–11; and Commission on Security and Cooperation in Europe, *Elections in the Baltic States and Soviet Republics* (Washington DC: US Government Printing Office, 1990).

70 See Taagepera, 'The Baltic states'.
71 *Pravda*, 14 March 1990, and *Izvestiia*, 5 March 1990.
72 *Pravda*, 4 March 1990, and 14 March 1990. On these elections, see Peter Potichnyj, 'Elections in the Ukraine, 1990', in Zvi Gitelman, ed., *The Politics of Nationality and the Erosion of the USSR* (London: Macmillan, 1992).
73 *Pravda*, 4 March 1990.
74 *Pravda*, 22 March 1990.
75 *Soviet Weekly*, 31 May 1990, p. 6; *Kommunist* (Yerevan), 29 May 1990.
76 *Kommunist* (Yerevan), 29 May 1990; *Izvestiia*, 4 June 1990.
77 *Zaria Vostoka*, 9 November 1990.
78 *Pravda*, 16 February 1990; *Izvestiia*, 18 February 1990; and *Pravda Vostoka*, 22 February 1990.
79 *Pravda*, 10 January 1990.
80 *Kommunist Tadzhikistana*, 2 March 1990.
81 *Elections in the Baltic Republics and Soviet Republics*, pp. 137–60.
82 The costs were 4–5 million rubles in the Ukraine, for instance: *Izvestiia*, 17 February 1990.
83 *Argumenty i fakty*, 1990, no. 17, p. 1.
84 For an up-to-date discussion of these issues, see Martin Harrop and William L. Miller, *Elections and Voters* (London: Macmillan, 1987).
85 *Pravda*, 7 February 1990.
86 *Moscow News*, 1990, no. 3, p. 4.
87 *Ibid.*
88 *Izvestiia*, 20 February 1990.
89 *Moscow News*, 1989, no. 22, p. 10; the need for judicial arbitration of this kind was also pointed out in *Politicheskoe obrazovanie*, 1989, no. 8, p. 21. A multi-party system obviously became legitimate after February–March 1990.
90 *Pervyi s"ezd narodnykh deputatov SSSR 25 maia–9 iiunia 1989 g. Stenograficheskii otchet*, 6 vols. (Moscow: Izdanie Verkhovnogo Soveta SSSR, 1989), I, p. 51.
91 *Izvestiia*, 19 March 1990.
92 *Vestnik MGU: Pravo*, 1989, no. 6, p. 11.
93 A. V. Berezkin et al., 'Geografiia vyborov narodnykh deputatov SSSR v 1989 g. (pervye itogi)', *Izvestiia Akademii nauk SSSR: seriia geograficheskaia*, 1989, no. 5, pp. 5–24.
94 *Pravda*, 19 March 1990.
95 *Narodnyi deputat*, 1990, no. 1, p. 64.
96 *Izvestiia*, 17 December 1989.
97 *Ibid.*, 4 March 1989.
98 *Ibid.*, 14 March 1989 (Barabashev).
99 *Pravda*, 15 February 1989.
100 *Izvestiia*, 23 December 1989 (Art. 100).
101 *Pravda*, 22 March 1989.
102 *Izvestiia*, 1 March 1990.
103 *Ibid.*, 6 April 1990.
104 *Ibid.*, 11 February 1990.
105 *Ibid.*, 8 February 1990.
106 *Pravda*, 16 June 1990.

107 *Moscow News*, 1990, no. 10, p. 5.
108 *Ibid.*, 1990, no. 7, p. 5.
109 *Sovetskaia Litva*, 11 October 1989.
110 *Narodnyi deputat*, 1990, no. 1, p. 67. For restrictions on the provision of finan-
     cial support, see for instance *Sovetskaia Moldaviia*, 26 November 1989.
111 *Sovetskoe gosudarstvo i pravo*, 1990, no. 1, p. 10.
112 *Vestnik MGU: Pravo*, 1989, no. 6, p. 18. Others suggested that (for instance)
     donations from abroad or the use of electoral funds for other purposes should be
     prohibited: *Pravovedenie*, 1991, no. 1, p. 12.
113 *Pravda*, 3 February 1989; for another instance see *ibid.*, 6 May 1989.
114 *Ibid.*, 27 March 1989.
115 *Izvestiia*, 22 April 1990.
116 *Sovetskaia Rossiia*, 8 March 1990.
117 *Trud*, 14 March 1990.
118 *Izvestiia*, 28 March 1990.
119 *Pravda*, 18 June 1991.
120 *Pravovedenie*, 1992, no. 1, pp. 14–15.
121 *Narodnyi deputat*, 1991, no. 14, pp. 18–21.
122 *Sovetskoe gosudarstvo i pravo*, 1991, no. 7, pp. 31–2.
123 *Narodnyi deputat*, 1991, no. 17, pp. 25–8.

3   STRUCTURES OF GOVERNMENT

1 There are useful discussions of the development of Soviet representative institutions in Peter Vanneman, *The Supreme Soviet: Politics and the Legislative
   Process in the Soviet Political System* (Durham NC: Duke University Press,
   1977); Robert T. Huber and Donald R. Kelley, eds., *Perestroika-Era Politics*
   (Armonk NY: Sharpe, 1991); Ottorino Cappelli, 'The Soviet representative
   system at the crossroads: towards parliamentary representation?', *Journal of
   Communist Studies*, vol. 7, no. 2 (June 1991), pp. 170–201, and N. I. Rich-
   mond, 'One step forwards, two steps back: the USSR Supreme Soviet in the age
   of *perestroika*', *ibid.*, pp. 202–16. For an orthodox but informed Soviet view, see
   D. L. Zlatopol'sky, *Verkhovnyi Sovet SSSR: Vyrazitel' voli sovetskogo naroda*
   (Moscow: Iuridicheskaia literatura, 1982).
2 Jean Blondel, *Comparative Legislatures* (Englewood Cliffs NJ: Prentice-Hall,
   1973), pp. 56–60.
3 Wolfgang Leonhard, *The Kremlin since Stalin* (London: Oxford University
   Press, 1965), p. 93. See also Vanneman, *The Supreme Soviet*, p. 92, for an early
   procedural dispute.
4 See for instance G. A. Arbatov, *Zatianuvsheesia vyzdorovlenie* (Moscow: Mezhdunarodnye otnosheniia, 1991), p. 256.
5 *Moskovskie novosti*, 1988, no. 50, p. 4.
6 See D. Richard Little, 'Soviet parliamentary committees after Khrushchev',
   Soviet Studies, vol. 24, no. 1 (July 1972), pp. 41–60; Robert W. Siegler, *The
   Standing Commissions of the Supreme Soviet* (New York: Praeger, 1982); and
   Shugo Minagawa, *Supreme Soviet Organs* (Nagoya: University of Nagoya
   Press, 1985).

7 Merle Fainsod, *How Russia is Ruled*, rev. edn (Cambridge MA: Harvard University Press, 1965), p. 384.

8 See 'On improving the activity of the soviets of people's deputies and strengthening their links with the masses' (1957), in *KPSS v rezoliutsiiakh i resheniiakh s"ezdov, konferentsii i plenumov TsK*, 9th edn, 15 vols. (Moscow: Politizdat, 1983–9), IX, pp. 156–66. For a more general discussion, see Ronald J. Hill, 'The development of Soviet local government since Stalin's death', in Everett M. Jacobs, ed., *Soviet Local Politics and Government* (London: Allen and Unwin, 1983).

9 See *KPSS v rezoliutsiiakh*, XII, pp. 8–13, and the Law on the Status of the Deputy, *Spravochnik partiinogo rabotnika*, XIII (Moscow: Politizdat, 1973), pp. 256–69.

10 Roy Medvedev, *Kniga o sotsialisticheskoi demokratii* (Amsterdam/Paris: Fond imeni Gertsena/Grasset et Fasquelle, 1972), p. 166; similarly Sakharov and others in *Posev*, 1970, no. 7, p. 40.

11 Zhores Medvedev, *Andropov: His Life and Death*, rev. edn (Oxford: Blackwell, 1984), pp. 220–1. A commission on energy was added in late 1982: see Iu. V. Andropov, *Izbrannye rechi i stat'i*, 2nd edn (Moscow: Politizdat, 1983), p. 213.

12 L. I. Brezhnev, *Leninskim kursom: rechi i stat'i*, VII (Moscow: Politizdat, 1979), p. 616.

13 *Materialy plenuma TsK KPSS 27–28 ianvaria 1987 goda* (Moscow: Politizdat, 1987), pp. 11–15, 24–5. For some of what follows I have drawn upon Stephen White, '"Democratisation" in the USSR', *Soviet Studies*, vol. 42, no. 1 (January 1990), pp. 3–24, and White, *Gorbachev and After*, 3rd edn (Cambridge and New York: Cambridge University Press, 1992).

14 M. S. Gorbachev, *Izbrannye rechi i stat'i*, 7 vols. (Moscow: Politizdat, 1987–90), IV, p. 397.

15 *Ibid.*, p. 431.

16 *Materialy plenuma TsK KPSS 25–26 iiunia 1987 goda* (Moscow: Politizdat, 1987), pp. 81–2.

17 Gorbachev, *Izbrannye rechi i stat'i*, V, pp. 410–13.

18 *Ibid.*, vol. 6, pp. 66–7.

19 *Ibid.*, p. 215.

20 *Materialy XIX Vsesoiuznoi konferentsii KPSS 28 iiunia–1 iiulia 1988 goda* (Moscow: Politizdat, 1988), pp. 35–7.

21 *Pravda*, 23 November 1988.

22 *Sovetskoe gosudarstvo i pravo*, 1988, no. 5, pp. 3–13.

23 *Kommunist*, 1988, no. 8, pp. 28–36.

24 *Materialy XIX konferentsii*, pp. 43–55.

25 For this discussion, see White, '"Democratisation"'.

26 *Pravda*, 27 November 1988. The evening paper *Vecherniaia Moskva* reported that it had received no letter suggesting a change (10 November 1988).

27 *Literaturnaia gazeta*, 9 November 1988, p. 2.

28 *Ibid.*, 16 November 1988, p. 10; similarly *Sotsialisticheskaia industriia*, 2 November 1988.

29 *Pravda*, 17 November 1988.

30 *Ibid.*, 10 November 1988.

31 *Sovetskaia Rossiia*, 4 November 1988.

32 *Pravda*, 22 November 1988.
33 *Vecherniaia Moskva*, 11 November 1988.
34 *Pravda*, 2 December 1989.
35 *Izvestiia*, 6 May 1989 (based on 2,044 deputies); 85.3 per cent of all candidates were party members.
36 *Vestnik statistiki*, 1990, no. 1, p. 47.
37 *Moscow News*, 1989, no. 24, p. 13.
38 *Izvestiia*, 6 May 1989.
39 *Pervyi s"ezd narodnykh deputatov SSSR: Stenograficheskii otchet*, 6 vols. (Moscow: Izvestiia, 1989), I, p. 137.
40 *Vtoroi s"ezd narodnykh deputatov SSSR: Stenograficheskii otchet*, 6 vols. (Moscow: Izvestiia, 1990), II, p. 373.
41 *Sovetskaia kul'tura*, 8 April 1989, cited in *Izvestiia*, 6 May 1989.
42 *Pervyi s"ezd*, I, p. 6.
43 *Ibid.*, p. 109.
44 *Ibid.*, p. 60.
45 *Ibid.*, p. 66.
46 *Ibid.*, p. 64.
47 *Ibid.*, pp. 68–9.
48 L. I. Sukhov in *Izvestiia*, 26 May 1989; the version that appeared in the official protocol (*Pervyi s"ezd*, I, p. 71) was more discreetly worded.
49 *Pervyi s"ezd*, I, pp. 346–7.
50 *Ibid.*, II, pp. 89–96.
51 *Ibid.*, pp. 40–3.
52 *Ibid.*, pp. 43–9.
53 *Ibid.*, III, pp. 77–84.
54 *Ibid.*, II, pp. 221–7.
55 *Ibid.*, III, pp. 77–84.
56 *Ibid.*, III, pp. 325–8 (incorporating his 'Decree on Power', which also appears in Sakharov, *Trevoga i nadezhda* (Moscow: Inter-Verso, 1990), pp. 260–6).
57 *Pervyi s"ezd*, II, pp. 289–90.
58 *Ibid.*, p. 363.
59 *Ibid.*, III, pp. 209–20, and II, pp. 169–74.
60 *Ibid.*, II, pp. 185–90.
61 *Ibid.*, III, pp. 99–105.
62 *Ibid.*, pp. 111–16, 119–23.
63 *Ibid.*, pp. 411 (pensions), 414 (privileges), 402–4 and 399–400 (commissions).
64 *Ibid.*, I, pp. 431, 433. The full list of deputies elected to the Supreme Soviet is in *Vedomosti S"ezda narodnykh deputatov SSSR i Verkhovnogo Soveta SSSR*, 1989, no. 1, item 12.
65 *Pervyi s"ezd*, I, pp. 223–4.
66 *Pravda*, 20 July 1989.
67 *Ibid.*, 8 June 1989.
68 *Moscow News*, 1989, no. 20, p. 8.
69 *Pravda*, 18 July 1989. For the discussion of the nominations see N. I. Ryzhkov, *Perestroika. Istoriia predatel'stv* (Moscow: Novosti, 1992), pp. 288–91. The full list of ministerial posts was published in *Pravda*, 6 July 1989.
70 *Vtoroi s"ezd*, I, pp. 209–49.

71 G. Popov in *ibid.*, I, p. 289.
72 *Ibid.*, I, p. 336.
73 *Ibid.*, I, p. 400.
74 *Izvestiia*, 16 December 1989.
75 *Vtoroi s"ezd*, II, pp. 193–8.
76 *Ibid.*, III, p. 398.
77 *Vneocherednoi tretii s"ezd narodnykh deputatov SSSR 12–15 marta 1990 g.: Stenograficheskii otchet*, 3 vols. (Moscow: Izvestiia, 1990), I, p. 45.
78 *Ibid.*, pp. 126–7.
79 *Ibid.*, p. 125.
80 *Pravda*, 13 March 1990.
81 *Ibid.*, 14 March 1990.
82 *Ibid.*, 16 March 1990.
83 *Vneocherednoi tretii s"ezd*, III, p. 193.
84 *Pravda*, 18 December 1990.
85 *Ibid.*, 25 December 1990.
86 *Ibid.*, 19 December 1990.
87 *Ibid.*, 20 December 1990.
88 *Ibid.*, 21 December 1990.
89 *Izvestiia*, 23 December 1990.
90 *Pravda*, 22 December 1990.
91 *Izvestiia*, 6 September 1991.
92 *Vedomosti Verkhovnogo Soveta SSSR*, 1991, no. 52, p. 2,015.
93 *Izvestiia*, 18 December 1991.
94 The years were 1954, 1956, 1959 and 1961.
95 See Inter-Parliamentary Union, *Parliaments of the World*, 2nd edn (Aldershot: Gower, 1986), I, table 8; most parliaments met from 25–49 days a year (p. 271).
96 *Izvestiia*, 3 June 1991. For the work of commissions in earlier convocations see Daniel Nelson and Stephen White, eds., *Communist Legislatures in Comparative Perspective* (Albany: State University of New York Press, 1982), pp. 138–44.
97 *Izvestiia*, 3 June 1991.
98 See *Zasedaniia Verkhovnogo Soveta SSSR, desyatyi sozyv, vtoraia sessiia, 28–30 noiabria 1979 g.* (Moscow: Izvestiia, 1979) and *piataia sessiia, 23–24 iiunia 1981 g.* (Moscow: Izvestiia, 1981).
99 *Sovetskoe gosudarstvo i pravo*, 1988, no. 5, p. 3.
100 Robert K. Furtak, ed., *Elections in Socialist States* (Hemel Hempstead: Harvester Wheatsheaf, 1990), p. 47; *Moskovskie novosti*, 1988, no. 50, p. 4.
101 Giulietto Chiesa, *Transizione alla democrazia* (Rome: Lucarini, 1990), p. 151.
102 *Glasnost'*, 1991, no. 4, p. 4; *Istoriia SSSR*, 1992, no. 1, p. 2 (an analysis based on roll-call voting).
103 M. P. Georgadze, ed., *Verkhovnyi Sovet SSSR* (Moscow: Izvestiia, 1975), p. 188.
104 Zlatopol'sky, *Vyrazitel' voli*, p. 136.
105 See Nelson and White, *Communist Legislatures*, p. 138.
106 *Izvestiia*, 3 June 1991.
107 *Narodnyi deputat*, 1992, no. 1, pp. 5–6.
108 *Izvestiia*, 3 June 1991; Ryzhkov, *Perestroika*, p. 282.
109 *Izvestiia*, 29 May 1989.

110 *Pravda*, 20 July 1989.
111 Marsha Siefert, ed., *Mass Culture and Perestroika in the Soviet Union* (New York: Oxford University Press, 1991), p. 177.
112 *Izvestiia*, 27 June 1989.
113 *Moscow News*, 1989, no. 29, p. 10.
114 *Argumenty i fakty*, 1989, no. 26, p. 1.
115 *Izvestiia*, 1 January 1990.
116 *Dialog*, 1991, no. 1, pp. 10–12.
117 *Izvestiia*, 13 April and 1 June 1992.
118 *Ibid.*, 20 April 1992.
119 *Ibid.*, 23 April 1992.
120 *Ibid.*, 8 June 1992; *Kommunist*, 1991, no. 6, p. 69.
121 *Izvestiia*, 6 April 1992 (slightly adapted).
122 *Ibid.*, 14 May 1990.
123 *Kommunist*, 1990, no. 2, p. 37.
124 *Vestnik statistiki*, 1990, no. 1, pp. 72, 75.
125 *Ibid.*, p. 73; *Izvestiia*, 27 December 1990.
126 *Pravovedenie*, 1991, no. 5, p. 15.
127 *Ibid.*, pp. 6–7.
128 *Ibid.*, pp. 8–9. One particularly notable inquorate meeting was when the Supreme Soviet voted to include the discussion of Article 6 on the Congress of People's Deputies agenda; there was a majority in favour, but the vote was invalid: *Izvestiia*, 13 November 1989.
129 *Izvestiia*, 27 September 1990.
130 *Ibid.*, 22 November 1991.
131 *Ibid.*, 25 June 1991.
132 *Ibid.*, 22 November 1991.
133 *Pervyi s"ezd*, I, pp. 145–6, 152–3.
134 S. Stankievich in *Dialog*, 1990, no. 2, p. 48.
135 Burlatsky in *Literaturnaia gazeta*, 6 March 1991, p. 4.
136 *Narodnyi deputat*, 1990, no. 1, p. 35.
137 Iu. Burtin, ed., *Pul's reform* (Moscow: Progress, 1989), p. 68.
138 *Dialog*, 1990, no. 2, p. 49.
139 *Izvestiia*, 25 November 1991; and (for the Russian Federation) *Proekt Konstitutsii Rossiiskoi Federatsii* (Moscow: Izdanie Verkhovnogo Soveta, 1992), ch. 25.
140 *Pravda*, 15 May 1990.
141 *The Guardian* (London), 18 July 1992.
142 *Izvestiia*, 22 April 1992.

4   THE PRESIDENCY AND CENTRAL GOVERNMENT

1 Speech to the third session of the Supreme Soviet, *Pravda*, 3 July 1985.
2 Articles 121 and 122 of the Constitution.
3 Although Gromyko was active in at least one area of controversy. Following the demonstration by Crimean Tartars in Red Square in mid-1987, a special commission was set up under his chairmanship to investigate their call for the right to return to their traditional homelands.
4 M. S. Gorbachev, 'O khode realizatsii reshenii XXVII s"ezda KPSS i zadachakh

po uglubleniiu perestroiki', *Pravda*, 29 June 1988, and the resolution 'O demokratizatsii sovetskogo obshchestva i reforme politicheskoi sistemy', *Pravda*, 5 July 1988.

5 This was ostensibly to 'enhance' the role of the representative bodies. 'O demokratizatsii . . .'

6 Gorbachev, 'O khode . . .'

7 M. S. Gorbachev, 'O prakticheskoi rabote po realizatsii reshenii XIX vsesoiuznoi partiinoi konferentsii', *Pravda*, 30 July 1988. The resolution was of the same name.

8 For the report, see *Izvestiia*, 2 October 1988. On the day before (30 September) Gromyko had requested that he be relieved of his duties as a member of the Politburo and CC. *Pravda*, 1 October 1988.

9 M. S. Gorbachev, 'K polnovlastiiu sovetov i sozdaniiu sotsialisticheskogo pravovogo gosudarstva', *Pravda*, 30 November 1988. For the law on the constitutional changes see 'Ob izmeneniiakh i dopolneniiakh Konstitutsii (Osnovnogo Zakona) SSSR', *Pravda*, 3 December 1988.

10 All 42 members of the Presidium of the Supreme Soviet were to be *ex officio*: Chairman and First Deputy Chairman of the Supreme Soviet, the chairmen of the two chambers of the Supreme Soviet, Chairman of the People's Control Committee, the chairmen of the fifteen republican Supreme Soviets and the chairmen of the twenty-two permanent commissions and committees of the Supreme Soviet.

11 For the debate and voting, see *Pervyi s"ezd narodnykh deputatov SSSR. 25 maia–9 iiunia 1989 g. Stenograficheskii otchet*, 6 vols. (Moscow: 1989), I, pp. 56–110.

12 Respectively Logunov and Kryzhkov, *Pervyi s"ezd*, pp. 60 and 62.

13 Golovlev, *Pervyi s"ezd*, p. 72.

14 Emel'ianenkov, *Pervyi s"ezd*, p. 79.

15 An unidentified delegate, *Pervyi s"ezd*, p. 70.

16 For example, Bekhtereva and Zvonov, *Pervyi s"ezd*, pp. 74 and 76.

17 Konev, *Pervyi s"ezd*, p. 82.

18 *Pervyi s"ezd*, pp. 90–1.

19 *Pervyi s"ezd*, III, p. 265.

20 'O vnesenii izmenenii i dopolnenii v Konstitutsiiu (Osnovnoi Zakon), SSSR i uchrezhdenii posta Prezidenta SSSR', *Pravda*, 13 March 1990.

21 Although the first President was to be elected by the Congress of People's Deputies.

22 For example, Alekseev and Afanasev, *Izvestiia*, 13 and 14 March 1990.

23 For example, Gumbaridze and Salaev, *Izvestiia*, 13 March 1990.

24 Dabizha, *Izvestiia*, 14 March 1990.

25 *Izvestiia*, 13 March 1990.

26 Likhachev, *Izvestiia*, 16 March 1990.

27 *Izvestiia*, 15 March 1990.

28 'Ob uchrezhdenii posta Prezidenta SSSR i vnesenii izmenenii i dopolnenii v Konstitutsiiu (Osnovnoi Zakon) SSSR', *Pravda*, 16 March 1990.

29 The Chairman of the USSR Supreme Court was explicitly excluded from the list of people who the President could suggest be relieved of their posts, although this position was one that the President could nominate for filling.

30 He argued that all the amendments should be approved as a single package (thereby bracketing those concerning the presidency with that removing the constitutional basis for the party's leading and guiding role), after which minor changes could be considered on individual issues. However when it came time to consider proposed changes, it was argued that these constituted changes to the Constitution and therefore required a two-thirds majority.

31 For a brief comparison with the French and American models, see Elizabeth Teague and Dawn Mann, 'Gorbachev's Dual Role', *Problems of Communism*, vol. 39, no. 1 (January–February 1990), pp. 1–14.

32 The law on legal conditions applying in a state of emergency adopted on 3 April 1990 made specific provision for the imposition of presidential rule in an area where a state of emergency had already been declared and failed to restore order. However, this did not restrict presidential rule to such situations. The law allowed the President to suspend local governing bodies and replace them with his own executive organ or plenipotentiary. For the need for presidential rule to be based on the law and conducted within the Constitution, see *Argumenty i fakty*, 1991, no. 3.

33 Yeltsin was popularly elected in June 1991. Gorbachev was never thus elected, obtaining his position as a people's deputy on the CPSU's list of 100 deputies nominated by the CC.

34 'Ob obespechenii obsluzhivanii i okhrane Prezidenta SSSR', *Vedomosti S"ezda narodnykh deputatov i Verkhovnogo Soveta SSSR*, 1990, no. 22, pp. 488–9.

35 'O zashchite chesti i dostoinstva Prezidenta SSSR', *ibid.*, p. 487. The law is dated 14 May.

36 See the decision of the Supreme Soviet, 'O poriadke primeneniia i vvedeniia v deistvie Zakone SSSR "O zashchite chesti i dostoinstva Prezidenta SSSR"', *ibid.*, pp. 487–8.

37 The most prominent case of this was that of Democratic Union activist Novodvorskaia who was accused of labelling Gorbachev a fascist. See *Moscow News*, 1991, no. 16.

38 See the report of the proceedings of the Supreme Soviet in *Izvestiia*, 25 September 1990.

39 *Pravda*, 26 September 1990.

40 This is separate from the personal apparatus used to sustain the position. By the middle of 1991 this apparatus, headed by Valerii Boldin, consisted of nine sections: Administration of Affairs, Committee for Co-ordination of Activities of Law-Enforcement Organs, Press Service, General Department, Department for Questions of Defence and State Security, Department for Socio-economic Development and Political Prognosis, Department for Juridical Expertise, Information Service, and Group for Letters and Reception of Citizens. Alexander Rahr, 'The Soviet Leadership on the Eve of the Coup', RFE/RL Research Institute, *Report on the USSR*, 23 August 1991, pp. 4–5.

41 'Ob izmeneniiakh i dopolneniiakh Konstitutsii (Osnovnogo zakona) SSSR v sviazi s sovershenstvovaniem sistemy gosudarstvennogo upravleniia', *Pravda*, 27 December 1990. For Gorbachev's speech proposing the measures, see *Pravda*, 5 December 1990 and for Luk'ianov's explanation of the changes, *Pravda*, 22 December 1990.

42 For a list of decrees, see *Argumenty i fakty*, 1990, nos. 39 and 50, and 1991, no. 11.

43 The Committee's finding was announced on 14 September. For the original decree, see *Pravda*, 21 April 1990.

44 The speaker was Leningrad party secretary Gidaspov. *Pravda*, 6 July 1990.

45 Richard Sakwa, *Gorbachev and His Reforms 1985–1990* (London: Philip Allan, 1990), p. 149.

46 For an outline of the interim, and short-lived, state structure introduced in the wake of the coup, see 'The interim state structure of the USSR', *Report on the USSR*, 6 December 1991, pp. 10–11.

5 FROM UNION TO INDEPENDENCE

1 A report comparing the Soviet and Russian military industrial complex appeared in *Moscow News*, 1992, no. 9, p. 10.

2 See Graeme Gill, *The Origins of the Stalinist Political System* (Cambridge: Cambridge University Press, 1990).

3 This process of concentrating power in the ministries and other branch agencies was especially pronounced in the Brezhnev era, after the dismantling of the regional economic councils (*sovnarkhozy*) created by Khrushchev. Even before this, however, Khrushchev's reform had been undermined by the continued role of Gosplan and its branch-oriented departments.

4 For more on this aspect of Soviet politics, see Darrell Slider, 'Regional aspects of policy innovation in the Soviet Union', in Thomas F. Remington, ed., *Politics in the Soviet System: Essays in Honour of Frederick C. Barghoorn* (London: Macmillan, 1989), pp. 139–69.

5 For a review of the republic acts, see Ann Sheehy, 'Fact sheet on declarations of sovereignty', *Report on the USSR*, 9 November 1990, pp. 23–5.

6 Based on comments by a Minsk factory manager in *Pravitel'stvennyi vestnik*, no. 51 (December 1990).

7 For more on the Georgian case, see Darrell Slider, 'The politics of Georgia's independence', *Problems of Communism*, vol. 40, no. 6 (November–December 1991), pp. 63–79.

8 *Izvestiia*, 26 July 1990.

9 A review of military forces in the republics, both official and unofficial, was presented in *Komsomol'skaia pravda*, 12 March 1991.

10 See the interview with Victor Alksnis, nicknamed the 'black colonel', in *Sovetskaia Rossiia*, 21 November 1990. Bakatin was forced to resign from his post in December 1990 and was replaced by Boris Pugo, the former party first secretary in Latvia who adopted a much harsher line toward the republics. Bakatin discussed his role in the MVD in *Komsomol'skaia pravda*, 30 December 1990. Pugo later committed suicide after the failure of the August 1991 coup.

11 *Izvestiia*, 8 January 1991.

12 A report on the Ukrainian measures appeared in *Izvestiia*, 30 April 1991.

13 A collection of some of the most important pieces of Russian legislation adopted in the fall of 1990 were collected in *Novye zakony Rossii*, supplement to the journal *Za i protiv* (Moscow, 1991).

14 See, for example, the efforts by L. Mikhailov in *Ekonomika i zhizn'*, 1990, no. 10; Goskomstat in *Vestnik statistiki*, 1990, no. 3, pp. 36–53; M. Gorshkov in *Planovoe khoziaistvo*, 1991, no. 2, pp. 15–23.

15 Based on a study by the Central Mathematical Economics Institute (TsEMI) reported in *Kommunist*, 1990, no. 15, p. 69.

16 An effort by Gorbachev to stop this by decree was, like similar attempts in other areas, ineffective. The decree was published in *Izvestiia*, 13 April 1991.

17 Appeal from the USSR Supreme Soviet to the Supreme Soviets of the republics. *Izvestiia*, 5 April 1991.

18 An interview with the then Central Committee Secretary for nationality relations, Andrei Girenko, on the drafting process appeared in *Izvestiia TsK KPSS*, 1990, no. 9, p. 110.

19 The list of signatories appeared in *Izvestiia*, 12 March 1991. In an interview, the chairman of the Russian Supreme Soviet, Ruslan Khasbulatov, opposed the agreement as an attempt to break up the Russian federation. *Kuranty*, 22 March 1991.

20 Yeltsin's speech to the Russian parliament on the creation of the commonwealth. *Rossiiskaia gazeta*, 13 December 1991.

21 One of the authors, Darrell Slider, was present at the foreign affairs commission of the Georgian parliament during efforts to organise the forum in March 1991. Negotiations on setting up the group were conducted at the parliamentary level by the head of the foreign affairs commission of the Moldavian parliament, a member of the Moldavian popular front.

22 Declarations and resolutions adopted by the Kishinev Forum were published in the Georgian newspaper *Svobodnaia Gruziia*, 4 June 1991 and 6 July 1991. A lengthy interview with the Armenian representative to the talks, David Shakhnarzyan, appeared in *Respublika Armeniia*, 11 September 1991.

23 These figures include both cities and the surrounding rural areas. For a detailed analysis of the referendum, see Darrell Slider, 'The first Soviet "national" referendum and referenda in the republics: Voting on union, sovereignty, and independence', *Journal of Soviet Nationalities* (forthcoming).

24 *Pravda*, 20 August 1991.

25 This interrepublic group first met in March 1991, under the chairmanship of the deputy chairman of the Soviet government, Vitalii Doguzhiiev. Under Doguzhiiev, the committee sought to impose economic sanctions on republics refusing to join the new union.

26 *Izvestiia*, 4 October 1991.

27 The Alma Ata agreement was published in *The New York Times*, 23 December 1991. The Russian text appeared in *Rossiiskaia gazeta*, 24 December 1991.

28 For details on the inner workings of the Commonwealth see the interviews with a primary participant in the talks, the then first deputy chairman of the Russian foreign ministry, Fedor Shelov-Kovediaev in *Rossiiskie vesti*, 19 March 1992, and *Nezavisimaia gazeta*, 30 July 1992.

29 The speaker of the Russian parliament, Ruslan Khasbulatov, was elected chairman of the council of the assembly. An Azerbaijani delegation attended but only as observers. Russian evening television news, 16 September 1992. The March agreements appeared in *Rossiiskaia gazeta*, 1 April 1992.

30 The venue and chairmanship of these sessions rotated each time, and they were preceded in each case by a meeting of the Council of Foreign Ministers.

31 The decision on the UN seats was adopted as part of the Alma Ata agreement. Belarus (then Belorussia) and Ukraine were given seats in the General Assembly when the UN was founded.

32 Presidents of the Academies of Science and ministers of higher education from Azerbaijan, Kyrgyzstan, Kazakhstan, Tajikistan, Turkmenistan and Uzbekistan gathered in Tashkent in March 1992 and called for Soviet research facilities to be transferred to international control. *Poisk*, 7–13 March 1992.
33 *Izvestiia*, 7 July 1992.
34 *Rossiiskaia gazeta*, 2 September 1992.
35 The text of documents approved by CIS leaders on military matters appeared in *Rossiiskaia gazeta*, 25 March 1992.
36 Report on Russian evening news, 15 April 1992.
37 The agreement was published in *Rossiiskaia gazeta*, 8 August 1992.
38 The structure was described in *Izvestiia*, 9 July 1992.
39 *Izvestiia*, 7 July 1992.

6 PATTERNS OF REPUBLIC AND LOCAL POLITICS

1 On the popular front and its role in parliament, see the reports in *Nezavisimaia gazeta*, 24 October 1991 and 28 July 1992.
2 *Izvestiia*, 24 July 1991 and *Moscow News*, no. 26 (26 June–5 July 1992).
3 *Moscow News*, no. 24 (14–21 June 1992).
4 *Nezavisimaia gazeta*, 5 June 1992.
5 *Izvestiia*, 20 August 1992. The Ukrainian Central Electoral Commission registered the initiative groups in September. *Izvestiia*, 17 September 1992.
6 *Nezavisimaia gazeta*, 12 September 1992.
7 Just before the August coup, local communist parties continued to own 3,583 newspapers according to a report in *Nezavisimaia gazeta* reported in *The New York Times*, 9 August 1991.
8 *Rossiiskaia gazeta*, 1 September 1992.
9 An account by observers of the June 1992 election was compiled by the UN Congress, Commission on Security and Cooperation in Europe, *The Presidential Election in Azerbaijan*, 26 June 1992.
10 Later Manukian, in September 1992, ended his opposition role and rejoined the Armenian government of President Ter-Petrosian.
11 This followed Ivan Silaev's appointment to head the interrepublic economic council. The economist Yegor Gaidar became the 'acting' prime minister in Yeltsin's government until his removal in December 1992.
12 *Moscow News*, no. 15 (12–19 April 1992), p. 5.
13 One of the few studies to focus on local elections is that of Timothy Colton, who examines elections to the Moscow city soviet in 'The politics of democratization: The Moscow election of 1990', *Soviet Economy*, vol. 6 (1990), pp. 285–344.
14 The classic study of the role of the party at the local level – though the focus is on relations between the party and enterprise managers – is Jerry F. Hough, *The Soviet Prefects: The Local Party Organs in Industrial Decision-Making* (Cambridge MA: Harvard University Press, 1969).
15 The head of the Supreme Soviet commission that prepared the draft of the law, Nikolai Pivovarov, commented that recognition of the rights of republics and autonomous republics in this area was the most important change in the law. Interview in *Pravda*, 13 November 1989. The law was passed on 9 April 1990 and appeared in *Izvestiia*, 14 April 1990.
16 *Izvestiia TsK KPSS*, no. 6 (June 1991), pp. 17–24.

17 In Tomsk region, for example, the average rural district had 1,500 voters while urban districts had around 4,000. *Izvestiia*, 4 October 1991.

18 *Nezavisimaia gazeta*, 10 April 1992. The study was conducted by VTsIOM.

19 The decision, by the USSR Committee on Constitutional Supervision, was published in *Izvestiia*, 13 March 1991.

20 Among the first to resign their party posts were the first secretary of the Komi Autonomous Republic in the RSFSR (Iu. Spiridonov), the Ukrainian first secretary (V. Ivashko), and the city party leader in Kursk (N. Golovin).

21 *Izvestiia* (1 November 1991) presented a list of some examples from Ulianovsk, Penza, Kirov, Cheliabinsk and Rostov provinces.

22 *Izvestiia*, 22 July 1991.

23 *Izvestiia*, 11 April 1990.

24 *Izvestiia*, 16 September 1990; and *Komsomol'skaia pravda*, 21 September 1990.

25 *Izvestiia*, 2 May 1991 and 2 November 1991.

26 *Moscow News*, no. 7 (16–23 February 1991); *Izvestiia*, 29 February 1992. See also V. A. Kriazhkov, 'Mestnoe samoupravlenie: pravovoe regulirovanie i struktury', *Sovetskoe gosudarstvo i pravo*, 1992, no. 1, pp. 16–24.

27 This description comes from an interview with then chairman of the Volgograd soviet Valerii Makharadze, *Rossiiskaia gazeta*, 29 June 1991.

28 On relations between the party and soviets, see Ronald Hill, 'The development of Soviet local government since Stalin's death', in Everett M. Jacobs, ed., *Soviet Local Politics and Government* (London: Allen and Unwin, 1983), pp. 18–33.

29 *Moscow News*, no. 26 (8–15 July 1990), p. 5.

30 *Rabochaia tribuna*, 19 April 1991.

31 Complaints of this sort from Volgograd, including an example of the city *ispolkom* independently introducing price increases, were published in *Izvestiia*, 4 October 1990.

32 Kriazhkov, 'Mestnoe samoupravlenie', pp. 21–2.

33 *Izvestiia*, 27 September 1990.

34 *Izvestiia*, 7 July 1990.

35 *Izvestiia*, 4 October 1990.

36 *Sovetskaia Kirgiziia*, 22 February 1991.

37 *Chto delat'* published in Moscow, November 1990. A later version of Popov's proposals appeared almost a year later, in an article entitled 'What next?', *Izvestiia*, 3 October 1991.

38 In other cities the term was used informally to mean the chairman of the soviet.

39 *Izvestiia*, 9 August 1990.

40 This section draws in part on Darrell Slider, 'Republican leaders confront local opposition', *RFE/RL Research Report*, 6 March 1992, pp. 7–11.

41 *Rossiiskaia gazeta*, 20 February 1992.

42 *Rossiia*, 4–10 January 1991, p. 2.

43 *Trud*, 18 April 1991.

44 *Nedel'ia*, no. 29 (1990), p. 3.

45 *Sovetskaia Rossiia*, 1 December 1988.

46 *Nedel'ia*, no. 29 (1990), p. 3.

47 According to a report in *Izvestiia*, 17 September 1990, radical soviets in Ukraine formed an Association of Democratic Soviets at the end of July 1990. The democratic regional soviets of the western Ukraine were also included in the group: L'viv, Ivano-Frankovsk, and Ternopil.

48 *Nezavisimaia gazeta*, 16 March 1991.

49 The idea of prefects was initially proposed by Vakhtang Khmaladze, from the moderate party Democratic Choice for Georgia, assuming that prefects would merely report to Tbilisi on violations by local officials. Based on an interview with Khmaladze, then serving as deputy chairman of the Central Electoral Commission, in Tbilisi in July 1991.

50 The law on the prefecture was published in *Svobodnaia Gruziia*, 27 April 1991.

51 The law governing the *sakrebulo* appeared in *Svobodnaia Gruziia*, 24 May 1991.

52 *Svobodnaia Gruziia*, 5 September 1991.

53 On the law, see *Izvestiia*, 31 January 1991 and 13 June 1991.

54 *Izvestiia*, 11 July 1991; the law appeared in *Sovetskaia Moldova*, 15 August 1991.

55 V. Makharadze, the Russian Chief State Inspector and who was discussed above as chairman of the Volgograd oblast soviet, was the first official named to serve as coordinator of their activities. Interview with Makharadze in *Izvestiia*, 1 November 1991. The decree establishing the post was issued by Yeltsin on August 22. In March 1992 Makharadze was promoted to the post of deputy chairman of the Russian government, where he continued to oversee regional issues. Another highly visible radical deputy, Yuri Boldyrev, replaced Makharadze as Chief of the Control Administration. *Rossiiskaia gazeta*, 5 March 1992.

56 Based on the analysis of the presidential representative undertaken by Boris Bogatov in *Nezavisimaia gazeta*, 6 November 1991.

57 *Nezavisimaia gazeta*, 14 August 1992.

58 In the case of Ulianovsk, Yeltsin reversed his decision and appointed the head of the oblast soviet. *Izvestiia*, 5 November 1991. The case of Krasnodar was mentioned in *Izvestiia*, 26 August 1991.

59 The law 'On Elections for Chiefs of Administration' was adopted by the Russian Supreme Soviet on 25 October 1991 and appeared in *Rossiiskaia gazeta*, 14 November 1991.

60 *Rossiiskaia gazeta*, 5 November 1991.

61 Yeltsin's directive appeared in *Rossiiskaia gazeta*, 15 September 1992.

62 Test of Akaev's speech to the Kirgiz Supreme Soviet, in *Slovo Kyrgzystana*, 23 April 1991.

63 A report on the first meeting of the district administrators appeared on the Russian evening television news, 15 April 1992.

64 *Nezavisimaia gazeta*, 28 March 1992.

65 *Sovetskaia Moldaviia*, 30 January 1991.

66 *Rossiia*, 6–12 June 1991.

67 *Izvestiia*, 25 June 1991.

68 *Bakinskii rabochii*, 6 October 1990.

69 *Rossiiskaia gazeta*, 20 March 1992.

70 Report on Moscow evening television news, 13 March 1992.

71 The text of the federation treaty appeared in *Rossiiskaia gazeta*, 18 March 1992.

7   THE WITHERING AWAY OF THE PARTY

1 See Graeme Gill, *The Origins of the Stalinist Political System* (Cambridge: Cambridge University Press, 1990).

2 For example, see M. S. Gorbachev, 'Politicheskii doklad Tsentral'nogo Komiteta KPSS', *Pravda*, 26 February 1986.

3 For example, see M. S. Gorbachev, 'Korennoi vopros ekonomicheskoi politiki partii', *Pravda*, 12 June 1985.
4 Section 4(b) of the new party Rules adopted at the XXVII Congress in February–March 1986. *Pravda*, 7 March 1986.
5 Section 19(e) of the new party Rules adopted at the XXVII Congress, *Pravda*, 7 March 1986.
6 'Iz besedy v TsK KPSS s pervymi sekretariami nekotorykh oblastnykh komitetov partii', in M. S. Gorbachev, *Izbrannye rechi i stat'i* (Moscow: Politizdat, 1987), II, pp. 16–25. There was some discussion of this in the press: see *Kommunist*, 1985, no. 17, pp. 79–83. Also for minimum compulsory turnover levels in party organs: *Kommunist*, 1985, no. 18, pp. 61–5.
7 'O perestroike i kadrovoi politike partii', *Pravda*, 28 January 1987.
8 The national CC was not included in this list, although Gorbachev did say that further democratisation should apply to the formation of the central leading bodies of the party.
9 'O perestroike i kadrovoi politike partii', *Pravda*, 29 January 1987.
10 *Pravda*, 10 February 1987, *Sovetskaia Rossiia*, 10 February 1987 and 19 February 1987, and *Pravda*, 1 March 1987.
11 *Partiinaia zhizn'*, 1988, no. 11, p. 15.
12 M. S. Gorbachev, 'O zadachakh partii po korennoi perestroike upravleniia ekonomikoi', *Pravda*, 26 June 1987.
13 'O sozyve XIX Vsesoiuznoi konferentsii KPSS', *Pravda*, 27 June 1987.
14 For example, see *Sovetskaia Rossiia*, 1 June 1988, *Pravda*, 6 June 1988, *Izvestiia*, 18 June 1988 and *Moscow News*, 1988, no. 24. For a discussion of the election campaign, see Aryeh L. Unger, 'The travails of intra-party democracy in the Soviet Union: The elections to the 19th Conference of the CPSU', *Soviet Studies*, vol. 43, no. 2 (1991), pp. 329–54.
15 *Sovetskaia Rossiia*, 13 March 1988. For the response to it, see *Pravda*, 5 April 1988.
16 *Pravda*, 27 May 1988.
17 M. S. Gorbachev, 'O khode realizatsii reshenii XXVII s"ezda KPSS i zadachakh po uglubleniiu perestroiki', *Pravda*, 29 June 1988.
18 'Ob izmeneniiakh i dopolneniiakh Konstitutsii (Osnovnogo Zakona) SSSR', *Pravda*, 3 December 1988. For the resolution of the XIX Conference, see 'O demokratizatsii sovetskogo obshchestva i reforme politicheskoi sistemy', *Pravda*, 5 July 1988.
19 'Instruktsiia o provedenii vyborov rukovodiashchikh partiinykh organov', *Partiinaia zhizn'*, 1988, no. 16, pp. 30–5.
20 *Izvestiia TsK KPSS*, 1989, no. 1, pp. 81–6. On the re-organisation of the lower level apparatus see pp. 87–91. For references to the way in which economic departments in the obkoms formally were eliminated and then re-established as sub-departments of other departments, see *Pravda*, 14 June 1989 and *Partiinaia zhizn'*, 1989, no. 19, p. 7.
21 'O komissiiakh Tsentral'nogo Komiteta KPSS', *Pravda*, 29 November 1988.
22 The nine were Party work and cadres policy, Ideology, Social-economic policy, Agrarian policy, Defence, State and legal policy, International policy, General Department and *Upravlenie delami*. On the reduction in personnel, see M. S. Gorbachev, 'Narashchavit' intellektual'nyi potentsial perestroiki', *Pravda*, 8 January 1989.

23 For example, see 'Partiia i kadry', *Pravda*, 12 September 1989. According to one report, in the latest round of party elections, only 8.6 per cent of local secretaries and 1 per cent of regional secretaries were chosen on a competitive basis. *Pravda*, 10 July 1989.

24 Respectively *Pravda*, 6 February 1990 and 13 February 1990. The latter was entitled 'K gumannomu, demokraticheskomu sotsializmu'.

25 Although this was not specified as the method of election of delegates to the XXVIII Congress. The procedure of election was to be determined by individual party organisations. *Pravda*, 17 March 1990. This suggests continuing opposition to the notion of competitive elections in the party.

26 *Pravda*, 12 March 1990.

27 For example, 'Partiia i kadry', *Pravda*, 12 September 1989. For earlier suggestions that multi-candidate elections would be the means of undermining the exclusive nature of the nomenklatura, including clientelistic and kinship links, see *Partiinaia zhizn'*, 1987, no. 2, p. 30 and *Pravda*, 24 February 1987.

28 *Pravda*, 15 October 1989.

29 Radianska Ukraina 23 January 1990, in FBIS, *Soviet Union Daily Report*, 12 March 1990.

30 *Pravda*, 27 April 1989.

31 Gorbachev argued that deputies should adopt united positions on those questions of principle on which party organs adopted decisions, while having full freedom of initiative, judgement and voting on others. Such a distinction was impossible to realise in practice. M. S. Gorbachev, 'Perestroika raboty partii – vazneishchaia kliuchevaia zadacha dnia', *Pravda*, 19 July 1989.

32 Regular reports of its proceedings in the press ceased in 1989. According to one report, it met on only nine occasions during 1990 compared with thirty-eight in 1985. *Moscow News*, 10–17 March 1991.

33 *Sovetskaia Rossiia*, 22 June 1990. The speaker was Ligachev.

34 *Pravda*, 5 July 1990. Speech by Ligachev. Also see the discussion at the meeting between Gorbachev and party secretaries in July 1989, *Pravda*, 21 July 1989. Both appear to have become more active following their reconstitution at the XXVIII Congress.

35 The CC met in plenary sessions as follows: 1985: 4, 1986: 3, 1987: 3, 1988: 5 (including two directly linked with the Conference), 1989: 8, 1990: 5 and 1991: 3.

36 This was a common theme at the July 1989 meeting between Gorbachev and party secretaries. *Pravda*, 21 July 1989.

37 *Pravda*, 19 July 1989 and 21 July 1989. This meeting was remarkable at the time for the frankness of the criticisms of policy and its implementation made by regional and central party leaders.

38 For one discussion of reformist elements in the party, see Igor Chubais, 'The democratic opposition: An insider's view', Radio Liberty, *Report on the USSR*, 3 May 1991, pp. 4–15.

39 For example, see 'Iz besedy v TsK KPSS s pervymi sekretariami nekotorykh komitetov partii', Gorbachev, *Izbrannye rechi i stat'i*, II, pp. 16–25.

40 'Vystuplenie M. S. Gorbacheva na Plenume Ts.K. KPSS po voprosam II S"ezda narodnykh deputatov SSSR', *Pravda*, 10 December 1989.

41 *Pravda*, 6 February 1990.

42 *Pravda*, 16 March 1990.

43 This reinforced the fears that had been created by Gorbachev's accession to the

Chairmanship of the Supreme Soviet in March 1990. These concerns were stimulated by Gorbachev's accession to this post when, in 1985, he had said that such a move was inappropriate because the General Secretary should devote his energies principally to the party and its affairs. *Pravda*, 3 July 1985. His move to this post clearly suggested a downgrading of the party.

44 For an overview of the discussion of these documents, see Stephen White, 'Rethinking the CPSU', *Soviet Studies*, vol. 43, no. 3 (1991), pp. 405–28.

45 These changes were introduced at the October 1990 plenum. The commissions were to be Renewal of the activity of primary party organs (based on the former Party construction and cadre policy), Ideology, Socio-political, Agricultural, International policy, Socio-economic policy, Nationality policy, Women and family questions, Science, education and culture, Youth policy and Military policy. New departments: Organisational (based on former Party work and cadre policy department), Ideology, Socio-economic policy, Humanitarian, Agricultural policy, International, Legislative initiatives and questions of law, Centre for Information (based on former Defence department), Women and the family, General, Chancellery, Nationality policy, Press centre, and Ties with socio-political organisations. *Pravda*, 10 October 1990.

46 According to CC Secretary Shenin, its current total of 1,493 officials was to be reduced by 40.4 per cent or 603, following a reduction in the previous year of 536 officials. *Pravda*, 10 October 1990.

47 For an interesting discussion, see Ronald J. Hill, 'The CPSU: From monolith to pluralist?', *Soviet Studies*, vol. 43, no. 3 (1991), pp. 217–35.

48 *Pravda*, 21 July 1989.

49 It also occurred later in some of the other republics; for example, both Georgia and Armenia in December 1990.

50 'Ob obrazovanii rossiiskogo biuro TsK KPSS', *Pravda*, 10 December 1989.

51 For an unconvincing attempt to distinguish between the Khrushchev experience and the new Bureau, see the interview with CC Secretary Manaenkov in *Pravda*, 9 November 1989.

52 *Pravda*, 13 February 1990.

53 *TASS*, 17 July 1990.

54 'O proekte platformy TsK KPSS k XXVIII s"ezdu partii', *Pravda*, 6 February 1990.

55 'K gumannomu, demokraticheskomu sotsializmu', *Pravda*, 13 February 1990.

56 The initial all-union conferences of both bodies occurred in January (DP) and April (MP).

57 *Pravda*, 3 March 1990 and 16 April 1990.

58 *Pravda*, 11 April 1990.

59 For example, see the comments of Moscow party leader Prokof'ev: *Moskovskaia Pravda*, 15 June 1990. His attempt to distinguish between a platform and a fraction is specious and illustrates the futility of the position official speakers sought to defend.

60 This was not only frequently commented upon in the press, but was given graphic proof by the swelling numbers leaving the party in the first half of 1990. For some figures see *Argumenty i fakty*, 16–22 June 1990.

61 *Moskovskaia Pravda*, 17 June 1990.

62 *Sovetskaia Rossiia*, 20 June 1990.

63 For some examples, see the articles about Gidaspov and Polozkov in *Moscow News*, 8–15 July 1991. Also see *ibid.*, 25 November–2 December 1990. For a discussion of the fears of party secretaries, see Vladimir Brovkin. 'First party secretaries: An endangered Soviet species?', *Problems of Communism*, vol. 39, no. 1 (January–February 1990), pp. 15–27.

64 *Izvestiia TsK KPSS*, 1989, no. 1, p. 132 and J. H. Miller, 'The mass party membership: Steady as she goes', in R. F. Miller, J. H. Miller and T. H. Rigby, eds., *Gorbachev at the Helm. A New Era in Soviet Politics* (London: Croom Helm, 1987), p. 91.

65 *Izvestiia TsK KPSS*, p. 134.

66 *Pravda*, 26 July 1991. Gorbachev cited this figure in his address to the CC plenum on 25 July 1991. Some three million left during 1990.

67 For the drawing of explicit linkages between disillusionment and party membership developments, see *Rabochaia Tribuna*, 8 May 1990, *Moskovskaia Pravda*, 15 June 1990 (Prokof'ev) and *Sovetskaia Rossiia*, 21 June 1990 (Mel'nikov).

68 *Pravda*, 21 May 1990.

69 *Glasnost'*, 28 June 1990.

70 *Rabochaia Tribuna*, 8 May 1990.

71 *Vestnik MID*, August 1990, p. 27. This is the journal of the Soviet Foreign Ministry.

72 *Moskovskaia Pravda*, 17 June 1990 (V. S. Afanas'ev).

73 *Moscow News*, 4–11 November 1990.

74 Radio Liberty, *Report on the USSR*, 19 October 1990, p. 39.

75 *Krasnoe znamia*, 30 January 1990, 20 February 1990, 15 March 1990 and 15 May 1990.

76 'O merakh po okhrane neprikosnovennosti prava sobstvennosti v SSSR', *Vedomosti S"ezda narodnykh deputatov SSSR i Verkhovnogo Soveta SSSR*, 1990, no. 42, pp. 1057–8.

77 *Moscow News*, 4–11 November 1990.

78 And a reluctance to pay. In October 1990 more than one million members were behind in their payments. *Pravda*, 12 October 1990.

79 In November 1990 *Pravda* had 30.3 per cent of the subscribers it had at the start of the year. *Argumenty i fakty*, 1990, no. 48.

80 See the Tass report of comments by CC Secretary Shenin, in Radio Liberty, *Report on the USSR*, 26 October 1990, p. 43.

81 *Nezavisimaia gazeta*, 9 August 1991.

82 For example, despite registering as an all-union party on 11 April 1991 under the terms of the Law on Public Associations (*Glasnost'*, 18 April 1991), the party refused at the XXVIII Congress to the proposal that the party be considered a parliamentary rather than a vanguard party and therefore that the PPOs be transformed from workplace organisations to territorial, electorate, bodies. In practice in some enterprises the party was forced to close its branches and relocate to rented accommodation elsewhere. *Moscow News*, 2–9 September 1990.

83 See Elizabeth Teague and Julia Wishnevsky, 'Yeltsin organized political activity in state sector', Radio Liberty, *Report on the USSR*, 16 August 1991, pp. 21–5.

84 *Pravda*, 5 August 1991. The party's reluctance to accept such a move which threatened its workplace control is reflected in an earlier episode. On 3 September 1990 Gorbachev issued a presidential decree transferring control of the Main

Political Administration in the armed forces from the party to the state. On 15 November the CC Secretariat ordered the MPA to develop new measures to improve soldiers' patriotic education in the spirit of Marxism-Leninism.

85 *Izvestiia*, 7 November 1991. Similar measures were taken in some of the other republics.

8 THE EMERGENCE OF COMPETITIVE POLITICS

1 'The Novosibirsk report', *Survey*, vol. 28, no. 1 (Spring 1984), pp. 88–108.

2 *Ibid.*, p. 103.

3 For example, see the comments of CC Secretary V. A. Medvedev in *Pravda*, 4 October 1988 and M. S. Gorbachev, 'Oktiabr' i perestroika: revoliutsiia prodolz-haetsia', *Pravda*, 3 November 1987. However not all were positive about this concept. For example, see the comments of future first secretary of the Russian Communist Party I. K. Polozkov: *Pravda*, 27 April 1990.

4 For his call for a 'truthful analysis', of Soviet history, see M. S. Gorbachev, 'Oktiabr' i perestroika: revoliutsiia prodolzhaetsia', *Pravda*, 3 November 1987.

5 The first significant case of this occurred in the Kazakh capital Alma Ata in December 1986 over the replacement of Kazakh First Secretary Kunaev by the Russian Kolbin.

6 Although on 28 July 1988 a nation-wide ban on 'anti-Soviet' demonstrations was introduced, and formally promulgated in September. But even this made provision for demonstrations by making these dependent upon special permission from the local soviet.

7 For discussions of informals, see M. V. Maliutin, 'Neformaly v perestroike: opyt i perspektivy', in Iu. Afanas'ev, *Inogo ne dano* (Moscow: Progress, 1988), pp. 210–27; Geoffrey Hosking, 'Informal associations in the USSR', *Slovo*, vol. 1, no. 1 (May 1988), pp. 7–10; Vera Tolz, *The USSR's Emerging Multiparty System* (New York: Praeger, 1990); Vera Tolz, 'Informal groups in the USSR in 1988', Radio Liberty, *Research Bulletin*, 30 October 1988; Nick Lampert, 'Russia's new democrats. The club movement and *perestroika*', *Detente*, nos. 8–9, 1988, pp. 10–12; Vladimir Brovkin, 'Revolution from below: informal political associations in Russia 1988–1989, *Soviet Studies*, vol. 42, no. 2 (April 1990), pp. 233–57; and Judith B. Sedaitis and Jim Butterfield, eds., *Perestroika from Below* (Boulder: Westview Press, 1991).

8 *Pravda*, 5 February 1988 and 10 February 1989. For reports on the extent of membership, see *Argumenty i fakty*, 1988, no. 31, and Tolz, *The USSR's Emerging Party System*, p. 7.

9 An analysis of some 2,000 unofficial groups in Moscow toward the end of 1988 showed that about a quarter sought to influence state policy in one form or another while the remainder were devoted principally to leisure activities. *Pravda*, 11 November 1988.

10 Following David Lane, *Soviet Society Under Perestroika* (Boston: Unwin Hyman, 1990), p. 96. A particularly useful handbook has been produced in Moscow, *Spravochnik po neformal'nym obshchestvennym organizatsiiam i presse* (Moscow: SMOT Informatsionnoe agenstvo, 1989, Informatsionnyi biulleten' no. 16). See also *Neformal'naia Rossiia. O neformal'nykh politizirovannykh dviz-*

heniiakh i gruppakh v RSFSR (opyt spravochnika) (Moscow: Molodaia gvardiia, 1990).

11 *Spravochnik*, p. 100.

12 Cited in note 10.

13 The USSR Writers' Union and the Soviet Cultural Foundation later also became sponsors. Julia Wishnevsky, 'Conflict between state and "Memorial" Society', *Report on the USSR*, 20 January, 1989, pp. 8–9.

14 For reports on the Week of Conscience, see *Moscow News*, 1988, nos. 48 and 49.

15 Often with different names, for example, Pamiatnik in Kamensk-Uralskii and Initiative group for the establishment of a monument to the victims of Stalinism (Initsiativnaia gruppa po sozdanii pamiatnika zhertvam stalinizma) in Tallinn in Estonia. For a discussion of Memorial in Ukraine, see Bohdan Nahaylo, 'Ukrainian "Memorial" Society confronts Stalinist heritage in Ukraine', *Report on the USSR*, 17 March 1989, pp. 15–18.

16 *Spravochnik*, p. 51.

17 In the words of the description of the concerns of the patriotic group Meeting Movement (Vstrechnoe Dvizhenie) in Magnitogorsk. *Spravochnik*, p. 24.

18 *Spravochnik*, p. 64.

19 *Spravochnik*, p. 62.

20 The description of it refers to affiliates in 30 cities. *Spravochnik*, p. 61.

21 Specifically religious groups developed throughout the non-Russian republics. For examples from Latvia, Lithuania, Georgia and Uzbekistan, see *Spravochnik*, pp. 109, 117, 122 and 127.

22 'The Charter of the Estonian People's Front' (Adopted at the Congress of the People's Front, 2 October 1988), reprinted in Lane, pp. 204–5.

23 Russian informals did hold some joint meetings to try to coordinate their activity in August 1987 and 1988. Mike Urban, 'Politics in an unsettled climate. Popular fronts and "informals"', *Detente*, no. 14 (1989), p. 6. Also *Moscow News*, 1990, no. 21, and Tolz, *The USSR's Emerging Party System*, ch. 3.

24 Lane, *Soviet Society*, p. 205.

25 Although an initiative group in Tartu University had suggested the establishment of a front in April 1988. Urban, 'Politics', p. 4. Some details on the founding congress are also presented here.

26 For a discussion of the congresses, see Boris Kagarlitsky, *Farewell Perestroika. A Soviet Chronicle* (London: Verso, 1990), ch. 3. For the announcement of the initiative group in Estonia, see *Sovetskaia Estoniia*, 7 June 1988.

27 Respectively Lane, *Soviet Society*, p. 193, and *Spravochnik*, pp. 110 and 117.

28 In February 1990, people's deputy Mikhail Poltoranin declared that in the Transcaucasus and other parts of the USSR, popular fronts have become more powerful forces than party and government bodies, and that the only way party leaders could retain any power was through the establishment of partnerships with these fronts. *Moscow News*, 1990, no. 7.

29 For the electoral platform of Renewal, the Belorussian Popular Front, see 'Belorussian Popular Front announces its electoral platform', *Report on the USSR*, 12 January 1990, pp. 20–2. The Moldavian Democratic Movement in Support of Perestroika was established in June 1988 while Rukh, or the Popular Movement of Ukraine for Perestroika, held its founding congress in September 1989.

30 *Spravochnik.* Also see Urban, 'Politics', pp. 6–7. By early 1990, there were some 140 popular fronts throughout the RSFSR. *Moscow News,* 1990, no. 7.

31 For example, see the comments on the Leningrad Popular Front made by Boris Kagarlitsky, radical socialist activist in the movement for the creation of a Moscow Popular Front. Kagarlitsky, *Farewell Perestroika,* pp. 170–2.

32 This is based on the account in Kagarlitsky, *Farewell Perestroika, Spravochnik,* p. 60 and *Neformal'naia Rossiia,* pp. 288–91.

33 *Spravochnik,* p. 60.

34 Kagarlitsky, *Farewell Perestroika,* pp. 9–10.

35 *Neformal'naia Rossiia,* p. 289.

36 Of the total of sixteen candidates the Front supported, twelve were elected as People's Deputies.

37 For a characterisation of these, see Vera Tolz, 'The emergence of a multiparty system in the USSR', *Report on the USSR,* 27 April 1990, pp. 1–11. Also see *Moscow News,* 1990, no. 28, and the stimulating paper by Michael Urban, 'Party formation and deformation on Russia's Democratic Left' (mimeo). For discussions of the individual parties in the organ of the CC CPSU, see *Izvestiia TsK KPSS,* 1990, no. 4, pp. 150–6 and no. 8, pp. 145–61, and Eberhard Schneider, 'The new political forces in Russia, Ukraine and Belorussia', *Report on the USSR,* 13 December 1991, p. 12.

38 For a discussion of this, see J. Aves, 'The Democratic Union – a Soviet opposition party', *Slovo,* vol. 1, no. 2 (November 1988), pp. 92–8.

39 *Spravochnik,* p. 56. Also see the discussion in Brovkin, 'Revolution from Below', pp. 242–5.

40 For a discussion of this tactic, see Sergei Ivanenko, 'What's the alternative to demos?', *Moscow News,* 1990, no. 50.

41 See the discussion of the relationship between these bodies in the work of Front activist Boris Kagarlitsky.

42 This is based principally upon John B. Dunlop, 'Christian Democratic party founded in Moscow', *Report on the USSR,* 13 October 1989, pp. 1–2.

43 Although see the argument advanced by the Director of the Moscow Bureau of Information Exchange, Viacheslav Igrunov, that its commitment to democracy is purely tactical. Michael E. Urban, 'The Soviet multi-party system. A Moscow roundtable', *Russia and the World,* 1990, no. 18, p. 3. On the party's congresses, see *Glasnost',* 7 November 1990.

44 This claim is disputed by the Liberal Democratic Party which held its founding congress in March 1990 and claims such a pedigree for itself. Its programmatic aims are very similar to those of the Union of Constitutional Democrats. On the Liberal Democratic Party, see 'Coup or operetta?', *Moscow News,* 1990, no. 45. For an interview with its chairman, Vladimir Zhirinovsky, see 'Liberalism: "A thing in itself?"', *Moscow News,* 1990, no. 17.

45 *Paket programmnykh dokumentov, Soiuz Konstitutsionnykh Demokratov* (Moscow, 1989). For the view that the party's policy discussions have been isolated from the course of events in the country, see Urban, 'Soviet multi-party system', p. 3.

46 Brovkin, 'Revolution from Below', pp. 243–4.

47 See 'Manifest Orgkomiteta Uchreditel'nogo S"ezda Pravoslavnoi Konstitutionno-monarkhicheskoi Partii Rossii', *Rossiiskie vedomosti,* December 1989 (samizdat). For one discussion of the conference, see Sergei Ivanenko, 'They want to restore the Russian monarchy', *Moscow News,* 1990, no. 43.

48 For a report on its second congress, see 'Social Democrats adopt programme', *Moscow News*, 1990, no. 44.

49 *Argumenty i fakty*, 1990, no. 20, and *Moscow News*, 1990, no. 21. Also see the discussion in Elizabeth Teague, 'Soviet television features new political party', *Report on the USSR*, 29 June 1990, pp. 4–5 and the interview with prominent party member Gary Kasparov in *The Times Saturday Review*, 1 September 1990.

50 Dmitry Miknev, 'Democratic Party of Russia', *Moscow News*, 1990, no. 21.

51 For earlier moves in this direction, see Kagarlitsky, *Farewell Perestroika*, especially p. 205. Also see the report in *Moscow News*, 1990, no. 26.

52 For reports see Sergei Mulin, 'Mensheviks turn republican. Only for three months?', *Moscow News*, 1990, no. 47, and Michael McFaul, 'The Social Democrats and Republicans attempt to merge', *Report on the USSR*, 18 January, 1991, pp. 10–13.

53 For example, on the emergence of Democratic Union, Social Democrat and Christian Democrat groups, as well as human rights, independence and other groups in Ukraine, see Taras Kuzio, 'Unofficial groups and publications in Ukraine', *Report on the USSR*, 24 November 1989, pp. 10–21. For an Islamic party, see Bess Brown, 'The Islamic Renaissance Party in Central Asia', *Report on the USSR*, 10 May 1991, pp. 12–14.

54 *Pravda*, 16 March 1990.

55 *Pravda*, 16 October 1990. The draft appeared in *Pravda*, 4 June 1990. On the problems in formulating an acceptable draft earlier, see the discussion in Nina Beliaeva, 'Form unions according to the law', *Moscow News*, 1990, no. 34, p. 12. The earlier draft discussed by Beliaeva is criticised for according the state too intrusive a role, contradicting Soviet international commitments, and being selective in its coverage. For a call for the legalisation of all opposition groups, see the article by Lilia Shevtsova in *Izvestiia*, 27 February 1990. Some republics, including Lithuania and Armenia, introduced laws on political parties which forbade those organised outside the republic. This was directed specifically against the Communist Party.

56 For a report from August 1990 that the Moscow city soviet had established a commission to register all new political parties, public associations and media organisations, see *Report on the USSR*, 7 September 1990, p. 31. For one view of the effect registration was thought to have on the CPSU, see the interview with CC Secretary Manaenkov in *Glasnost'*, 10 January 1991. On the registration of the first parties in the RSFSR, see *Moscow News*, 1992, no. 12, and on difficulties in gaining registration, *Moscow News*, 1990, no. 34.

57 According to one report, in early 1990 there were some 2,000–3,000 political groups with a membership of 2–2.5 million. *Moscow News*, 1990, no. 7. For some other figures, see Schneider, 'New political forces', p. 17.

58 These views are expressed by Andrei Vasilevsky and Sergei Mitrokhin of the Moscow Bureau of Information Exchange. Urban, 'Soviet multi-party system', p. 4.

59 Respectively Urban, 'Soviet multi-party system', p. 4 and Sergei Mulin, 'The party of entrepreneurs', *Moscow News*, 1990, no. 51.

60 Ivanenko.

61 *Pravda*, 16 October 1990.

62 Urban, 'Soviet multi-party system', pp. 4–5.

63 In the middle of 1990, copies of many parties' newspapers could be purchased

near Oktiabr'skaia metro station. Moscow State University was another fertile source of such publications. Among the publications available at these locations were *Golos izbiratelia* (Moscow Association of Voters), *Novaia zhizn'* and *Alternativa* (Social Democrats), *Rossiiskie vedomosti* (Orthodox Russian Monarchists), *Grazhdanskoe dostoinstvo* (Union of Constitutional Democrats), *Vestnik Khristianskoi Demokratii* (Christian Democrats), *Svobodnoe slovo* (Democratic Union), *Ekspress-khronika* (independent non-party), *Baltiiskoe vremia* (Latvian Popular Front) and *Nabat* (Anarcho-syndicalists).

64 For a discussion about how a dispute over whether decision-making should be decentralised and democratic or more centralised led to a split in the Democratic Party of Russia, see *Moscow News*, 1990, no. 22.

65 For an interesting discussion, see Viktor Sheinis, 'Kakaia platforma nam nuzhna', *Rabochii klass i sovremennyi mir*, 1990, no. 3.

66 There have been a number of these blocs in legislatures at different levels. In the USSR Congress of People's Deputies and the Supreme Soviet were the Inter-regional Group of Deputies and Soiuz. In the Congress of People's Deputies and the Supreme Soviet of the RSFSR were Democratic Russia and the conservative Communists of Russia. In the Moscow city soviet have been Democratic Russia, Moskva (those around the Moscow *gorkom*) and the conservative Otechestvo. Julia Wishnevsky, 'Multiparty system, Soviet style', *Report on the USSR*, 23 November 1990, pp. 3–4. On the Communists of Russia, see the report in *Glasnost'*, 13 December 1990.

67 The wide diversity of views within this body was a major factor preventing the emergence of a coherent party. For one view of the weaknesses of this group, see the interview with a former member in *Glasnost'*, 22 November 1990. Indeed, towards the end of 1990, the Inter-Regional Group of Deputies called for a two-three year moratorium on the activities of all parties. *Argumenty i fakty*, 1990, no. 52. This may have been a tactical measure designed to eliminate the CPSU from political activity.

68 For example, Travkin, Burbulis and Murashev of the Democratic Party of Russia were USSR deputies, while Astaf'ev of the Constitutional Democrats and Iakunin of the Russian Christian Democratic Movement were RSFSR deputies. According to one observer, in Ukraine 'nearly all the leaders of existing parties and those not yet founded are members of the Supreme Soviet'. Gorevskaia in Urban, 'Soviet multi-party system', p. 5.

69 Of course this has not been the only path to prominence. Travkin became well known through his work as a labour organiser while Iakunin is a former political prisoner.

70 On factions in the Democratic Union, see Ivanenko. For reports of some splits, see *Moscow News*, 1990, no. 22 (Democratic Party of Russia) and 28 (Constitutional Democrats) and *Moskovskaia pravda*, 30 June and 20 July 1990.

71 *Pravda*, 25 November 1988, 16 February 1989, 26 August 1989 and 26 March 1990. Many of the comments at the April 1989 CC plenum are relevant here: *Pravda*, 27 April 1989. Also see Chebrikov in *Kommunist*, 1989, no. 8.

72 Compare the statements by Gorbachev and Ligachev at the July 1989 meeting in the CC. *Pravda*, 21 July 1989.

73 See Boris Kurashvili, *Moscow News*, 1988, no. 6. It was assumed that this

structure would ensure that organisations like the Democratic Union that rejected cooperation and compromise would become isolated.

74 *Pravda*, 19 November 1990. A new CC Department for Work with Socio-Political Organisations was created. For an interview with its deputy head, see *Glasnost'*, 1 November 1990. The department was not headed by someone conspicuously sympathetic to these groups, so the extent to which the commitment to negotiation with them would have been carried out remains uncertain.

75 The predominantly ethnic Russian Intermovement in the Baltic area and the United Front of Workers of Russia are often seen as examples of this tactic. The latter gained its genesis through the United Front of Workers in Leningrad, which was sponsored by the Leningrad regional committee. Some have suggested that the similarity in names of the parties reflects in part an attempt by the CPSU to foster small party groups with similar names as independent potential challengers with a view to complicating the ability of the latter to establish themselves as major political forces. Wishnevsky (23 November 1990), p. 5.

76 For example, see Gorbachev's declaration at the February 1990 plenum that the CPSU was willing 'to cooperate and maintain dialogue with all the organisations which base themselves on the USSR Constitution and the social system inherent in it'. *Pravda*, 6 February 1990. There have also been calls for the conduct of roundtables as in Eastern Europe where the future of the country would be discussed between the authorities and 'the democratic opposition'. See *Moscow News*, 1990, no. 4, p. 5.

77 At least this is the interpretation that comes from reports of two seminars in a leading party journal. *Partiinaia zhizn'*, 1990, no. 2, pp. 31–6, and no. 3, 1990, pp. 29–33. Also see the discussion in Vera Tolz, 'A new approach to informal groups', *Report on the USSR*, 9 March 1990, pp. 1–3.

78 *Argumenty i fakty*, 1990, no. 46.

79 Vasilevskii in Urban, 'Soviet multi-party system', p. 2.

80 Elizabeth Fuller, 'Round Table coalition wins resounding victory in Georgian Supreme Soviet elections', *Report on the USSR*, 16 November 1990, pp. 13–14. Round Table won 54.03 per cent of the vote.

81 According to chairman of the organising committee, A. Murashev. *Argumenty i fakty*, 1990, no. 46. A congress was held on 20–1 October 1990 designed to consolidate the movement. At that gathering, Democratic Russia was declared to be the alternative to the CPSU. For one discussion of the congress, see *Glasnost'*, 1 November 1990. A continuing organ, the coordinating council, was created in December 1990.

82 For example, in June 1990 negotiations in Moscow resulted in the establishment of an alliance between the Constitutional Democrats, the Social Democratic Party of Russia, the organising committee of the Free Labour Party and the Russian Democratic Party (not the Democratic Party of Russia led by Travkin). Radio Moscow World Service cited in *Report on the USSR*, 6 July 1990, p. 34. This became the hub of the so-called Centrist Bloc of Political Parties and Movements. On this see 'Coup or operetta?'. Later in the year a leftist bloc was formed, consisting of a radical faction of the Moscow Popular Front, the Russian Democratic Forum and the Association for Soviet-American Integration. TASS cited in *Report on the USSR*, 12 October 1990, p. 40.

83 RFE/RL *Research Report*, 31 January 1992, pp. 66–7.

9 THE POLITICS OF ECONOMIC INTERESTS

1 The most influential work on the question of interest groups was H. Gordon Skilling and Franklyn Griffiths, *Interest Groups in Soviet Politics* (Princeton: Princeton University Press, 1971); see also Susan Gross Solomon, ed., *Pluralism in the Soviet Union* (New York: St. Martin's Press, 1982).

2 See *Izvestiia*, 14 August 1990.

3 Based on table 3.2 in Darrell Slider, 'Political elites and politics in the republics', in David Lane, ed., *Russia in Flux: The Political and Social Consequences of Reform* (Aldershot: Elgar, 1992), p. 44.

4 See Mary McAuley, 'Politics, economics, and elite realignment in Russia: a regional perspective', *Soviet Economy*, vol. 8, no. 1 (1992), pp. 46–88. The quote is from p. 64.

5 *Kommersant*, 6–13 April 1992.

6 A speech by Tiziakov appeared in *Ekonomika i zhizn'*, no. 13 (March 1991).

7 He also served at Gorbachev's request as the Moscow-appointed administrator of Nagorno-Karabakh, the object of an intense territorial dispute between Armenia and Azerbaijan.

8 See *Ekonomika i zhizn'*, no. 11 (March 1991).

9 On the structure of the NPS, see *Ekonomika i zhizn'*, no. 37 (September 1991). See also *Izvestiia*, 4 April 1991.

10 On Vol'sky, see the interview in *Moscow News*, 8–15 March 1992.

11 The original appeal to form the party was published in *Rabochaia tribuna*, 30 April 1992. The founding conference was reported in the same publication on 2 June 1992.

12 See the interview with Vladislavlev in *Nezavisimaia gazeta*, 2 June 1992.

13 Lengthy 'programmatic declarations' appeared in *Rabochaia tribuna*, 16 June 1992 and 11 September 1992.

14 Nikolai Vishnevskii in the Russian government paper *Rossiiskie vesti*, 8 June 1992. For comments by former Moscow mayor, Gavriil Popov, see *Kuranty-Daidzhest*, no. 19 (May 1992).

15 On the initial agreement to organise the Civic Union, see *Rossiiskaia gazeta*, 30 May 1992. The founding forum of the union was the subject of reports in *Nezavisimaia gazeta*, 22 and 23 June 1992, *Moscow News*, 28 June–5 July 1992, and *Rossiiskaia gazeta*, 22 June 1992. See also Elizabeth Teague and Vera Tolz, 'The Civic Union: the birth of a new opposition in Russia?', *RFE/RL Research Report*, 24 July 1992, pp. 1–11.

16 See *Nezavisimaia gazeta*, 19 and 22 September 1992.

17 For more on the Civic Union programme, see the article by Philip Hanson and Elizabeth Teague, 'The industrialists and Russian economic reform', *Radio Free Europe/Radio Liberty Research Report*, 8 May 1992, pp. 1–7; also, see the interview with Vladislavlev in *Nezavisimaia gazeta*, 25 September 1992. Vol'sky's position on bankruptcy was outlined in *Rabochaia tribuna*, 23 June 1992. For a critique of the alternative programme by an advocate of the Gaidar programme, see the article by Mikhail Leont'ev in *Izvestiia*, 23 July 1992.

18 *Kommersant*, 16–23 March 1992.

19 See the lengthy article by Vol'sky in *Rabochaia tribuna*, 29 September 1992, and *ibid.*

20 *Nezavisimaia gazeta*, 26 September 1992.

21 *Moscow News*, 28 June-5 July 1992; *Nezavisimaia gazeta*, 9 October 1992.

22 On the first meetings, see *Ekonomika i zhizn'*, no. 9 (February 1992) and *Izvestiia*, 12 June 1992. The group met again in Kiev in October 1992; *Rabochaia tribuna*, 9 October 1992.

23 On the role of cooperatives in Soviet economic reform, see Darrell Slider, 'Embattled entrepreneurs: Soviet cooperatives in an unreformed economy', *Soviet Studies*, vol. 43, no. 5 (1991), pp. 797–821.

24 *Poisk*, 6–12 June 1992; see also *Ekonomika i zhizn'*, no. 17 (April 1992).

25 *Rossiiskaia gazeta*, 4 August 1992 and *Kommersant*, 20–7 July 1992.

26 *Izvestiia*, 19 November 1991; and *Ekonomika i zhizn'*, no. 23 (June 1992).

27 *Ekonomika i zhizn'*, no. 24 (June 1992).

28 *Ekonomika i zhizn'*, no. 23 (June 1992).

29 *Moscow News*, 12–19 April 1992, p. 5.

30 *Ekonomika i zhizn'*, no. 23 (June 1992).

31 Tarasov resigned his seat in 1991 and left the country in the midst of a controversy over his business dealings and after indications that he might be prosecuted for charges he had made against Gorbachev on the issue of concessions to Japan.

32 Borovoi was trained as a mathematician, and he first became involved in business in 1987 with a computer software consulting firm. On the Russian commodity exchange, see *Ekonomika i zhizn'*, no. 44 (October 1991).

33 *Rossiiskaia gazeta*, 15 May 1992.

34 Report by Joanne Levine in *The Moscow Times*, 19 May 1992.

35 A draft of the new party's programme appeared in *Nezavisimaia gazeta*, 11 June 1992.

36 *Ibid.*, also interviews with Fedorov in *Trud*, 23 June 1992 and with Borovoi in *Ekonomika i zhizn'*, no. 31 (August 1992).

37 *Rossiiskaia vesti*, 19 September 1992; earlier Borovoi had rejected such efforts. See *Rossiiskaia gazeta*, 15 May 1992.

38 Based on reports on the evening Russian television news, 9 April 1992 and 17 October 1992.

39 *Nezavisimaia gazeta*, 21 May 1992.

40 *Ekonomika i zhizn'*, no. 9 (February 1992).

41 *Nezavisimaia gazeta*, 25 and 31 July 1992.

42 Darrell Slider, 'The first independent Soviet interest groups: unions and associations of cooperatives', in Judith B. Sedaitis and Jim Butterfield, eds., *Perestroika from Below: Social Movements in the Soviet Union* (Boulder, CO: Westview, 1991), pp. 153–4.

43 Based on interviews with SOK officials in June 1990.

44 *Pravitel'stvennyi vestnik*, no. 27 (July 1990).

45 *Pravitel'stvennyi vestnik*, no. 51 (December 1990).

46 The directive and list of members of the council can be found in *Ekonomika i zhizn'*, no. 42 (October 1991). A report of one session appeared in *Izvestiia*, 30 November 1991.

47 *Kommersant*, 2–9 March 1992. The council had twenty-seven members; Vladislavlev was designated chairman, and Borovoi was also a member.

48 *Delovye liudi*, no. 9 (September 1992), pp. 20–1 and the interview with Konstan-

tin Zatulin, member of the council, in *Nezavisimaia gazeta*, 5 August 1992. The chairman of the council reportedly met with Yeltsin for the first time on 18 July 1992. See *Kommersant*, 20–7 July 1992.

49 *Rossiiskaia gazeta*, 18 July 1992.
50 *Vestnik merii Moskvy*, no. 5 (March 1992), pp. 4–6.
51 *Izvestiia*, 13 May 1992.
52 Interview with Nazarbaev in *Ekonomika i zhizn'*, no. 28 (July 1991).
53 *Ekonomika i zhizn'*, no. 9 (February 1992).
54 *Ekonomika i zhizn'*, no. 10 (March 1992).
55 For biographies of each, see *Rossiiskie vesti*, 5 June 1992. Shumeiko's role in Renewal was indicated in *Nezavisimaia gazeta*, 2 June 1992. On Khizha's activities in Leningrad, see Mary McAuley, 'Politics', p. 73.
56 *Izvestiia*, 23 May 1992.
57 *Nezavisimaia gazeta*, 1 August 1992 and 3 February 1993.
58 *Los Angeles Times*, 14 October 1992 and *Nezavisimaia gazeta*, 15 October 1992.
59 See Elizabeth Teague, 'Russian government seeks "social partnership"', *RFE/RL Research Report*, 19 June 1992, pp. 16–23.
60 Based on remarks by deputy minister of labour, Pavel Kudiukin, at the Institute of Employment Problems, Moscow, 28 April 1992.
61 Pavel Kudiukin, quoted in *Nezavisimaia gazeta*, 5 June 1992.
62 *Izvestiia*, 14 August 1990.
63 See the series of articles in *Sovetskaia Rossiia*, 25 February 1990, 4 March 1990, and 8 March 1990.
64 A Russian legal scholar, Viktor Danilenko, has called for a law on lobbies and has defended lobbying as a part of the political process in *Izvestiia*, 9 October 1991 and 29 September 1992. Another call for legal regulation was voiced in *Rossiiskie vesti*, 10 October 1992.
65 *Izvestiia*, 17 April 1992.
66 *Delovye liudi*, no. 9 (September 1992), p. 21.
67 Such complaints were voiced frequently at the organisational congress of the Russian Union of Industrialists and Entrepreneurs, reported in *Trud*, 21 January 1992.

10 PUBLIC OPINION AND THE POLITICAL PROCESS

1 For a thorough discussion of the traditional role of journalists, see Thomas Remington, *The Truth of Authority: Ideology and Communication in the Soviet Union* (Pittsburgh: University of Pittsburgh Press, 1988).
2 A detailed review of the development of glasnost in the Soviet media is contained in Stephen White, *Gorbachev and After*, 3rd edn (Cambridge: Cambridge University Press, 1992), pp. 76–103.
3 Based on secret Politburo documents from the party archives summarised by the chairman of Yeltsin's commission on archives, Mikhail Poltoranin, at a press conference in June 1992. See *Kuranty-Daidzhest*, no. 22 (June 1992).
4 On the role of Soviet television see Ellen Mickiewicz, *Split Signals: Television and Politics in the Soviet Union* (New York: Oxford University Press, 1988).
5 Kravchenko had previously served as director of TASS. Interview with Kravchenko in *Rabochaia tribuna*, 13 March 1991.
6 A poll of Muscovites conducted in late January 1991 found that 53 per cent felt

that the quality of Central Television had declined in the months after Krav-chenko took over. VTsIOM poll reported in *Komsomol'skaia pravda*, 5 February 1991. (Telephone poll, N = 500.)

7 *Pravda*, later also accepted the partial sponsorship of a Greek businessman.

8 See Vera Tolz, 'The plight of the Russian media', *RFE/RL Research Report*, 28 February 1992, pp. 54–9.

9 *Moscow News*, 19–26 July 1992. *Trud* continued to reflect the conservative views of the official unions as well as managers of state enterprises. *Komsomol'skaia pravda*, on the other hand, was generally antiestablishment and remained oriented toward young people.

10 These figures are undoubtedly generous in what they define as 'sociological'. *Vestnik Akademii Nauk SSSR*, no. 10 (October 1985), p. 66.

11 Chernenko, before becoming General Secretary, was the head of the Brezhnev Central Committee's General Department, the office responsible for the analysis of letters and other secretarial functions.

12 Darrell Slider, 'Party-sponsored public opinion research in the Soviet Union', *The Journal of Politics*, vol. 47, no. 1 (February 1985), pp. 209–27. Shevard-nadze's interest in public opinion continued when he was named Soviet foreign minister; in that post he commissioned a number of studies of public opinion on foreign policy issues and organized a Centre for the Study of Soviet Public Opinion on Foreign Policy Problems within its diplomatic training institute. See *Vestnik Ministerstva inostrannykh del SSSR*, no. 8 (1 May 1988), p. 42. Results commissioned by the Foreign Ministry from other institutes were published in *ibid.*, no. 9 (15 May 1988), p. 35 and no. 23 (15 December 1988), pp. 20–1.

13 Sergei Voronitsyn, 'New center created for the study of public opinion', *Radio Liberty Research*, 7 May 1986.

14 According to a letter by nine of the most prominent Soviet sociologists, the director named to head the institute in 1972, M. N. Rutkevich, forced over 120 leading specialists to leave – a blow from which it had still not recovered in 1987. The letter appeared in *Sovetskaia kul'tura*, 19 December 1987.

15 *The New York Times*, 27 May 1988.

16 *Sobranie postanovlenii pravitel'stva SSSR*, no. 38 (1987), pp. 809–14.

17 *Trud*, 29 March 1988, and *Ekonomicheskaia gazeta*, no. 14 (April 1988), p. 19. Tatiana Zaslavskaia had previously announced the creation on Moscow television in October 1987; reported in *FBIS Daily Report: Soviet Union*, no. 204 (22 October 1987), p. 55.

18 *Pravda*, 6 February 1987.

19 This was the main theme of the famous 'Novosibirsk report' that brought her international attention (and official rebuke) when it was leaked to the foreign press in August 1983. A translation, along with commentary by Philip Hanson, appeared in *Survey*, vol. 28, no. 1 (Spring 1984), pp. 83–108.

20 Reports on VTsIOM's early efforts appeared in *Moscow News*, 4–11 September 1988, pp. 9–10; and *Trud*, 28 December 1988.

21 *Trud*, 29 March 1988.

22 *Sotsiologicheskie issledovaniia*, 1991, no. 9, p. 18.

23 A sharp critique of the methodological soundness of VTsIOM's work was published by the Leningrad sociologist Vasilii Ovsianikov in *Sotsiologicheskie issledovaniia*, 1991, no. 9, pp. 18–21.

24 A critique and brief guide to how public opinion results should be presented was published in *Izvestiia*, 22 February 1991, by the head of the Institute of Sociology, V. Iadov.

25 One such poll was reported in *The New York Times*, 5 November 1989. See also the interview with Rutgaizer in *Kommersant*, 9 April 1990, p. 8.

26 *Pravitel'stvennyi vestnik*, no. 34 (August 1990).

27 The subcommittee was mentioned in a report in *Rossiiskaia gazeta*, 13 December 1991. Results from a survey preceding the April 1992 session of the Congress of People's Deputies were published in *ibid.*, 6 April 1992.

28 One of the best known of the new groups was Vox Populi, headed by Boris Grushin.

29 *Moscow News*, 19–26 March 1989, p. 13. The poll was conducted by public opinion study section of the Komsomol Higher School's Scientific Research Centre in Moldova, Ukraine, Latvia, Kyrgyzstan as well as in five regions of the Russian republic with an overall sample size of 'over 1,000'.

30 *Poisk*, 8–14 February 1991 and *Polis*, 1991, no. 3, pp. 67–76. Centre for the Study of Public Opinion, Institute of Sociology. 1989: N = 1,052 in 'various cities'; 1990: N = 760 in Moscow and Volgograd.

31 *The New York Times*, 27 May 1988.

32 *Kommersant*, no. 10 (March 1990). VTsIOM; N = 1,134, conducted in twenty-one regions, including thirteen cities and eight rural areas.

33 *Partiinaia zhizn'*, 1990, no. 7. Centre for Sociological Research, Academy of Social Sciences; N = 1,510 in seventeen regions.

34 *Pravda*, 23 October 1989. The sample, described as all-union, comprised 4,075 respondents in June 1986, 2,741 in February 1988, and 3,687 in February 1989.

35 *Moscow News*, 22–9 April 1990, p. 7. VTsIOM; N = 2,500.

36 *Moscow News*, 29 December 1991–5 January 1992, pp. 6–7.

37 Arthur H. Miller, William M. Reisinger, and Vicki L. Hesli, 'Public support for new political institutions in Russia, the Ukraine, and Lithuania', *Journal of Soviet Nationalities*, vol. 1, no. 4 (Winter 1990–1), pp. 82–107.

38 Richard B. Dobson and Steven A. Grant, 'Public opinion and the transformation of the Soviet Union', *International Journal of Public Opinion Research*, vol. 4, no. 4 (Winter 1992), pp. 302–20. The survey was conducted by Vox Populi in eight Soviet republics; N = 2,504.

39 *Rossiiskaia gazeta*, 31 December 1991. VTsIOM poll.

40 Based on material in *Data-express*, no. 9 (October 1991), p. 8.

41 Ratings for each month of 1990 are given in *Nezavisimaia gazeta*, 24 January 1991, p. 2. VTsIOM. The survey was conducted each month in the same thirty locations, each time with a new representative sample of approximately one thousand adults.

42 Results reported in VTsIOM publication *Data-express*, no. 9 (October 1991), p. 7. The sample for October was national, with N = 2,053.

43 *Sotsiologicheskie issledovaniia*, 1991, no. 9, p. 5. VTsIOM data.

44 *Argumenty i fakty*, 15–21 April 1989. Telephone survey conducted by the Institute of Sociology, with N = 1,000.

45 V. Rukavishnikov, et al., *Predvybornaia situatsiia: mneniia izbiratelei* (Moscow: Institute of Sociology, 1990); summarized in Darrell Slider, 'Soviet public

opinion on the eve of the elections', *Journal of Soviet Nationalities*, vol. 1, no. 4 (Spring 1990), pp. 155–62.

46 *Sotsiologicheskie issledovaniia*, 1991, no. 8, p. 14; VTsIOM.

47 Survey conducted by VTsIOM. From the text of a speech by Zaslavskaia to the first congress of Soviet sociologists, *Izvestiia*, 18 January 1991.

48 *Nezavisimaia gazeta*, 8 August 1992 and 29 August 1992. The surveys were conducted by the Centre for Social Monitoring and Marketing of the Russian Independent Institute of Social and Ethnic Problems. The polls were conducted in at least ten regions, though the number of respondents was not indicated. The wording of the questions, which did not permit an answer between 'good' and 'bearable', reflected the bias of the researchers, several of whom formerly worked in the Academy of Social Sciences of the party Central Committee.

49 *Izvestiia*, 21 September 1992. VTsIOM, conducted in twenty cities, N = 2,000.

50 *Izvestiia*, 21 September 1992. VTsIOM, in cities and rural areas, N = 1,600.

51 *Nezavisimaia gazeta*, 8 August 1992; conducted by the Russian Independent Institute for Social and Ethnic Problems.

52 *Obshchestvennoe mnenie v tsifrakh*, vyp. 4 (October 1989), p. 5. The survey was conducted by VTsIOM in all regions, N = 1,148.

53 See *Izvestiia*, 29 July 1990; conducted by VTsIOM in eleven urban and rural regions, N = 1,048.

54 Shpil'ko in *Voprosy ekonomiki*, 1991, no. 4, pp. 108–16; survey conducted by VTsIOM in seven republics, N = 3,399.

55 *Nezavisimaia gazeta*, 8 August 1992; conducted by the Russian Independent Institute for Social and Ethnic Problems.

56 See, in particular, the findings of Irina Boeva and Viacheslav Shironin, *Russians Between State and Market: The Generations Compared* (Glasgow: University of Strathclyde Studies in Public Policy, 1992). The survey reported therein was conducted in Russia in January 1992 by VTsIOM, N = 2,106.

57 The same pattern was discovered by Shpil'ko, *Voprosy ekonomiki*, 1991, no. 4, pp. 113.

58 Reported in *Nezavisimaia gazeta*, 10 September 1992. Conducted by Vox Populi in twelve regions. N = 1,990. February results appeared in *RFE/RL Research Report*, 19 June 1992, pp. 72–3; N = 1,985. Somewhat different results were achieved in another poll conducted in February and May by the Centre for Comparative Social Research, because the wording of the question did not permit four responses – only trust 'completely' (12 per cent in May), 'not much' (44 per cent), or 'not at all' (28 per cent). *Rossiiskaia gazeta*, 3 June 1992.

59 *Nezavisimaia gazeta*, 29 July 1992. The survey was conducted by the Centre of Social Research of the Culture Foundation together with the Russian parliament's Subcommittee on the Study of Public Opinion. No information was given on the size of the sample, though it included Moscow, other large cities, and rural areas.

60 *Ibid.*

11 LETTERS AND PUBLIC COMMUNICATIONS

1 *Izvestiia*, 20 September 1991.

2 *Literaturnaia gazeta*, 4 December 1991, p. 3.

3 The literature on Soviet letter-writing includes Claudio Fracassi, ed., *Cara Pravda* (Rome: Napoleone, 1972); Mark Rhodes, 'Letters to the Editor in the USSR', PhD dissertation, University of Michigan, 1977; Christine Revuz, *Ivan Ivanovich écrit à la Pravda* (Paris: Editions sociales, 1980); Jan S. Adams, 'Critical letters to the Soviet press', in Donald E. Schulz and Adams, eds., *Political Participation in Communist Systems* (New York: Pergamon, 1981); Stephen White, 'Political communications in the USSR: letters to party, state and press', *Political Studies*, vol. 31, no. 1 (January 1983), pp. 43–60; Nicholas Lampert, *Whistle-blowing in the Soviet Union* (London: Macmillan, 1985); Dmitri Shlapentokh and Vladimir Shlapentokh, 'Letters to the editor on ideologies in the USSR during the 1980s', in Anthony Jones, ed., *Research on the Soviet Union and Eastern Europe*, vol. 1 (Greenwich CT: JAI Press, 1990), pp. 167–93; James W. Riordan, 'The revolution from below: the role of letters to the editor under *perestroika*', *Coexistence*, vol. 27, no. 4 (December 1990), pp. 269–84; and James Riordan and Susan Bridger, eds., *Dear Comrade Editor* (Bloomington: Indiana University Press, 1992). I have additionally drawn, in this chapter, with interviews with the letters departments of *Argumenty i fakty*, *Izvestiia* and *Moskovskie novosti* and with the National Public Opinion Research Centre (VTsIOM), and upon the CPSU Central Committee declassified archives.

4 Soviet journalists, by the early 1990s, were well aware that readers' letters 'did not reflect the attitudes of the average reader' and that only properly conducted opinion polls could do so; the broadcast media also made use of listeners' or viewers' phone calls for this purpose. See Radio Liberty, *Report on the USSR*, 25 October 1991, p. 5.

5 VTsIOM interviews, December 1990.

6 *Izvestiia*, interviews, March 1991.

7 *Argumenty i fakty*, 1992, no. 42, p. 1.

8 V. D. Pel't, ed., *Teoriia i praktika sovetskoi periodicheskoi pechati* (Moscow: Vysshaia shkola, 1980), p. 141.

9 N. K. Verzhbitsky, *Zapiski starogo zhurnalista* (Moscow: Sovetskii pisatel', 1961), pp. 183–4.

10 E. N. Roshchepkina, 'O rabote s pis'mami grazhdan v pervye gody Sovetskoi vlasti (1917–1924 gg.)', *Sovetskie arkhivy*, 1979, no. 6, p. 23.

11 See particularly *Novyi mir*, 1992, no. 6, pp. 281–300.

12 Robert C. Tucker, *Stalin in Power: The revolution from above, 1928–1941* (New York: Norton, 1990), p. 356.

13 *Ibid.*, pp. 357–8.

14 In the Khrushchev period, however, as Zhores Medvedev notes, 'practically all the relatives of those who were in the camps began to bombard the Central Committee with letters, petitions and appeals, demanding rehabilitation whether or not their relatives were still alive . . . When one thinks of the number of the victims of the purges and the size of the Gulag in 1953, it is clear that the Central Committee was suddenly deluged with appeals' (*Andropov* (Oxford: Blackwell, 1983), pp. 142–3).

15 Text in *KPSS v rezoliutsiiakh s"ezdov, konferentsii i plenumov TsK*, 9th edn, 15 vols. (Moscow: Politizdat, 1983–9), VIII, p. 242.

16 Text in *Spravochnik partiinogo rabotnika*, IX (Moscow: Politizdat, 1969), pp. 398–404 and 404–5).

17 Text in *KPSS v rez.*, XIII, pp. 92–5.
18 A similar resolution was adopted after the 26th Congress in 1981: *Partiinaia zhizn'*, 1981, no. 8, pp. 9–11.
19 *Spravochnik partiinogo rabotnika*, XXI (Moscow: Politizdat, 1981), pp. 355–60, 361–2.
20 L. I. Brezhnev, *Leninskim kursom*, 9 vols. (Moscow: Politizdat, 1971–83), VIII, p. 293.
21 *Leninskim kursom*, IX, pp. 676–7.
22 Brezhnev referred to work with letters at both the 25th and 26th Congresses: *Leninskim kursom*, V, p. 524, and VIII, pp. 720–1.
23 See Konstantin Chernenko, *Narod i partiia ediny. Izbrannye rechi i stat'i* (Moscow: Politizdat, 1984), pp. 351–2.
24 *Spravochnik partiinogo rabotnika*, XXI, pp. 503–4.
25 *Ibid.*
26 *Partiinaia zhizn'*, 1979, no. 17, pp. 26–7.
27 White, 'Political communications', p. 48.
28 *Ibid.*, p. 49.
29 *Ibid.*, pp. 51–2.
30 G. S. Vychub, *Pis'ma trudiashchikhsia v sisteme massovoi raboty gazety* (Moscow: Izdatel'stvo MGU, 1980), pp. 8–9.
31 See S. D. Indrusky, *Gazeta vykhodit vecherom* (Moscow: Mysl', 1979), pp. 117, 121; and B. M. Morozov, et al., *Sotsiologicheskie issledovaniia kak sredstvo povysheniia effektivnosti rukovodstva pressoi* (Moscow: AON, 1980), pp. 29–30.
32 White, 'Political communications', pp. 53–4.
33 B. A. Grushin and L. A. Onikov, eds., *Massovaia informatsiia v sovetskom promyshlennom gorode* (Moscow: Politizdat, 1980), pp. 410, 414.
34 Quoted in Thomas F. Remington, *The Truth of Authority* (Pittsburgh: University of Pittsburgh Press, 1985), p. 127.
35 Ellen Mickiewicz, *Media and the Russian Public* (New York: Praeger, 1981), p. 67; *Guardian* (London), 29 July 1980.
36 Brezhnev, *Leninskim kursom*, VI, p. 518–19.
37 *Voprosy istorii KPSS*, 1990, no. 10, pp. 73–7. For an earlier discussion by the same author, see V. P. Smirnov, *Referendum v pechati* (Moscow: Mysl', 1978).
38 M. S. Gorbachev, *Izbrannye rechi i stat'i*, 7 vols (Moscow: Politizdat, 1987–90), I, p. 87.
39 *Ibid.*, pp. 103–9; for a further article on letters see pp. 160–75.
40 *Ibid.*, III, p. 342.
41 *Ibid.*, II, p. 404.
42 *Ibid.*, VII, p. 329.
43 *Ibid.*, II, p. 164.
44 *Ibid.*, IV, p. 321.
45 *Ibid.*, V, pp. 135–6.
46 *Pravda*, 19 October 1987.
47 Mikhail Gorbachev, *Perestroika: New Thinking for Our Country and the World* (London: Collins, 1987), pp. 77, 68, 72.
48 Raisa Gorbachev, *I Hope* (New York: HarperCollins, 1991), p. 136.
49 *Ibid.*, pp. 137–9.
50 *Izvestiia*, 7 August 1991.

51 Lloyd S. Fischel, ed., *Dear Mr Gorbachev* (Edinburgh: Canongate, 1990), p. 240.
52 *Sovetsko-amerikanskaia vstrecha na vysshem urovne. Zheneva 19–21 noiabria 1985 goda* (Moscow: Politizdat, 1985), p. 23.
53 Gorbachev, *Izbrannye rechi*, V, p. 497.
54 *Vizit General'nogo sekretaria TsK KPSS M. S. Gorbacheva v SShA 7–10 deka-bria 1987 goda* (Moscow: Politizdat, 1987), pp. 3–4.
55 Fischel, ed., *Dear Mr Gorbachev*, pp. 187, 266, 184–5, 57–8.
56 V. Korotich, S. Koen, intr., *Amerikantsy pishut Gorbachevu* (Moscow: Progress, 1988), pp. 38, 46, 247, 71 and 102 (assignments), 300. In 1985 the Central Committee received 89,300 letters from foreign citizens; in 1988 the total was 261,500: see *Izvestiia TsK KPSS*, 1989, no. 7, p. 122.
57 Fischel, *Dear Mr Gorbachev*, pp. xv–xvi and 6.
58 *Narodnyi deputat*, 1990, no. 3, p. 13.
59 *Pravda*, 27 February 1991.
60 *XXVII s"ezd Kommunisticheskoi partii Sovetskogo Soiuza: Stenograficheskii otchet*, 3 vols (Moscow: Politizdat, 1986), I, p. 124; *Izvestiia TsK KPSS*, 1990, no. 9, p. 31.
61 *Izvestiia TsK KPSS*, 1990, no. 9, p. 32, and 1991, no. 7, p. 88.
62 *Ibid.*, 1990, no. 4, p. 158, and no. 9, p. 33.
63 *Izvestiia*, 19 May 1990.
64 *Pravda*, 6 January 1990.
65 This letter is discussed below. On the paper more generally, see Angus Rox-burgh, *Pravda* (London: Gollancz, 1987).
66 *Pravda*, 6 January 1987 and 20 April 1989.
67 *Ibid.*, 6 January 1990; and personal communication, *Pravda* letters department.
68 White, 'Political communications', p. 52; interviews, *Izvestiia*, March 1991; and *Izvestiia*, 2 January 1992.
69 White, 'Political communications', p. 52; and for the more recent figure S. M. Gurevich, ed., *Rabota s pis'mami v redaktsii* (Moscow: Vysshaia shkola, 1991), p. 24.
70 Riordan, 'The revolution from below', p. 277, and Ron McKay, *Letters to Gorbachev* (London: Michael Joseph, 1991), p. 2.
71 Christopher Cerf and Marina Albee, eds., *Voices of Glasnost* (London: Kyle Cathie, 1990), pp. 14, 17.
72 Riordan, 'The revolution from below', p. 277.
73 *Yezhegodnik Bol'shoi Sovetskoi Entsiklopedii, 1980* and *1990* (Moscow: Sovetskaia entsiklopediia, 1980 and 1990), pp. 93 and 95.
74 *Pravda*, 4 January 1988.
75 *Ibid.*, 2 March 1988.
76 *Izvestiia*, 3 September 1991, and 11 September 1991.
77 Riordan, 'The revolution from below', p. 278.
79 *Ibid.*, p. 277; *Pravda*, 23 February 1987.
80 *Pravda*, 21 September 1987. The discussion that follows draws in part upon Stephen White, 'Dear comrade, sir', *Detente*, no. 11 (1988), pp. 14–16.
81 *Pravda*, 20 July 1987.
82 *Ibid.*, 13 July 1987.
83 *Ibid.*, 12 October 1987 and 5 October 1987.
84 *Ibid.*, 28 September 1987.

85 *Ibid.*, 29 November 1987.
86 *Ibid.*, 17 August 1987.
87 *Ibid.*, 21 September 1987.
88 *Ibid.*, 28 September 1987.
89 *Izvestiia TsK*, 1991, no. 2, p. 94.
90 *Pravda*, 26 December 1990.
91 *Izvestiia TsK*, 1991, no. 2, p. 92; *Pravda*, 20 October 1990.
92 *Pravda*, 25 March 1991.
93 *Ibid.*, 24 December 1990.
94 *Izvestiia TsK KPSS*, 1990, no. 9, p. 41.
95 *Pravda*, 29 January 1991.
96 *Izvestiia TsK KPSS*, 1990, no. 9, p. 41.
97 *Pravda*, 15 April 1991.
98 *Izvestiia*, 13 June 1991.
99 *Izvestiia TsK KPSS*, 1991, no. 2, p. 92.
100 *Pravda*, 15 July 1991.
101 *Izvestiia*, 16 December 1990.
102 *Pravda*, 3 August 1987.
103 *Ibid.*, 15 July 1991.
104 *Ibid.*, 25 February 1991.
105 *Ibid.*, 17, 16 and 24 August 1987, and 23 November 1987.
106 *Ibid.*, 6 July 1987.
107 *Ibid.*, 5 February 1987.
108 *Ibid.*, 6 July 1987.
109 *Ibid.*, 12 October 1987, 20 April 1987, and 11 May 1987.
110 *Ibid.*, 25 May 1987.
111 *Ibid.*, 18 January 1988.
112 *Komsomol'skaia pravda*, 21 February 1988.
113 *Izvestiia*, 17 September 1991.
114 *Pravda*, 9 October 1982.
115 *Sovetskaia Rossiia*, 13 March 1988. A similar letter appeared in *Molodaia gvardiia*, 1989, no. 7, pp. 272–7.
116 *Kommunist*, 1989, no. 7, pp. 68–9.
117 *The People and the Party are United?* (Moscow: Novosti, 1990), p. 63.
118 *Soviet Weekly*, 24 June 1989, p. 10.
119 *Argumenty i fakty*, 1991, no. 19, p. 3.
120 *Izvestiia*, 24 September 1991.
121 Cited in the *Glasgow Herald*, 20 January 1992.
122 *Pravda*, 26 December 1990.
123 *Ibid.*
124 *Ibid.*, 6 May 1991.
125 For the letters and resolution of party branches and members during 1991 see the Centre for the Preservation of Contemporary Documentation (TsKhSD), Moscow, fond 89, perechen' 11, documents 181–7 and elsewhere.
126 *Izvestiia TsK KPSS*, 1990, no. 9, pp. 132–5.
127 *Pravda*, 1 September 1990.
128 *Izvestiia*, 17 September 1991, and *Pravda*, 1 September 1990.
129 *Moscow News*, 1991, no. 38, p. 5.

130 See for instance Victor Zaslavsky and Robert J. Brym, 'The functions of elections in the USSR', *Soviet Studies*, vol. 30, no. 3 (July 1978), pp. 362–71, and Ronald J. Hill, *Soviet Politics, Political Science and Reform* (Oxford: Martin Robertson, 1980).

131 See Jerry F. Hough, 'Political participation in the USSR', *Soviet Studies*, vol. 28, no. 1 (January 1976), pp. 3–20, and Jan S. Adams, *Citizen Inspectors in the Soviet Union* (New York: Praeger, 1977).

132 See David Wedgwood Benn, *Persuasion and Soviet Politics* (Oxford: Blackwell, 1989), p. 156.

133 See Harry Rositzke, *The KGB: Eyes of Russia* (New York: Doubleday, 1981), pp. 63–5, 79–80 and elsewhere.

134 V. I. Remnev, *Predlozheniia, zaiavleniia i zhaloby grazhdan* (Moscow: Iuridicheskaia literatura, 1972), p. 15.

135 *Pravda*, 25 March 1991; Gurevich, ed., *Rabota s pis'mami*, p. 55.

136 V. I. Vlasov et al., *Gazeta, avtor i chitatel'* (Moscow: Politizdat, 1975), p. 33 and elsewhere.

137 *Sovetskoe gosudarstvo i pravo*, 1986, no. 8, p. 19.

138 *Guardian* (London), 21 June 1982.

139 *Pravda*, 11 December 1982.

140 *Ibid.*, 9 January 1983.

141 Dusko Doder and Louise Branson, *Gorbachev: Heretic in the Kremlin* (New York: Viking, 1990), p. 191.

142 *Izvestiia TsK*, 1989, no. 1, pp. 156–99.

143 *Ibid.*, no. 4, p. 117.

144 *Ibid.*, 1990, no. 9, p. 33.

145 Riordan, 'The revolution from below', p. 279.

146 *Sobesednik*, 1989, no. 9, p. 4.

147 Riordan, 'The revolution from below', p. 278.

148 *Pravda*, 13 February 1986.

149 McKay, *Letters to Gorbachev*, p. 16; *Arguments and Facts International*, January 1990, pp. 2–3.

150 *Moscow News*, 24 April 1988, p. 7.

151 McKay, *Letters to Gorbachev*, pp. 36–7.

152 *Argumenty i fakty*, 1991, no. 39, p. 6.

153 *Ibid.*, 1992, no. 10, p. 8.

154 *Ibid.*, nos. 38–9, p. 13; 41, p. 1; 38–9, p. 2; and 41, p. 5.

155 Iu. A. Levada, ed., *Est' mnenie* (Moscow: Progress, 1990), p. 284.

156 *Mir mnenii i mneniia o mire*, 1992, no. 9, p. 5.

157 *Izvestiia*, 19 May 1990.

158 White, 'Political communications', p. 55.

159 Cited in the *Daily Express* (London), 24 December 1991.

160 *Pravda*, 3 January 1992.

161 *Izvestiia*, 21 October 1991.

12 THE SOVIET TRANSITION AND 'DEMOCRACY FROM ABOVE'

1 For example, for Gorbachev's recognition of this, see 'Oktiabr' i perestroika: revoliutsiia prodolzhaetsia', *Pravda*, 3 November 1987. Also Gorbachev in *Pravda*, 2 August 1986.

2 'Sotsialisticheskaia ideia i revoliutsionnaia perestroika', *Pravda*, 26 November 1989.

3 'O khode realizatsii reshenii XXVII s"ezda KPSS i zadachakh po uglubleniiu perestroiki', *Pravda*, 29 June 1988.

4 'O pravovoi reforme', *Pravda*, 5 July 1988. For discussions of this concept, see *Pravda*, 2 August 1988 and *Kommunist*, 1988, no. 11.

5 Guillermo O'Donnell and Philippe C. Schmitter, *Transitions from Authoritarian Rule. Tentative Conclusions about Uncertain Democracies* (Baltimore: Johns Hopkins University Press, 1986), pp. 48–56.

6 This initial phase of reform is discussed in terms of 'democratisation from above', in Michael E. Urban, *More Power to the Soviets* (Aldershot: Elgar, 1990).

7 For example, see Iu. A. Rozenbaum, 'K razrabotke proekta Zakona SSSR o svobode sovesti', *Sovetskoe gosudarstvo i pravo*, 1989, no. 2, pp. 91–8.

8 *Pravda*, 9 October 1990.

9 There are also deficiencies in the law as adopted in the eyes of the church, particularly its refusal to grant the status of legal entity to the church as a whole (individual parishes could apply for this but not the church as an institution) and to make provision for the use of school premises for religious instruction outside school hours.

10 See Gorbachev's speech to the UN, *Pravda*, 8 December 1988.

11 *Izvestiia*, 20 June 1990.

12 Censorship had been relaxed in June 1986 with the abolition of the censorship functions of Glavlit, the Chief Administration of Literature and State Publishing Houses.

13 This seems to be a shift from the position adopted in the new regulations for cooperatives adopted in December 1988 which specifically banned independent cooperatives in the sphere of ideology and publishing. *Izvestiia*, 31 December 1988.

14 She apparently carried a banner calling Gorbachev a 'fascist pig' at an anti-government rally in Moscow on 16 September 1990.

15 For an early review of the effects of the law in the Russian Republic, see the comments of Deputy Minister of the Press and Means of Information in the RSFSR V. Logunov, 'Rossiia obretaet golos', *Argumenty i fakty*, 1990, no. 46.

16 *Pravda*, 1 July 1987.

17 *Pravda*, 18 March 1988.

18 For example, on 11 August 1987 in response to the demonstration by Crimean Tatars in Red Square, the Moscow city soviet introduced a set of 'Temporary Regulations' banning demonstrations in the city.

19 *Izvestiia*, 14 October 1989.

20 *Pravda*, 17 May 1991.

21 'O pravakh professional'nykh soiuzov SSSR', *Trud*, 29 April 1989.

22 *Pravda*, 15 December 1990.

23 *Pravda*, 16 October 1990.
24 *Pravda*, 7 September 1991.
25 This was consistent with the liberalisation of emigration rights in June 1991. Departure could be refused those deemed to be in possession of state secrets or with some form of legal obligation to fulfil, and required the consent of parents and under-age children remaining behind. These were to take effect from 1993. *Izvestiia*, 6 June 1991. It was also consistent with the decision of the Committee for Constitutional Supervision that all regulations concerning the system of residence permits would be abolished as from 1 January 1992.
26 For surveys, see Anders Aslund, *Gorbachev's Struggle for Economic Reform*, 2nd edn (London: Pinter, 1991) and Richard Sakwa, *Gorbachev and His Reforms 1985–1990* (London: Philip Allen, 1990), ch. 7.
27 This includes not only matters like pricing and resource supply questions, but also while control over things like access to premises remained administratively-based, entrepreneurs could not act solely on the basis of market considerations.
28 Crucial in this is private ownership of property, something which some of the republics were faster to legitimise than the all-union government.
29 This does not mean that commitment to law is supreme. There were many instances of the law not being observed by the authorities, both before the coup and after. Paradoxically among the latter were many of the initial moves against the party: its suspension, closure of a number of its newspapers, and the nationalisation of its property were all strictly illegal. So too was Yeltsin's suspension of local elections and appointment of presidential plenipotentiaries.
30 Gorbachev, 'O khode realizatsii'. For the Law on Constitutional Supervision in the USSR, see *Izvestiia*, 26 December 1989.
31 For example, *Izvestiia*, 15 September 1990. This related to a presidential decree dating from April 1990 which passed responsibility for demonstrations and public events in Moscow from the Moscow Soviet to the USSR Council of Ministers. *Pravda*, 21 April 1990. For a review of its functions, see Carla Thorson, 'Legacy of the USSR Constitutional Supervision Committee', RFE/RL Research Report, 27 March 1992.
32 *Pravda*, 3 July 1987.
33 In a symbolic sense, so too was the release of dissidents, particularly Andrei Sakharov.
34 For discussions of the South American experience, see Guillermo O'Donnell, Philippe C. Schmitter and Laurence Whitehead, eds., *Transitions from Authoritarian Rule. Latin America* (Baltimore: Johns Hopkins University Press, 1986) and James M. Malloy and Mitchell A. Seligson, eds., *Authoritarians and Democrats. Regime Transition in Latin America* (Pittsburgh: University of Pittsburgh Press, 1987).
35 A good example of the problems caused by the rush to republican sovereignty, and then independence, and one of direct relevance to the question of the construction of a democratic society was the question of citizenship. In some of the republics, including Belarus and the Baltic states, it was mooted that only people of the titular nationality of the republic should be citizens of that republic. This would effectively debar often substantial communities of other ethnic groups from playing a role in republican political life.
36 For example, see Andrew Arato, 'Civil society against the state: Poland 1980–81',